W9-DGA-409

The Berkeley DB Book

Himanshu Yadava

Apress®

The Berkeley DB Book

Copyright © 2007 by Himanshu Yadava

All rights reserved. No part of this work may be reproduced or transmitted in any form or by any means, electronic or mechanical, including photocopying, recording, or by any information storage or retrieval system, without the prior written permission of the copyright owner and the publisher.

ISBN-13: 978-1-59059-672-2

ISBN-10: 1-59059-672-2

Printed and bound in the United States of America 9 8 7 6 5 4 3 2 1

Trademarked names may appear in this book. Rather than use a trademark symbol with every occurrence of a trademarked name, we use the names only in an editorial fashion and to the benefit of the trademark owner, with no intention of infringement of the trademark.

Lead Editor: Jonathan Gennick
Technical Reviewer: Mike Olson
Editorial Board: Steve Anglin, Ewan Buckingham, Gary Cornell, Jonathan Gennick, Jason Gilmore,
    Jonathan Hassell, Chris Mills, Matthew Moodie, Jeffrey Pepper, Ben Renow-Clarke, Dominic Shakeshaft,
    Matt Wade, Tom Welsh
Project Manager: Sofia Marchant
Copy Editor: Nicole Abramowitz
Assistant Production Director: Kari Brooks-Copony
Production Editor: Lori Bring
Compositor: Susan Glinert Stevens
Proofreader: Linda Seifert
Indexer: Brenda Miller
Artist: April Milne
Cover Designer: Kurt Krames
Manufacturing Director: Tom Debolski

Distributed to the book trade worldwide by Springer-Verlag New York, Inc., 233 Spring Street, 6th Floor, New York, NY 10013. Phone 1-800-SPRINGER, fax 201-348-4505, e-mail orders-ny@springer-sbm.com, or visit http://www.springeronline.com.

For information on translations, please contact Apress directly at 2855 Telegraph Avenue, Suite 600, Berkeley, CA 94705. Phone 510-549-5930, fax 510-549-5939, e-mail info@apress.com, or visit http://www.apress.com.

The information in this book is distributed on an "as is" basis, without warranty. Although every precaution has been taken in the preparation of this work, neither the author(s) nor Apress shall have any liability to any person or entity with respect to any loss or damage caused or alleged to be caused directly or indirectly by the information contained in this work.

The source code for this book is available to readers at http://www.apress.com in the Source Code/Download section. You will need to answer questions pertaining to this book in order to successfully download the code.

Contents at a Glance

Contents

■CHAPTER 9 Distributed Transactions and Data-Distribution Strategies 273

■CHAPTER 10 Berkeley DB Utilities 323

About the Author

HIMANSHU YADAVA is a software developer who provides software design and development consultancy through his company, BitSeer Inc. His areas of interest include embedded databases, fault tolerance, and monitoring/management frameworks. Previously, he has worked in various technical roles at Oracle, Kineto Wireless, ProactiveNet (now a part of BMC Software), and Infosys Technologies. He maintains a Berkeley DB information page on his company's web site (http://www.bitseer.com).

About the Technical Reviewer

MIKE OLSON, vice president of Embedded Technologies at Oracle, is a technology industry veteran with more than 20 years of experience in engineering, marketing, sales, and business management. He joined Oracle after its acquisition of Sleepycat Software, makers of the open source embeddable database engine Berkeley DB. Olson served in sales and marketing roles at Sleepycat before being named its Chief Executive Officer in 2001.

Prior to joining Sleepycat, Olson served in technical and business management positions at database vendors Britton Lee, Illustra, and Informix. He holds BA and MA degrees in computer science from the University of California, Berkeley.

Acknowledgments

This book is dedicated to my parents—my mother Sarla Yadav and my father Om Prakash. They taught me everything I know, and they guided and inspired me at every important step in my life.

I couldn't have written this book without my wife, Shivani. She not only had to deal with my insane schedule, a full-time job, and nights and weekends of writing this book, but she also single-handedly took loving care of our son Samyak, who was born when I had just started working on this book.

First and foremost, I'd like to thank Mike Olson for reviewing the book. Being one of Berkeley DB's original developers, he has a unique perspective on it. He helped me explain many complex topics, he provided detailed comments, and he helped me fix numerous technical errors. Also, many thanks to Keith Bostic, Ciaran Carthy, and Dennis Zhou for reviewing the book.

I cannot thank Jonathan Gennick, the editor of this book, enough. He kept my spirits high during the difficult periods. It was his determination and passion that brought this project to fruition. Thanks, Jonathan! Special thanks also to Sofia Marchant for managing the project and encouraging me and cheering me up during the entire process. Matt Wade signed me up for writing this book—thanks, Matt, for giving me this opportunity.

Thanks to Nicole Abramowitz, for the copy edit, and to Lori Bring, for preparing the final layout of the book and for doing the final review. I would also like to thank all of the other people from Apress who contributed in the production of the book.

Introduction

The database technology landscape has been changing rapidly over the last few years. The server-based relational databases, which were so successful in solving the data-storage problem for traditional client/server and web-based applications, are no longer able to meet the requirements of newer applications, such as handheld devices, appliance-based solutions, and distributed applications. Berkeley DB is not a new technology that was designed to meet the requirements of this new breed of applications, but it is flexible enough to be used in these applications nevertheless. Berkeley DB doesn't fulfill all the requirements of these applications, so new database technologies will evolve to fill the void. However, its versatility and flexibility will certainly influence the design of any new database product.

This book's target audience ranges all the way from developers who don't know anything about Berkeley DB to fairly knowledgeable users. Therefore, I expect that not all readers will be interested in reading the entire book. I have given a brief outline of each chapter below to help you decide which chapters you may want to read or skip.

Chapter 1: This chapter offers a general introduction to Berkeley DB. It includes a brief history of its development and a basic description of its architecture. If you're already familiar with Berkley DB, you can skip this chapter.

Chapter 2: This chapter explains the pros and cons of using Berkeley DB. If you're evaluating Berkeley DB to decide whether to use it in your application, then you should read this chapter. If you've already decided to use Berkeley DB, you may skip this chapter.

Chapter 3: This chapter describes the process of compiling and installing different Berkeley DB products. Experienced Berkeley DB users can safely skip this chapter.

Chapter 4: This chapter introduces the Berkeley DB API with code examples. It provides an introductory discussion about Berkeley DB architecture and different types of access methods available in Berkeley DB. This chapter is a must for new users of Berkeley DB.

Chapter 5: The chapter introduces the various data stores available in Berkeley DB. Once again, this chapter is essential for new users.

Chapters 6 and 7: These two chapters contain a detailed discussion on the various design issues involved in using the Transactional Data Store (TDS), which is the most complex and also the most widely used data store. Experienced users will find these chapters useful.

Chapter 8: This chapter deals with database replication. The material in this chapter assumes that you have a good understanding of TDS. If you're not interested in replication, you can skip this chapter.

Chapter 9: This chapter discusses distributed transactions (XA) and data-distribution strategies. Experienced users will find this chapter useful.

Chapter 10: This chapter discusses the use of Berkeley DB utilities for tuning and trouble-shooting Berkeley DB–based applications. Both new and experienced users will find this chapter useful.

Chapter 11: This chapter introduces the Berkeley DB Java API. Users interested in using the Java API should read this chapter.

Chapter 12: This chapter discusses the Berkeley DB C API.

In spite of my best effort, I know for a fact that readers will find many errors in the book. I apologize in advance for any grammatical or technical errors that could not be caught during the production process. I'll be more than happy to discuss and clarify them if you bring them to my attention. You can reach me at hy@bitseer.com. I hope you will enjoy reading the book.

Best wishes.

CHAPTER 1

■ ■ ■

Introduction to Berkeley DB

There exist only a few pieces of software that are so versatile and so well engineered that they can be used with ease in applications as diverse as a simple web browser and a highly sophisticated telecom switch connecting millions of calls every hour. Berkeley DB is one of such pieces of software. What started as a research project at the University of California, Berkeley (UC Berkeley), has become a widely deployed and highly successful database management package, with more than 200 million known installations. And this is not the end of it—Berkeley DB has barely scratched the surface in terms of exploiting its full potential. Berkeley DB is often the most suitable database for the new breed of applications. Like search engines, peer-to-peer networking, cellular telephone and radio-frequency identification (RFID) systems, and mesh and sensor networks. What makes Berkeley DB such a success? I'll explore the answer to this question in this first chapter. I'll begin by reviewing its creation, then I'll survey its architecture and unique features.

A Brief History

Until the early 1990s, the UNIX operating system (OS) wasn't freely available to researchers and users. Anyone interested in using or studying UNIX had to get a license from AT&T. It also wasn't possible to modify the OS and make the changes available to others because AT&T owned the copyrights to the source code. In 1991, the Computer Systems Research Group at UC Berkeley decided to produce a version of UNIX that didn't require a source-code license from AT&T. It needed cheap labor to produce clean versions of key utilities that were a part of UNIX. Keith Bostic, who was leading the research group at that time, convinced Margo Seltzer and Mike Olson to work on a replacement for a UNIX utility called *ndbm*. ndbm is a UNIX utility that allows applications to manage data within the process memory. It's used in a wide variety of UNIX applications. They decided to name this utility *Berkeley DB*.

Seltzer and Bostic perfected the original 1.0 version over several releases and finally released version 1.85 in 1992. This version was rolled into Berkeley Software Distribution (BSD) version 4.4 (4.4BSD), which proved to be an instant success. Many projects, both commercial and academic, picked up the Berkeley DB code and incorporated it into applications and servers. In particular, the Lightweight Directory Access Protocol (LDAP) team at the University of Michigan chose Berkeley DB as the backing store for its directory server. By 1996, Berkeley DB became widely adopted as an in-memory database.

The University of Michigan LDAP team went on to work for an Internet startup called Netscape. It wanted to use Berkeley DB in Netscape's directory server but realized that Berkeley DB lacked a number of key features that were essential for building a commercial product on top of it. Netscape convinced Seltzer and Bostic to add transactions, recovery, and support for concurrency to the academic version of Berkeley DB. Seltzer and Bostic incorporated Sleepycat Software, as the owner of their work, to enhance and market Berkeley DB. Sleepycat adopted *dual licensing*, a hybrid open source and proprietary strategy, to encourage the use of Berkeley DB and create a sustainable business model. Under Sleepycat, Berkeley DB was extensively improved and enhanced; a number of new products and features were added to the Berkeley DB ecosystem. The new products that were introduced include High Availability (2001), Berkeley DB XML (2003), and Berkeley DB Java Edition (2004).

By 2006, Berkeley DB had truly become a mainstream product, as companies such as Google, Yahoo!, Microsoft, Cisco, and MySQL adopted it. Eager to extend its reach in the open source world, Oracle acquired Berkeley DB in 2006.

What Is Berkeley DB?

Now that you know how Berkeley DB came into existence, let's take a look at what it actually is and what it does. Berkeley DB is a library for transactional data management. This description is simple, but it's deceptive. It doesn't give a sense of how powerful and useful it can be. Because of the ubiquity of relational databases all around us in the form of stand-alone database servers, we often associate record management with monstrous databases running on huge servers and managed by professional database administrators. It's hard for us to think of data management as something simple and closely related to the application. Part of the reason for such a perception is the success of the established relational vendors who extol the benefits of relational databases for all possible data-management problems. However, different applications need different services, and using a client/server relational engine isn't always the best way for an application to manage the data it uses.

To better understand Berkeley DB, let's take a look at the most popular types of databases.

Relational Databases

In a relational database, information is stored as a set of related tables. Each table consists of a collection of a particular type of record. You can access data in any random fashion from a relational database without having to reorganize the database tables. The biggest advantage with this approach is that a relational database can produce a different *view* of the data depending on the query executed on the database. The database is queried and modified through a generic query language called Structured Query Language (SQL). SQL statements are parsed, evaluated, and executed dynamically. The drawback with this approach is that query parsing and execution can impose a significant processing overhead.

The name *relational* comes from a branch of mathematics called *set theory*. Relations, or sets of data, can be combined or transformed in certain well-defined ways. The *relational model* is the formal definition that describes those sets and the operations that may be performed on them.

Hierarchical Databases

Hierarchical databases store information in a tree structure. Information that is closely related is stored under the same parent node in the tree. All the parent nodes that are closely related share the same grand-parent node, and so on. The advantage here is that you can retrieve information easily and efficiently in certain fixed patterns. It's easy to find the children of any parent, so applications that need to search trees in that way get exactly the data representation that they need. However, it's difficult to find data in the tree if you need to search by attributes other than the parent-child relationship. Hierarchical databases are commonly used in applications such as directory servers.

Object Databases

An object database stores and retrieves objects that are mapped to the objects in an object-oriented programming language such as C++ or Java. Since there is a very tight coupling between the objects used in the program and the objects stored in the database, there is little query parsing and execution overhead. Object databases usually make it easy to find an object by its name (possibly a unique object ID, an address in some virtual object space, or some other unique identifier). Object databases recognize relationships—usually pointers—among objects and make them easy to traverse and search. These links can create graphs more complex than the simple parent-child hierarchies supported by a hierarchical database.

Berkeley DB

So which category does Berkeley DB fall under? The answer: none. Berkeley DB falls into a category that's a level below these higher-level abstractions. In fact, Berkeley DB can be, and has been, used to implement all of the previously mentioned databases. MySQL, the popular relational database, can be configured to use Berkeley DB as its storage engine. OpenLDAP, which is a hierarchical database, uses Berkeley DB to store data internally. Many Common Object Request Broker Architecture (CORBA) implementations use Berkeley DB to do object caching and object replication.

Berkeley DB is essentially a transactional database engine. A *transaction* ensures that the data doesn't get corrupted as it changes from one state to another. Another way to think of transactions is in terms of the so-called ACID properties. I quote the definition of the ACID properties from the venerable *Transaction Processing: Concepts and Techniques* by Jim Gray and Andreas Reuter (Morgan Kaufmann, 1993):

- **Atomicity**: A transaction's changes to state are atomic: either all happen or none happen.

- **Consistency**: A transaction is a correct transformation of the state. The actions taken as a group don't violate any of the integrity constraints associated with the state.

- **Isolation**: Even though transactions execute concurrently, it appears to each transaction, T, that others executed either before T or after T, but not both.

- **Durability**: Once a transaction completes successfully (commits), its changes to the state survive failures.

The *type* of a database—relational, hierarchical, object-oriented, and others—is independent of whether the database supports transactional data access. In fact, these types are just different ways of presenting and querying the data that they store, in a way that best suits the needs of the application.

Berkeley DB is a transactional database engine. With Berkeley DB, the application designer chooses the best access infrastructure around the core engine to suit the needs of the application. You can use Berkeley DB to design a relational database that runs as a stand-alone server, or an embedded database that runs within the process memory. Berkeley DB is a core transactional database engine, which is extremely configurable and can be used to design all sorts of application-specific databases.

Architecture of Berkeley DB

The design philosophy of Berkeley DB can be summed up as follows:

- Create a pure data-management system devoid of any application-specific constraints.

- Make the core engine very efficient.

- Provide access to the internals of the engine through application programming interfaces (APIs).

The designers of Berkeley DB believed that anticipating all the possible ways in which a database might be used would be impossible. They decided to focus instead on the common functionality that every database has to provide. Since functions such as threading, interprocess communication, and query processing vary greatly from platform to platform and application to application, they were excluded. Berkeley DB provides only these components:

- **Access methods**: Methods for creating, updating, and deleting entries and tables in the database

- **Memory pool**: A chunk of shared memory used to cache the data and share it among the processes using the database

- **Transactions**: Used to provide atomicity to a bunch of separate operations on the database

- **Locking**: A mechanism to provide concurrent access and isolation in the database

- **Buffer management**: A cache of recently used data shared among processes to reduce the frequency of disk input/output (I/O)

- **Logging**: A write-ahead logging implementation to support transactions

A unique feature of Berkeley DB is that all the subsystems, except for access methods and logging, can be used independently by the applications, outside of the context of Berkeley DB. I'll go over the details in later chapters. Figure 1-1 shows the relationships of these subsystems.

■**Note** Relatively few applications actually use these subsystems independent of the database. This book doesn't discuss the independent use of these subsystems.

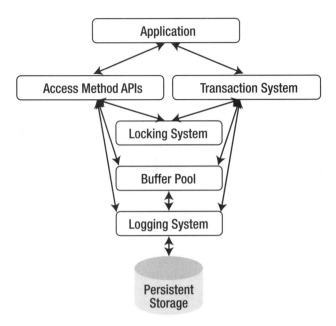

Figure 1-1. *Berkeley DB subsystems and relationships*

As shown in Figure 1-1, an application invokes the access method APIs to perform operations such as creating a database, deleting a database, inserting a record, reading a record, and so on. The application also calls the transactional subsystem to wrap multiple database operations into a single transaction.

The access methods acquire locks and then access the shared memory to retrieve the requested data and use the logging subsystem to record the operations performed. Similarly, the transactional subsystem acquires locks and accesses the shared memory region to access data and the logging module to record the operations. Finally, the buffer pool interacts with the persistent storage to service page faults and to persist data to the disk when requested.

I'll go over these subsystems in much more detail in later chapters. At this point, it's more important merely to understand the entire system at a high level than to understand the details of individual components.

Berkeley DB vs. RDBMS

Relational products are so ubiquitous and have such a huge market share that almost every conversation about database management assumes the relational model. Any database product will inevitably be compared with the relational database model. The biggest reason why the relational model is so popular and so successful is because it's extremely versatile, and exposes a single well-known standard query language—SQL—for data manipulation. The biggest problem with RDBMS is that it adds a lot of complexity and processing overhead to data management in order to support SQL. Let's look at the compromises a relational database makes to provide uniformity.

The relational model was designed to free database designers from the restriction of having to know the queries that would be run on the database in advance. The challenge is that different applications, even when they're looking at the same data, require different types of queries. For example, a database containing the performance data for a network would be queried by the reporting application to find all the machines on which the central processing unit (CPU) usage maxed out in the last hour. A graphing application, on the other hand, might want to get all the CPU usage data gathered in the last hour. To solve this problem, the early database researchers abstracted out the query component. IBM introduced a querying language (SQL, in most of today's implementations), which could be used to express any query. This made it simple to express queries, but it introduced a significant overhead at runtime. In order to find the data a user wants, a relational system must parse a query, make a plan to find and fetch the desired records from storage, and consider ways to make the fetches efficient. Only after parsing, planning, and optimizing can the user's request actually execute. This causes the following problems:

- **Unnecessary overhead**: Applications that don't need to run different types of queries have to bear the overhead of doing query parsing and optimization, which could dominate the total query-processing time.

- **Complex query language**: To please all the vendors participating in the standards process, SQL got loaded with a large number of esoteric but rarely used features. Few SQL programmers know how to use all the language constructs correctly.

- **Unpredictable performance**: Due to a complex parsing and optimization component, it's very difficult to accurately estimate the time it takes to execute a query in a typical relational database management system (RDBMS). For real-time systems, deterministic query performance is a must.

- **Large administrative overhead**: Most relational databases are designed to handle a wide variety of data-storage needs, and usually they're deployed to take care of a number of the data-management needs of an organization. For example, a company may be managing its payroll, inventory, and production data from the same Oracle relational database instance. Administering such databases is a time-intensive and expensive proposition.

- **Large footprint**: To cater to different types of applications from a single code base, RDBMS vendors typically include a large number of features and tools with their software. Most users need only a fraction of the total feature set available. As a result, RDBMS offerings usually have a huge resource footprint (i.e., they require a lot of disk space, memory, and powerful processors to run).

Relational databases provide a good, cost-effective solution for applications that need more or less static data management, but for which the queries may vary widely over time. This combination of static data and dynamic queries is common to most relational applications. Relational applications don't perform so well when presented with dynamic data, which is mostly accessed through a fixed number of known, static queries.

Berkeley DB, in contrast, has the following features:

- **No query-processing overhead**: The application writer has to know what type of data resides in the database and must explicitly program data access according to the query patterns he expects. This is definitely more work than writing a SQL query, but this approach eliminates overhead for applications that don't need a generic querying capability.

- **No complex query language**: There's no need to learn a complex query language if all you want is a simple data store.

- **Predictable performance**: Threading, inter-process communication (IPC), and query processing introduce the most runtime overhead and performance uncertainty in a database system. Berkeley DB leaves decisions such as threading model, network boundaries, and query patterns to the application developer. As a result, the database operates using the data model and computational framework of the application. In essence, the database disappears into the application, rather than being an independent component of the deployed system.

- **Zero administrative overhead**: Berkeley DB administers itself through the database-management tasks programmed into the application by the application developer. All the management policies can be implemented using Berkeley DB API calls from inside the application.

- **Ability to be optimized for the application's access pattern**: The application developer can easily customize the database to support any access pattern.

- **Small footprint**: Berkeley DB's designers worked diligently to keep the footprint of the database extremely small. The entire package takes about 350KB of space on most platforms to install.

Berkeley DB allows you to define the access pattern most suitable for an application. Implementing the data-access layer in the application is definitely more work than writing a SQL query, but when the performance cannot be compromised, there's really no other alternative available.

Why Berkeley DB Isn't As Popular As RDBMS

After reading about all the good things about Berkeley DB, you may be asking yourself, "If Berkeley DB is so great, why isn't it as popular as RDBMS?" There are a couple of reasons behind the perception that Berkeley DB is less popular. First of all, it doesn't always get the credit it deserves. You might have used it numerous times without even noticing. For example, it's used in numerous open source applications such as Sendmail (the popular e-mail daemon) and RPM (the Linux package manager), commercial applications such as Tibco messaging products and Cisco routers, and popular online services such as Google and Amazon.com. But most of us don't know that.

And second, the relational database vendors use their huge marketing budgets and large sales teams to push any competitor out of the market. To justify the enormous investment in their complex technology, they hard-sell it even in places where it's not the best choice. That's not to say that they've succeeded only because of excessive marketing. Relational databases have proved to be extremely versatile and flexible in meeting a wide variety of data-management requirements through an easy-to-use interface. It's just that they're not suitable for applications that require a customized database solution.

Why Berkeley DB May Become More Popular

Relational databases have been tremendously successful, but that success may undermine future growth. Some developers choose to use relational systems in every application imaginable, from huge data centers to handheld organizers. There's an enormous difference between these two computing environments, and it's reasonable to look for different ways to manage data for them.

Over the past decade, the number and variety of computing devices has exploded, from servers to desktops to laptops to palmtops and beyond. At the same time, high-speed networking is becoming ubiquitous using wired and wireless technologies. The combination of distributed computing power and fast communication has created a new wave of applications. Most of these applications have internal data-management requirements and are good prospects for Berkeley DB. Some of the industry trends that drive these applications include the following:

- **Search**: Most applications and services are moving toward a search-based infrastructure, because in the new, connected world, keeping track of every resource is impossible. It's easier to search what you want when you need it than to organize everything according to a known pattern. This requires databases optimized for fast and frequent read operations.

- **Special-purpose appliances**: A number of applications that used to be run and maintained as software solutions on general-purpose hardware are being transformed into stand-alone specialized appliances. Examples include firewalls, log servers, and access points. Since applications are becoming complex and IT budgets are shrinking, companies prefer to buy solutions that don't need an administrator to install and maintain them. Appliances need self-administrating databases.

- **Miniaturization**: The size of gadgets is shrinking. Laptops are replacing desktops, and multimedia cell phones are replacing the music player, the cell phone, and the digital camera. Small footprint databases are a must for smaller devices.

- **Move toward open source**: Companies are getting fed up with the exploitative licensing schemes and expensive support contracts of the proprietary technology vendors. They now prefer to use open source technologies wherever possible.

These emerging applications are generally ill-suited to heavyweight client/server relational database management. Berkeley DB addresses the needs of these applications much better. It's only a matter of time before Berkeley DB will capture a bigger share of the database market.

Oracle Dual License

An introduction to Berkeley DB cannot be complete without an explanation of the innovative licensing scheme under which it's distributed. Berkeley DB is distributed with the a *dual license*, which states the following:

- Open source applications can freely use and redistribute Berkeley DB without paying any license fee to Sleepycat.

- Proprietary application vendors can redistribute Berkeley DB either if they make their source code, which uses Berkeley DB, public or if they buy a license from Oracle.

In essence, the dual license behaves like the GNU General Public License (GPL) for open source products and like a proprietary license for proprietary software products.

An important point to note in the case of proprietary applications is that you must buy the license only if the Berkeley DB library is *redistributed* with the application. Applications that are installed in a single location—for example, in an in-house data center—can use Berkeley DB without paying anything to Oracle and without releasing the source code of the application.

The Oracle engineering team does most of the product development and product enhancement, as it fully owns the intellectual property behind Berkeley DB. The absence of third-party components within Berkeley DB allows Oracle to sell commercial licenses without any legal ramifications. The dual license has worked very well for Berkeley DB. Adoption by the open source community has created an enormous installed base, and the licensing revenue, derived from the proprietary vendors, has allowed Oracle to keep enhancing the product.

Summary

Berkeley DB offers a set of unique features with a unique licensing scheme designed with the application designer in mind who needs a simple, effective, flexible, and reliable data-management solution. RDBMS is a versatile, general-purpose database technology that has proved its worth in a wide range of applications; however, it imposes significant processing and administrative overhead on the systems using it. Many emerging applications cannot tolerate that overhead or complexity. Berkeley DB provides an alternative for those applications, but requires more work than a relational database to integrate. In the next chapter, I'll go over the components that you'll have to build in order to use Berkeley DB.

■ ■ ■

CHAPTER 2

When to Use Berkeley DB

Berkeley DB is different from a traditional client/server relational database. Most relational databases support standard interfaces such as SQL and Open Database Connectivity (ODBC). Although easy to use, these interfaces don't allow you to manipulate the guts of the database framework. Berkeley DB APIs are designed to allow you to take full control of every aspect of the database framework. Careful thought went into making them flexible and providing the right level of semantics. Certain features that you might expect to be present in a database aren't available in Berkeley DB; they're left for you to implement so you can optimize them for the application at hand. This chapter will help you understand how Berkeley DB is different from a traditional database so that you're prepared when you start using this powerful technology in your application.

What Berkeley DB Does and Doesn't Provide

Before jumping to the list of components that Berkeley DB does or doesn't provide, let's first look at all the components that are usually present in a functioning database system. Figure 2-1 shows a simplified view of the subsystems in a typical database in the client/server configuration. I chose this configuration because it contains all the subsystems that a database can have, and that will help in comparing the features of a traditional database with those of Berkeley DB. Depending on the database vendor and the type of driver, some of the components shown in the figure may be placed differently, but for the most part, you can find these components in all client/server databases.

Out of the components shown in Figure 2-1, Berkeley DB provides the following:

- Access method APIs

- Transaction manager

- Buffer cache

- Lock manager

- Transaction logging

- Replication manager

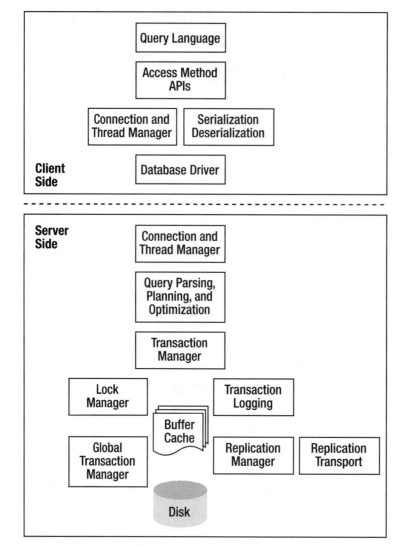

Figure 2-1. *Typical database subsystems in a stand-alone configuration*

Additionally, while Berkeley DB doesn't provide a global transaction manager (GTM), it does provide support for distributed transactions and two-phase commits. Third-party GTMs make use of that support to provide you with the ability to execute transactions spanning multiple database environments.

All the remaining components—the query language, the connection and thread manager, the serialization/deserialization layer, and the database driver—are not included in Berkeley DB. You may be thinking, "What kind of database doesn't even provide a query language? Aren't we supposed to be unaware of the details of the database structure in our applications? Haven't we accepted the superiority of the relational database theory?" So you might think, but the reality is that the relational technology is not the panacea. It's a useful tool that's comparable to the Swiss Army knife in its versatility. However, relational technology leaves a lot be desired when it comes to applications that have demanding data-management requirements. You can use a Swiss Army knife to build yourself a shack in the middle of nowhere, but if you're building a million dollar home, you'll need something better than that. You'll see, in the coming sections and chapters, when it's not a good idea to use an RDBMS.

Berkeley DB comes packaged as a library that you can link with any program on most operating systems. This aspect of Berkeley DB causes some confusion, because many are accustomed to thinking of databases as client/server applications. However, as you'll see later, all data-management operations can be adequately performed in the context of application threads and processes.

The next logical question would be, "Why does Berkeley DB include only the components listed earlier?" As it turns out, there's a very good reason behind every inclusion and every omission. The designers of Berkeley DB built a well-engineered database engine that exposes necessary components through clean and simple interfaces.

Why Berkeley DB Doesn't Provide Everything

As a principle, Berkeley DB includes only those components that you can implement without making any assumptions about the application that will be using the database or about the OS on which the application will run on. This principle is followed in the broadest possible sense; as a result, Berkeley DB doesn't include any threading infrastructure, any communication support, any querying and serialization support, or any process structure. In other words, Berkeley DB provides basic data-management tools, and it leaves the policy up to you by allowing you the flexibility to choose how to integrate with OS services and the application.

Threading

To understand the reason behind the key principle of Berkeley DB design, let's take the specific example of threading infrastructure. Suppose you want to design a multithreaded database engine, you will have to foresee every kind of threading model that an application, intending to use your engine, can use. An application could be a single-threaded process or a multithreaded process, or it could run on an OS that doesn't even support threads. In addition to the question of which threading model to use, numerous threading libraries are available on most operating systems that differ vastly in the way they work. In the presence of so many possible design options, if you had to come up with a design that would work in most cases, you'd either have to support all the permutations and combinations, or you'd have to cut corners and produce something not capable of delivering the best possible performance. Neither alternative is accept-able to the designers of Berkeley DB.

In the first case, the database system would have an enormous disk and memory footprint. And in the second case, the database system would have severe limitations, as is the case with various lightweight database systems. The ideal solution then would be to allow the application developer to plug a threading framework that's most suitable for the application into the database, and that is exactly what Berkeley DB does. Other database systems choose the threading regime because (a) they're usually stand-alone engines and entirely in charge of the execution model, and (b) they're targeted at a reasonably narrow deployment scenario like a big-iron server in a data center. Berkeley DB was designed to be able to run not only on big iron, but also on cell phones. Those are very different platforms with different threading and scheduling models. Leaving those policy decisions in the hands of the application developer allows Berkeley DB to be used in more places, and in more ways, than a monolithic database product could be.

Communication Support

IPC and connection management is required in a database for the following reasons:

- To enable applications to communicate with the database

- To replicate data from one database to another

- To perform distributed transactions

- To provide locking, logging, and other low-level internal database tasks

It's difficult to envision the ideal communication abstraction for every application. For an embedded database running in the context of an application, there's no need to incur the overhead of establishing and maintaining socket connections; simple method invocations on the database interface would be sufficient. In comparison, for a CORBA-based distributed application, a much higher level of communication abstraction, based on interface description language (IDL), would be more suitable. Instead of cramming every possible communication method into the database and then forcing you to use inflexible and complex interfaces in your programs, Berkeley DB allows you to build the most suitable communication layer for your applications. Berkeley DB does provide several implementations of IPC based on common OS abstractions— shared memory, pthread mutexes, and so on—for the locking, logging, and other low-level IPC requirements of the Berkeley DB engine itself. In version 4.5.x, a communication framework based on Transmission Control Protocol and Internet Protocol (TCP/IP) has been added for replication, since most applications predominantly use TCP/IP-based IPC for replication. However, you can still choose to implement a custom IPC framework.

Query Support

The hardest argument for a Berkeley DB proponent to fight is the absence of query support in Berkeley DB. There's no support for running random queries against a database without having to change application code. In other words, you have to know in advance what kind of queries would be required to run on a database, and you have to write code to make that happen, since the database doesn't support a generic query language such as SQL. During a typical evaluation process for selecting the database system for a new application, developers and their managers are usually impressed by the flexibility and speed of Berkeley DB, but the lack of SQL-based query support often becomes the basis of Berkeley DB's rejection.

The need for SQL can be justified only for certain types of applications. SQL is a must in applications where you routinely need to run different types of queries on the data (e.g., in data-mining applications). In such applications, you need to slice and dice huge amounts of data to deduce various trends and patterns. It would be hard for anyone to foresee all the possible queries that would be run on the data. Usually, such applications don't have a requirement to run these queries blindingly fast. Such applications are usually executed as batch jobs overnight when systems are least loaded. Berkeley DB should not be used in these kinds of applications.

A large number of applications, however, don't really need the generic querying capability that SQL provides. Here's an easy way to figure out if your database really needs SQL. Ask yourself the following questions:

- Is the database schema published to the outside world?

- Is the database going to be queried frequently from outside your application?

- Does your program generate new queries to be run on the database?

- Is minimal code change required in your program if the queries that it runs change?

If you answered "no" to all the questions, then your application code is tightly coupled with the database and you won't gain much by having SQL to run random queries on the database. If you answered "yes" to a couple of the questions, then you need to sit down and think carefully about whether you really need SQL. Sometimes there's no clear answer to the questions. For those cases, you should design your application in such a way that allows you to experiment with various database systems and select the one that works best.

Serialization Support

In order for the data to be stored in the database, it has to be serialized. Relational database systems provide serialization of the application data structures; they can do that because they understand the schema of the application data through SQL. On the other hand, since Berkeley DB has no knowledge of the schema of the data being stored, it cannot serialize the application data automatically. As a result, the application has to implement the serialization code. It's important to understand that relational database systems have to incur a significant overhead of parsing and understanding every SQL query in order to provide this functionality. If your application doesn't really need SQL (see the discussion in the previous section), then it may not be worth it to incur the SQL parsing overhead in order to have automatic data serialization.

WHAT'S SO BAD ABOUT SQL?

SQL may not always be required, but what's the harm in having the capability to run SQL in the database system? Maybe there will be a need in the future to run random queries. Or maybe it's just cool to have a command-line interface to view what is stored in the database. The problem with SQL is that it complicates everything. It introduces more complexity to the system than it reduces by providing a generic query interface. To make it possible to run arbitrary queries on a database, a full-fledged expression language is required. Once you have a language, you have to parse it, optimize the parsed query, and then plan its execution. These tasks aren't easy. There are numerous ways of executing a SQL statement, and you could execute it differently even on the same system under different circumstances. The performance of a database system then becomes unpredictable, because you don't know what execution path will be selected at runtime.

Over the years, numerous esoteric features have been added to the SQL standard upon the insistence of the vendors participating in the standards process. Not all RDBMS vendors implement all the features. So even though SQL is standard, most vendors implement only a subset of the standard.

It's easy to write trivial queries in SQL, but most real-world applications require complex queries. You would need to hire a SQL expert if you want to develop a serious SQL-based application; your regular programmer probably won't know the intricacies of SQL. You would also need a database administrator to do database maintenance and tuning as the application matures. Pretty soon, you'll realize that an entire ecosystem has evolved around your database.

The tasks of designing queries and doing database maintenance are also required in systems using Berkeley DB, but the programmer writing the application can perform them easily. The capability of running arbitrary queries on a database doesn't come cheap, and you don't have to have it if you don't really need it.

What Type of Data Store Do You Want?

You must have figured out by now that Berkeley DB leaves a significant portion of the database implementation for you to implement. To decide whether Berkeley DB would be the right choice for your application, you have to weigh its advantages against the development effort required to implement the missing pieces. To accurately estimate the development effort, you first have to decide what kind of data store you need. You should think of the following aspects of your application to help yourself answer that question.

Data-Access Patterns

How your application accesses the database affects the design of the database infrastructure to a great extent. If your application is single-threaded, then you don't have to worry about concurrency. In that case, the database framework will be quite simple. On the other hand, if your application is multithreaded and you want multiple threads or processes in your application to access the database concurrently, then you'll either have to use locking at the database level or serialize the access to the database at the application level.

Transaction and Recovery

One of the key benefits provided by a database is that it ensures that you can recover the data stored in the database even if the application or the database system crashes. Recoverability is made possible through support for transactions. I'll go over the details of how that support is achieved in Chapters 5 and 6. However, not all applications need recoverability. Many applications may want to repopulate the database every time they're restarted. Such applications may not need recoverability. You should determine whether your application needs transaction and recovery support.

Another related aspect that you should consider is whether you need to make groups of changes in a single operation. Transactions give you a way to make multiple changes *atomically,* thereby ensuring that either all changes succeed or none of them succeed.

Fault Tolerance and High Availability

Mission-critical solutions have to be available all the time (typically 99.999% of the time). It's impossible to guarantee such a high availability just by depending on the quality of hardware and software components, because even the best systems have a much higher rate of failure than 0.001%. One way to provide high availability is to build redundancy into the system, which allows the system to be operational even if individual components fail.

You should determine whether your application has to be fault-tolerant as well. One problem that is introduced by making a system fault-tolerant is that the redundant components have to be aware of the application state at all times so that they can pick up where the failed component left off. This problem is usually solved by replicating the application state from the active components to the redundant components via database replication. You can configure the database to provide either a *cold* failover or a *hot* failover:

- **Cold failover**: In a cold failover, the backup system has to be brought online manually when the active system fails. It's simpler than a hot failover to implement. You can achieve a cold failover by taking hot backups of the active database at regular intervals.

- **Hot failover**: In a hot failover, the backup system becomes active automatically after the active system fails. It is complex to implement.

Scalability

As the volume of traffic handled by an application grows, the database framework usually becomes one of the performance bottlenecks. One way of dealing with increased load is through replication. In addition to providing fault tolerance, replication also provides support for scale-out. As your workload increases, you add more replicas, and each of them can handle a share of the workload. This allows systems to handle growth in data volume and user load over time.

Data Organization

You should determine in advance the data organization in your application. Consider the answers to the following questions:

- Is the data produced from a single location or from multiple locations?

- Is the data consumed from a single location or from multiple locations?

- Is the data stored in one location or in multiple locations?

In Berkeley DB, a set of databases (or tables, in the parlance of relational database systems) that are administered and managed as a single entity represent a database environment. If all your data resides in a single location, you have to deal with only one database environment. For complex applications, a single environment may not be sufficient. There could be various reasons for having multiple environments—for example, the amount of data to be managed may be too big to be managed efficiently in a single environment, or various components of the application may be running in physically diverse locations. To deal with multiple environments, you'd have to implement a distributed transaction manager for your application.

Berkeley DB Data Stores

You can configure the Berkeley DB library into four distinct products by using different configure and runtime options, which allow you to build the data store suitable for your application. I'll talk about how to do that in Chapter 3. For now, you just need to get an overview of the four products so that you can create a component checklist:

- **Data Store (DS)**: Provides a simple data store with a single writer and multiple readers.

- **Concurrent Data Store (CDS)**: Allows multiple readers and writers, but the application has to ensure that only a single application thread or process accesses the database at any given time. The database doesn't provide locking.

- **Transactional Data Store (TDS)**: Provides ACID transactions and recovery. The database manages concurrent access internally.

- **High Availability (HA)**: Provides replication and distributed transaction support.

As you can see, the various product offerings have been tailored to fit the needs of the commonly used application architectures. This makes your task slightly easier because you can simply choose the configuration that best suits your needs instead of having to fine-tune hundreds of available parameters.

A Checklist of Components to Be Built

After you've decided which Berkeley DB product will suit your application, the next step is to create a checklist of the components that you'll have to build for yourself. The following is a list of components that you'll have to build:

- **Marshalling and unmarshalling layer:** This layer is required for every application using Berkeley DB. Since Berkeley DB doesn't interpret the data being stored (or retrieved) in the database according to a predefined schema, it's the application's responsibility to format the data. Formatting the data is conceptually a very simple task, but it entails significant maintenance overhead. In certain projects, the formatting becomes an ongoing task where you have to keep adding support for new structures and modifications to the existing structures. This is especially true in cases where there is a lot of variability in the structure of different items stored in a table, or if the items are deeply nested trees of pointers. For some applications, the application-level data structures can be directly persisted in the database.

- **Threading framework:** You need to develop a thread-pool manager if you're planning to use the database concurrently from multiple threads. For RDBMS-based applications, you only have to worry about the threads on the client side. But with Berkeley DB, you have to worry about the threads on the server side also, in case the application needs to provide a client/server-based interface for the database. There are numerous ways in which you can access a database when using Berkeley DB. You can design a client/server model around Berkeley DB and deal with server issues in a single process, or you can link with Berkeley DB directly from your application threads and not have a separate server at all. In the second case, you'll have to deal with database-management issues from your application process, which could become messy if you don't design your application properly. But in either case, you should set aside some time in the schedule to devote to the threading issues.

- **Communication layer:** If you decide to also provide a server-based interface (some applications may want to expose the database through a server for some external or certain distrusted third-party components) to your database, you'll need to build a communication layer between your database server and your application. Of course, if you decide to link to the database directly from your application threads, you won't need a communication layer. Another place where you would need a communication layer is in a replication framework (which you might build should your application need fault tolerance). You can build the communication layer using TCP/IP sockets, UNIX sockets, CORBA, or any other mechanism available on your platform. Berkeley DB will work with everything. Even though it takes some effort to develop a communication layer, not too many changes are required once it is built.

- **Table relationships manager**: In Berkeley DB, there's no way to establish relationships between databases (similar to tables in relational databases), except for making a database a secondary database of another database. You can use a secondary database to sort the database entries based on a key that is not the primary key. However, if you need some kind of foreign-key relationship, you'll have to build it on your own. Building a generic foreign-key functionality can be a significant amount of work.

- **Schema management framework**: Berkeley DB doesn't understand the structure of the data that's being stored in it. It treats all data as key-value pairs. If you like, you can store different types of structures in the same table. It's the responsibility of the application to manage the database schema in the application layer. It's not difficult to do, but you'll have to plan for it from the very beginning. Think about the extensibility, the upgrade, and the migration issues while implementing the schema management framework.

- **Database administration framework**: You must implement various administrative tasks such as checkpoints, transaction-log cleanup, and backups. The database allows you to take care of these tasks programmatically from within your application. In a traditional database, a database administrator handles these tasks. There is, however, a bright side to this: in the long run, the one-time cost of the development effort will be much less than the ongoing cost of a database administrator.

- **Global transaction manager**: Some applications require distributed transactions. Berkeley DB provides distributed transaction support. You can execute transactions spanning multiple environments by using two-phase commits. However, Berkeley DB doesn't provide a global transaction manager, which is required for managing the two-phase commits. If your application needs distributed transactions, you'll have to implement the transaction manager on your own. It's not very hard to implement, but it's an additional work item to worry about.

Plan for the Future

Berkeley DB provides immense flexibility for you to design the best database solution for your application, and it does that by leaving a lot of design for you, the application developer, to fill in. The database framework can become very complex if you're building a serious application using Berkeley DB. Once you've built the framework, it becomes difficult to make significant changes down the line, so you should ensure that the framework design is flexible and extensible. Many projects either fail or overshoot their schedule because their initial design didn't factor in future requirements. Consider these key things when designing a database framework around Berkeley DB:

- **The load**: If your current requirements can be met by, say, 10 database queries per second, you should plan for 100. Keep your framework flexible enough to scale to 100 queries per second without significant code changes. You should think about distributing the load among multiple threads or processes from the very beginning. Even if a single-threaded database can handle your current application load, you shouldn't tightly couple your design to that fact. Your design should be configurable enough to allow multiple threads in the future.

- **High availability and fault tolerance**: Most products start with prototypes. In the proof-of-concept phase, the focus is always on getting the product out of the door soon enough. No one has fault tolerance and high availability on their mind. However, fault tolerance usually is a must-have feature for any serious product. In fact, fault tolerance often becomes the key differentiator for products with similar features. If there's one thing that can propel a product to the front of a pack of contenders, it's support for high availability and fault tolerance. It's never too early to think about such support.

- **Upgrades**: A company busy with rolling out a new product doesn't care about upgrades. Upgrades are always way ahead in the future. The common argument against planning for upgrades is that if a product reaches the stage of needing to be upgraded, the company will then have enough money to deal an upgrade. However, that's not often true. In many cases, messy upgrades lead to bad impressions from which a young company can never recover. If you have a database schema, no matter how small, it will change, and you should plan for dealing with such change from the very beginning.

- **Code generation**: Since Berkeley DB doesn't understand the data format it stores, you have to write the marshalling/unmarshalling routines for the database entries. Writing these routines manually for each structure is boring and error-prone. It's no big deal to write these routines for only a couple of structures, but that is seldom the case. The number of data structures to be stored in the database usually increases as an application grows. You should think of ways to generate the marshalling/unmarshalling routines automatically through scripting, code generation, and so on. Putting some effort in this area early on pays off handsomely on an ongoing basis when you have the ability to add or modify schemas in your database at the drop of the hat.

Berkeley DB Licensing

Last but not least, you must keep licensing issues in mind. Berkeley DB licensing is innovative. It's a common misperception that Berkeley DB is an open source product and hence, you don't have to pay for it. In essence, Berkeley DB has a dual license that tries to capture the hearts of both the open source community and the proprietary software industry. To quote part of the license statement from Oracle's web site:

> *Our open source license permits you to use Berkeley DB at no charge under the condition that if you use the software in an application you redistribute, the complete source code for your application must be available and freely redistributable under reasonable conditions. If you do not want to release the source code for your application, you may purchase a license from Oracle.*

The open source community loves this license, because it forces companies who are trying to reduce their costs to open up their source code to the public. The license allows a company to make money from its product without paying Oracle any fee, if the product source code is open sourced. On the other hand, the license allows proprietary vendors to buy legal licenses of Berkeley DB and make their products immune to the viral nature of the Oracle public license (similar to the GPL license). The dual license allows Oracle to reap the benefits of both the huge user base and the word-of-mouth advertising of the open source community. It also provides Oracle with enough licensing revenue to keep Berkeley DB financially viable.

As an evaluator of Berkeley DB, you have to consider the pros and cons of paying a license fee vs. making your code open source. If you cannot go the open source route, you might consider going with a proprietary vendor if you have to pay for the license anyway. However, proprietary database technology isn't necessarily superior. You should consider the following facts before you make up your mind:

- **Database technology is complex**: The more open the technology is, the more likely that design issues will be found and corrected.

- **Open source is becoming mainstream**: A number of vendors, such as IBM and Computer Associates, have decided to make their database technology open source. Open source is no longer a taboo like it used to be. In other words, you won't get fired for selecting an open source technology.

- **Berkeley DB may cost less**: Even if you end up paying the license fee to Oracle, it will be much less than what you would have to pay for a proprietary product. It's possible to pay a one-time license fee (if you choose that option). You can then sell any number of copies of your product without paying anything extra beyond the initial amount. The one-time license is slightly more expensive than the per-copy license, but it's a good investment if you've decided to use the technology. Proprietary vendors can charge by the number of users, the number of CPU cores in the servers, CPU clock cycles, or some other ridiculously insane metric that will earn them more money.

Summary

A database system is a critical part of any application, and selecting a database system for an application is a very important decision. You shouldn't just follow the latest industry trend when making that decision. Database technology has matured quite a bit, and options are available to suit every kind of requirement. Your decision should be based on a thorough evaluation of your requirements against the database features available from various vendors. In the next chapter, I'll go over how to configure and install Berkeley DB.

■■■

CHAPTER 3

Products, Compilation, and Installation

When learning to use a new software product, the first hurdle you must overcome is getting the software compiled and installed. Unfortunately, software developers don't follow any particular standard for packaging and building their products. Every product has its own quirks and tricks when it comes to installation, and Berkeley DB is no exception.

This chapter will explore the various products available under the Berkeley DB umbrella and show you how to compile and install them. The chapter will also go over the various options available in the build configuration, which you can use to customize Berkeley DB according to your requirements.

Berkeley DB Product Family

After taking the open source university project under its wings, Sleepycat Software (founded by the original developers of Berkeley DB) transformed the original software beyond recognition. Berkeley DB now has three separate product lines:

- **The Berkeley DB core**: The transactional database technology, which is the subject of this book

- **Berkeley DB XML**: An XML schema–aware layer written on top of Berkeley DB, which allows you to use XPath and XQuery to store and query XML documents

- **Berkeley DB Java Edition**: A Berkeley DB–like database written purely in Java

Figure 3-1 shows the relationship among these products and the various APIs supported on top of them.

In the above list Berkeley DB core and Berkeley DB XML are packaged as libraries, while Berkeley DB Java Edition is packaged as JAR files. The applications access the database through the various APIs, which are supported on top of Berkeley DB. Berkeley DB is one of the most portable software packages out there. Language support includes C, C++, Java, Perl, Python, PHP, and TCL, to name a few. In terms of platform support, Berkeley DB has been ported to more than 50 operating systems, including UNIX, Linux, Mac OS, Windows, VxWorks, and Plan 9. Most of the code examples in this book will be based on the C++ API.

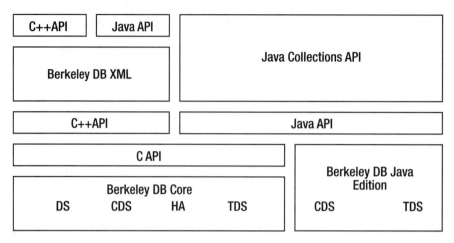

Figure 3-1. *Berkeley DB products and their relationships[1]*

The Berkeley DB core forms the basis of the C, C++, and Java APIs and the Berkeley DB XML product. The C++ and Java APIs are thin wrappers over the C API. Berkeley DB Java Edition is a totally independent product with no relation to the core. The Java APIs for the core and Java editions are very similar, and they support a common Java Collections API. The Java applications that use the Berkeley DB Collections API can seamlessly switch between the core and the Java editions.

Berkeley DB XML and the Berkeley DB core share a common database engine, which provides high-performance transactional data storage. The main difference between the Berkeley DB core and Berkeley DB XML is the support for running generic queries. Berkeley DB XML contains a full-fledged XML parser and a query optimizer and planner, whereas the Berkeley DB core doesn't support generic queries.

■**Note** You can create both Berkeley DB XML and the Berkeley DB core databases in the same Berkeley DB environment, and you can have transactions that span the two database types within the common environment.

Berkeley DB Java Edition was created to fulfill the need of having a fast and reliable caching mechanism for Java applications. Numerous caching frameworks are available for Java, but most of them either cache the data within the Java Virtual Machine (JVM) memory (which doesn't scale) or don't support ACID transactions (if they use disk-based persistence). Before the arrival of Berkeley DB Java Edition, the only way to create large, reliable caches was through traditional relational databases. Although you can use the Berkeley DB core for caching data in a Java application, Berkeley DB Java Edition, which itself is written in Java, provides better performance.

---

1. Courtesy: Dave Segleau, Vice President of Engineering, Sleepycat Software Inc. I took this picture from Dave's Berkeley DB training material.

Another difference between the Java and core editions, apart from the language, is that the core edition uses write-ahead logging to provide transactional semantics, whereas the Java Edition uses the transaction log itself to store the data. A detailed discussion on the differences between the two approaches is outside the scope of this book. As you can see in Figure 3-1, the Java Edition doesn't provide HA, but that might change in the upcoming releases.

The Berkeley DB core and the Berkeley DB Java Edition can be customized to provide specialized data stores. The following types of data stores are available:

- **Data Store (DS)**: Nontransactional simple data store with no locking.

- **Concurrent Data Store (CDS)**: Nontransactional concurrent data store that supports a single writer and multiple readers with database-level (table-level, in RDBMS lingo) locking.

- **Transactional Data Store (TDS)**: Transactional data store with ACID semantics. Provides page-level or record-level locking and supports multiple readers and writers concurrently.

- **High Availability (HA)**: Replication support for high availability and fault tolerance.

If you've ever attempted to download one of these products from Oracle's web site, you've probably noticed that no matter which data store you select, the same file gets downloaded. That happens because Oracle provides a single source code distribution, and the different products are made available as compile-time or runtime options. However, this information isn't mentioned anywhere on the download page. In the next section, I'll show you how to build and install Berkeley DB.

Compiling and Installing

Building Berkeley DB libraries from the source distribution is a straightforward process. You can download the distribution from Oracle's web site.[2] The source distribution comes in two flavors: one with strong encryption support, and one without. The specific instructions for compiling the source code are available in the distribution and are also on Oracle's web site.[3] For UNIX platforms, follow these steps:

1. Specify the type of product you want, along with a number of other options.

2. Compile the source code.

3. Install the compiled code.

The first step is significant, because it's where you decide what kind of Berkeley DB library you want to build and install. A large number of configuration options are available in the `configure` command. Here's a list of some of the more important ones:

---

2. http://www.oracle.com/technology/software/products/berkeley-db/db/index.html
3. http://www.oracle.com/technology/documentation/berkeley-db/db/ref/build_unix/intro.html (for UNIX platforms)

- --enable-cxx, --enable-java: By default, the Berkeley DB library is built with support only for the C API. If you want to use the C++ API or the Java API, you must specify those options while running configure.

- --disable-cryptography: Berkeley DB provides the support to encrypt the data stored in the database. This feature can be useful for enhancing the security of your system. However, if you know you have other ways of securing your application and you want to squeeze every bit of performance out of the database, you can disable this feature. Simply building your library with this option doesn't mean that all data will be encrypted in the database automatically; you'll have to set a runtime flag to enable encryption.

■**Tip** Most modern devices support encrypted file systems. If you know your application is always going to run on an encrypted file system, you should set the --disable-cryptography option.

- --enable-diagnostics: You can use this option to enable runtime diagnostics checks and detailed debug messages in the Berkeley DB code. This feature is extremely useful during the development phase. I usually build two versions of the library—one with diagnostics and one without—so that I can enable diagnostic messages easily when I have to troubleshoot a problem. However, diagnostics cause a significant performance overhead, so it's not advisable to use this option for production and during benchmarking.

■**Caution** The --enable-diagnostics option alters the control flow of the Berkeley DB library. An application should not link with an environment that's been created with a library built with this option, while it's also linking with another Berkeley DB environment created from a library built without this option.

- --enable-debug: The --enable-debug option is different from --enable-diagnostic. If you need symbols for debugging, use --enable-debug. If you want internal checking in the Berkeley DB code, enable --enable-diagnostic. Generally, you should compile with --enable-debug so you can get stack traces and so on, but you shouldn't compile with --enable-diagnostic unless you'd like to run the extra checks in case of corruption or other major errors.

- --enable-posixmutexes: Portable Operating System Interface (POSIX) mutexes are better than non-POSIX–complaint mutexes for your platform, but they cannot be used for interprocess mutual exclusion. If your application isn't multiprocess, you could override the default choice and use POSIX mutexes anyway. Therefore, blocking mutexes are better, but Berkeley DB won't choose them unless they work interprocess. If your application isn't multiprocess, you can use --enable-posixmutexes to override the default choice.

■Tip It's best not to use the `--enable-posixmutexes` option. Usually Berkeley DB picks the correct mutex implementation on a system. Unless you know something about your operating system that's not common knowledge, Berkeley DB will pick the best mutex library. To check whether the mutex implementation selected is performing properly, you can use the db_stat utility. The number of times a thread is forced to wait for a mutex—one of the parameters reported by db_stat—should not be significant.

- `--with-mutexalign`: On multiprocessor machines, each processor has its own cache that caches the frequently accessed memory for the thread it's running. If the mutexes being used by two separate threads, running on separate processors, are placed too close together in the memory, then the caches of both processors will cache the mutexes for both the threads. That will force the cache of both the processors to be refreshed every time any mutex is modified. This phenomenon is called *cache sloshing*. Cache sloshing can seriously degrade the performance of a multiprocessor machine. To prevent that from happening, you can set the value of this option to prevent any two mutexes from being aligned on the same cache line.

- `--enable-smallbuild`: This option creates a very small footprint library. On most systems, this option results in a library size of just around 350KB. A number of optional features are disabled when this option is specified. This option is equivalent to specifying `--disable-cryptography`, `--disable-hash`, `--disable-queue`, `--disable-replication`, `--disable-statistics`, and `--disable-verify`. Typically, you use the `--enable-smallbuild` option when embedding Berkeley DB in small devices such as cell phones and personal digital assistants (PDAs).

- `--disable-replication`: You can use this option to create a Berkeley DB library that doesn't support replication. Since replication support adds a significant overhead in terms of library size and performance, it has been made optional.

Most of the other options available in the `configure` script are self-explanatory. You won't normally need to use them, but if you have an unusual requirement, you can browse through the list to see if it's met by one of the available options. Since Berkeley DB is supported on a wide array of operating systems, it isn't feasible to explain the compilation procedure for every platform. The online documentation is sufficient to help you with the installation. Listing 3-1 shows the compilation and installation steps that I go through to install Berkeley DB on my Linux machine.

Listing 3-1. *Compiling and Installing Berkeley DB from the Source Distribution*

```
hy@linux:~/bdb> ls -l
-rw-r-r-1 hy users 6103264 2005-10-26 20:20 db-4.3.29.tar.gz
hy@linux:~/bdb> tar -zxf db-4.3.29.tar.gz
hy@linux:~/bdb> cd db-4.3.29
hy@linux:~/bdb/db-4.3.29> cd build_unix
hy@linux:~/bdb/db-4.3.29/dist_unix> ../dist/configure \
--prefix=/home/hy/bdb/install -enable-cxx
hy@linux:~/bdb/db-4.3.29/dist_unix> make
hy@linux:~/bdb/db-4.3.29/dist_unix> make install
```

■**Tip** To see the list of all the `configure` options, you can run `configure` with the `--help` option. For more information, the Berkeley DB Reference Guide has a discussion of the configuration options.

After I follow these steps, the files appear in the `~/bdb/install` directory, as shown in Listing 3-2.

Listing 3-2. *Berkeley DB Installation Directories*

```
hy@linux:~/sw/install> ls -l
total 14
drwxr-xr-x   6 hy users    168 2005-10-30 14:03 .
drwxr-xr-x   4 hy users     96 2005-10-29 10:17 ..
drwxr-xr-x   2 hy users   1464 2005-10-30 13:56 bin
drwxr-xr-x  12 hy users    336 2005-10-30 13:56 docs
drwxr-xr-x   7 hy users    216 2005-10-30 13:56 include
drwxr-xr-x   3 hy users  13712 2005-10-30 13:56 lib
```

Listing 3-3 shows the Berkeley DB utilities that are bundled with the Berkeley DB distribution. You'll be using them quite a lot for configuring, tuning, and administering the databases; the most useful utility here is db_stat.

Listing 3-3. *Berkeley DB Utilities*

```
hy@linux:~/sw/install> ls -l bin
-r-xr-xr-x  1 hy users   6224 2005-10-30 13:56 bin/db_archive
-r-xr-xr-x  1 hy users   7896 2005-10-30 13:56 bin/db_checkpoint
-r-xr-xr-x  1 hy users   7160 2005-10-30 13:56 bin/db_deadlock
-r-xr-xr-x  1 hy users   9736 2005-10-30 13:56 bin/db_dump
-r-xr-xr-x  1 hy users  18572 2005-10-30 13:56 bin/db_load
-r-xr-xr-x  1 hy users  40796 2005-10-30 13:56 bin/db_printlog
-r-xr-xr-x  1 hy users   7104 2005-10-30 13:56 bin/db_recover
-r-xr-xr-x  1 hy users   8708 2005-10-30 13:56 bin/db_stat
-r-xr-xr-x  1 hy users   6556 2005-10-30 13:56 bin/db_upgrade
-r-xr-xr-x  1 hy users   6940 2005-10-30 13:56 bin/db_verify
```

Listing 3-4 shows the libraries that are created when you compile Berkeley DB. The files with _cxx in the name are libraries with C++ support, and the rest are the libraries with C support. The .so files are the dynamic libraries, and the .a files are the static libraries.

Listing 3-4. *Berkeley DB Libraries*

```
hy@linux:~/sw/install> ls -l lib/
-rw-r--r--  1 hy users 1087050 2005-10-30 13:56 lib/libdb-4.3.a
-rw-r--r--  1 hy users     805 2005-10-30 13:56 lib/libdb-4.3.la
-rwxr-xr-x  1 hy users  860337 2005-10-30 13:56 lib/libdb-4.3.so
lrwxrwxrwx  1 hy users      12 2005-10-30 13:56 lib/libdb-4.so -> libdb-4.3.so
```

```
-rw-r--r--  1 hy users 1087050 2005-10-30 13:56 lib/libdb.a
-rw-r--r--  1 hy users 1212676 2005-10-30 13:56 lib/libdb_cxx-4.3.a
-rw-r--r--  1 hy users     855 2005-10-30 13:56 lib/libdb_cxx-4.3.la
-rwxr-xr-x  1 hy users  970430 2005-10-30 13:56 lib/libdb_cxx-4.3.so
lrwxrwxrwx  1 hy users      16 2005-10-30 13:56 lib/libdb_cxx-4.so ->
libdb_cxx-4.3.so
-rw-r--r--  1 hy users 1212676 2005-10-30 13:56 lib/libdb_cxx.a
lrwxrwxrwx  1 hy users      16 2005-10-30 13:56 lib/libdb_cxx.so -> libdb_cxx-4.3.so
lrwxrwxrwx  1 hy users      12 2005-10-30 13:56 lib/libdb.so -> libdb-4.3.so
hy@linux:~/sw/install>
```

The include directory includes the header files for the C and C++ APIs, as shown in Listing 3-5.

Listing 3-5. *Berkeley DB Include Files*

```
hy@linux:~/sw/install> ls -l include/
total 187
-r--r--r--  1 hy users 33606 2005-10-30 13:54 db_cxx.h
-r--r--r--  1 hy users 88907 2005-10-30 13:54 db.h
hy@linux:~/sw/install>
```

If, for some reason, you want to change the configuration options (for example, if you want to enable diagnostics to troubleshoot some problem), you can rebuild the library with the code shown in Listing 3-6.

Listing 3-6. *Rebuilding Berkeley DB with a New Configuration*

```
hy@linux:~/bdb/db-4.3.29/dist_unix> make realclean
hy@linux:~/bdb/db-4.3.29/dist_unix> ../dist/configure --prefix=/home/hy/bdb/install
\
--enable-cxx --enable-diagnostics

hy@linux:~/bdb/db-4.3.29/dist_unix> make
hy@linux:~/bdb/db-4.3.29/dist_unix> make install
```

■**Tip** It's difficult to remember all the options you used when you last ran configure. And knowing these options is the only way to know what's enabled or disabled in a particular Berkeley DB library. The configure script creates a log of its output that it stores in the build directory (build_unix in the example) in a file called config.log. This file also stores the options with which configure was run.

Also, you should always check the instructions for building and installing the latest Berkeley DB distribution for any changes in the steps for compiling and installing the library. You can check the instructions either online or in the docs directory. It's possible that some options and steps might change in future releases.

Berkeley DB Versioning

If you plan to use Berkeley DB in your application, you should be aware of how Berkeley releases are versioned. That will help you decide when to upgrade to the newer version of Berkeley DB and also when to migrate your existing application to a newer version. The version number included in the distribution consists of three parts (for example, it's 4.3.29 in the example):

- Major version number: This number changes every time any major functionality is introduced. For example, the major version number was bumped from 3 to 4 when replication support was added to the database. A major version-number change could happen if, say, Berkeley DB starts supporting row-level locking for the Btree access method (there are no actual plans for that). In the example, the major version number is 4.

- Minor version number: A minor version number can change when a minor functionality changes. For example, support for sequences in the database caused version 4.2 to jump to 4.3. A minor version number can also change due to minor API changes and transaction-log format changes. The log format changes don't usually require data migration. Running database recovery usually takes care of it. You can find specific instructions for each release on Oracle's web site or in the release notes in the distribution. In the example, the minor version number is 3.

- Patch number: Patch number changes usually consist of bug fixes and no API changes. You should be prepared to make minor code changes every time you upgrade. Oracle believes in deprecating the APIs. It prefers to change the APIs rather than maintain a large number of obsolete APIs. This helps Oracle keep the code base clean and small. In the example, the patch number is 29.

■**Note** In the past, Oracle has changed the format of the internal database pages. The last format change happened in the 3.x.x release when transactions were added to the database. Oracle understands the difficulty developers have to face because of page-format changes, and it tries to keep the format unchanged as much as possible. With the growing user base, it's getting better at keeping the upgrades simple and manageable.

Summary

Berkeley DB provides a flexible configuration scheme that allows you to use Berkeley DB on numerous platforms with the smallest possible footprint from a common code base. The flexible compilation and installation process is still simple enough for a novice to use. In the past, some people have expressed concerns about the changing table formats, but Oracle has assured that this won't be the case in the future. Now that you have Berkeley DB installed on the platform of your choice, you're ready to write your first program. In the next chapter, I'll show you how to write a "Hello World" program the Berkeley DB way.

CHAPTER 4

Building a Simple Application Using Berkeley DB

The best way to get a feel for a new software product is to try it out by using it in a simple program. Since Berkeley DB is a developers' database, it's important that you get introduced to the API as quickly as possible.

In this chapter, I'll show you how to build a simple data store using Berkeley DB. This will allow you to become familiar with the main methods and terminology used in the Berkeley DB APIs. You'll learn about the Berkeley DB environment, which is one of the most important concepts for a Berkeley DB programmer to understand. Berkeley DB allows you to choose an access method for your application. I'll go over the various access methods available in Berkeley DB and explain why it's important to use the right access method for your application.

But first, in the time-honored tradition followed by all computer-programming books, let's print "Hello World"—Berkeley DB style!

Storing "Hello World"

"Hello World" has long been used in computer-programming books, and for good reason. It allows you to build a working prototype quickly without having to understand all the details of a new system. Before proceeding with the code example, I'll go over some terminology used in Berkeley DB. What is normally referred to as a *table* in most database systems is called a *database* in Berkeley DB, and what is referred to as a *database* in other databases is called a *database environment* in Berkeley DB. I'll try to stick to the Berkeley DB terminology most of the time in this book. Sometimes, however, especially when comparing Berkeley DB with another database, I'll use the conventional terms.

■**Tip** A *table* is called a *database*, and a *database* is called a *database environment* in Berkeley DB.

Listing 4-1 shows you how to create a simple database without creating an environment. An environment is required when you want to have multiple databases (or tables) that are related to each other, or when you want to use transactions concurrently from multiple threads (or processes). However, for this example, you just need a stand-alone nonshared database. In Chapters 5, 6, and 7, I'll go over situations in which you'll need an environment.

First, let's store the string "Hello World - Berkeley DB Style !!" in a database and then print it out after reading it from the database. This exercise may seem trivial, but it will help you understand how to create a database and how basic database operations are performed in Berkeley DB.

■**Note** Most of the code examples in this book use the Berkeley DB C++ API and have been compiled and tested on SUSE Linux 10.0.

Listing 4-1. *How to Store "Hello World" in Berkeley DB*

```cpp
#include <iostream>
#include <db_cxx.h>

using std::cout;
using std::endl;
using std::cerr;

int main(int argc, char *argv[])
{
    try
    {
        /* 1: create the database handle */
        Db db(0, 0);

        /* 2: open the database using the handle */
        db.open(NULL, "./chap4_db", NULL, DB_BTREE, DB_CREATE, 0644);

        /* 3: create the key and value Dbts */
        char *first_key = "first_record";
        u_int32_t key_len = (u_int32_t)strlen(first_key);

        char *first_value = "Hello World - Berkeley DB style!!";
        u_int32_t value_len = (u_int32_t)strlen(first_value);

        Dbt key(first_key, key_len + 1 );
        Dbt value(first_value, value_len + 1);

        /* 4: insert the key-value pair into the database */
        int ret;
        ret = db.put(0, &key, &value, DB_NOOVERWRITE);
```

```
    if (ret == DB_KEYEXIST)
    {
        cout << "hello_world: " << first_key << ➥
            " already exists in db"<< endl;
    }

    /* 5: read the value stored earlier in a   Dbt object */
    Dbt stored_value;

    ret = db.get(0, &key, &stored_value, 0);

    /* 6: print the value read from the database */
    cout << (char *)stored_value.get_data() << endl;

    /* 7: close the database handle */
    db.close(0);
}
catch(DbException &dbex)
{
    cerr << "hello_world: exception caught: " << ➥
        dbex.what() << endl;
}
}
```

Let's go over this hello_world.cc program step by step. The following steps correspond with the numbers shown in Listing 4-1:

1. **Create a database handle**: A database handle serves as a reference to the physical database. All database operations are performed using this reference. The method for creating the handle takes two arguments. The first one is the environment handle, which you set to NULL. This means that this database handle will refer to a stand-alone database. The second argument is used to pass a set of flags (after bitwise or-ing the individual flags together). You'll find that the flags argument is present in almost all Berkeley DB APIs. You use it to modify the runtime behavior of various components. In this call, you're not setting any flags.

2. **Open the database handle**: In this step, the handle becomes associated with a physical database. Until open is called on the handle, you cannot use it to access the entries stored in the database. The first argument is a pointer to a transaction object, which you set to NULL. This is used to transactionally protect the open operation. You'll learn more about this when I go over transactions in Chapter 5. The second argument is the file backing up the database that will be associated with the handle. If you're creating multiple databases in the physical file, the third argument will name the database; otherwise, the database name will be the same as the file name. I'll discuss this option in detail later in the chapter. The fourth argument specifies the access method, or the database type, to use for this database. The fifth argument is the set of flags; you use only one flag, DB_CREATE, because you want to create a new database. The last argument specifies the file permissions on the physical file associated with the database.

3. **Create the Dbt objects for the key and the value that you'll store in the database:** The Dbt class encapsulates all the entries—both keys and values—stored in Berkeley DB. I'll go over the details of the Dbt class in the "Dbt Class" section later in this chapter.

4. **Insert the key/value pair using the put method in the database that you opened in step 2:** You use the first argument, which is NULL, to pass the transaction object, similar to what you saw in the open method. The next two arguments specify the key and the value pair that you must insert. The last argument is the set of flags for the put method. You use DB_NOOVERWRITE to tell the database not to overwrite the record if it already exists.

5. **Read the record that you inserted in the database:** Create a Dbt object to receive the value found in the database for the key you used to store the value. You already have the Dbt key that you constructed earlier. In the get method, pass the Dbt key and an empty value Dbt to the database. The first and the last arguments in the get call are the transaction reference and the flags, respectively, both of which are NULL.

Note You could have used the Dbt value that you used to store the record earlier, but you should create another Dbt for the sake of clarity. The library doesn't impose any restriction on the reuse of a Dbt object.

---

6. **Read the value in the Dbt using the get_data method and print it out to stdout:** You have the value in the value Dbt returned by the get call.

7. **Close the database handle:** It's important to close the database after you're done; otherwise, the resources associated with the handle won't be freed. However, if other threads or processes are using the database handle, you shouldn't close it until they're done. Once it's closed, the handle becomes unusable.

Now compile and run the program to see the output:

```
hy@linux:~/ws/bdb_book/chap_4> ./hello_world
Hello World - Berkeley DB style!!
```

As expected, you can see the string you stored in the database. Now if you run your program once more, you will see the following results:

```
hy@linux:~/ws/bdb_book/chap_4> ./hello_world
hello_world: first_record already exists in db
Hello World - Berkeley DB style!!
```

Since you specified the DB_NOOVERWRITE flag, the put method returned DB_KEYEXIST. After running your program, you'll notice that a file called chap4_db has been created in your current working directory. This is the Berkeley DB database file that you specified in the open method. Since you passed the DB_CREATE flag, the library created this file. If you hadn't passed the DB_CREATE flag, the open method would have returned a file-not-found error. Specifying the DB_CREATE flag won't cause a new database to be created if a database already exists with the same name.

Note Listing 4-1 uses a configuration called the *data store*. It's not thread-safe, it provides no locking during concurrent operations, and it doesn't support transactions. This is the simplest data store that you can build using Berkeley DB.

Named, Unnamed, and In-Memory Databases

You just learned how to create a simple stand-alone database backed by a physical file. It's possible in Berkeley DB to create in-memory databases that exist only in the process memory and are never persisted to a file. Such databases are used on diskless systems and for temporary data storage. It's also possible to create multiple databases in a single file. Such databases are useful when you have to access a large number of databases without incurring the overhead of opening too many files. These choices are available implicitly in the Db::open method through various combinations of the file-name and database-name arguments. Table 4-1 summarizes these combinations.

Table 4-1. *Database Persistence Options*

File Name	Database Name	Description
NULL	NULL	Unnamed in-memory database. You can only access it through the handle it was created with.
Not NULL	NULL	Named database backed by a physical file. The database name is the same as the file name. This is the most commonly used configuration.
NULL	Not NULL	Named in-memory database. It was introduced in version 4.4 and is not backed by a file.
Not NULL	Not NULL	Multiple databases backed by a single file.

Error Reporting in Berkeley DB

Berkeley DB methods return three types of return codes:

- **Positive values**: These are returned when the Berkeley DB library encounters a system-related error condition. For example, positive values are returned if the file permissions on a database file don't allow read access. In this case, the error codes are the POSIX error mappings of the actual error codes returned by the operating system.

- **0**: This is returned if an operation is successful.

- **Negative values**: These are returned for Berkeley DB–specific error conditions. For example, DB_KEYEXISTS is returned if a put is tried with a key that's already present in a database that was opened with the DB_NOOVERWRITE flag.

■Note You can configure Berkeley DB to throw an exception instead of returning an error code when the C++ or the Java API is being used. Every exception thrown by the library also has an error code associated with it—this discussion applies to those error codes as well.

In addition to the return codes, Berkeley DB also provides detailed error messages if error reporting is enabled. It's always a good idea to enable error reporting, because you won't get too many error messages. Three reporting channels are available:

- **Error stream**: You can use the set_error_stream() method to set a C++ stream that the Berkeley DB library uses to display error messages.

- **Error file**: You can use the set_errfile() method to set a C library FILE * where the library dumps all the error messages.

- **Error callback**: You can use the set_errcall method to register a user-defined callback to report the errors. This is useful if you already have an error-reporting infrastructure in place, and you'd like to use it for reporting Berkeley DB library error messages.

You can specify multiple error-reporting channels—that is, if you specify a callback function and a FILE *, the message will get sent to both. Unless it's absolutely essential to do otherwise, it's usually better to use only one reporting method in your program, because it can be confusing for someone who is troubleshooting a problem to see the same error being reported in multiple places.

Apart from the reporting channels, you can also set one prefix to the error messages per database handle. If multiple databases are being accessed from multiple threads, then it can become difficult to identify which messages a given database handle reported. If you have a unique prefix that's based on the database handle, debugging in the error messages will be much easier. Listing 4-2 shows you how to add the error callback to the hello_world example.

■Note For database handles opened inside of Berkeley DB environments, calling the Db.set_errpfx method affects the entire environment and is equivalent to calling the DbEnv.set_errpfx method. This is a known issue that should soon get fixed in one of the upcoming releases.

Listing 4-2. *hello_world.cc with Better Error Reporting*

```
#include <iostream>
#include <db_cxx.h>

using std::cout;
using std::endl;
using std::cerr;
```

```cpp
void errCallback (const DbEnv *env, const char *prefix,
                  const char *errMsg)
{
    cout << prefix << " " << errMsg << endl;
}

int main(int argc, char **argv)
{
    Db db(0, 0);
    try
    {
        db.set_errpfx("hello_world");
        db.set_errcall(errCallback);

        db.open(NULL, "./chap4_db", NULL, DB_BTREE, DB_CREATE, 0644);

        char *first_key = "first_record";
        u_int32_t key_len = (u_int32_t)strlen(first_key);

        char *first_value = "Hello World - Berkeley DB style!!";
        u_int32_t value_len = (u_int32_t)strlen(first_value);

        Dbt key(first_key, key_len + 1 );
        Dbt value(first_value, value_len + 1);

        int ret;
        ret = db.put(0, &key, &value, DB_NOOVERWRITE);
        if (ret == DB_KEYEXIST)
        {
            db.err(ret, "");
        }

        Dbt stored_value;
        ret = db.get(0, &key, &stored_value, 0);
        cout << (char *)stored_value.get_data() << endl;
        db.close(0);
    }
    catch(DbException &dbex)
    {
        db.err(dbex.get_errno(), dbex.what());
    }
}
```

When you compile and run this version of hello_world, this is what you should see:

```
hy@linux:~/ws/bdb_book/chap_4> ./hello_world
hello_world : DB_KEYEXIST: Key/data pair already exists
Hello World - Berkeley DB style!!
```

Notice how the library returns a detailed error message for DB_KEYEXISTS error without you having to provide the specific error message, as you had to do in the previous version. The hello_world prefix also appears in the error message; this can be useful if multiple databases are being used simultaneously.

Another advantage of using the error callback is that you can change the output method easily. Suppose that later on, you want to change your reporting method from cout to printf. All you need to change is the errCallback method. In the previous version, on the other hand, you would have had to replace cout with printf in numerous places. As you can see, using the error callback allows you to greatly simplify and enhance the error-reporting capability of your application.

Flags in Berkeley DB

As you must have noticed already, numerous flags are being passed around in the Berkeley DB APIs. Flags are used to modify the runtime behavior of Berkeley DB resources. A flags argument exists in most methods. If you go through the API documentation, you'll find a list of available flags for every method. You can specify any number of available flags by bitwise or-ing them together. For example, in the Db constructor (which creates an empty database handle), there are two possible flags: DB_CXX_NO_EXCEPTIONS and DB_XA_CREATE. Listing 4-3 shows how you can specify these flags.

Listing 4-3. *Setting Configuration Flags*

```
/* no flags set */
Db(0, 0);

/* A Db handle that returns error codes instead of exceptions.*/
Db(0, DB_CXX_NO_EXCEPTION);

/* A Db handle that throws no exceptions and participates in
distributed transactions */
Db(0, DB_CXX_NO_EXCEPTIONS | DB_XA_CREATE);
```

Each flag falls under one of these three categories:

- **Preinitialization flags:** These are set before a resource is initialized. For example, the flags available in the Db constructor fall under this category.

- **Initialization flags:** These are used when initializing a resource. For example, the flags available in the Db::open method fall under this category.

- **Post-initialization flags:** These can be specified at any time during the lifetime of a resource.

Not every resource has all three types of flags. Not all flag combinations may be valid for a given method. When that's the case, the API reference will explicitly mention that. Usually, if the library detects an illegal combination, it will return a sufficiently detailed error message (if you've enabled error reporting). However, sometimes the error message isn't very specific. You'll have to read the documentation carefully to figure out the illegal combination in those cases.

Dbt Class

Berkeley DB doesn't understand the structure of either the keys or the values that are being stored in the database. All keys and values are treated as chunks of binary data. The Dbt class is the encapsulation of the binary data, which is passed to Berkeley DB as keys or values. As is the case with most of the classes in the Berkeley DB C++ API, the Dbt class is a thin wrapper around its Berkeley DB C API counterpart—the DBT structure. It's easier to understand the Dbt class if you can see what the DBT structure contains, as shown in Listing 4-4.

Listing 4-4. *The DBT Structure*

```
typedef struct {
    void     *data;        /* Key/data */
    u_int32_t size;        /* key/data length */
    u_int32_t ulen;        /* RO: length of user buffer. */
    u_int32_t dlen;        /* RO: get/put record length. */
    u_int32_t doff;        /* RO: get/put record offset. */
    u_int32_t flags;
} DBT;
```

data points to the beginning of the key/data byte array, and size specifies the length of that array. You'll be using these two members most of the time. When you do a get on the database, the library stores the pointer to the retrieved record in the data element, and the size of the record in the size element of the DBT structure you passed. By default, the library allocates the buffer that contains the retrieved record. When you do a put, you have to set the pointer of the value that you want to store in the data element and the size in the size element.

■**Caution** When the library allocates the buffer containing the record in the get operation, the buffer is valid only until you do the next get operation on the database handle you used for the get. You should make sure that the record has been copied to a buffer owned by you before you do another get on the handle. The buffer gets reused in subsequent get operations.

However, sometimes when there is a requirement to read/write only a part of the record rather the entire record at once, you'll be using dlen and doff as well. You use ulen to specify the length that the user wants to read or write, and you use doff to set the offset in the actual record from where the read or write should start.

Let's examine partial reads. To do partial reads, you have to set the DB_DBT_PARTIAL flag. Partial reads are needed when you want to process just a part of the record. For example, let's say you've stored a message in the database that's comprised of a fixed-size header and the body. If you're interested only in the body, you can use the DB_DBT_PARTIAL flag to do a partial read of only the body. You'll rarely need this feature; it's easier and simpler to read the entire record and then discard what you don't need. You should use partial reads only if there is a significant overhead involved in reading the entire record. Suppose you have a record in the database that stores the string PARTIAL READ. If you have to read only the "READ" substring, you will initialize the DBT as shown in Listing 4-5 before passing it to the get method.

Listing 4-5. *Preparing DBT for a Partial Read*

```
DBT d;
memset(&d, 0, sizeof(d));
d.dlen = 4;
d.doff = 8;
```

Now let's look at a partial write example. Suppose you want to replace just the "READ" portion of the record to "WRITE". You must perform the operation shown in Listing 4-6.

Listing 4-6. *Preparing DBT for a Partial Write*

```
DBT d;
memset(&d, 0, sizeof(d));
const char *newstr = "WRITE";
d.data = newstr;
d.size = strlen(newstr);
d.dlen = 4;
d.doff = 8;
```

Notice that the record's size will grow after this replacement, because the size of "WRITE" is five characters long, whereas "READ" was only four characters long. You cannot perform this operation if your database supports duplicate records for the same key, because then the put operation will become ambiguous. The library won't know which one of the duplicate records it has to change.

Another important flag in the DBT structure is DB_DBT_USERMEM. You use this flag to tell the library that the requested record should be copied to a user-allocated memory location. This is useful when you want to keep the record in the program memory, but you don't want to incur the overhead of copying the record from the library-allocated memory to your own memory location. When this flag is used, data should point to the user-allocated memory location, and ulen should be set to the size of the allocated buffer. On return, the library sets size to the actual size of the data returned. If the user-defined buffer is smaller than the actual size of the record, size is still set to the actual record size, and the DB_BUFFER_SMALL error is returned (or the DbMemoryException is thrown if the library was configured for throwing exceptions).

Basic Database Operations in Berkeley DB

Now that you're somewhat familiar with Berkeley DB, let's look at how some of the basic operations are performed. If you've worked with relational databases, you'll notice some differences.

Table 4-2 summarizes the basic database operations supported by Berkeley DB. The last column in the table shows the equivalent commands in relational databases.

Table 4-2. *Basic Operations*

Operation	Berkeley DB API	Relational Counterpart
Read	get	SELECT
Insert	put	INSERT
Update	put	UPDATE
Delete	del	DELETE

You're already familiar with get and put. You must have noticed that no UPDATE method is available; you'll have to use put for doing updates as well. Berkeley DB treats inserts and updates in the same way. If the DB_NOOVERWRITE flag isn't set when put is invoked, the supplied record will simply replace the existing record. A side effect of this peculiarity is that even if you want to update only a portion of a record, you'll still have to read the entire record and pass in the entire record (with the modification of course) while doing a put. You could use DB_DBT_PARTIAL and modify only a portion of the record, but calculating the exact offset and length of the modification can be even more cumbersome than reading the entire record.

The reason why the update is missing from Berkeley DB is that it's impossible to update a record if you have no knowledge of the schema of record. Since Berkeley DB doesn't understand the database schema, it has no way to figure out which fields to update. In Chapter 6, I'll show you how you can implement a data-access layer over Berkeley DB to hide this complexity from your application.

■**Note** For doing updates, it would be nice if Berkeley DB provided an interface that said, "Replace bytes X through Y in record Z with the string at location A." There are two reasons why such an interface wasn't added. First, it would have added a difficult-to-use interface to the API. Second, it would have been difficult to handle changes in record size during updates. For example, if the record got longer, the library would have to move the record to a new page, and the act of moving a record would involve multiple API calls to Berkeley DB from inside Berkeley DB, raising new possibilities for deadlocks. It's simple enough to do a delete and then an insert for an update.

Access Methods in Berkeley DB

An *access method* determines how the data gets stored and retrieved in the database under the covers. Some database systems also refer to an access method as a *table type*. A database is a high-level abstraction of the actual data storage. Internally, a database system can store data in numerous ways. For example, it can store it in flat files with records appended one after the other, or it can store it in a hash table with records stored against keys. An access method can be as simple as an American Standard Code for Information Interchange (ASCII) file containing comma-separated values (CSV), where all new records are appended to the end of the file, and retrieval is done by searching for the requested record from the beginning of the file. You've probably already devised and used numerous such systems.

The key characteristic of an access method is the speed with which you can store and retrieve data from the storage. The speed of storage and retrieval is not solely dependent on how you store your data, but it's also dependent on how you access your data. For example, in a logging server, inserts always happen at the end of the log file, and reads almost always go over the records in sequence. For such a system, a sequential access method will work best. On the other hand, a sequential access method won't work that well for an application that looks up individual records based on a known key, because it will have to start searching from the first record every time a record has to be read (as no index is maintained here to enable random access). In this case, a hash table would be a better choice. No single access method can provide the best performance for every type of application.

Common Access Method Configuration Parameters

Berkeley DB not only provides various access methods, which I've covered in the next section, but it also provides a number of configuration parameters that you can use to tune the access methods. Using the access method configuration, you can provide the library with the system and application-specific information that affects the access method performance. You can find some of the biggest performance-tuning knobs among these parameters.

Page Size

A database page is not unlike a disk page. A disk page is the smallest amount of data that it will read or write at a time from the disk. Databases, which do page-level locking, will lock at least the amount of data that fits on a single page. You can set the page size for a database using the following method:

```
Db::set_pagesize(u_int32_t pagesize)
```

Berkeley DB reads and writes data from and to the disk in fixed-size chunks called pages. The page size affects the following characteristics of the database:

- **Locking:** Locking is used to protect data during concurrent operations. It allows each concurrent thread to assume that it's the only one operating on a data set. All access methods (except Queue) use page-level locking at the most granular level. (Depending on which data store you're using, the locking could be courser than page-level.) This means that a lock is acquired over all the records present on a page, even if it's meant to be acquired over some of the records on the page. If you select a page size that's too big, you'll end up unnecessarily locking more records than you need to for every lock, and that will reduce the throughput of concurrent operations.

- **Overflow records:** An overflow record is created if a particular record doesn't fit entirely on one page. The portion that doesn't fit is written on another page, and a reference to it is stored on the original page. Processing overflow records is expensive, because it might involve multiple disk reads. If you select a very small page size, most of the records will overflow page boundaries, resulting in bad performance.

- **Disk I/O**: Disk access is the most expensive operation in a database system. You should avoid it as much a possible. The minimum amount of data that can be written to the disk is the size of a disk block. If the database page is smaller than a disk block, additional disk reads may be required to fill up the block before it can be written to the disk. As a general rule, you shouldn't select a page size that's smaller than the block size of the disk. By default, the page size always is set equal to the block size. If you select a very large page size, the database will needlessly read more data from the disk than required, thereby reducing performance.

■**Tip** Don't try to simulate record-level locking by selecting the page size closest to the size of your records. As you'll see later, page-level locking is often not the reason behind bad performance. It's best not to set the page size on your own unless you're very sure of what you're doing. The default page size (which is set to the disk block size) works pretty well for most applications.

Cache Size

To avoid going to the disk for every piece of data, Berkeley DB uses an in-memory cache of the recently accessed data. If the cache size is big enough and if the queried keys display some degree of locality of reference, disk I/O can be avoided for most database operations. You can find the optimal cache size for an application only by trying out various cache sizes. You can use the following method for setting the cache size:

```
Db::set_cachesize(u_int32_t gbytes, u_int32_t bytes, int ncache)
```

The method has the following arguments:

- gbytes: The number of gigabytes to be allocated for the cache.

- bytes: The number of bytes (in addition to the gigabytes) to be allocated for the cache.

- ncache: The number of caches to be created. Some operating systems have a limit on the amount of memory that can be allocated in a contiguous chunk.

Theoretically, if you keep increasing the cache size, the performance should keep increasing until the entire database fits in the cache. However, that's not always the case. If the cache becomes larger than the physical memory of the system, virtual memory–swapping will start degrading the performance. The best way to evaluate the cache performance in Berkeley DB is to look at the cache hit rate. You can use db_stat (with the –m option) utility to find out the cache hit rate of your application, as you can see in Listing 4-7.

Listing 4-7. *Output of db_stat -m*

```
> db_stat -m
131072  Cache size (128K).
4273    Requested pages found in the cache (97%).
134     Requested pages not found in the cache.
18      Pages created in the cache.
```

116	Pages read into the cache.
93	Pages written from the cache to the backing file.
5	Clean pages forced from the cache.
13	Dirty pages forced from the cache.
0	Dirty buffers written by trickle-sync thread.
130	Current clean buffer count.
4	Current dirty buffer count.

The second line in the output shows the cache hit rate (97%). The default cache size is 256KB, which is almost never sufficient for most applications. You should always set the cache size to a value that suits your application. This is one of the most overlooked tunable parameters, which significantly affects the performance of the database.

■Tip *Always* change the default cache size. To get the best cache size for your application, start with a reasonable cache size of, say, 2MB. Note the cache hit ratio by using db_stat. Increase the size, and note the hit ratio again. Keep doing this until you stop observing a significant improvement in the hit ratio. You then will have the optimal cache size for your application.

Logical Record Numbers

Every record in a relational database has a logical record number associated with it. Logical record numbers are assigned by the database and are used as the default primary key for all tables. Berkeley DB also provides the concept of logical record numbers, but not for all access methods. For Queue and Recno, the database, by default, creates logical record numbers, which are used as primary keys. For Btree, the database can be optionally configured to create logical record numbers. Hash doesn't support them.

When logical record numbers are enabled, every record stored in the database is assigned a unique number, which you can use to access the database without using the key against which the record was stored. The record numbers start from 1; the first record to be inserted in the database is assigned the record number 1. New record numbers are generated by incrementing the maximum existing record number. By default, Berkeley DB doesn't maintain logical record numbers for the databases (except when Queue or Recno access methods are being used), because in most cases, that can significantly reduce the performance of the database. Logical record numbers are maintained differently for different access methods. You'll learn more about them in the next few sections when I discuss the access methods in detail.

■Tip It's tempting to use the logical record number to keep track of the total number of records in the database. However, this can impose a significant penalty on the performance of the database. It's only advisable to do this when the data set is very large and fairly static. If the record numbers aren't maintained in a large data set, it can be very inefficient to count all the records every time a record count is needed. If the new records are not being added frequently, you can ignore the overhead of maintaining the record count.

Btree Access Method

The Btree is the most commonly used access method in databases. A Btree stores data in a balanced, sorted tree structure. This access method has the following characteristics:

- **Insertions, deletions, and lookups take the same amount of time**: The time taken is of the order of $O(\log_B N)$, where B equals the number of records per page, and N equals the total number of records.

- **Lexicographically similar keys are placed close to each other**: This results in better performance when locality of reference is present in the queried keys. You can modify this behavior by supplying a custom comparison function to the library.

- **It performs page-level locking**: This means that if a lock is being acquired for modifying or reading an element, the entire node on which the element is located will be locked.

- **It supports duplicate records**: This means that multiple records can be stored against the same key.

Figure 4-1 shows the structure of a Btree. For efficient lookups, the root page and the internal nodes should always be read into the memory, because that way any record can be accessed with a single disk access even if none of the records (key/data pairs) are present in the memory. However, placing the internal nodes in the memory isn't under the application's control. The only way that can happen is if the keys have some locality of reference and the working set can fit into the cache. The arrangement of the elements within the Btree depends on the following parameters:

- **Tree height**: This specifies the number of levels in the tree. In the example in Figure 4-1, it is three.

- **Minimum number of elements per node**: During a split, this number determines the points at which the node is split. In the example, it is two.

- **Maximum number of elements per node**: When the elements in a node exceed this number, the node is split. In the example, it is three.

Let's see how some of the operations are performed on the Btree:

- **Read**: All reads start at the root (except when a cursor is being used). During a read, a binary search is performed for the requested key until either a match is found, an element bigger than the key is found, or all the elements have been compared. The search ends if the match is found. If a bigger element is found, the child of the element just left of the element is selected. If neither a match nor a bigger element is found, the child of the right-most element is selected for further search.

- **Insert**: The position where the element should be inserted is found through the method described in the previous bullet. After the insertion, if node exceeds the maximum element limit, it's split by pushing one element to the parent node, which itself will be split if it also exceeds the limit, and so on until the root node is reached.

- **Delete**: The element to be deleted is searched as mentioned previously.

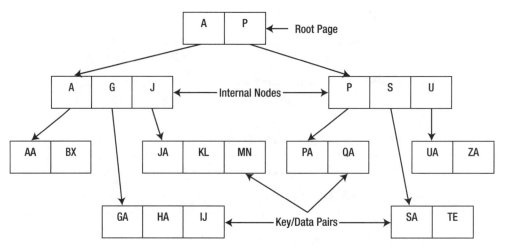

Figure 4-1. *Structure of a Btree*

Types of Applications

Usually the size of the nodes in the Btree is set to be the same as the page size of the disk. When an element has to be read from the disk, the entire page containing the element is read, which brings all the other elements present on that page into the memory as well. Since the elements in a Btree are sorted, the elements on the page are lexicographically similar to each other. If an application queries for lexicographically similar keys in a sequence, the probability of finding the keys in memory will increase if the Btree access method is being used. Suppose, in the Figure 4-1, that key KL is being looked up. If KL isn't already present in the memory, the disk page containing KL will be read into the memory (assuming the page size for the database has been set equal to the size of the disk page). This will bring the elements JA and MN into the memory as well. If the application usually queries similar keys one after the other, then it will most likely query JA or MN, which will be found in the memory without incurring a disk read. In general, applications that request keys having a locality of reference—for example, queries that request a range of adjacent entries—benefit from using the Btree access method.

■**Tip** It can be difficult to determine whether an application's access pattern displays a locality of reference. There are few applications that access data in a truly random pattern, so if you're in doubt, you can safely assume that your application's access pattern shows some degree of locality of reference.

Using the Btree access method isn't a good idea if the memory isn't big enough to hold the root page and all the internal nodes, because then every lookup would involve multiple disk reads.

Logical Record Numbers

A database using the Btree access method can be configured to maintain logical record numbers by setting the DB_RECNUM flag through the following method:

```
Db::set_flags(DB_RECNUM)
```

Once configured, you can use the logical record numbers to access records, as shown in Listing 4-8.

Listing 4-8. *Using Logical Record Numbers*

```
Dbt key, value;
db_recno_t  recnum = 100;
key.set_data (&recnum);
key.set_size(sizeof(recnum));
db.get(0, &key, &value, DB_SET_RECNO);
```

Upon return, the Dbt key will have the key for record number 100, and the Dbt value will have the value for record number 100.

Logical record numbers in Btree access methods are *always* mutable, which means that every time a record is deleted or inserted, all the records with record numbers greater than that of the inserted or deleted record will be reassigned to keep the numbers consistent.

Hash Access Method

The Hash access method uses the extended linear hash (ELH) algorithm. To understand the ELH algorithm, let's look at how hashing works. A hash table creates an index, which you can use to do a random key lookup. The index is created by applying a hashing function on the keys. Figure 4-2 shows how a hashing function maps a set of keys into a hash table.

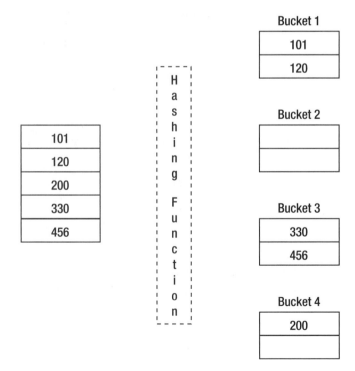

Figure 4-2. *A hash table representation*

The hashing function resolves all keys into a fixed number of indices, represented by buckets in the figure. A key is inserted into the hash by calculating the hash (using the hashing function) and adding the key to the bucket associated with the calculated hash. If more than one key maps to the same bucket, then all of them are stored in the same bucket (or database page). As the number of keys increase, more keys will map to the same bucket. After a while, the bucket will overflow. In the ideal case, all the keys should map to a unique bucket, but the size of such a hash table will be infinite. Bucket overflow can be handled by one of following techniques:

- **Chaining**: A linked list of buckets (or database pages) is created to hold the overflow entries. During a lookup, all chained buckets are searched to find the requested key. As the number of buckets with overflows increases, the performance degrades.

- **Rehashing**: Once the buckets start overflowing, the keys are rearranged by creating more buckets through a modified hashing function. The rehashing of all keys can be very expensive. Once rehashed, the performance is good.

- **Linear hashing**: This dynamic rehashing algorithm dynamically modifies the hashing function in order to keep increasing the number of buckets as the number of keys increases. A detailed description of the algorithm is outside the scope of this book.[1] ELH is one of the best performing algorithms for managing dynamic hashes.

A hash can be very efficient if the number of buckets is large enough to avoid chaining. However, that also results in a large number of empty buckets and wasted storage. ELH provides an efficient trade-off between chained and empty buckets. The Hash access method has the following characteristics:

- **Quick random access**: Any key can be accessed with, at the most, one disk read.

- **Page-level locking**: This access method locks at least one database page at a time while acquiring a lock.

- **Unsorted storage**: The keys aren't sorted, so the Hash access method cannot benefit from locality of reference.

- **Logical record numbers**: Hash doesn't automatically generate a logical record number for every record. However, you can configure a Hash-based database to generate logical record numbers, just like the Btree.

- **Duplicate records**: Multiple records can be stored against the same key.

The Hash access method is useful when random access is required for a large data set. If some degree of locality of reference is present in the queried keys—which is almost always the case—then the Btree will perform better than the hash. However, if the data set is so big that the internal nodes of the Btree cannot be entirely cached in memory, then the hash will perform better. In other words, the Hash access method serves as the last resort for providing random access for large data sets. The Hash access method does not support logical record numbers.

---

1. For more information please visit http://www.oracle.com/technology/documentation/berkeley-db/db/ref/refs/refs.html.

■Tip If you're using the Hash access method, try out the Btree access method as well, and compare the performance. Btree usually performs better than the Hash because it provides locality of reference as well as random access.

Queue Access Method

The Queue access method is a file-based access method that stores all records sequentially. All records that are stored in a Queue have to be of a fixed length. Even though random reads and insert operations are supported, the Queue optimizes the access to the head and the tail of the Queue. Therefore, access to the first and the last record is always very efficient.

Figure 4-3 shows how the Queue access method stores the records. It is the simplest and also the fastest access method available in Berkeley DB.

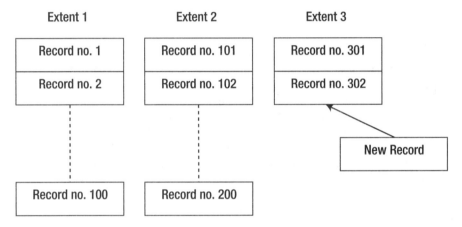

Figure 4-3. *Layout of a Queue*

The *extents* shown in Figure 4-3 represent the backing files that store the records. By default, all records are stored in a single file. The records are accessed in a Queue by calculating the offset from the top of the file using the record number. For example, record 2 in the figure will be located at 2x(record_size) bytes off of the beginning of the file 1. Since no metadata is stored in the Queue access method, the record numbers cannot have gaps. All gaps are filled with empty records, unless extents are being used (extents are explained in the next section). If a record is deleted from the middle, it is replaced by an empty record. If, in the figure, Record no. 310 is inserted instead of Record no. 303, the library will create seven empty records after Record 302 and then insert Record no. 310. The main properties of this access method are

- Fixed-length records

- Record-level locking

- Immutable record numbers

- Supports logical record numbers

Extents

If all records in a Queue are stored in a single file, it's impossible to reclaim the space occupied by the deleted records, because if the file is shrunk (to reflect the deleted records), the offset of the remaining records cannot be calculated with record numbers alone. To allow cleanup of the deleted records, you can divide the Queue storage into fixed-sized extents, which map to fixed-size backing files. When the head of the Queue moves away from an extent, it can be safely deleted. An extent is deleted only when all threads have closed the extent. Once the extent size has been set using the Db::set_q_extentsize(u_int32_t extentsize) method, the extent creation and deletion happens automatically. This method has to be called before open is called on the Db handle.

■Tip The extent size should not be set too small; otherwise, the overhead of opening and closing files will degrade the database performance.

Types of Applications

The Queue access method is best suited for applications that store fixed-length records and access them only through logical record numbers. The perfect use case of the Queue is a publish/subscribe message queue system. In a typical implementation, the messaging system is built by storing the message queues for each subscriber in a Berkeley DB database, which uses the Queue access method. All subscribers wait in the Db::get method, which has the DB_CONSUME_WAIT flag set. DB_CONSUME_WAIT causes the calling thread to wait until a record becomes available to be consumed. The publisher simply inserts messages into the subscriber's Queue databases. Since all operations happen either on the head or the tail of the Queue, they're very efficient (remember that the head/tail access is optimized for the Queue).

■Tip Even if all the records aren't of the same length, you can store them in a Queue by selecting a record size that's bigger than (or equal to) the biggest record. Some space will be wasted as a result of that, but that can be ignored if the records are of roughly the same size.

Recno Access Method

The Recno access method uses a Btree underneath and provides an interface like the Queue access method to the applications. You can use it to store variable-length records based on record numbers. This access method is of limited use. Its main characteristics include

- Variable-length records

- Fixed or mutable record numbers

- The ability to be backed by flat-text files

Logical Record Numbers

Logical record numbers are used as the keys in the Recno access method. This is the only access method that allows a choice of either fixed or mutable logical record numbers; they're fixed by default. You can use the DB_RENUMBER flag in the Db::set_flags method to configure mutable record numbers.

Backing Flat-Text Files

You can configure the Recno access method to be backed with a flat-text file by calling Db::set_re_source. This is useful for providing fast read access to data that's created and stored in a flat-text file—for example, if you want to read the output from a device driver that writes to a flat-text file. Instead of dealing with file offsets and other file-management tasks on your own, you can create a read-only Recno database based on the device driver output file. By default, the ASCII newline character is used as the record relimiter, but you can change that by calling Db::set_re_delim on the Db handle. You can also create a read/write database backed by a flat-text file, but you cannot use it reliably if multiple processes are accessing the file.

Types of Applications

Most applications won't need this access method. Record-based databases that contain variable-length records should use this access method, but even those databases can sometimes use the Queue access method by setting the record size equal to that of the largest record. The use of this access method becomes necessary only when either the maximum record length is not known or there's a big difference among the sizes of the records.

■**Note** Berkeley DB presents a common data access API for all access methods. Minimal application code change is required to change the access method.

Berkeley DB Environment

So far, I've only talked about single stand-alone database (or tables). The code example also used a stand-alone database. However, when you're designing the database for a real-world application, you'll have to deal with multiple databases. You can theoretically store all data in a single database; however, organizing your data into logical namespaces (or tables) simplifies the design of your application and makes it easier for you to maintain and enhance it in the future.

Most applications also have multiple threads of control (which could be threads or processes) that use a common database. The database must work with multiple threads of control reliably. Most relational databases are based on the client/server architecture, where the stand-alone server manages all the tables in its independent address space and provides access to the database over some form of IPC. Berkeley DB, in contrast, is a library that links into the application address space. There's no server process that can coordinate the client threads and manage the tables. The Berkeley DB environment serves as a common location from where the various management and coordination tasks can be staged. The actual tasks still happen within the individual threads of processes, but the states and addresses of the managed resources are stored in the Berkeley DB environment. In other words, the environment serves as a shared repository of control information.

The Berkeley DB environment contains the following information:

- **References to the databases**: The list of all the databases sharing the environment

- **Shared memory segments**: The shared memory segments for caching databases and caching control information

To get a better understanding of the Berkeley DB environment, take a look at Listing 4-9, which shows how to create a Berkeley DB environment. I've added a Berkeley DB environment to the hello_world example from the beginning of the chapter.

Listing 4-9. *Berkeley DB Environment*

```
#include <iostream>
#include <db_cxx.h>

using std::cout;
using std::endl;
using std::cerr;

void errCallback (const DbEnv *env, const char *prefix, const char *errMsg)
{
    cout << prefix << " " << errMsg << endl;
}

int main(int argc, char **argv)
{
    /* Step 1: Create the environment handle */
     DbEnv dbenv(0);

    try
    {
        /* Step 2: Define the environment directory */
        const char *envhome = "./chap4_env";

        /* Step 3: Set up error reporting for the environment */
        dbenv.set_errpfx("env_ex");
        dbenv.set_errcall(errCallback);

        /* Step 4: Open the environment */
        dbenv.open(envhome, DB_CREATE | DB_INIT_MPOOL, 0);
```

```
    /* Step 5: Associate the Db handle with the environment */
    Db db(&dbenv, 0);

  db.open(NULL, "chap4_db", NULL , DB_BTREE, DB_CREATE, 0644);

    char *first_key = "first_record";
    u_int32_t key_len = (u_int32_t)strlen(first_key);

    char *first_value = "Hello World - Berkeley DB style!!";
    u_int32_t value_len = (u_int32_t)strlen(first_value);

    Dbt key(first_key, key_len + 1 );
    Dbt value(first_value, value_len + 1);

    int ret;
    ret = db.put(0, &key, &value, DB_NOOVERWRITE);

    if (ret == DB_KEYEXIST)
    {
        db.err(ret, "");
    }

    Dbt stored_value;
    ret = db.get(0, &key, &stored_value, 0);

    cout << (char *)stored_value.get_data() << endl;

    db.close(0);

    /* Step 6: Close the env handle */
    dbenv.close(0);

}
catch(DbException &dbex)
{
    /* Step 7: Use the Env error handler to report errors */
    dbenv.err(dbex.get_errno(), "Db exception caught");
}
catch(...)
{
    cout << "unknown exception caught" << endl;
}
}
```

As you can see, most of the code here is similar to the hello_world example. Let's step through the modified code. I've referred to the Berkeley DB environment as Env. Here we go:

1. **Create an empty Env handle:** You'll notice that for most Berkeley DB resources, the creation and initialization of resource handles is done in two separate steps. Here you create an empty environment handle, which you will initialize later.

2. **Identify a directory in which to create the Env:** The library uses this directory to store the shared memory backing files. You can also use the same directory for storing the physical backing files for the databases and the transaction logs; the library doesn't impose any restriction on where you keep those files.

3. **Set up the error-handling routines for this Env:** You can use this setup for all the databases associated with this Env. Remember that you had to do this earlier for the database because it wasn't associated with an Env.

4. **Initialize the Env handle:** The first argument in the open method is the Env directory from step 2. Then we have the flags argument. Two flags are set: DB_CREATE to indicate that Env should be created if it doesn't exist, and DB_INIT_MPOOL to initialize the shared memory segment for holding the data cache. An Env handle cannot be initialized without the DB_INIT_MPOOL flag. The last argument is the mode of the files, which Berkeley DB creates to set up the Env. If it isn't set, the default file permissions will be used.

5. **Associate the Env handle with the Db handle:** This is the only way you can associate a database with an Env.

6. **Close the Env handle to clean up the resources associated with the handle:** In order to shut down the environment gracefully, it's important to call close on the environment handle.

7. **Use the Env error-reporting routine to report the errors:** By properly reporting the exceptions thrown by the library, you can enhance the debuggability and maintainability of your application.

When you run this program, you'll see the following output:

```
hy@linux:~/ws/bdb_book/chap_4> ./env_ex
env_ex ./chap4_env/__db.001: No such file or directory
env_ex Db exception caught: No such file or directory
```

The error is returned because the library couldn't find the directory you identified for creating the Env. Let's create the directory and try again:

```
hy@linux:~/ws/bdb_book/chap_4> mkdir chap4_env
hy@linux:~/ws/bdb_book/chap_4> ./env_ex
Hello World - Berkeley DB style!!
```

This time, the database was created, and get found the first_record in the database. Let's look at the files that were created:

```
hy@linux:~/ws/bdb_book/chap_4> ls -al chap4_env/
total 41
drwxr-xr-x  2 hy users     120 2005-11-26 13:47 .
drwxr-xr-x  4 hy users     664 2005-11-26 13:47 ..
-rw-r--r--  1 hy users    8192 2005-11-26 13:47 chap4_db
-rw-r-----  1 hy users   24576 2005-11-26 13:47 __db.001
-rw-r-----  1 hy users  278528 2005-11-26 13:47 __db.002
```

chap4_db is the database file with which you associated the Db handle. By default, all the database files are created in the Env directory. You can change the default behavior by calling DbEnv::set_data_dir to point to a different directory. __db.001 and __db.002 are the shared memory region files that are used for creating the database cache and the lock table. Some additional files are created when the environment is set up for transactions and replication; I'll go over these in Chapters 5 and 6.

Types of Shared Memory Regions

You can create the Berkeley DB environment in any one of the following ways by setting different flags in the DbEnv::open call:

- **Heap memory of the process**: If the environment is supposed to be neither shared with other processes nor backed by the file system, you should open it with the DB_PRIVATE flag. In this case, the environment is wiped out when the process dies. DB_PRIVATE is useful because intraprocess mutexes are faster than interprocess mutexes on some systems, and cleanup is easier since no files are created.

- **System shared memory**: On many operating systems, such as UNIX SystemV systems and VxWorks systems, shared memory based on system memory is available, which isn't backed by the file system. If the environment has to be shared with other processes but it should not be backed by the file system, you can open it with the DB_SYSTEM_MEM flag. This method is not system-independent.

- **File-based shared memory**: If no flag is specified, then file-based system memory will be used, as is the case with the code example. The library uses either the mmap, the shmget interface, or some other form of memory map, depending on the platform, to create the shared memory region.

■**Tip** The file-based shared memory is the most common and the most portable option.

DB_CONFIG and DB_HOME

You can see in Listing 4-9 that the location of the environment is hard-coded in the program. That's clearly a problem, because if you want to change the location of the environment, you'll have to recompile the program. You can mitigate this problem somewhat by providing the Env directory as an argument to the program. However, the environment directory isn't the only configurable property in the environment configuration. You might want to change a number of other properties dynamically without recompiling the program. The DB_CONFIG file allows you to change the environment configuration dynamically.

Before going over the syntax of DB_CONFIG, let's understand how the library locates the environment directories and files. There are two ways you can supply the location of the environment directory.

- **Use the db_home argument in the DbEnv::open method**: This is the method that Listing 4-9 uses.

- **Use the DB_HOME environment variable**: You can set this environment variable and instruct the library to use it by setting the DB_USE_ENVIRON flag in the DbEnv::open method.

The environment directory specified is used as the base directory, and all the file names are treated relative to it. The library uses the following rules to construct the complete path of a file:

- If neither db_home nor DB_HOME is set and the file names aren't absolute, they're treated relative to the current working directory.

- If the file names are absolute, they're used as is without any modification.

- If the environment directory has been specified through db_home or DB_HOME and file names aren't absolute, all file names are appended to the environment directory to compute the file location.

The values in DB_CONFIG override the ones specified in the program. Listing 4-10 shows you how to create DB_CONFIG for the example program and save it in the Berkeley DB environment directory.

Listing 4-10. *Contents of DB_CONFIG*

```
# Berkeley DB Environment configuration for hello_world
# the location of the database files
set_data_dir    hello_world_data
# set the cache size to 0 GBytes 512 KBytes and 1 segment
set_cachesize   0 524288 1
```

The format of the file is a list of name-value pairs (separated with one or more spaces), one per line. Any line starting with a # is ignored and can be used for comments. If you run the program again, you'll see the following results:

```
hy@linux:~/ws/bdb_book/chap_4> ./env_ex
env_ex Db exception caught: No such file or directory
```

The error is thrown because in the DB_CONFIG file, you set the data directory (where all database files are located) to be hello_world_data. Since all file locations are relative to the environment directory (which is set to "./chap4_env" using the db_home argument in Db::open), the library will look for a directory called hello_world_data in the chap4_env directory, which it cannot find. Let's create the directory and try again:

```
hy@linux:~/ws/bdb_book/chap_4> mkdir chap4_env/hello_world_data
hy@linux:~/ws/bdb_book/chap_4> ./env_ex
Hello World - Berkeley DB style!!
```

■**Note** To find out if you can set a particular configuration parameter through the DB_CONFIG file, you should check the API documentation for the method that's used to set the parameter programmatically. If it can be set through DB_CONFIG, there will be a note in the documentation, along with the keyword to be used for setting the parameter value.

Remote File Systems and Berkeley DB

A common question that new Berkeley DB users often ask about the environment is whether they can create it on a remote file system such as Network File System (NFS), Server Message Block (SMB), or Andrew File System (AFS). You might want to do that to access the database from multiple machines or to share the database on a network. The shared memory segments in the environment maintain various mutexes to synchronize database operations, so they should be visible to all the processes using the environment. Since remote file systems rarely allow mapping of remote files to process memory, and no commercial file system allows distributed shared memory for remote files, it's impossible to share mutexes across machines. Therefore, you cannot use remote file systems to host a Berkeley DB environment.

You can, however, host read-only databases from a remote file system, as no locking is required in read-only databases. You can also host read/write databases on remote file systems, but you cannot share them. In other words, the locks have nothing to do with the physical database file, so the file can live anywhere, but the locks must be local. Since it's impossible to acquire locks on a remote file system, you cannot host a modifiable database from a remote file system, even if only a single process is modifying the database. When there is a single modifying process and multiple readers, the readers won't know when the database is being modified, as the locks cannot be shared across machines, and as a result, the readers can read inconsistent data.

Access Control and Security

There's no server process in Berkeley DB that can do sophisticated access control for the database. The file permissions on the database files and the environment directory determine which users and groups can access and modify the database. The usual issues with file permissions–based access control apply to Berkeley DB as well. On UNIX systems, applications using setuid and setguid can assume permissions that aren't granted to the user running the application.

In the case of an unnamed in-memory database, the database is paged to a temporary file on the disk when it gets too big to be held completely in the process memory. The /tmp directory or the directory pointed to by the TMPDIR environment variable is used to create the temporary files. Even though the files created like this are created with permissions to allow read/write access to only the owner on some systems, the /tmp directories are not sufficiently protected. All unnamed in-memory databases should use the DbEnv::set_tmp_dir method to specify a secure temporary directory.

Viewing the Berkeley DB Environment State

Chapter 10 will offer a more detailed look at the utilities available in Berkeley DB, but let's take a quick look at the db_stat utility to see how you can use it to view the state of your Berkeley DB environment. Two options, -e and -E, are available in the db_stat utility and show information related to the environment. Let's run db_stat with -e for the chap4_env, which you created before.

Various types of statistics are printed out by db_stat -e. The most useful ones are the ones related to the cache, which are the same as reported by db_stat -m, as you saw earlier. These statistics are most useful when you're trying out different configuration settings and want to see how they're affecting the performance. Sometimes when the database performance is inexplicably bad, you can look at the environment statistics to get a clue about the problem. Here's what you'll see when you run db_stat on chap4_env:

```
hy@linux:~/ws/bdb_book/chap_4/chap4_env> db_stat -e
4.3.29   Environment version
0x120897      Magic number
0        Panic value
1        References
0        The number of region locks that required waiting (0%)
=-=-=-=-=-=-=-=-=-=-=-=-=-=-=-=-=-=-=-=-=-=-=
264KB 48B      Total cache size
1        Number of caches
272KB    Pool individual cache size
0        Maximum memory-mapped file size
0        Maximum open file descriptors
0        Maximum sequential buffer writes
0        Sleep after writing maximum sequential buffers
0        Requested pages mapped into the process' address space
12       Requested pages found in the cache (75%)
4        Requested pages not found in the cache
0        Pages created in the cache
4        Pages read into the cache
2        Pages written from the cache to the backing file
0        Clean pages forced from the cache
0        Dirty pages forced from the cache
0        Dirty pages written by trickle-sync thread
4        Current total page count
4        Current clean page count
0        Current dirty page count
37       Number of hash buckets used for page location
20       Total number of times hash chains searched for a page
1        The longest hash chain searched for a page
12       Total number of hash buckets examined for page location
0        The number of hash bucket locks that required waiting (0%)
0        The maximum number of times any hash bucket lock was waited for
0        The number of region locks that required waiting (0%)
14       The number of page allocations
```

```
0        The number of hash buckets examined during allocations
0        The maximum number of hash buckets examined for an allocation
0        The number of pages examined during allocations
0        The max number of pages examined for an allocation
Pool File: chap4_db
4096     Page size
0        Requested pages mapped into the process' address space
6        Requested pages found in the cache (75%)
2        Requested pages not found in the cache
0        Pages created in the cache
2        Pages read into the cache
1        Pages written from the cache to the backing file
```

db_stat -E reports the details of the environment's shared memory region and is used for debugging problems within the Berkeley DB library.

Summary

Berkeley DB provides a very simple data-access API. No single access method is optimal for every type of application; Berkeley DB is one of the few databases that allow you to choose the best access method for a particular application. Another unique feature of Berkeley DB is that it provides a common API for all four access methods (Btree, Hash, Queue, and Recno). This allows you to change the access method without much change to your application code. The Berkeley DB environment allows multiple processes to share a set of databases. A rich set of environment tuning parameters is available in the Berkeley DB API, which you can use to build the optimal database solution for any type of application on any platform. In the next chapter, I'll go over the different data-store wrappers, which include CDS and TDS.

■ ■ ■

CHAPTER 5

Introduction to Advanced Data Stores

You can't master a software product unless you build a sophisticated application that uses most, if not all, of the product's features. No amount of theoretical discourse can replace the experience gained from building a real application.

In this chapter, you'll learn how to use Berkeley DB to build applications that employ more sophisticated data stores. I'll explain CDS, which allows you to access the database from multiple threads with limited concurrency, and TDS, which allows you to build ACID-compliant database access with no restriction on the number of concurrent reader and writer threads. I'll aim to provide you with a good understanding of locking, logging, and deadlocks to work with TDS. You'll notice that a large number of topics are introduced at a rather high level in this chapter. I'll cover most in much more detail in subsequent chapters. This chapter is intended to provide a background so you can understand the more-involved discussions in the later chapters.

Database Locking

In Chapter 4, you learned how to build an application that uses a simple DS. You learned how to use a single-threaded program to demonstrate the creation and usage of a DS. The main limitations of a DS are that it doesn't do any locking, logging, transactions, and recovery; therefore, it doesn't provide features associated with ACID-compliant databases.

Take a look at Figure 5-1 to understand why locking is required if multiple threads are accessing the database concurrently.

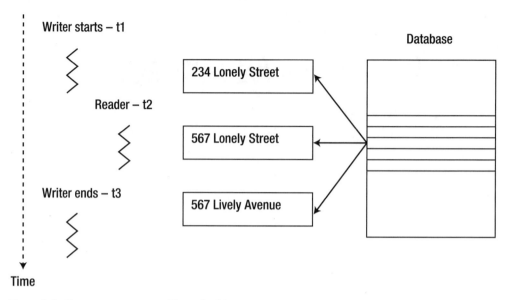

Figure 5-1. *Concurrent access without locking*

Figure 5-1 shows a reader and a writer accessing an address database concurrently. The writer thread wants to update a stored street address, which is 234 Lonely Street. It starts modifying the street address at time t1. It modifies the address to 567 Lively Street by time t3. In between t1 and t3, the reader accesses the same record. Since the writer didn't block the record, the reader is able to read it even while it's being modified. The reader reads 567 Lonely Street as the address, which is neither the address before the writer modified it nor the address after the modification. Concurrent access without locking can therefore result in data corruption.

Now let's introduce locking to the address database. A lock can be defined as a *token*, which indicates that a resource is in use. If a thread has acquired a lock for a resource, then another thread will wait until that lock is released before it can acquire another lock on that resource for itself. Generally speaking, there are two types of locks: shared and exclusive. An *exclusive lock* blocks everyone, other than the entity that owns the lock, from using the locked resource. A write lock (W), which indicates that the locked resource is about to be modified, is an exclusive lock. A *shared lock*, such as the read lock (R), allows other readers to access the resource but blocks all the writers from accessing the resource. Figure 5-2 shows the access sequence with locking.

The writer thread starts at t1 and acquires a lock W on the record. At t2, the reader thread comes in but gets blocked, because it finds that the record has a lock W on it. At t3, the writer is done with the modification, and it releases the lock W. At t4, the reader finds that the record has no locks on it. It acquires its own lock R on the record and reads it. As you can see, the reader is able to read the record only after the modification is completed, so it gets a consistent record.

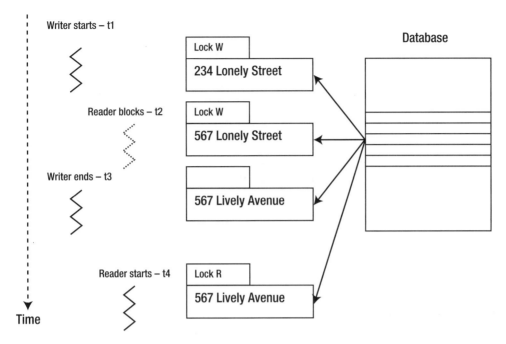

Figure 5-2. *Concurrent access with locking*

Lock Granularity

In Figure 5-2 the threads are shown acquiring a lock on the record that they're accessing. The figure doesn't show the scope, or the granularity, of the acquired lock. The record could have been locked using one of the following types of locks:

- **Record-level lock**: Locks only the memory location occupied by the record

- **Page-level lock**: Locks the entire page in the database cache that holds the record

- **Database-level lock**: Locks the entire database where the record resides

- **Environment-level lock**: Locks the entire environment in which the database was created

The record-level locks have the finest granularity, and the environment-level locks have the coarsest granularity. Record-level locking has a couple of advantages:

- **Increased concurrency**: Only one single record is locked by a lock, so more threads can access the database without blocking.

- **Increased throughput**: More threads are able to operate on the database without blocking, so the throughput can increase.

Record-level locking has a few disadvantages as well, including the following:

- **Complexity**: Record-level locking is much more complex to implement, test, and debug compared to page-level locking, because it has a large number of possible locking states for every database page. (The possible locking states are n^2, where n is the number of records per page.) In addition, it becomes complicated to implement, because database recovery has to take into account multiple threads of control while simultaneously making structural changes to a page, such as splitting it.

- **Bigger lock tables**: Every thread has to acquire a lock on every record accessed by it, so the data structures required to hold the locks can become huge. After a certain point, the management of the lock table can degrade the database performance.

- **Deadlocks**: If the threads modify multiple records at a time, it's possible to have deadlocks, in which two or more threads wait for each other forever because they all hold locks on records needed by the other threads.

Lock granularity plays an important role in database performance. Different types of applications require different levels of lock granularity to perform optimally.

■**Note** In practice, many database systems "promote" a large number of record locks to a page lock, and a large number of page locks to a table lock. Berkeley DB uses page-level locking to avoid this problem. Again, it's a question of complexity. When there are more code paths to test, and more code to execute at runtime, page-level locking provides less complexity along with good performance.

Optimal locking granularity is also dependent on the access pattern of the application using the database. Low-concurrency applications that deal with small amounts of data, such as a router storing its configuration information, work fine with table-level locking. On the other hand, a stock exchange that manages price information for thousands of stocks and executes millions of trades every minute needs record-level locking.

Lock Types

There are two types of locks:

- **Shared locks**: Multiple threads can acquire shared locks at a given time for a given resource. Read locks are shared locks.

- **Exclusive locks**: Only one thread at a time can acquire exclusive locks. Write locks are exclusive locks.

Figure 5-2 shows that it's possible for another reader thread at time t4 to acquire another read lock on the record. This is a simple description of lock types. In practice, things are more complicated. The database maintains a lock-conflict graph for every locked resource. When a thread of control tries to access a resource, the conflict graph of the resource is evaluated to either permit or to deny access to the resource. Read locks can be shared with other readers, but not with writers. Write locks can't be shared with anybody.

Concurrent Data Store

You now have sufficient background for me to introduce a slightly more sophisticated data store than the simple DS you saw in Chapter 4. The CDS allows multiple threads to access the database concurrently, with one restriction. The restriction is that either multiple readers or a single writer can access the database at any given time. (Other database systems call this a "table-level lock," since Berkeley DB calls tables "databases.") If multiple writers try to access the database, only one will be allowed; the rest will have to wait until the writer is done. Likewise, if a writer wants to access a database while one or more readers is using it, then the writer must wait until all the readers are done reading.

It's easier to understand the behavior in terms of lock semantics. CDS enables concurrent access by enforcing database-level locks, which means that if a thread is modifying any record in the database, the entire database will be locked until the thread is done. Since read locks are shared locks, multiple readers can acquire a read lock on the database concurrently and therefore read the database concurrently. Since write locks are exclusive, only one thread can acquire it at a time; all other threads, whether readers or writers, have to wait until the write lock is released.

Let's now go through a code example that shows you how to create a database based on CDS. The code will help you understand the various flags and options used in the CDS. I'll discuss the design issues after the code example.

A Note About the Code Example

The code examples in this chapter use cursors and some open source C++ libraries. You might not be familiar with the cursor concept and the C++ libraries I'm using, so I'm taking a small detour in this section, to introduce them, before going over the code example. I'll cover cursors in more depth in the next chapter. If you'd like, you can read the section on cursors in the next chapter before going over the rest of this chapter. Since a complete treatment of cursors isn't possible before introducing the topics covered in this chapter, I've placed it in the next chapter.

A Brief Introduction to Cursors

A *cursor* is a location within a database. A good analogy for a cursor, from the world of programming language patterns, would be an *iterator*. If you have to access all the entries in a hash table without knowing in advance all the keys that are stored in it, then the only way you can do that is by using an iterator. Similarly, if you have to access all the entries in a database without knowing all the keys that are stored in it, then you'll have to use a cursor. A cursor is used for the following purposes.

- **Sequentially accessing all entries in a database**: If all the keys stored in a database aren't known, then the only way to access all the entries in the database is through a cursor.

- **Accessing duplicate entries**: If a database supports duplicates, then the only way to access all the values stored against a key is through a cursor.

You can create a cursor on a Db handle by calling the cursor method on it, as shown in Listing 5-1.

Listing 5-1. *Creating a Cursor from a Db Handle*

```
Dbc *dbcur;
db->cursor(NULL, &dbcur, 0); // where db is an instance of Db class
```

Listing 5-2 shows how you can iterate through all the entries using the cursor.

Listing 5-2. *Iterating a Database Using a Cursor*

```
Dbt key, value;
while (dbcur->get(&key, &value, DB_NEXT) == 0)
{
    char *key = (char*)key.get_data(); // assuming the key is a string
    char *data = (char*)key.get_data(); // assuming data is a string
}
dbcur->close();
```

■Tip It's important to close the cursor after you're done with it because the resources allocated to the cursor by the library don't get released unless the cursor is closed.

Cursor Positions

You can give a cursor a specific position by specifying certain flags in the get method of the cursor. Here's the list of those flags:

- DB_FIRST, DB_LAST: For positioning at the first or the last record of the database.

- DB_NEXT, DB_PREV: For moving to the next or previous record. When specified for the first time after opening the cursor, DB_NEXT is identical to DB_FIRST, and DB_PREV is identical to DB_LAST.

- DB_NEXT_DUP, DB_NEXT_NODUP, DB_PREV_NODUP: If the database supports duplicates, using DB_NEXT_DUP flag will let you go over all the data values stored against a particular key. If no duplicate records are present for a key and DB_NEXT_DUP is set, then DB_NOT_FOUND is returned. DB_NEXT_NODUP skips over the duplicate values and positions the cursor on the next nonduplicate record in the database. Similarly, DB_PREV_NODUP skips over the duplicate values to position the cursor on the previous key.

- DB_CURRENT, DB_SET: DB_CURRENT lets you refer to the location where the cursor is currently positioned. DB_SET lets you position the cursor on a known key.

Cursor Operations

Cursors support the following operations:

- get: Reads a record. The location is specified using one of the flags described in the previous section.

- put: Stores or updates a record. The location of the inserted record is specified by DB_AFTER, DB_CURRENT, DB_BEFORE, DB_KEYFIRST (the first of the duplicates) or DB_KEYLAST (the last of the duplicates).

- del: Deletes a record. Only the record at which the cursor is currently positioned can be deleted.

- count: Counts the number of duplicate records for a given key. It doesn't count the total number of records in the database.

Open Source C++ Libraries

I've extensively used the following C++-based open source libraries in this book's code examples:

- **Standard Template Library (STL):** This template-based library provides containers, iterators, and algorithms. It's available on Windows as well as most UNIX platforms.

- **Adaptive Communication Environment (ACE):** This template-based library provides threading, messaging, logging, and many other useful design patterns. ACE is freely available; it is open source and has been ported to most operating systems.

- **Boost:** It provides memory management, file-system utilities, parsing utilities, and many other utility classes. Boost is open source and is known to work on most operating systems.

Using just C in my code examples would have addressed the largest subsection of programmers. However, I decided to use C++ and the previously mentioned libraries so I could focus on the database issues without spending too much time on the infrastructure. C++, along with these libraries, exposes intuitive, high-level design patterns. For example, ACE provides ready-made, neatly organized thread classes that you can use to build multithreaded applications quickly. If I had to write the same code in C, it would have taken a lot more time, and it would've been difficult to organize it as neatly into individual class-based modules. It shouldn't be difficult to convert this code to C or to use other C++ libraries. I'll introduce you to the features I've used in my program from these libraries.

ACE_DEBUG

ACE_DEBUG is a macro from the ACE library that allows you to do logging from your programs. This useful tool lets you send the output to stdout or to a file, depending on the configuration. It also allows you to control the log level and print the thread IDs by using the %t format directive.

ACE_Task_Base

ACE_Task_Base is an ACE wrapper around pthread. By putting the code that has to be run in a thread in a class derived from ACE_Task_Base, you can easily create, suspend, and wait for a thread.

Creating a CDS Data Store

Listing 5-3 shows the code for creating a simple CDS database. The file name for the code is
cds.cc. This program creates a CDS-based Berkeley DB environment. A database is opened in
the environment and then two threads are created—one writer thread and one reader thread—
to demonstrate that multiple threads can access a CDS database concurrently. The code is
organized in such a way that you can easily create any number of reader and writer threads.

Listing 5-3. *Creating Multiple Reader/Writer Threads for Accessing CDS*

```
 1 #include <iostream>
 2 #include <sstream>
 3 #include <string>
 4
 5 #include <db_cxx.h>
 6
 7 #include <ace/Task.h>
 8
 9 using std::cout;
10 using std::endl;
11 using std::cerr;
12 using std::stringstream;
13 using std::string;
14
15 #define NUM_RECS 5
16
17 void errCallback (const DbEnv *env, const char *prefix, const char *errMsg)
18 {
19     ACE_DEBUG((LM_ERROR, "(%t) %s errMsg: %s\n", prefix, errMsg));
20 }
21
22 class CDSWorker: public ACE_Task_Base
23 {
24     public:
25         CDSWorker(DbEnv *env, Db *db, bool reader, int id);
26         virtual int svc();
27
28     private:
29         void runReader();
30         void runWriter();
31
32         DbEnv   *env_;
33         Db      *db_;
34         bool    reader_;
35         int     id_;
36 };
37
38 CDSWorker::CDSWorker(DbEnv *env, Db *db, bool reader, int id)
```

```
39        :env_(env), db_(db), reader_(reader), id_(id)
40 {}
41
42 int CDSWorker::svc()
43 {
44     try
45     {
46         if(reader_)
47             runReader();
48         else
49             runWriter();
50     }
51     catch(...)
52     {
53         ACE_DEBUG((LM_ERROR, "CDSWorker: exception caught\n"));
54     }
55 }
56
57 void CDSWorker::runReader()
58 {
59     Dbc *dbcur;
60     db_->cursor(NULL, &dbcur, 0);
61     Dbt key;
62     Dbt value;
63
64     while (dbcur->get(&key, &value, DB_NEXT) == 0)
65     {
66         ACE_DEBUG((LM_ERROR, "Reader %d: key \"%s\" data \"%s\"\n",
67                     id_, (char*)(key.get_data()),
68                     (char*)(value.get_data()) ));
69         ACE_OS::sleep(1);
70     }
71     dbcur->close();
72 }
73
74 void CDSWorker::runWriter()
75 {
76     for(int i=0; i < NUM_RECS; i++)
77     {
78         stringstream keyss;
79         keyss << id_;
80         keyss << "_";
81         keyss << i;
82         string keystr = keyss.str();
83
84         stringstream valss;
85         valss << id_;
```

```
86            valss << "_";
87            valss << i*i;
88            string valstr = valss.str();
89
90            Dbt key((void*)(keystr.c_str()), keystr.size() + 1);
91            Dbt value((void*)(valstr.c_str()), valstr.size() + 1);
92
93            int ret = db_->put(0, &key, &value, 0);
94            if(ret)
95                env_->err(ret, keystr.c_str());
96            else
97                ACE_DEBUG((LM_ERROR, "Writer %d: key \"%s\" data \"%s\" \n",
98                          id_,
99                          keystr.c_str(),
100                         valstr.c_str() ));
101           ACE_OS::sleep(1);
102       }
103 }
104
105 int main(int argc, char **argv)
106 {
107     DbEnv dbenv(0);
108
109     try
110     {
111         const char *envhome = "./chap5_env";
112
113         dbenv.set_errpfx("env_ex");
114         dbenv.set_errcall(errCallback);
115
116         dbenv.open(envhome, DB_CREATE | DB_INIT_MPOOL | ➥
117                                 DB_INIT_CDB | DB_THREAD, 0);
118         Db db(&dbenv, 0);
119         db.open(NULL, "chap5_cds", NULL , DB_BTREE, DB_CREATE | ➥
120                            DB_THREAD, S_IRUSR | S_IWUSR );
121         CDSWorker *w1 = new CDSWorker(&dbenv, &db, false, 1);
122         if(w1->activate((THR_NEW_LWP | THR_JOINABLE), 1) != 0)
123             ACE_DEBUG((LM_ERROR, "Could not launch w1\n"));
124
125         CDSWorker *r1 = new CDSWorker(&dbenv, &db, true, 2);
126         if(r1->activate((THR_NEW_LWP | THR_JOINABLE), 1) != 0)
127             ACE_DEBUG((LM_ERROR, "Could not launch r1\n"));
128
129         w1->wait();
130         r1->wait();
```

```
131
132        delete r1;
133        delete w1;
134
135        db.close(0);
136        dbenv.close(0);
137
138    }
139    catch(DbException &dbex)
140    {
141        dbenv.err(dbex.get_errno(), "Db exception caught");
142    }
143    catch(...)
144    {
145        cout << "unknown exception caught" << endl;
146    }
147 }
```

Let's go through the program, starting from main. You'll notice that I start with line 107 and then describe the smaller line numbers later on. That's because main is located after the other methods in the program:

- **Lines 107–119**: Create and open a DbEnv handle. This time, you specify two extra flags. DB_INIT_CDB indicates that you want to create a CDS. DB_THREAD tells the environment that you'll be using the database in a multithreaded environment.

■**Caution** If DB_THREAD isn't used in multithreaded applications, all database locks for a given Db handle will be created with the same locker ID. In addition, data corruption could happen if the same Db handle is used from multiple threads simultaneously. (It's safe to do that if the use of the handle is serialized.)

- **Lines 121–127**: Create and launch one reader thread and one writer thread. CDSWorker is a class derived from ACE_Task_Base (a wrapper around pthread). CDSWorker takes the DbEnv handle, Db handle, a flag (to indicate whether it's a reader or a writer), and an ID as arguments. The activate method launches the thread.

- **Lines 129–130**: Wait for the threads to finish.

- **Lines 132–136**: Delete the thread objects and close the Db and DbEnv handles.

- **Lines 22–36**: Declare the CDSWorker class, which is derived from ACE_Task_Base. The svc method is invoked when activate is called on an instance. There are two private methods defined to execute the reader and the writer threads, and there are four private variables for storing the Db handle, the DbEnv handle, the ID, and the mode of the thread.

- **Lines 38–40**: Define the constructor.

- **Lines 42–55:** Define the svc method. It looks at the mode flag and runs either runReader or runWriter.

- **Lines 57–71:** Define runReader. A cursor is created on the Db handle, and all the records are read in a while loop.

- **Lines 74–103:** Define runWriter. Five records are created (or updated if they already exist) here. The key is created by appending the thread ID to the loop count. The value is created by appending the thread ID to the square of loop count. This scheme ensures a unique key for every record created by every writer thread.

When you run the program from Listing 5-3, this is what you get:

```
hy@linux:~/ws/bdb_book/chap_5> ./cds
Writer 1: key "1_0" data "1_0"
Reader 2: key "1_0" data "1_0"
Writer 1: key "1_1" data "1_1"
Writer 1: key "1_2" data "1_4"
Writer 1: key "1_3" data "1_9"
Writer 1: key "1_4" data "1_16"
```

You created and launched one writer thread and one reader thread. The writer first creates the record for key 1_0. Since the writer loop uses the put method, the locks are released at the end of the operation. Since the CDS locks the entire table for every operation, and since write locks are exclusive, the reader thread blocks until the writer is done. The reader creates a cursor to read all the records, since only one record exists by the time it reads it, and closes the cursor and releases the locks on the table. A cursor holds a read lock until it is closed, so the writer gets blocked until the reader closes the cursor, after which it creates the rest of the four records.

Let's run the program again. Now the database already contains five records. You would expect the reader to iterate through all ten records before the writer gets a chance to write. Let's see what happens:

```
hy@linux:~/ws/bdb_book/chap_5> ./cds
Writer 1: key "1_0" data "1_0"
Reader 2: key "1_0" data "1_0"
Reader 2: key "1_1" data "1_1"
Reader 2: key "1_2" data "1_4"
Reader 2: key "1_3" data "1_9"
Reader 2: key "1_4" data "1_16"
Writer 1: key "1_1" data "1_1"
Writer 1: key "1_2" data "1_4"
Writer 1: key "1_3" data "1_9"
Writer 1: key "1_4" data "1_16"
```

As expected, the writer blocks until the reader iterates through all the existing records, and then it gets a chance to update the records. By introducing more threads in this program, you can simulate a real multithreaded application and use it as a benchmark for evaluating various database configurations. I'll be using this program with variations in the rest of the book.

Using DB_THREAD Correctly in CDS

To highlight the importance of DB_THREAD as used in lines 107-119 of Listing 5-3, let's try out one variation of the program. Replace lines 116-119 in cds.cc with the following lines:

```
116             dbenv.open(envhome, DB_CREATE | DB_INIT_MPOOL | DB_INIT_CDB, 0);
117
118             Db db(&dbenv, 0);
119             db.open(NULL, "chap5_cds", NULL , DB_BTREE, DB_CREATE, ➥
                                S_IRUSR | S_IWUSR);
```

You've simply removed the DB_THREAD flag from the open calls of DbEnv and Db. If you run the modified program, you'll see the following output:

```
hy@linux:~/ws/bdb_book/chap_5> ./cds
Writer 1: key "1_0" data "1_0"
Reader 2: key "1_0" data "1_0"
Writer 1: key "1_1" data "1_1"
Reader 2: key "1_1" data "1_1"
Writer 1: key "1_2" data "1_4"
Reader 2: key "1_2" data "1_4"
Writer 1: key "1_3" data "1_9"
Reader 2: key "1_3" data "1_9"
Writer 1: key "1_4" data "1_16"
Reader 2: key "1_4" data "1_16"
```

Neither the writer nor the reader blocks if you don't set the DB_THREAD flag. In the absence of the DB_THREAD flag, the library creates all locks (for both the reader and the writer threads) with the same locker ID, resulting in no lock protection at all. This can lead to serious errors in highly concurrent applications.

Another important thing to keep in mind when using DB_THREAD with CDS is that you must never mix cursor and noncursor operations in the same thread. When DB_THREAD is set, each method invocation on each Db handle and each cursor is assigned a unique locker ID, so that when a Db handle is used from multiple threads, there's no ambiguity as to which thread owns the lock for the handle (or the cursor). This approach, however, can cause a problem when the same thread mixes operations on a cursor and a Db handle. Since the same thread will create locks with two different locker IDs, it can result in a self-deadlock. A self-deadlock is unlike a normal deadlock, where multiple threads are involved, and it cannot be resolved like a normal deadlock.

So far in this chapter, you've learned about the issues that an application has to deal with at the database-access level, without looking at the issues involved at the system level.. You've been looking at the trees without worrying about the forest, so to speak. Now I'll take a small detour to look at the bigger picture, before going back to the CDS discussion. In the next section I'll consider various aspects of database administration and investigate questions such as, what happens when a process that's linked to a Berkeley DB environment crashes? Or, how can a process ensure that the database environment that it's using isn't corrupted? These administrative tasks are performed, through various Berkeley DB APIs, by an entity called a *watchdog*, which you'll have to implement.

Database Watchdog

A watchdog is a process (or a thread) that monitors something. It's a generic term that's used in numerous contexts; however, most watchdogs do some kind of monitoring. A database watchdog monitors a database. It ensures that the database isn't corrupted and that if it does get corrupted, all the threads (and processes) using the database will be notified of the corruption. In client/server-based databases, the database server also acts as the watchdog.

Architecting an industrial-strength solution using Berkeley DB can be a challenging exercise. The challenge stems mainly from the fact that Berkeley DB is a library. There is no watchdog entity that can coordinate proper initialization, usage, and recovery of database resources. The lack of a watchdog is both a strength and a weakness. It's a strength because it allows you to design a custom watchdog that does exactly what the application needs. It is a weakness because it's difficult to design a good watchdog.

To understand why the lack of a central monitoring process makes it difficult to manage concurrent database access, let's look at how Berkeley DB protects its shared memory region. Figure 5-3 shows a Berkeley DB shared memory region.

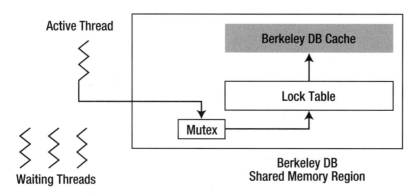

Figure 5-3. *Securing the Berkeley DB shared memory region*

The Berkeley DB cache is the cache of data stored in the database. The lock table holds the list of locks and the lockers who own those locks. When a thread acquires a lock on a page, a database (or any other database resource) creates an entry in the lock table against its own locker ID, which is issued by the library. If another thread is interested in that resource, it first checks the lock table to see if another locker has locked it already. If the resource has already been locked, the second thread will wait for the lock to be freed. This scheme still has a problem. If the second thread comes in while the first thread is creating the lock-table entry, then it's possible that both threads can acquire locks on the same resource. To protect the access to the lock table, Berkeley DB uses a mutex.

Every time a thread accesses the lock table, the library acquires a mutex on behalf of the thread and releases the mutex when the thread is done with the table. This mutex isn't held for the entire duration of the database operation on the locked resource, but rather only for the duration when the thread is reading or modifying the lock table. This arrangement works well as long as all the threads behave properly—that is, as long as they don't corrupt the lock table and the cache, and they release the mutex after accessing the lock table. However, in the real world, it's impossible to guarantee that all threads will behave properly. If a thread crashes before it is able to release the lock table mutex, the entire Berkeley DB environment will become unusable, as no other thread will be able to access the lock table and the database cache. To prevent such a thing from happening, you have to implement a watchdog that can monitor the activities of the threads accessing the database. The watchdog must perform the following tasks:

- **Monitor the threads entering the shared memory region**: If a thread dies while inside a Berkeley DB call, the environment can become corrupted.

- **Verify that the environment isn't corrupted**: It's possible that some threads of control can continue to use an environment that has been corrupted. The watchdog should try to prevent that by making sure that if a thread died in the library, it didn't corrupt the environment.

- **Recover the environment**: If the environment becomes corrupted, the watchdog should be able to recover it. In CDS and DS, the only way to recover an environment is to kill all the processes that are linked to the environment, remove the corrupted environment, re-create a new environment, and finally restart all the processes.

Process Monitoring

The primary task of the watchdog is to monitor the application processes or threads that are sharing the Berkeley DB environment. There are multiple ways in which a watchdog can keep track of the threads of control. The simplest way is to make the watchdog the parent process (or thread) of all the other threads of control. When a thread of control dies abnormally, the watchdog receives an indication of the abnormal exit of a child, so it can then kill all the other threads of control, recover the environment, and restart the children.

■**Note** You can find a more detailed discussion on the design of the watchdog in Chapter 6.

Database Verification

The process of database verification verifies the integrity of the data stored in the database. You can do database verification either to detect whether the data stored in the database is corrupted, or to salvage the data from a corrupted database. The verification process involves an analysis of every database page, so it can take a long time if a large amount of data is present in the database. Since it's an expensive operation, you should perform verification only when there is a reasonable possibility of database corruption.

You can enable database verification either by running the db_verify utility externally or by using the verify method within the program. If you were to add database verification to the code example from Listing 5-3, you would modify the program as follows:

```
118         Db db_ver(NULL, 0);
119         int verify = db_ver.verify( "./chap5_env/chap5_cds", NULL, NULL, 0);
120
121         ACE_DEBUG((LM_ERROR, "verify returned %d\n", verify));
122
123         Db db(&dbenv, 0);
124         db.open(NULL, "chap5_cds", NULL , DB_BTREE, DB_CREATE | DB_THREAD);
```

You can't reuse the Db handle that you used to perform database verification, not even for calling close on it. That's why I've used a different Db handle db_ver for verifying the database.

■**Caution** You shouldn't do database verification using db_verify or the Db::verify API while the database is being accessed through another thread or process, because Db::verify doesn't acquire a lock on the database during the verification process.

Database verification only verifies the structure of the physical database storage. It cannot detect other types of inconsistencies.

Let's try a simple exercise to see when database verification isn't of much help. After changing the code example in Listing 5-3, run the program again and interrupt it deliberately:

```
hy@linux:~/ws/bdb_book/chap_5> ./cds
verify returned 0
Writer 1: key "1_0" data "1_0"
Reader 2: key "1_0" data "1_0"
Reader 2: key "1_1" data "1_1"
Reader 2: key "1_2" data "1_4"
<CTRL C>
```

Before the reader thread is done iterating through the records, hit Ctrl+C to terminate the program without allowing it to close the database and the environment gracefully. Now if you run the program again, it will hang:

```
hy@linux:~/ws/bdb_book/chap_5> ./cds
<program hangs>
```

It hangs because the reader thread reads the records through a cursor, which acquires a read lock on the database until the cursor is closed. When you ran the program again after terminating it abruptly, the database couldn't be accessed because the lock acquired by the cursor from the previous run wasn't yet released. To verify if that's the case, you can run the db_stat utility to see the lock entries in the lock table. The db_stat utility is an extremely useful tool for inspecting the state of the database. It provides flags for viewing information about various subsystems within the database. You can find more information on using this utility in Chapter 10. When used with the flag combination –CA (which I'll show you how to do next), it shows the database lock structures:

```
hy@linux:~/ws/bdb_book/chap_5> db_stat -CA
-
-
<A lot of other information is dumped before this>
-
Locks grouped by lockers:
Locker   Mode        Count Status ---------------- Object --------------
      5 dd= 0 locks held 1     write locks 0
      5 READ            1 HELD    (74fd2 305 bb9263ad 529e 0) handle       0
      6 dd= 0 locks held 0     write locks 0
      7 dd= 0 locks held 0     write locks 0
      8 dd= 0 locks held 0     write locks 0
      9 dd= 0 locks held 1     write locks 0
      9 READ            1 HELD    (74fd2 305 bb9263ad 529e 0) handle       0
      a dd= 0 locks held 0     write locks 0
      b dd= 0 locks held 0     write locks 0
      c dd= 0 locks held 0     write locks 0
=-=-=-=-=-=-=-=-=-=-=-=-=-=-=-=-=-=-=-=-=-=-=
Locks grouped by object:
Locker   Mode        Count Status ---------------- Object --------------
      5 READ            1 HELD    (74fd2 305 bb9263ad 529e 0) handle       0
      9 READ            1 HELD    (74fd2 305 bb9263ad 529e 0) handle       0
```

You can see that the lockers 5 and 9 are holding READ locks even though no process or thread is currently reading the database. Until these locks are released, no other thread can acquire a write lock on the database. This is how you might end up with a database environment where some databases are permanently locked and therefore cannot be used by any thread of control. There's no way to recover from this situation if you're using either DS or CDS. The only recourse is to delete the database environment and re-create it by using a previously saved database snapshot or by reentering all the entries in the database. (I'll show you the procedure for creating a database snapshot in the "Database Backups" section.) Re-creating the database from a previous snapshot can result in data loss. This is unacceptable for many applications; if that's the case with your application, you should *not use* either DS or CDS. In this kind of environment corruption db_verify is not of much use.

■**Caution** You should never use DS or CDS if data loss due to unexpected crashes is unacceptable in your application, because certain types of corruptions are unrecoverable in DS and CDS. In such cases, you should use TDS, where you can recover all committed transactions after failures. I'll go over TDS in detail in Chapter 6.

Database Recovery

Database recovery involves bringing the database environment back to a consistent, uncorrupted state. Even if you can't recover all data present in the databases prior to the crash, the data should be consistent. In CDS and DS, the only way to recover the database is to delete and re-create it. In TDS, as you'll see in Chapter 6, a more sophisticated recovery mechanism is possible.

Watchdog for DS and CDS

Considering the limitations of DS and CDS, a watchdog cannot provide a very robust database framework, no matter how nicely it has been designed. There will always be cases of data loss due to unexpected crashes. However, even then a watchdog can minimize the chances of something like that happening. When designing the watchdog, keep these things in mind for managing the threads and processes participating in the shared database environment:

- **Single-threaded initialization**: The initialization of the environment includes the opening of the environment, verification of the databases, and the opening of the databases. The watchdog should always perform these functions in a single thread before any other thread can access the environment.

- **Monitoring**: The watchdog should monitor every thread accessing the database. If a thread crashes while doing a database operation, the watchdog should force all the other threads (or processes) to quit so that it can restore an uncorrupted environment. There are a number of ways of doing this; I'll go over a few examples in Chapter 7.

- **Re-creation after failure**: Once the watchdog has forced all the threads that were using the environment to quit after a crash, it should re-create a pristine environment either by using a previously saved snapshot or by reentering all the entries in the databases.

   The watchdog process itself should be simple and robust, so that it can perform these functions without crashing.

An Introduction to TDS

The TDS provides an ACID data store, which should possess the following four characteristics:

- **Atomicity**: The ability to execute a single or multiple database operations as a single atomic event. Atomic means that either all the operations succeed or all of them fail.

- **Consistency**: The ability to present a consistent view of the database to all the users. The effects of the operations that are in the process of being completed aren't visible to the users.

- **Isolation**: The ability to isolate every user from the rest of the users, giving every user the illusion that no one else is using the database.

- **Durability**: The ability to persist the result of all completed operations even after an unexpected application or system failure.

The DS doesn't possess any of these properties, and the CDS provides only consistency and isolation. As you saw in the previous section, CDS and DS have major limitations when it comes to preserving data in the face of unexpected failures. In the rest of this chapter, you'll see how the ACID characteristics of the TDS ensure that no data is ever lost, even after an unexpected crash.

Why ACID?

The main purpose of an ACID data store is to preserve the data in the face of unexpected crashes and allow multiple threads of control to access the database simultaneously with the minimum amount of locking. So how does an ACID data store accomplish that? Several key concepts are utilized in ensuring the ACIDity of a data store; let's review them.

First of all, an ACID data store provides the concept of *transactions*. A transaction transforms the database from one consistent state to another in an atomic fashion. The term *atomic* implies that either all the changes that are part of the atomic change are applied together or none are applied. Thereby, it is guaranteed that the database will always be in a consistent state. This concept of encapsulating a set of modifications into an atomic change is called a *transaction*. Transactions provide *atomicity*.

A transaction is considered to be *committed* if all individual operations constituting a transaction are processed successfully. If any operation in a transaction fails, then all the changes affected by the operations used until that point are undone or *rolled back* by the data store, and the transaction is considered to be *aborted*.

In a transactional data store, all modifications that are not yet committed are off limits for every other thread of control except for the one that's making the modifications. This can be achieved by *locking* the change made to the data until it is committed, so that the data that's visible is always *consistent*. Locking also ensures *isolation*, because during a modification, the user has exclusive access to the data, which no one else can see until the change is committed. The consistency and isolation properties in an ACID data store are made possible by appropriate locking.

To ensure that after a crash the data can be restored to the last committed transaction, the changes made by the transactions are written to some kind of persistent storage (a hard disk is the most common persistent storage), which can preserve data after system restarts. Durability in ACID is thus achieved. The most common persistent storage is the hard disk, which provides really slow I/O compared to system memory. If every transaction is written to the disk when it's committed, the performance of the system can suffer quite a lot. In order to speed up the system and at the same time achieve durability, a technique called *write ahead logging* (WAL) is used in most transactional data stores, including Berkeley DB TDS. "Write ahead" means that you write the log entries before you declare the transaction committed. You don't release the locks on the data until the transaction is declared committed, and thus preventing other threads from seeing the changes that weren't committed.

WRITE AHEAD LOGGING

WAL is a technique used in many transactional databases to achieve durability efficiently. Other techniques provide similar semantics, such as multiversion concurrency control (MVCC), available in more recent Berkeley DB releases. In WAL, instead of writing the actual changes in the database to the hard disk, a *log* of the change is created and persisted to the disk in the form of a *log file* during the commit operation. A transaction is considered to be committed only after the transaction log associated with it has been flushed to the disk. The transaction log is sequential—that is, every new transaction is appended at the end of the file. It's efficient to write it to the disk because sequential access is much faster than random access for disks. The log includes enough information to redo or undo every change, so you can commit or roll back any transaction. During recovery, you can reconstruct the database by applying the committed transactions from the transaction log to the data files. Writing modified data files to the disk for every transaction would be very inefficient, because it would require random accesses to the disk.

Transactions in Berkeley DB

The ACID properties provide a broad guideline of how a transactional system should behave; the actual implementation can differ vastly from one database to another. Most databases use one of the following architectures for implementing transactions:

- **Transactional log-based architecture**: A transaction log, independent of the actual database, is maintained on the disk. It is complex to implement but provides a good update as well as good lookup performance. Berkeley DB uses this approach.

- **Log-only architecture**: A single log file, which is also the database, is maintained. No separate transaction log is maintained. It provides a very good update performance, but the lookup performance is inferior as compared to the transactional log-based architecture. Berkeley DB Java Edition and PostgreSQL databases use this approach.

Before going over the design, let's first get acquainted with the terms used to describe the various concepts and components in the TDS:

- **Transaction**: A set of database operations that's treated as an atomic operation.

- **Commit**: When all changes made by a transaction are written to the transaction log successfully, it's considered to be committed.

- **Abort/rollback**: When all the changes that are a part of a transaction are undone (or rolled back) because of the failure of one or more operations, it's known as a rollback.

- **Recovery**: When a database is reconstructed using the transaction log after an application or system failure, it's known as database recovery.

Figure 5-4 shows the components of a transactional data store.

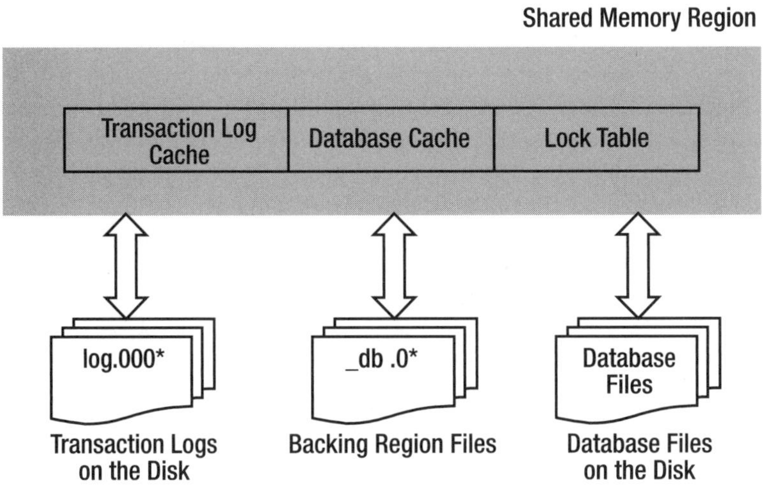

Shared Memory Region

Figure 5-4. *Components of a transactional data store*

The TDS uses three independent shared memory regions for managing the data store. These regions are used for the transaction log cache, the database cache, and the lock table. To understand how transactions work in Berkeley DB, let's go through the sequence of steps that happen during a transaction (this is a simplified description, the actual process of executing a transaction is much more complex):

1. When an application starts a transaction by invoking the txn_begin method, the library generates a unique transaction ID. The ID is used to associate the database operations, which are a part of the transaction.

2. The library creates an entry in the transaction log cache in the shared memory region. This entry will eventually contain information about the database modifications that happen as a part of the transaction.

3. Once a transaction has been started, the application can use it to execute database operations that are intended to be a part of the transaction. Each operation is recorded in the log cache, which is a circular buffer that gets flushed to disk in order to free up space. Appropriate locks are acquired using the transaction ID, and changes are made in the database cache.

4. If any operation fails, the changes made to the database cache so far by the previous operations will be undone using the log cache. In some cases, log records may need to be pulled in from disk in the event that the cache fills up and is partially flushed before a transaction commits or aborts. This procedure is known as the rollback or transaction abort.

5. If no operation fails, the contents of the log cache entry are written to the disk when the application invokes DbTxn::commit on the transaction. If the disk write fails, the transaction is rolled back. If the disk write succeeds, the transaction is considered committed.

6. After the transaction has either been committed or rolled back, the library releases the acquired locks.

The transaction log that gets created in this process holds a record on the disk of all the committed and aborted transactions. Each log record contains enough information to redo or undo the change, so that you can use it to redo or undo the entire transaction. After a system or an application failure, the transactions recorded in the transaction log on the disk can be rerun to restore the database to its most recent transaction-consistent state prior to the crash. Listing 5-4 shows how transactions actually get used in an application. I've modified the code in Listing 5-3 to create a TDS instead of a CDS; the code is same until line 114.

Listing 5-4. *Creating a TDS*

```
107     DbEnv dbenv(0);
108     try
109     {
110         const char *envhome = "./chap5_env";
111
112         dbenv.set_errpfx("env_ex");
113         dbenv.set_errcall(errCallback);
114
115         u_int32_t envFlags =
116             DB_CREATE | DB_INIT_MPOOL | DB_INIT_TXN |
117             DB_INIT_LOG | DB_INIT_LOCK | DB_RECOVER | DB_THREAD;
118
119         dbenv.open(envhome, envFlags, 0);
120
121         Db db(&dbenv, 0);
122         DbTxn *txn = NULL;
123         try
124         {
125             dbenv.txn_begin(NULL, &txn, 0);
126             db.open(txn, "chap5_tds", NULL ,
127                     DB_BTREE, DB_CREATE | DB_THREAD, S_IRUSR | S_IWUSR);
128             txn->commit(0);
129         }
130         catch(DbException &txn_ex)
131         {
132             if (txn != NULL)
133                 txn->abort();
134         }
```

Let's step through the code:

- **Lines 115–117**: These flags are used to open the environment. There are four new flags here: DB_INIT_TXN for transactions, DB_INIT_LOG for logs, DB_INIT_LOCK for locking, and DB_RECOVER for running recovery (this flag is optional). These flags indicate that the database will be created and accessed as a TDS. To run recoverable transactions in a scenario of multiple readers and multiple writers, you need the first three flags.

- **Line 122**: A pointer to a transaction handle is declared. This pointer will point to a transaction object after the transaction has been started.

- **Line 125**: This marks the beginning of a transaction. The pointer to the transaction handle declared earlier is passed in; the library creates a transaction object and sets its address to the pointer.

- **Line 128**: The transaction is committed using the transaction pointer created during `txn_begin`.

- **Line 132**: If a `DbException` is thrown while executing these operations, it's always a good idea to abort the transaction.

In this example, only one database operation is being performed inside a transaction—the opening of a database called `chap5_tds`. A shortcut is available in the API for executing single-operation transactions. You can replace lines 122-134 with the following lines:

```
126             db.open(NULL, "chap5_tds", NULL ,
127                     DB_BTREE, DB_CREATE | DB_THREAD | DB_AUTO_COMMIT, \
                            S_IRUSR | S_IWUSR)
```

Note You should always open Db handles inside a transaction. Starting from version 4.5.x, transactions can only be used with handles opened inside of a transaction. In earlier versions it was possible to use transactions even with handles that were not opened within transactions, since that could cause unrecoverable errors the newer versions don't allow it.

Locking in TDS

The CDS suffers from many drawbacks with respect to locking. First of all, since the locks are acquired over the entire database, the concurrency is reduced. Secondly, since the locker IDs are assigned on a per `Db` handle (or a per cursor) basis, the possibility of running into a deadlock is quite high when cursor and noncursor operations are mixed within a thread. In TDS, these drawbacks aren't there. TDS locks have the following characteristics:

- **Page- or record-level locking**: Depending on the type of access method being used, a TDS allows for either database page-level or record-level locking, which usually results in much better throughput. The `Queue` access method supports row-level locking for head and tail operations in Berkeley DB. Most Berkeley DB TDS applications end up using page-level locking, as most of them either use a `Btree` or `Hash` access method.

- **Transaction-based locker IDs**: Every transaction is assigned a unique locker ID, which makes it possible to mix cursor and noncursor operations within the case transaction.

Let's look at the locks acquired by a TDS application using `db_stat` while it's executing. In order to see the locks, you'll have to modify the CDS example further by wrapping the database operations within transactions. Listing 5-5 shows how you must modify the writer thread.

Listing 5-5. *Adding a Transaction for Db::put*

```
104          DbTxn *txn;
105          try
106          {
107              env_->txn_begin(NULL, &txn, 0);
108              int ret = db_->put(txn, &key, &value, 0);
109              if(ret)
110                  env_->err(ret, keystr.c_str());
111              else
112                  ACE_DEBUG((LM_ERROR,
"Writer %d: key \"%s\" data \"%s\"              \n",
113                              id_,
114                              keystr.c_str(),
115                              valstr.c_str() ));
116              txn->commit(0);
117          }
118          catch(DbException &txn_ex)
119          {
120              txn->abort();
121          }
```

Listing 5-6 shows how you must modify the reader thread.

Listing 5-6. *Adding a Transaction for Dbc::get*

```
63     DbTxn *txn;
64     try
65     {
66         env_->txn_begin(NULL, &txn, 0);
67         db_->cursor(txn, &dbcur, 0);
68         while (dbcur->get(&key, &value, DB_NEXT) == 0)
69         {
70             ACE_DEBUG((LM_ERROR, "Reader %d: key \"%s\" data \"%s\"\n",
71                         id_, (char*)(key.get_data()),
72                         (char*)(value.get_data()) ));
73             ACE_OS::sleep(1);
74         }
75         dbcur->close();
76         txn->commit(0);
77     }
78     catch(DbException &txn_ex)
79     {
80         txn->abort();
81     }
```

If you don't create a transaction handle and use it while invoking the database operations, you'll get an exception when you run the program that complains about a missing transaction handle. Since you opened the Db handle using a transaction, you cannot use it to perform a nontransactional operation. Now compile and run the program while the program is running; it will take around 10 to 15 seconds to finish. Execute db_stat -Cl from a separate terminal to view the locks in the environment. You'll see something like this:

```
hy@linux:~/ws/bdb_book/chap_5/chap5_env> db_stat -Cl
=-=-=-=-=-=-=-=-=-=-=-=-=-=-=-=-=-=-=-=-=-=-=-=
Lock REGINFO information:
Lock      Region type
4         Region ID
__db.004        Region name
0x4027a000      Original region address
0x4027a000      Region address
0x402e7f40      Region primary address
0         Region maximum allocation
0         Region allocated
REGION_JOIN_OK  Region flags
=-=-=-=-=-=-=-=-=-=-=-=-=-=-=-=-=-=-=-=-=-=-=-=
Locks grouped by lockers:
Locker   Mode        Count Status  ---------------- Object --------------
       5 dd= 0 locks held 1    write locks 0
       5 READ            1 HELD    chap5_tds               handle       0
       6 dd= 0 locks held 0    write locks 0
       7 dd= 0 locks held 0    write locks 0
       8 dd= 0 locks held 0    write locks 0
80000003 dd= 0 locks held 1    write locks 0
80000003 READ            3 HELD    chap5_tds               page         1
80000004 dd= 0 locks held 0    write locks 0
80000004 WRITE           1 WAIT    chap5_tds               page         1
```

In the section Locks grouped by lockers, you'll see a list of the locks held by various lockers. The locker ID 5 belongs to the Db handle created by the Db::open method, as mentioned in the second row under the Locks grouped by lockers section. The locker IDs 80000003 and 80000004 belong to the transactions under the reader and writer threads. As you can see, the transaction locks are page locks. In CDS, all locks are database-level locks, which is why the entire database gets locked during a database operation.

Configuring Locking in TDS

Berkeley DB maintains the locks as entries in a table called the *lock table*, which exists in the shared memory region. The lock table is created during the creation of the Berkeley DB environment. You cannot change the size of the lock table after initialization of the application. It's important, therefore, that you choose the size of the lock table carefully. If the table is too small, it won't be sufficient to hold all the locks that the application will need to function smoothly. On the other hand, if the table is too big, it will result in the waste of precious memory and computing resources. However, to be on the safer side, it's better to keep the lock table slightly bigger than what is actually required. The size of the lock table is determined by the following three parameters:

- **Maximum number of locks**: This is the maximum number of locks that can be requested simultaneously at any given time by all the threads of control. DbEnv::set_lk_max_locks is used to set this number.

- **Maximum number of lockers**: This is the maximum number of lock requesters that can be present at any given time. You can set it using DbEnv::set_lk_max_lockers. Since every transaction, every cursor, and every database handle is assigned a unique locker ID, you can calculate this number by adding the *expected number of simultaneous transactions + open database handles + open nontransactional cursors*.

- **Maximum number of lock objects**: This is the maximum number of objects (which can be database pages, or database records in the case of Queue) on which locks can be requested simultaneously. You can set it through DbEnv::set_lk_max_objects. This number isn't easy to calculate for a given system for two reasons. First, it's dependent on the access method being used, and second, there could be a variable number of objects involved in locking at different times for the same operation. As a rough estimate, the Btree and Recno access methods can lock up to six objects for a single access for a five-level deep tree (trees deeper than three levels are rare). A Queue locks up to three objects per access, and a Hash locks a single object per access.

Even with these guidelines, it can be challenging to estimate the perfect size of the lock table, because it's impossible to know exactly how many simultaneous accesses will happen at a given time in a running system. It's not of much use to theorize how many threads of control will do how many accesses simultaneously. Instead, it's much easier and practical to estimate those numbers by starting with ballpark estimates and then fine-tuning them using db_stat on a running system with different load levels. These numbers can be specified from the DB_CONFIG file to avoid recompilation for every trial. Let's try to do that for the TDS code example, in which you have the following parameters:

- **Number of concurrent threads**: Two

- **Number of simultaneous transactions**: Two (one in the reader, and one in the writer)

- **Number of open Db handles and nontransactional cursors**: One (just one Db)

- **Access method**: Btree

With this data, you get the following results:

- **Maximum lockers**: 2 (simultaneous transactions) + 1 = 3

- **Maximum object**: 2 (simultaneous transactions) × 5 (for Btree) + 1 (Db handle) = 11

- **Maximum locks**: Locker × objects = 2 × 11 = 22

Now let's run db_stat while the program is running to see the actual limits reached:

```
hy@linux:~/ws/bdb_book/chap_5/chap5_env> db_stat -CA
Default locking region information:
8          Last allocated locker ID
0x7fffffff      Current maximum unused locker ID
9          Number of lock modes
1000       Maximum number of locks possible
1000       Maximum number of lockers possible
1000       Maximum number of lock objects possible
3          Number of current locks
3          Maximum number of locks at any one time
6          Number of current lockers
6          Maximum number of lockers at any one time
2          Number of current lock objects
2          Maximum number of lock objects at any one time
```

The limits that you calculated for the maximum objects and the maximum locks are comfortably above the actual numbers. However, the maximum number of lockers calculated is half of the actual maximum. The estimates for the maximum lock objects and locks are much more than the actual numbers because you assumed a five-level Btree (the database is too small to need a five-level deep Btree). Let's look at the section where the all the lockers are listed:

```
Locks grouped by lockers:
Locker    Mode      Count Status  ---------------- Object ---------------
          5 dd= 0 locks held 1    write locks 0
          5 READ           1 HELD    chap5_tds              handle       0
          6 dd= 0 locks held 0    write locks 0
          7 dd= 0 locks held 0    write locks 0
          8 dd= 0 locks held 0    write locks 0
80000003 dd= 0 locks held 1    write locks 0
80000003 READ           5 HELD    chap5_tds              page         1
80000004 dd= 0 locks held 0    write locks 0
80000004 WRITE          1 WAIT    chap5_tds              page         1
=-=-=-=-=-=-=-=-=-=-=-=-=-=-=-=-=-=-=-=-=-=-=-=
```

Lockers 80000003 and 80000004 hold READ and WRITE page locks that correspond to the transactions, and locker 5 holds a READ handle lock that corresponds to the Db handle you created. The remaining locks are dd locks. The database creates these special locks (one for each locker ID) for running the deadlock detector. Since the dd locks are also stored in the same lock table, you should always double the number of lockers you estimate for your system.

■**Tip** To be on the safe side, set the maximum number of locks, lockers, and lock objects to twice the numbers you arrive at for your application. In the worst case, you would be wasting a few kilobytes of memory at the most.

Lock Time-Outs

If a database operation takes more time than expected, it can cause the application to come to a standstill because the locks acquired for performing the operation will be held until the operation is completed. There can be many reasons for an operation to take too long or even hang. For example, it could be a network problem, a hardware problem, or even an application bug. You can't guarantee that everything will work as planned. Lock time-outs provide a way to deal with these uncertainties in a graceful manner.

If a time-out has been set for a lock, the library clears the lock after the time-out expires. If a lock was acquired by a transaction, it is aborted when the lock expires. That allows other threads waiting to acquire the lock to proceed.

You can use the following methods to configure time-outs on locks:

- `DbEnv::set_timeout`: For setting the default time-out on all the locks and transactions in an environment.

- `DbTxn::set_timeout`: For setting a time-out specifically for a transaction. If an environment-wide time-out was also set earlier, this call will override it.

- `DbEnv::lock_vec`: For setting a time-out for individual locks. If either of the previous methods were called before this method, it will override them. If you read the API description of this method, you won't find a time-out argument. That's because the time-out is a part of the `DB_LOCKREQ` structure, which is one of the arguments.

Degrees of Isolation

Jim Gray and Andreas Reuter coined the phrase *degrees of isolation* in their famous book *Transaction Processing: Concepts and Techniques* (Morgan Kaufmann, 1993). Isolation is an important property of a transactional database. It's essential to maintaining the database's integrity during concurrent access. It's also required to maintain a record of the database activity, so that it can be stored in a transaction log. If the updates happening on a record aren't isolated from each other, there's no way for the library to figure out what changes were made by the individual updates.

Write locks always have to be exclusive and fully isolated, which means that when a transaction acquires a write lock on a record, no other transaction can read or modify it until the transaction ends.

A special lock called DB_RMW, which stands for read-modify-write, is used when a record is read with the intention to write. DB_RMW is like a write lock, but it's specified in a read call. Like a write lock, DB_RMW is always exclusive and fully isolated.

The read locks can have various degrees of isolation. By default in TDS, they use the highest level of isolation, which is known as *degree 3* isolation. Under degree 3 isolation, it is guaranteed that every time a thread of control reads a record within a transaction, no modification to it will be allowed until the transaction is either committed or aborted. In TDS, that means if a record is read inside a transaction (which results in a read lock on the record under the transaction's locker ID), it cannot be changed until the transaction ends. If the record is read more than once within the transaction, it is guaranteed that the same value will be returned. That's why degree 3 isolation is also known as *repeatable reads*.

Sometimes degree 3 isolation is too restrictive. In particular, if a cursor is being used within a transaction to read records, the entire database can eventually get locked because every record that the cursor reads will get locked for the duration of the transaction. To allow other transactions to modify the records already read by a transaction, Berkeley DB provides *degree 2 isolation*. Degree 2 isolation guarantees that the transaction will get to read only committed data, but other transactions can modify the records before the transaction ends. For long-living cursors, such as cursors created by a UI application that have to be kept open for long durations, this is very useful. You can specify degree 2 isolation by setting DB_READ_COMMITTED in DbTxn::open, Db::get, Dbc::get, and Dbc::pget methods.

■**Tip** You can specify degree 2 isolation for a cursor that's been created inside a degree 3 isolation transaction. In such a case, only records read by the cursor can be modified by other transactions before the transaction ends.

Degree 1 isolation basically means that uncommitted data currently under modification by a transaction can be read. You should be very careful in using this option, because it can result in inconsistencies. To specify degree 1 isolation, you can set the DB_READ_UNCOMMITTED flag in the DbTxn::open, Db::get, Db::c_get, and Db::c_pget methods.

Deadlocks

A *deadlock* is a condition where two or more threads are waiting for resources that have been locked by the same threads. Since the threads that hold the locks are themselves waiting for other locks, they can never release the locks. A deadlock can happen even within in a single thread when a thread tries to acquire a lock that it acquired earlier using a different locker ID. Figure 5-5 shows how a typical deadlock is created.

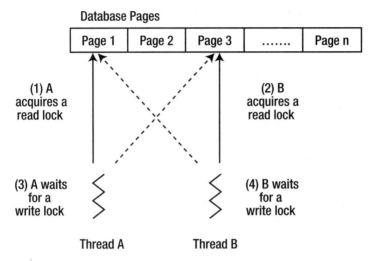

Figure 5-5. *Creation of a deadlock*

The following steps explain how the deadlock illustrated in Figure 5-5 came about:

1. Thread A acquires a read lock on page 1.

2. Thread B acquires a read lock on page 3.

3. Thread A tries to acquire a write lock on page 3. Thread B already has a read lock on the page. Since a write lock is an exclusive lock, Thread A has to wait for Thread B to release the read lock.

4. Thread B tries to acquire a write lock on page 1, but it gets blocked because Thread A already has a read lock on the page.

Any number of threads can be involved in a cyclic blocking condition such as this.

Why Deadlocks Are Created

Deadlocks are not entirely avoidable. Sometimes deadlocks happen because of the order in which the locks are acquired. Apart from such unavoidable deadlocks, avoidable deadlocks can be created due to any of the following reasons:

- **Poor design:** If the locks are held longer than necessary or if different threads acquire locks in a different order, the possibility of getting into a deadlock increases.

- **Poor configuration:** If the wrong access method is used or if the various configuration parameters aren't tuned properly for the application, deadlocks can result.

- **Choice of access method**: The access methods Btree and Recno (since it uses a Btree internally) are prone to deadlocks if multiple threads are adding and deleting data concurrently and their access pattern isn't designed to avoid deadlocks.

- **Page-level locking**: All access methods, except Queue, use page-level locking. In page level-locking, the entire page where the record exists is locked. If there are multiple records on one page, then the chances of a deadlock increase significantly.

You can take care of the first two cases with good design and proper tuning. However, if a Btree-based access method is being used in an application, deadlocks are inevitable, no matter how carefully you designed the system. Figure 5-6, which depicts a typical Btree access pattern, helps explain why you can't avoid deadlocks in a Btree.

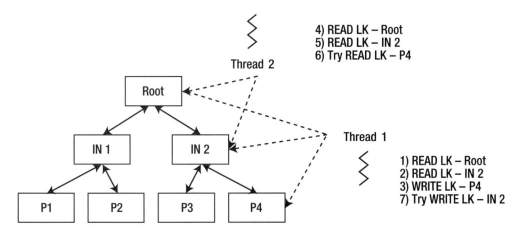

Figure 5-6. Btree deadlock

Two threads are interested in the same page, P4. Thread 1 is interested in adding a new record on P4, and Thread 2 wants to read a record present on P4. The following sequence of events lands the two threads in a deadlock:

1. Thread-1 acquires a read lock on the root node, internal node IN-2. Since it wants to add a record, it acquires a write lock on P4.

2. Thread-2 comes in at this point. It acquires a read lock on the root node and IN-2. It tries to acquire a read lock on P4. It has to wait because Thread-2 already has a write lock on P4.

3. Thread-1 finds out that the record it is adding on P4 won't fit entirely on the page. It has to do a page split to create more space. To do the split, it has to create an entry in IN-2 for the new page. It tries to acquire a write lock on IN-2. It gets blocked because Thread-1 already has a read lock on IN-2.

At this point, both Thread 1 and Thread 2 are blocked, waiting for each other.

■**Note** This page-split scenario has been greatly simplified to show how a deadlock can happen in a `Btree`. In reality, Berkeley DB doesn't deadlock that easily during a page split, because it uses a number of deadlock-avoiding algorithms to prevent deadlocks. The `Btree` access method, however, is prone to deadlocks during a page split.

Deadlock Detection

You cannot prevent deadlocks, but you can detect and resolve them. Berkeley DB performs deadlock detection by examining the lock table to find cyclic dependencies among the lockers waiting to acquire locks. If a cyclic dependency exists among a set of lockers, they're deadlocked. You can break the deadlock by evicting one of the lockers from the lock table. You choose the locker according to the eviction policy set for the environment. According to the Berkeley DB API, the following policies are available:

- `DB_LOCK_DEFAULT`: Uses the policy set for the environment, which is set to `DB_LOCK_RANDOM` by default

- `DB_LOCK_EXPIRE`: Rejects lock requests that have timed out

- `DB_LOCK_MAXLOCKS`: Rejects the lock request for the locker ID with the most locks

- `DB_LOCK_MAXWRITE`: Rejects the lock request for the locker ID with the most write locks

- `DB_LOCK_MINLOCKS`: Rejects the lock request for the locker ID with the fewest locks

- `DB_LOCK_MINWRITE`: Rejects the lock request for the locker ID with the fewest write locks

- `DB_LOCK_OLDEST`: Rejects the lock request for the locker ID with the oldest lock

- `DB_LOCK_RANDOM`: Rejects the lock request for a random locker ID

- `DB_LOCK_YOUNGEST`: Rejects the lock request for the locker ID with the youngest lock

You set the policy using the `DbEnv::set_lk_detect` method. It's possible that even after one locker has been evicted, the deadlock won't get resolved. That can happen if more than two threads are involved in a deadlock. Berkeley DB evicts one locker at a time, which means that the next locker will be evicted, if that's required, only when the detection routine is run again. This approach simplifies the deadlock-detection algorithm, but it makes the detection process slightly inefficient. When a locker is evicted, the thread of control running the transaction that owns the locker ID gets a `DbDeadlockException` thrown from an operation that is waiting to acquire the lock. The thread running the transaction should abort the transaction to release all the locks held by the transaction.

Deadlock Detection and Lock Time-Outs

You can resolve deadlocks by using lock time-outs instead of running deadlock detection. When a lock time-out is set, the lock is released when the time-out expires. If the locker is deadlocked with other lockers, the time-out will resolve the deadlock automatically. If you want to configure deadlock detection based purely on time-outs, you should set the `DB_LOCK_EXPIRE` flag in the `DbEnv::set_lk_detect` method.

Berkeley DB doesn't have any threads of its own. All database functions are performed through the application threads. Lock time-outs also are enforced through application threads. There is no database thread running in the background going through the lock table and evicting the timed-out lockers. Time-outs are checked only when a locker requests a lock. If a lock held by a locker isn't requested by another locker, it can keep holding it beyond the time-out set for the lock. Because of this limitation, lock time-outs are only as accurate as the frequency of deadlock detections. Therefore, it's a good idea to run db_deadlock periodically even when DB_LOCK_EXPIRE has been set.

■**Tip** It's a good idea to run db_deadlock periodically if the application depends on the database lock time-outs.

Berkeley DB provides numerous ways of doing deadlock detection and resolution. You can do deadlock detection programmatically or by running a Berkeley DB utility called db_deadlock. The detection routine can be executed synchronously when a deadlock is created, or it can be run asynchronously at fixed intervals. Let's look at the various ways of resolving deadlocks:

- **Asynchronously**: Running deadlock detection using db_deadlock is simple and easy to set up, but you can't use it to do synchronous detection. A cron job, or a service (in the Windows environment), can be set up to run db_deadlock at fixed intervals.

- **Synchronously**: Every time the library receives a lock request, it executes the deadlock detection routine to check if the request can result in a deadlock. You can't perform synchronous detection with db_deadlock. You must call the DbEnv::set_lk_detect method on the environment handle to set up automatic, synchronous deadlock detection. Synchronous detection imposes an overhead on transaction processing, because the library has to go over the lock table to identify potential deadlocks before acquiring each lock. However, this overhead is insignificant.

- **Using time-outs without detection**: You can use lock timeouts to resolve deadlocks by setting DB_LOCK_EXPIRE instead of running deadlock detection.

- **Using time-outs plus detection**: It's possible to use both deadlock detection and lock time-outs at the same time. When you set both time-outs and detection, deadlock detection happens as usual, but deadlocks are sometimes resolved because of lock time-outs. If the application wants to know whether a time-out resolved the deadlock, it should set the DB_TIME_NOTGRANTED flag using the DbEnv::set_flags method. The library will then return the DB_LOCK_NOTGRANTED error instead of DB_LOCK_DEADLOCK when deadlock resolution happens because of a time-out.

- **Synchronously and asynchronously with time-outs**: This is the most comprehensive deadlock detection scheme that you can set up. In this case, time-outs are set for the environment and transactions, db_deadlock is run periodically to check the lock table for deadlocks and time-outs, and DbEnv::set_lk_detect is called to do automatic synchronous deadlock detection. With all three deadlock-resolution methods in play, the chances of a database deadlock causing an application hang are reduced considerably.

Tip For applications that require fast database access, it's useful to try out both synchronous and asynchronous detection to evaluate if there is a significant performance impact due to synchronous detection.

Let's revisit the TDS code example to see how you can set up deadlock detection in an application. With the current tds.cc version, no deadlocks were reported because you weren't loading the database sufficiently and you were giving enough time for each operation to finish. To see how the deadlock detection helps an application, let's first cause the application to deadlock and then apply the techniques you just learned to resolve the deadlocks.

The simplest way to create a deadlock is to force a Btree page split while a read lock is present on an internal node of the tree. You'll have to make some changes to the program to achieve this:

- **Make the database page size smaller**: The smaller the page size, the more frequently new pages will be created.

- **Perform read operations outside of a cursor**: In the example, you're doing all reads from a cursor. The cursor holds read locks until it's closed, which blocks out the writer until all the reads are done. You want to allow the writer thread to add new records in between reads.

Now you can add a new type of worker thread that does a simple read instead of a cursor read:

```
145 void CDSWorker::runNonCursorReader()
146 {
147     DbTxn *txn;
148     env_->txn_begin(NULL, &txn, 0);
149     while(true)
150     {
151         int j = 0;
152         for(int i=0; i < NUM_RECS; i++)
153         {
154             stringstream keyss;
155             keyss << "1_";
156             keyss << i;
157             string keystr = keyss.str();
158
159             Dbt key((void*)(keystr.c_str()), keystr.size() + 1);
160             Dbt value;
161             value.set_flags(DB_DBT_MALLOC);
162
163             try
164             {
165                 int ret = db_->get(txn, &key, &value,0 );
166                 if(ret == DB_NOTFOUND)
167                 {
```

```
168                         ACE_DEBUG((LM_ERROR, "key not found\n"));
169                         txn->commit(0);
170                         env_->txn_begin(NULL, &txn, 0);
171                         i --;
172                         continue;
173                    }
174                    else if(ret != 0)
175                    {
176                         env_->err(ret, keystr.c_str());
177                    }
178                    else
179                    {
180                         ACE_DEBUG((LM_ERROR, ➥
                              "NonCursorReader %d: key \"%s\" data \"%s\" size %d \n",
181                                      id_,
182                                      keystr.c_str(),
183                                      (char*)(value.get_data()), ➥
                                          value.get_size() ));
184                    }
185                    j++;
186                    if(j >= 20)
187                    {
188                         txn->commit(0);
189                         env_->txn_begin(NULL, &txn, 0);
190                         j = 0;
191                    }
192               }
193          catch(DbException &txn_ex)
194          {
195               env_->err(txn_ex.get_errno(), "nonCursorReader");
196               txn->abort();
197               env_->txn_begin(NULL, &txn, 0);
198          }
199     }
200  }
201 }
```

This code is similar to the earlier reader thread. Let's look at the key differences:

- **Line 149**: The original reader thread used to exit once done. Now, however, you want to keep running the reader until a deadlock is created, so you add an infinite loop here.

- **Lines 154–162**: Earlier you were doing reads from a cursor, but you don't want to do that now, so you add the same code to create the keys that the writer thread uses for inserting the records.

- **Line 165**: Instead of using a cursor read, you're doing a simple read using the get method. Notice that when you used the cursor, you didn't need to know the keys in advance, but now you're passing the key you constructed earlier in the get method.

- **Line 171**: You decrement the counter if you hit a nonexistent record, so that you're not trying to read records that aren't yet present in the database.

- **Lines 186–191**: You commit after doing 20 get operations instead of committing after every operation. By extending the duration of the transactions, you increase the chances of causing a deadlock.

You also need to change the main method to reduce the database page size and to activate the new thread. Here's the modified code:

```
207          Db db(&dbenv, 0);
208          DbTxn *txn;
209          try
210          {
211              dbenv.txn_begin(NULL, &txn, 0);
212              db.set_pagesize(512);
213              db.open(txn, "chap5_tds", NULL ,
214                      DB_BTREE, DB_CREATE | DB_THREAD, S_IRUSR | S_IWUSR);
215              txn->commit(0);
216          }
217          catch(DbException &txn_ex)
218          {
219              txn->abort();
220          }
221
222          CDSWorker *w1 = new CDSWorker(&dbenv, &db, WRITER, 1);
223          if(w1->activate((THR_NEW_LWP | THR_JOINABLE), 1) != 0)
224              ACE_DEBUG((LM_ERROR, "Could not launch w1\n"));
225
226          ACE_OS::sleep(1);
227          // NON_CURSOR_READER is defined further down in this section
228          CDSWorker *r1 = new CDSWorker(&dbenv, &db, NON_CURSOR_READER, 2);
229          if(r1->activate((THR_NEW_LWP | THR_JOINABLE), 1) != 0)
230              ACE_DEBUG((LM_ERROR, "Could not launch r1\n"));
231
232          CDSWorker *r3 = new CDSWorker(&dbenv, &db, NON_CURSOR_READER, 3);
233          if(r3->activate((THR_NEW_LWP | THR_JOINABLE), 1) != 0)
234              ACE_DEBUG((LM_ERROR, "Could not launch r3\n"));
235
236          w1->wait();
237          r1->wait();
238          r3->wait();
239
240          delete r1;
241          delete w1;
242          delete r3;
```

Let's go over the modifications made here:

- **Line 212**: Set the page size to 512 bytes, which is the minimum possible page size.

- **Line 226**: Sleep for a second to allow the writer thread to insert some records before the reader threads start.

- **Lines 228–242**: Create and activate two noncursor reader threads. You have to change the third argument type in the CDSWorker class to accommodate more than two possible values. Earlier it was a bool, but now it's an int.

To increase the chances of a deadlock, increase the size of the record that gets stored for every key by changing this code in the runWriter method of CDSWorker:

```
118        Dbt key((void*)(keystr.c_str()), keystr.size() + 1);
119        char buff[6000];
120        strcpy(buff, valstr.c_str());
121        Dbt value((void*)(buff), 6000);
```

The value that gets stored now has a size of 6KB and the page size of the database is set to 512 bytes. Since the record size is greater than the page size, every insert will cause a page split, increasing the chances of a deadlock. You should add the following definitions:

```
16 #define NUM_RECS 50000
17
18 #define READER 1
19 #define WRITER 2
20 #define NON_CURSOR_READER 3
```

Let's see what has changed here:

- **Line 16**: Increase the number of records that are created in the database from 5 to 50,000, so that multiple Btree pages have to be created to accommodate them.

- **Lines 18–20**: The constants used for the worker types are defined here.

Finally, here's how you'll have to implement the new svc method of the CDSWorker class:

```
49 int CDSWorker::svc()
50 {
51     try
52     {
53         switch(type_)
54         {
55             case READER:
56                 runReader();
57                 break;
58             case WRITER:
59                 runWriter();
60                 break;
61             case NON_CURSOR_READER:
62                 runNonCursorReader();
63                 break;
64             default:
```

```
65                              ACE_DEBUG((LM_ERROR, "unknown type %d\n", type_));
66                        break;
67            }
68      }
69      catch(...)
70      {
71            ACE_DEBUG((LM_ERROR, "CDSWorker: exception caught\n"));
72      }
73 }
```

Let's take a look at the interesting lines:

- **Lines 55–66**: You launch a different method depending on the type of worker created.

Before running this program, you should remove all the existing files in the database environment directory. When you run this program, you'll notice that the program hangs after running for some time. It hangs because you're not performing any deadlock detection. Let's add deadlock detection to the code and see what happens:

```
202 int main(int argc, char **argv)
203 {
204      DbEnv dbenv(0);
205      try
206      {
207            const char *envhome = "./chap5_env";
208
209            dbenv.set_errpfx("env_ex");
210            dbenv.set_errcall(errCallback);
211            dbenv.set_lk_detect(DB_LOCK_DEFAULT);
```

On line 211, you invoke set_lk_detect and set DB_LOCK_DEFAULT as the eviction policy. By default, the locker to be booted out is selected randomly. If you clean up the environment files and run the program with this change, you'll notice that the program no longer hangs. On closer examination of the program output, you'll notice these messages:

```
NonCursorReader 3: key "1_20" data "1_400" size 6000
NonCursorReader 2: key "1_20" data "1_400" size 6000
NonCursorReader 3: key "1_20" data "1_400" size 6000
(1087826864) env_ex errMsg: nonCursorReader: DB_LOCK_DEADLOCK: Locker killed to \
resolve a deadlock
(1085725616) env_ex errMsg: nonCursorReader: DB_LOCK_DEADLOCK: Locker killed to \
resolve a deadlock
(1089928112) env_ex errMsg: nonCursorReader: DB_LOCK_DEADLOCK: Locker killed to \
resolve a deadlock
```

The messages indicate that the `nonCursorReader` thread was evicted due to a deadlock resolution. You might have to capture the output of the program in a file to see these messages, because too many messages will be showing up on the `stdout`. If you execute `db_stat -Cl` on the environment, you can see the total number of deadlocks resolved and other lock statistics:

```
102493  Total number of locks requested
102465  Total number of locks released
0       Total number of lock requests failing because DB_LOCK_NOWAIT was set
878     Total number of locks not immediately available due to conflicts
5       Number of deadlocks
0       Lock timeout value
```

The transaction that gets aborted due to a deadlock resolution can be retried by the application, but that is something that is application-specific. In general, the application should try executing the transaction a few times before returning an error to the user. An error should be returned if the transaction fails even after the retries.

Recovering from Deadlocks

Deadlocks aren't disasters; rather, they're to be expected in transactional systems. An application can recover from a deadlock by aborting and retrying the transaction. Retries are timing-dependent, so they often succeed. In practice, you might want to retry once or twice, but if you consistently get a deadlock and abort on a given transaction, you'll probably need to report an error to the user and quit.

How to Avoid Deadlocks

You cannot eliminate deadlocks entirely. Due to page-level locking and `Btree` page splits, there's always a small possibility of deadlock. However, by designing the database access within the application properly, you can significantly reduce the number of deadlocks. The following guidelines should help you:

- **Avoid long-running transactions**: The longer a transaction is active, the longer it will hold the locks. You should try to keep the transactions as small as possible.

- **Access databases in the same order**: All transactions should acquire locks on databases (or tables) in the same order. Suppose you have three databases (D1, D2, and D3), and you force all your transactions to acquire locks in the following order: D3-D2-D1. If an existing transaction holds locks on D3 and D2, it will be guaranteed that any new transaction cannot acquire a lock on D1 because it will have to follow the defined order D3-D2-D1 and will block on D3.

- **Avoid long-running cursors**: By default, cursors hold locks on all the records they've visited, so they can end up locking large portions of a database. Therefore, you should close cursors as quickly as possible. If you cannot avoid long-running cursors, you should use degree 2 isolation or degree 1 isolation for them.

Nested Transactions

A nested transaction is a child transaction. The advantage of using nested transactions is that they can be committed or aborted without affecting their bigger parent transaction. Nested transactions allow you to break up transactions that are made up of a large number of individual database operations into smaller subtransactions. The following rules govern nested transactions:

- When a nested child transaction is created, it inherits all the locks held by its parent.

- The locks created by a child transaction are created with a new locker ID, which is distinct from its parent's locker ID.

- Two children of the same parent cannot share any locks that they create on their own. However, they do share the locks owned by their parent.

- While a child transaction is in an unresolved state—that is, it has neither been aborted nor been committed—the parent transaction cannot be used to initiate any database operation. Once the child is resolved, the parent can perform database operations.

- Once the child has been resolved, the parent inherits the locks that it owns.

- The resolution of a child doesn't affect the resolution of the parent. However, the resolution of the parent affects that of its children. Let's say transaction P has two children, C1 and C2. If C1 commits while C2 aborts, P can still be committed even though one child aborted. If C1 and C2 commit but P gets aborted, then both C1 and C2 will be aborted (even though they got committed once).

Listing 5-7 illustrates how you can create and use a nested transaction. Notice that the parent can be committed even when the child is aborted in the exception handler.

Listing 5-7. *Creating a Nested Transaction*

```
DbTxn *parent;
try
{
    env->txn_begin(NULL, &parent, 0);
    db->get(parent, &key, &value, 0);

    DbTxn *child;
    try
    {
        env->txn_begin(parent, &child, 0);
        db->put(child, &key, &value1, 0);
        child->commit(0);
    }
    catch (DbException ex)
    {
        child->abort();
    }
```

```
    parent->commit(0);
}
catch (DbException& ex)
{
    parent->abort();
}
```

Database Recoverability

The next four sections—"Checkpoints," "Transaction Log Maintenance," "Database Backups," and "Database Recovery"—describe how an application should manage the recoverability of the database. Berkeley DB provides a number of APIs that the application can use to perform backups, run recovery, and create checkpoints. It's important to fully understand the issues involved in designing a recoverable database framework. The Berkeley DB reference manual contains a good discussion on database recoverability (http://www.oracle.com/technology/documentation/berkeley-db/db/ref/toc.html). I highly recommended that any developer designing an application around Berkeley DB read this.

Checkpoints

During an update, the modified database pages aren't written to the disk. Instead, the modification is written into the transaction log, which is written to the disk. Therefore, the transaction log keeps growing over time. Suppose you have a database with only one record in it that you keep updating. Over a period of time, the transaction log will become enormous, even though you have just one record in the database. Checkpointing allows you to reduce the number of log files you have to keep.

When you create a database checkpoint, all the dirty pages residing in the cache are written to the disk, and a checkpoint record is written to the transaction log. You can now clean up all transaction log files that don't contain information about any active transaction, because they'll no longer be needed if you have to recover the database. During recovery, the transaction logs are replayed from the beginning of the active transaction list until a checkpoint record is found in the transaction log.

■**Tip** Frequent database checkpoints reduce the time it takes to run database recovery because, as explained in the last section, a checkpoint record will be found sooner during recovery.

You can create a checkpoint either by running the script db_checkpoint or by calling the DbEnv::txn_checkpoint method programmatically. For the TDS code example, you can add a routine to create a checkpoint every minute, as Listing 5-8 shows.

Listing 5-8. *Creating a Checkpoint Routine*

```
209 void CDSWorker::runCheckpoint()
210 {
211     while(true)
212     {
213         try
214         {
215             env_->txn_checkpoint(0,0,0);
216         }
217         catch(DbException &ex)
218         {
219             env_->err(ex.get_errno(), "checkpoint");
220         }
221         ACE_OS::sleep(60);
222     }
223 }
```

This method runs a checkpoint every minute; however, it is possible that no modification was done to the database in the last minute. You can configure txn_checkpoint to create a checkpoint only if a change in the database occurred. You can use the first argument in the txn_checkpoint method to specify the number of kilobytes of data in the transaction log after which the checkpoint should be created. If that much data hasn't been added since the last checkpoint, the call to txn_checkpoint will be a no-op. Similarly, you can use the second argument to specify the number of minutes after which the next checkpoint will be created.

Checkpointing can be an I/O-intensive operation if a large amount of data has been modified since the last checkpoint; therefore, it is advisable to run txn_checkpoint from a separate thread. You can easily add the checkpoint thread to the code example by using the infrastructure you've built so far. All you need to do is add the runCheckpoint method in the svc method of the CDSWorker class and execute it when the mode is set to CHECKPOINT, like this:

```
19 #define READER 1
20 #define WRITER 2
21 #define NON_CURSOR_READER 3
22 #define CHECKPOINT 4
~
~
52 int CDSWorker::svc()
53 {
54     try
55     {
56         switch(type_)
57         {
58             case READER:
59                 runReader();
60                 break;
61             case WRITER:
62                 runWriter();
```

```
63                    break;
64                case NON_CURSOR_READER:
65                    runNonCursorReader();
66                    break;
67                case CHECKPOINT:
68                    runCheckpoint();
69                    break;
70                default:
71                    ACE_DEBUG((LM_ERROR, "unknown type %d\n", type_));
72                    break;
73            }
74        }
75        catch(...)
76        {
77            ACE_DEBUG((LM_ERROR, "CDSWorker: exception caught\n"));
78        }
79 }
```

Next, simply create a new thread for creating checkpoints, as Listing 5-9 shows.

Listing 5-9. *Adding the Checkpointing Thread*

```
278        CDSWorker *r4 = new CDSWorker(&dbenv, &db, CHECKPOINT, 5);
279        if(r4->activate((THR_NEW_LWP | THR_JOINABLE), 1) != 0)
280            ACE_DEBUG((LM_ERROR, "Could not launch r5\n"));
281
282        ACE_Thread_Manager *tm = ACE_Thread_Manager::instance();
283        tm->wait();
```

Notice that on lines 282-283, you add a call to get an instance of the ACE_Thread_Manager and then call wait on it. This is a shortcut available in ACE to wait for all threads created in the process. With a large number of threads, it becomes cumbersome to wait for each one of them individually.

■**Note** Even though txn_checkpoint can be an I/O-intensive operation, it doesn't acquire any locks on the database. It can block other database operations, but only for very short periods through mutexes. It may be worthwhile to look at the DbEnv::memp_trickle method as a way to speed up the checkpointing. The memp_trickle method ensures that a specified percent of the pages in the shared memory pool are cleaned up by writing dirty pages to their backing files whenever the available memory pool shrinks below the specified limit.

Transaction Log Maintenance

If you let the TDS code example program run for a few minutes and then list the files in the environment directory, you should see something like this:

```
hy@linux:~/ws/bdb_book/chap_5/chap5_env> ls -l
total 30480
-rw-r--r--  1 hy users   6762496 2005-12-27 22:57 chap5_tds
-rw-r-----  1 hy users     24576 2005-12-27 22:57 __db.001
-rw-r-----  1 hy users    278528 2005-12-27 22:57 __db.002
-rw-r-----  1 hy users     98304 2005-12-27 22:57 __db.003
-rw-r-----  1 hy users    450560 2005-12-27 22:57 __db.004
-rw-r-----  1 hy users     16384 2005-12-27 22:57 __db.005
-rw-r-----  1 hy users  10485760 2005-12-27 22:57 log.0000000001
-rw-r-----  1 hy users  10485760 2005-12-27 22:57 log.0000000002
-rw-r-----  1 hy users  10485760 2005-12-27 22:57 log.0000000003
-rw-r-----  1 hy users  10485760 2005-12-27 22:57 log.0000000004
-rw-r-----  1 hy users  10485760 2005-12-27 22:57 log.0000000005
-rw-r-----  1 hy users  10485760 2005-12-27 22:57 log.0000000006
```

In just a few minutes, three log files of 10MB each were created. Clearly, this is a problem. You have to start removing some of these log files after some time. A transaction log can be removed if it meets the following criteria:

- It doesn't contain information about an ongoing transaction.

- At least one checkpoint has been written since it got created.

- It's not the only log file in the environment.

Now how do you find out if a log file meets these criteria? It's quite simple. You can use any of the following methods to automatically remove all the files that meet all the criteria:

- Run db_archive -d to remove all the *removable* log files from the environment.

- Set the DB_LOG_AUTOREMOVE flag using the DbEnv::set_flag method so that the moment a log file becomes removable, it gets removed automatically.

- Call DbEnv::log_archive with the DB_ARCH_REMOVE flag from your program, which has the same effect as running db_archive -d externally.

▮**Caution** Setting DB_ARCH_REMOVE or DB_LOG_AUTOREMOVE will make catastrophic recovery impossible. If your application needs the ability to run catastrophic recovery, you should use log_archive for log-file removal after doing a database backup.

If you run db_archive -d for the TDS code example environment, you'll notice that some log files got removed:

```
hy@linux:~/ws/bdb_book/chap_5/chap5_env>db_archive -d
hy@linux:~/ws/bdb_book/chap_5/chap5_env> ls -l
total 58013
-rw-r--r--  1 hy users 22179328 2005-12-27 23:23 chap5_tds
-rw-r-----  1 hy users    24576 2005-12-27 23:21 __db.001
-rw-r-----  1 hy users   278528 2005-12-27 23:21 __db.002
-rw-r-----  1 hy users    98304 2005-12-27 23:21 __db.003
-rw-r-----  1 hy users   450560 2005-12-27 23:21 __db.004
-rw-r-----  1 hy users    16384 2005-12-27 23:21 __db.005
-rw-r-----  1 hy users 10485760 2005-12-27 23:22 log.0000000005
-rw-r-----  1 hy users 10485760 2005-12-27 23:22 log.0000000006
```

The number of log files that get cleaned up depends on how frequently checkpoints are being created; the more frequent the checkpoints, the more log files that get removed.

Database Backups

It's important to do database backups periodically. Database backups are important for two reasons:

- **To recover from hardware failure**: No matter how you store data on a disk, you cannot recover your database if the disk crashes. To guarantee the safety of your data, you should either keep a backup on a different machine or maintain a tape archive. You can also replicate the database to a different machine (replication is covered in detail in Chapter 8).

- **To recover from transaction log corruption**: When the database gets corrupted due to a failure, you can use the transaction log to re-create it up to the last committed transaction. However, if the transaction log itself gets corrupted due to a failure, you cannot do anything to get your database up. But if you've backed up your database, you can recover up to a certain point in time.

There are two ways to do a database backup: through a cold backup or a hot backup. Cold backups require that all the database transactions be either committed or aborted and that no database operation takes place while the backup is in progress. There are no such restrictions for a hot backup. However, it's not guaranteed that every transaction that got committed while the hot backup was in progress will be present in the backup. In other words, a cold backup is more accurate than a hot backup if you want to ensure that all transactions at a given point in time have been captured in the backup. A hot back, however, is less disruptive than a cold backup. Let's look at the procedures for taking the two types of backups.

Cold Backup

You must perform the following steps to create a cold backup:

1. Commit or abort all active transactions.

2. Stop processing any new database operations.

3. Create a checkpoint as described in the previous section.

4. Run db_archive -s to get a list of all database files known to the database environment. Copy the files to the backup location.

5. Use db_archive -l to get a list of all the log files that have to be copied for a backup, and copy them to the backup location.

■**Caution** If you have any databases in your environment that weren't opened since the current transaction log files got created, they won't be reported by db_archive. You should copy all the files from your database directory to the backup location to avoid missing some database files.

Hot Backup

For a hot backup, you don't need to stop database processing. You just have to follow these steps:

1. Back up all your database files, as described in the step 4 of creating a cold backup.

2. Copy all the log files sequentially to the backup locations. Always maintain the order of backing up the data files before the log files.

These steps will create a very large backup if a lot of log files are present in the environment. Although not required, you can perform the following steps before creating a hot backup to reduce the size of the backup:

1. Create a database checkpoint.

2. Clean up unused log files.

You can use the DbEnv::log_archive method instead of the db_archive utility to get a list of data files and log files programmatically. Let's add the hot backup functionality to the TDS code example. Since you can use log_archive for a number of things, let's wrap it in a separate method, as shown in Listing 5-10.

Listing 5-10. *Creating the Archiving Routine*

```
245 void CDSWorker::archive(u_int32_t flags)
246 {
247     int ret;
248     char **file_list = NULL;
249
250     ret = env_->log_archive(&file_list, flags);
251     if(ret)
252     {
253         env_->err(ret, "runCheckpoint: archive failed");
```

```
254     }
255     else if(file_list != NULL)
256     {
257         char **begin = file_list;
258         for(; *file_list != NULL; ++file_list)
259         {
260             ACE_DEBUG((LM_ERROR, "%s\n", *file_list));
261         }
262         free(begin);
263     }
264 }
```

In this method, you can copy the files returned by log_archive to a backup destination. To keep the example simple, let's simply print the file names to stdout. In an actual program, you would perhaps FTP the files to a different machine or copy them to a mounted drive. The archive method should be called periodically so that the backup is always up to date. The checkpoint thread is a good place from which to run backups. Since you're creating a checkpoint every minute, you can add the archive call in the same thread but invoke it every hour, as shown in Listing 5-11.

Listing 5-11. *Running Database Archival from the Checkpointing Thread*

```
214 void CDSWorker::runCheckpoint()
215 {
216     int ARCH_INTERVAL = 60 * 60;
217     ACE_Time_Value last_arch = 0;
218
219     while(true)
220     {
221         try
222         {
223             env_->txn_checkpoint(0,0,0);
224             ACE_Time_Value curr_time = ACE_OS::gettimeofday();
225             if(curr_time.sec() - last_arch.sec() > ARCH_INTERVAL)
226             {
227                 ACE_DEBUG((LM_ERROR, "removing unused log files\n"));
228                 archive(DB_ARCH_REMOVE);
229
230                 ACE_DEBUG((LM_ERROR, "archiving data files\n"));
231                 archive(DB_ARCH_DATA);
232
233                 ACE_DEBUG((LM_ERROR, "archiving log files\n"));
234                 archive(DB_ARCH_LOG);
235             }
236         }
237         catch(DbException &ex)
238         {
239             env_->err(ex.get_errno(), "checkpoint");
```

```
240              }
241              ACE_OS::sleep(60);
242     }
```

The thread wakes up once every minute, creates a checkpoint, and checks if the last archive was done more than an hour ago. If that's the case, it first removes the unused log files by using the DB_ARCH_REMOVE flag, then archives the data files using the DB_ARCH_DATA flag and finally archives log files using DB_ARCH_LOG.

■**Note** If your database is very big, then copying the data files during a backup can take a long time. Since file copy is an I/O-intensive operation, the system might slow down during backups. It's advisable to take backups when the system isn't very busy—for instance, if your database is relatively free around midnight, you should schedule the backups around that time. Alternatively, you can design the application to throttle the backup mechanism so that it uses only a fraction of the available I/O bandwidth.

Database Recovery

One of the key features that transactions provide to a database is the ability to survive system, application, and hardware failures. When configured properly, the TDS can recover every committed transaction after an unexpected failure.

The Basic Concept Behind Database Recovery

The transaction log is the source that drives database recovery. When an application modifies a database record, the modification is first written to the transaction log cache, which then is persisted to the disk. Next, the database page in the cache is updated with the change. Only after the modification record is written to the transaction log on the disk will the change be marked as *committed*. If there is a system or application failure, you can reconstruct the database up to the last committed transaction by replaying the modifications recorded in the transaction log, because no change could have been *committed* if it wasn't written to the transaction log. Database recovery can be defined as *the reconstruction of a database* after a failure, carried out by applying the undo and redo data in the log to either reapply or remove changes for transactions, depending on their commit/abort status.

Types of Recovery

Database recovery is a very broad term; different applications have different requirements when it comes to recovery. Some applications can afford to lose the data stored in the database after a crash, whereas any data loss is unacceptable for other applications. Berkeley DB provides a number of configurable options that allow you to tailor the most suitable recovery scheme for your application. Since recovery procedures can be very expensive, no recovery mechanism is enabled by default. The recovery procedures can be categorized into no recovery, simple recovery, or catastrophic recovery, depending on what degree of recoverability the application requires.

No Recovery

This option should be used if the application can afford to lose data after a crash because the data being stored may be of a temporary nature or it may have been replicated to a different machine. In this case, there is no need to enable any recovery mechanism; in fact, you can even disable some parts of the transactional subsystem. I'll discuss this in detail in Chapter 7. If you don't need recoverability, you don't need to create transaction logs. Instead, you should use the DB_TXN_NOT_DURABLE flag when creating the database handle.

Simple Recovery

The application requires data recovery after an application crash, but it can live with the possibility of losing some or all data after an unusual hardware or power failure. Databases that you can re-create or recover from another source have this type of requirement. A good example is a proxy server that maintains a cache of information downloaded from the main server. It's possible for such applications to reload the data from the main server, but it's an expensive operation and it cannot be done every time there's an application failure or a hardware reboot. However, after a catastrophic failure, such as disk failure, you can easily reload the database from the main server. For such applications, you have to perform the following procedures:

- **Checkpointing**: Checkpoints are needed to flush the database cache to the disk periodically. You can do this from a thread within the application.

- **Transaction log maintenance**: You have to maintain the transaction logs generated since the last checkpoint in order to perform recovery.

- **Database recovery**: You can perform simple recovery either by running the db_recover utility or by opening the environment using DbEnv::open with the DB_RECOVER flag.

During simple recovery, the transaction logs are replayed on the database environment since the last checkpoint record. If the data stored on the disk wasn't corrupted by the failure, simple recovery is usually sufficient to bring the environment back into operation. However, certain events, such as disk failure or a power failure, can cause some of the disk pages to get corrupted. When that happens, you need catastrophic recovery to recover the environment.

Catastrophic Recovery

Catastrophic recovery replays all the transactions that can be found in the environment. Therefore, if all the transaction logs that were ever created since the creation of the environment are available, the entire environment can be re-created. Catastrophic recovery is required if the simple recovery fails, which happens when the data on the disk gets corrupted. Some extra procedures, in addition to the ones needed for simple recovery, are required to perform catastrophic recovery:

- Checkpointing

- Transaction log maintenance

- Database recovery

- Backup snapshot maintenance

- Catastrophic recovery

You're already familiar with these procedures except for catastrophic recovery. In order to run catastrophic recovery, you have to perform the following steps:

1. Create a new directory for doing catastrophic recovery. Although it isn't necessary, it's best to create a new directory to avoid any confusion.

2. Copy the log files and data file from the latest backup snapshot to the new directory.

3. Copy all the log files created since the last snapshot was taken in the directory, if they're available. It's important to copy the newer log files after you copy the backup snapshot, because if log files with the same name are in the snapshot, they should be overwritten. You should, however, be mindful of the possibility that some of the newer log files could be corrupted. If the recovery fails with the newer logs, then you'll have no other option than to go back to the plain snapshot and thereby lose some of the recent transactions.

4. Either run `db_recover -c` or open the environment using `DbEnv::open` with the `DB_RECOVER_FATAL` flag.

Catastrophic recovery lets you recover the database up to the last uncorrupted log file available.

Note You can recover the database in a directory other than the one where the original database was located if you've used relative path names for your data and log files (using `set_data_dir` and `set_log_dir` either programmatically or through the `DB_CONFIG` file). All you need to do to re-create the database in a different directory is to specify the new directory using the `-h` option in `db_recover`.

Summary

Berkeley DB provides a rich set of features that you can utilize to implement sophisticated data stores. This chapter was a high level introduction to the CDS and TDS, you learned how to design a CDS and a TDS, and you also learned how to utilize the various APIs to make your data store more functional and robust. In the next chapter I will discuss TDS in a lot more detail. I will also continue to explore the Berkeley DB APIs and show you how to use some of the more advanced features.

CHAPTER 6

■■■

Advanced Operations

In the last two chapters, I introduced you to the basic database operations and database architecture. I broke up the discussion on database operations into multiple parts, to be covered in different chapters, because it's impossible to introduce everything at once. Without an understanding of the basic operations, it's difficult to understand the architecture. And without an understanding of the architecture, it's difficult to grasp advanced operations. Now that you're familiar with the architecture, you're ready to learn advanced operations.

The last two chapters covered the basic insert, retrieve, update, delete, and cursor operations. In this chapter, I'll go over advanced cursor operations, data-alignment issues, joins, secondary indices, and partial/bulk retrieval. I'll also show you how to build a functional data-access layer on top of the Berkeley DB API.

Enhancing the Data Store

In order to explore the advanced operations, first let's enhance the tds.cc code example you developed in Chapter 5. In Chapter 5, you learned about access methods, database locking, and transactions, and you tried to simulate a multithreaded application with concurrent readers and writers. In that chapter, you weren't too interested in how and what kind of data was being stored and retrieved. In this chapter, you'll beef up the data-definition and data-loading portions of the code example so that you can create a rich enough data set to demonstrate the advanced operations.

One of the main strengths, and also one of the weaknesses, of Berkeley DB is that it doesn't recognize the structure of the data that's being stored in the database. All data stored in Berkeley DB is in the form of key-value pairs. Not dealing with the schema is a strength, because unlike a SQL-based relational database, Berkeley DB doesn't have to process the metadata, resulting in a much better and deterministic performance. However, it's also a weakness, because the schema management in Berkeley DB has now to be done by the application, which makes the application much more complicated than an application using a relational database.

To understand what it takes to do schema management within the application, let's try to store a simple data structure in a Berkeley DB database. The structure contains the following information about a person:

- Name

- Social Security number (SSN)

- Date of birth

If you were using a relational database, you would have written an SQL script similar to what is shown in Listing 6-1, to define the schema for the Person table.

Listing 6-1. *SQL Query for Creating the Person Table*

```
CREATE TABLE Person (
  name VARCHAR(64) default NULL,
  ssn INT default NULL,
  dob DATE default NULL,
  PRIMARY KEY (ssn)
)
```

Once you execute the script on an active database instance, the relational database takes care of converting the data to the appropriate format while storing and retrieving data from the Person table. To insert the following record in the table

```
Name - James Wood, SSN - 229113345, DOB - January 13, 1975
```

you just have to execute the following SQL command:

```
INSERT INTO Person (name, ssn, dob) values ('James Wood', 229113345, 1975-01-13);
```

Berkeley DB wasn't designed to understand SQL; it works with only byte arrays. Anything that has to be written to or read from a Berkeley DB database has to be in the form of a byte array. To store the same record in a Berkeley DB database, you would have to write something like what is shown in Listing 6-2 (assume for now that the date of birth is a string).

Listing 6-2. *Storing a Person Record in Berkeley DB*

```
unsigned long ssn = 123456789;
std::string name = "James Wood";
std::string dob = "January 13, 1975";

//create a buffer big enough to hold all the fields
char serializedData[1000];
memset (serializedData, 0, 1000);
char *buf= serializedData;
int elemLen = 0;
int totalLen = 0;

//write the ssn in the buffer
elemLen = sizeof(unsigned long);
memcpy(buf, &ssn, elemLen);
totalLen += elemLen;
buf += elemLen;
```

```
//write the name in the buffer
elemLen = name.length() + 1;
memcpy(buf, name.c_str(), elemLen);
totalLen += elemLen;
buf += elemLen;

//write the date of birth
elemLen = dob.length() + 1;
memcpy(buf, dob.c_str(), elemLen);
totalLen += elemLen;

//prepare the Dbt structures
Dbt keyDbt(&ssn, sizeof(ssn));
Dbt valueDbt(serializedData, totalLen);

//insert the Dbts in the database
int ret = db->put(txn, &keyDbt, &valueDbt, 0);
```

As you can see, the process is more complicated in Berkeley DB than in a relational database. The extra lines of code needed for Berkeley DB comprise only part of the complexity. The bigger problem is the implicit schema information embedded within the application code. Suppose you want to change the primary key from ssn to name. You would not only need to change the application code, but you would also have to remove and re-create your database. It isn't as easy as running the ALTER TABLE command, as in a relational database. In Berkeley DB, you would have to dump the data stored in the database in a text or some other kind of file, truncate the database, and reload the data with name as the key. A relational database can simplify the process of modifying the primary key, because it understands the structure of the stored data. The application, in which you want to use Berkeley DB for data management, should be able to do the following:

- Define the schema of the structures to be stored in the database

- Serialize/deserialize the data structure stored in the database

- Dump/load the database

■**Note** These capabilities are needed only if the application has to deal with changes in the data structures stored in the database. If the data stored in the database never changes, which is almost never the case, then you can hard-code this logic into the application.

Let's try to implement these features in the tds.cc code example. The main purpose of having these capabilities built into the applications is to make it easier to add, remove, or modify the schema. The goal should be to minimize the impact of schema changes on the application code; you should restrict the code changes to the database-specific code within the application. You can use the base class shown in Listing 6-3 to derive specific classes for each structure.

Listing 6-3. *Base Class Definition for Database Entries*

```
37 class DbEntry
38 {
39     public:
40         DbEntry();
41
42         void dbPut(Db *db);
43     protected:
44         virtual char* serialize()=0;
45         virtual int deserialize(char *buf)=0;
46         virtual void getPKey(void*& key, int& length)=0;
47
48         char serializedData_[1000];
49         int serializedLen_;
50 };
```

DbEntry is an abstract class that serves as the base class for specific structure-based classes. It has the following important methods and variables:

- **Line 42**: dbPut inserts a serialized record in a database.

- **Line 44**: serialize serializes a structure into a byte array.

- **Line 45**: deserialize constructs a structure from a byte array.

- **Line 46**: getPKey returns the primary key and its length associated with a record.

- **Line 48**: serializedData holds the serialized record.

Note The size of the buffer to hold the serialized record doesn't need to be fixed. The buffer can be allocated dynamically. It has been preinitialized in the code example to keep it simple, so that you can focus on the discussion of Berkeley DB.

Now define a class based on DbEntry for the Person database, as shown in Listing 6-4.

Listing 6-4. *Definition of the Person Class*

```
52 class Person : public DbEntry
53 {
54     public:
55         Person();
56         Person(std::string& line);
57
58     protected:
59         char* serialize();
60         int deserialize(char *buf);
```

```
61          void getPKey(void*& key, int& length);
62
63      private:
64          unsigned long       ssn_;
65          std::string         name_;
66          std::string         dob_;
67 };
```

Let's go over the declaration of the Person class line by line:

- **Line 56**: A constructor takes a text-based string to create an instance of the class. This constructor will be used to load the Person database from a text file.

- **Lines 59–61**: serialize and deserialize are virtual methods in the base class.

- **Lines 64–66**: ssn_, name_, and dob_ are fields in the database record.

Before implementing the Person class, you need to decide the format of the text file that you'll use for dumping and loading the database. Any format that allows you to represent the primitive data types will work. For example, you could use a sophisticated format such as XML, which is very flexible and allows you to implement constraint checking using the XML schema. However, XML would also complicate the simple example code. You could also use a simple format such as CSV, which wouldn't allow you to do fancy constraint checking but would be perfect for the simple example code. Let's go with CSV. Parsing a CSV file is very easy. CSV is extremely versatile for representing primitive data types. For the Person database, a CSV file containing the records will look like what's shown in Listing 6-5.

Listing 6-5. *CSV Representation of Some Person Records*

```
111223333,Manish Pandey,jan 13 1971
111223334,Shirish Rai,dec 23 1974
111443335,Roland Hendel,feb 13 1973
```

Each line is treated as a single record. Within each record, the fields are separated by commas.

■**Note** For a nontrivial application, it pays to implement an XML-based schema definition framework, because it allows you to implement automatic schema-update, data-migration, and data-verification utilities. You can also use the Berkeley DB XML engine to manage the XML-based database schema.

In the subsequent code snippets, you'll notice methods from a class called DbUtils being used. DbUtils is an aggregation of mostly static, miscellaneous utility methods that I'll use for schema management in the code example.

Going back to the definition of the Person class, the implementation of the second constructor, shown in Listing 6-6, creates an instance from a line in the CSV file you saw in Listing 6-5.

Listing 6-6. *Creating a* Person *Object from the CSV Representation*

```
164 Person::Person(std::string& line)
165 {
166     std::istringstream iss (line, std::istringstream::in);
167     std::string strVal;
168
169     iss >> ssn_;
170
171     char c;
172     iss >> c;
173
174     DbUtils::getStrVal(iss, strVal);
175     name_ = strVal;
176
177     DbUtils::getStrVal(iss, strVal);
178     dob_ = strVal;
179
180     ACE_DEBUG((LM_ERROR, "readPerson: ssn-%u name-%s, dob-%s\n",
181                 ssn_, name_.c_str(), dob_.c_str()));
182 }
```

The code here is pretty simple. An input stream is created on the string from the CSV file, and various fields are read out from the stream. On line 172, the comma is ignored after reading ssn_. The comma after the name_ field is discarded in the DbUtils::getStrVal method, as shown in Listing 6-7.

Listing 6-7. *Parsing a Field from CSV Input*

```
136 void DbUtils::getStrVal(std::istream& instrm,
                            std::string& value)
137 {
138     char c;
139     value.clear();
140     while(instrm.get(c))
141     {
142         switch(c)
143         {
144             case ',':
145             case '\n':
146                 return;
147             default:
148                 value += c;
149         }
150     }
151 }
```

Since the length of a string isn't fixed, unlike the other primitive data types, you have to read in all the characters until you find either the comma character or the newline character. That's all that is there in parsing a CSV file. You'll have to enhance your code slightly to take care of multiline entries and escaping commas (if some values contain the comma character). However, this implementation will suffice for this example.

Now you have a way to specify the data to be loaded into the database through a CSV file and a constructor to construct the data structures for the Person database from the CSV file. Now you need a serialize method to create a byte array out of the data structure, as shown in Listing 6-8.

Listing 6-8. *Implementation of the serialize Method*

```
220 char* Person::serialize()
221 {
222     memset (serializedData_, 0, 1000);
223
224     char *buf= serializedData_;
225
226     int elemLen = 0;
227     int totalLen = 0;
228
229     elemLen = sizeof(unsigned long);
230     memcpy(buf, &ssn_, elemLen);
231     totalLen += elemLen;
232     buf += elemLen;
233
234     elemLen = name_.length() + 1;
235     memcpy(buf, name_.c_str(), elemLen);
236     totalLen += elemLen;
237     buf += elemLen;
238
239     elemLen = dob_.length() + 1;
240     memcpy(buf, dob_.c_str(), elemLen);
241     totalLen += elemLen;
242
243     serializedLen_ = totalLen;
244     return serializedData_;
245
246 }
```

The implementation of the serialize method is very similar to Listing 6-2, which showed you how to insert a record into a Berkeley DB database. The deserialize method does the opposite of what serialize does, as shown in Listing 6-9.

Listing 6-9. *Implementation of the deserialize Method*

```
248 int Person::deserialize(char *buf)
249 {
250     char *tmpBuf = buf;
251     int totalLen = 0;
252     int elemLen = 0;
253
254     elemLen = sizeof(ssn_);
255     ssn_ = *((unsigned long *)tmpBuf);
256     totalLen += elemLen;
257     tmpBuf += elemLen;
258
259     name_ = tmpBuf;
260     elemLen = name_.length() + 1;
261     totalLen += elemLen;
262     tmpBuf += elemLen;
263
264     dob_ = tmpBuf;
265     elemLen = dob_.length() + 1;
266     totalLen += elemLen;
267
268     return 0;
269 }
```

You just have to read in each element in the same order as was written in the serialize method. It's important to keep the order of serializing and deserializing the fields identical; otherwise, you'll end up with corrupted data. These are the little details that make it difficult to build and maintain a Berkeley DB–based application.

■**Caution** You should always read (and write) fields from (and to) the serialized record in the same order, because Berkeley DB doesn't understand the structure of the data that's being stored in the database.

You now need a mechanism to insert the serialized data into the database. The dbPut method declared in the DbEntry base class helps you do that, as shown in Listing 6-10.

Listing 6-10. *Implementation of the dbPut Method*

```
188 void DbEntry::dbPut(Db *db)
189 {
190     serialize();
191
192     void *pkey = NULL;
193     int keyLen = 0;
194
```

```
195        getPKey(pkey, keyLen);
196
197        Dbt pkeyDbt(pkey, keyLen);
198        Dbt valueDbt(serializedData_, serializedLen_);
199
200        DbTxn *txn;
201        try
202        {
203            DbUtils::dbEnv_->txn_begin(NULL, &txn, 0);
204            int ret = db->put(txn, &pkeyDbt, &valueDbt, 0);
205            if(ret)
206                DbUtils::dbEnv_->err(ret, "DbEntry::dbPut" );
207            txn->commit(0);
208        }
209        catch(DbException &txn_ex)
210        {
211            DbUtils::dbEnv_->err(txn_ex.get_errno(), "DbEntry::dbPut");
212            txn->abort();
213        }
214
215 }
```

Here's what happens in the dbPut method:

- **Line 190**: serialize is called to create the byte array to be inserted.

- **Line 195**: getPKey is used to get the key against which the data will be stored. For the Person database, ssn is the key.

- **Lines 197–198**: Key-value Dbts, to be used by put, are prepared.

- **Lines 200–213**: A transaction is created, which is used for doing the insert, and then the transaction is committed. This portion is identical to what you did in Chapter 5 for inserting a record in the database within a transaction.

Listing 6-11 shows how you can define getPKey.

Listing 6-11. *Implementation of getPKey*

```
271 void Person::getPKey(void*& key, int& length)
272 {
273     key = &ssn_;
274     length = sizeof(ssn_);
275 }
```

You now have all the components for populating the Person database; however, you still need something to read in the CSV file. You can write a small program to read in the text file, which has the records in CSV format. If you write this program to take the database and the text file as arguments, you can reuse it for other databases as well. You can use the structure shown in Listing 6-12 to associate a database and the CSV-based text file that will be used to load the database. You can use the id to identify the database.

Listing 6-12. *Structure for Holding the Database Name to ID Mapping*

```
typedef struct
{
    const char*    dbName;
    const char*    fileName;
    int            id;
} DbDesc;

static const DbDesc dbDescArr[] =
{
    { "Person_Db", "person.txt", 1 }
}
static const size_t numDb = 1;
```

You can use the utility method shown in Listing 6-13 to load all the databases listed in
dbDescArr. For now, there's just one database to load.

Listing 6-13. *Implementation of loadDbs*

```
67 void DbUtils::loadDbs(DbEnv *env)
68 {
69     dbEnv_ = env;
70
71     for(int i=0; i < numDb; i++)
72     {
73         DbDesc dd = dbDescArr[i];
74         Db *db = new Db(env, 0);
75         DbTxn *txn;
76         try
77         {
78             env->txn_begin(NULL, &txn, 0);
79             db->set_pagesize(512);
80             db->open(txn, dd.dbName, NULL ,
81             DB_BTREE, DB_CREATE | DB_THREAD, S_IRUSR|S_IWUSR);
82             txn->commit(0);
83             dbMap_[dd.id] = db;
84         }
85         catch(DbException &txn_ex)
86         {
87             txn->abort();
88         }
89
90         load(dd.fileName, dd.dbName, dd.id);
91     }
92 }
```

Let's see what happens in the loadDbs method:

- **Line 71**: You loop through the array of databases defined Listing 6-12.

- **Lines 74–88**: You create a database handle using the name listed in the array.

- **Line 83**: The Db handle is stored in a map against the id of the database. You'll use the map later on to access the databases and also to close the database handles at the end of the program.

- **Line 90**: The load method reads in the CSV files and loads the database.

You can define the load method as shown in Listing 6-14.

Listing 6-14. *Implementation of load Method*

```
94  void DbUtils::load(const char *file, const char *dbName, int id)
95  {
96      std::ifstream fileStrm(file, std::ios::in);
97      if ( !fileStrm )
98      {
99          ACE_DEBUG((LM_ERROR, "LoadDb::load: unable to open %s\n", file));
100         throw std::exception();
101     }
102
103     Db *db = NULL;
104
105     DbMapIter it = dbMap_.find(id);
106     if(it != dbMap_.end())
107         db = it->second;
108
109     while (!fileStrm.eof())
110     {
111         std::string line;
112         std::getline(fileStrm, line);
113         if(line.length() <= 0)
114             break;
115         switch(id)
116         {
117             case PERSON_DB:
118                 {
119                     Person p(line);
120                     p.dbPut(db);
121                 }
122                 break;
129             default:
130                 ACE_DEBUG((LM_ERROR, "LoadDb::load: unknown Db id %d\n", ➡
                                            id));
```

```
131                    break;
132          }
133     }
134 }
```

Let's go over the important lines in the implementation of the load method:

- **Lines 96–101**: You open an input stream on the CSV file specified in the array.

- **Lines 105–107**: You find the Db handle by looking up the database id in the handle map created earlier. You could have passed the Db handle as an argument to this method, but I wanted to show you how the map gets used for looking up a database handle.

- **Line 109**: You read one line at a time from the file and process it. Remember, each line in the CSV-formatted text file represents one record.

- **Line 115**: You do a switch based on the database being loaded.

- **Lines 117–120**: If the database is the Person database, you create an instance of the Person class and then invoke dbPut on the instance.

After compiling all the classes, this is what you see when you run the program:

```
hy@linux:~/ws/bdb_book/chap_6> ./tds
readPerson: ssn-111223333 name-Manish Pandey, dob-jan 13 1971
readPerson: ssn-111223334 name-Shirish Rai, dob-dec 23 1974
readPerson: ssn-111443335 name-Roland Hendel, dob-feb 13 1973
```

Now let's dump the database to see what got inserted:

```
hy@linux:~/ws/bdb_book/chap_6/chap5_env> db_dump Person_Db
VERSION=3
format=bytevalue
type=btree
db_pagesize=512
HEADER=END
 2522a106
 2522a1064d616e6973682050616e646579006a616e2031332031393733100
 2622a106
 2622a10653686972697368820526169006465632032333203139373400
 877da406
 877da406526f6c616e642048656e64656c006665622032031332031393733300
DATA=END
```

In the dump, the records start after the HEADER=END line and continue to the DATA=END line. The key-value pairs appear on separate lines and are hex-encoded. The dump shows that three records got inserted in the database.

Endian Issues

In the database dump just shown, the first key is 2522a106. If you convert 111223333 (which is the ssn in the first record), you get 06a12225. The four bytes in the ssn integer are inserted in the reverse order in the database. The order gets reversed, because I used an x86 machine to run the program. Since x86 machines store integers in the little-endian format, the least significant byte (LSB) 06 is stored as the first byte of the word in the memory.

This reversal is harmless as far as data integrity is concerned. However, it has a significant impact on the way the keys are stored and searched in the underlying Btree by Berkeley DB. Berkeley DB doesn't know that the key is actually an integer; it uses the actual physical representation of the integer in the memory. The main advantage of using a Btree is the locality of reference it provides for lexicographically similar keys. The locality of reference means that the keys that are similar, such as 111223333 and 111223334, will most likely be located on the same page in the database. Therefore, when 111223333 is read from the disk, 111223334 will also be brought into the memory because it's on the same page. However, because of the reversal in the order of the bytes, Berkeley DB sees the keys as 623026438 and 639803654, which aren't very close to each other, so the locality of reference is lost. On a little-endian machine, therefore, integer keys in a Btree access method can cause the following problems:

- **Bad lookup performance**: The locality of reference is lost, causing poor lookup performance.

- **Sparsely populated** Btrees: The keys may get converted to values that are far apart from each other.

There are two ways of fixing these problems. First, you can manually reverse the order of bytes in the integers that are used as keys. Second, you can define your own comparison method for the Btree access method. Let's explore both methods.

Byte Order Reversal

You can reverse byte order by writing a simple reversal routine that swaps the bytes in an integer. The routine shown in Listing 6-15 does the swap for an unsigned integer. This routine isn't very efficient, but I've used it to demonstrate the concept.

Listing 6-15. *Method to Change the "Endian-ness" of an Integer*

```
218 void DbEntry::reverseEndian(unsigned long *intVal)
219 {
220     ACE_DEBUG((LM_ERROR, "original value %x\n", *intVal));
221     unsigned long tmpInt = *intVal;
222     char *buf = (char*)intVal;
223     char *bufOrig = (char*)(&tmpInt);
224     int size = sizeof(unsigned long);
225     for(int i=0; i < size; i++)
226     {
227         buf[size - i - 1] = bufOrig[i];
228     }
229     ACE_DEBUG((LM_ERROR, "converted value %x\n", *intVal));
230 }
```

A more efficient way would be to define a macro like the one shown in Listing 6-16.

Listing 6-16. *A Macro to Change the "Endian-ness" of an Integer*

```
#define long_swap(A) ((((u_int32_t)(A) & 0xff000000) >> 24) | \
                      (((u_int32_t)(A) & 0x00ff0000) >> 8)  | \
                      (((u_int32_t)(A) & 0x0000ff00) << 8)  | \
                      (((u_int32_t)(A) & 0x000000ff) << 24))
```

Listing 6-17 shows how you can use DbEntry::reverseEndian to reverse the order of ssn while loading the Person database by calling the method in getPKey.

Listing 6-17. *Implementation of the getPkey Method*

```
void Person::getPKey(void*& key, int& length)
{
    reverseEndian(&ssn_);
    key = &ssn_;
    length = sizeof(ssn_);
}
```

When you load the database and do a dump again, you'll see the following results:

```
hy@linux:~/ws/bdb_book/chap_6/chap5_env> db_dump Person_Db
VERSION=3
format=bytevalue
type=btree
db_pagesize=512
HEADER=END
 06a12225
 2522a1064d616e6973682050616e646579006a616e203133203139373100
 06a12226
 2622a10653686972697368682052616900646563203203233203139373400
 06a47d87
 877da406526f6c616e642048656e64656c00666656220331332031393733300
 080507a4
 a40705080000
DATA=END
```

The ssn field shows up as 06a12225 now, which is what you want to get the benefit of locality of reference and a compact Btree.

These routines still have a problem. What if you want to port your database to a big-endian machine? These routines would still reverse the order of the integers, which isn't what you would want, because the byte ordering would be correct by default on a big-endian machine. To avoid having to check for the endian-ness of the platform, you can use the system-defined conversion routines htonl or htons for converting the integers to the network byte order, which is always big-endian. The routines htonl and htnons are no-ops on big-endian machines. The getPKey method, shown in Listing 6-18, automatically takes care of endian-ness without any code changes when you move to a new platform.

Listing 6-18. *Implementation of getPKey*

```
void Person::getPKey(void*& key, int& length)
{
    ssn_ = htonl(ssn_);
    key = &ssn_;
    length = sizeof(ssn_);
}
```

Btree Comparison Function

Another way of making your database immune to the endian issues is to define a custom Btree comparison function for your database. By default, the Btree access method uses lexicographical comparison to compare keys, as mentioned earlier. Berkeley DB allows you to register your own comparison routine by calling Db::set_bt_compare on the database handle. The library invokes the registered callback every time the keys are compared within the Btree. Since the key comparison happens during insertions both and retrievals, the method will be called for every database access; therefore, it should be very efficient. Listing 6-19 shows how you could write a comparison function.

Listing 6-19. *Implementation of a Btree Comparison Function*

```
static int btreeCompare(Db *db, const Dbt *d1, const Dbt *d2);

int btreeCompare(Db *db, const Dbt *d1, const Dbt *d2)
{
    unsigned int d1_int;
    unsigned int d2_int;
    memcpy(&d1_int, d1->get_data(), sizeof(unsigned int));
    memcpy(&d2_int, d2->get_data(), sizeof(unsigned int));
    int ret = d1_int - d2_int;
    ACE_DEBUG((LM_ERROR, "d1 %d d2 %d returning %d\n", d1_int, d2_int, ret));
    return ret;
}
```

btreeCompare converts the raw data stored in the Dbts to integers and returns a negative value if d1_int < d2_int, 0 if d1_int == d2_int, and a positive value if d1_int > d2_int. You can register the comparison callback before opening the database, as shown in Listing 6-20.

Listing 6-20. *Registering the Comparison Callback*

```
db->set_pagesize(512);
db->set_bt_compare(btreeCompare);
env->txn_begin(NULL, &txn, 0);
db->open(txn, dd.dbName, NULL ,
            DB_BTREE, DB_CREATE | DB_THREAD, 0644);
txn->commit(0);
```

If you load the database again after compiling this change, you'll see the following results:

```
hy@linux:~/ws/bdb_book/chap_6> ./tds
readPerson: ssn-111223333 name-Manish Pandey, dob-jan 13 1971
d1 111223333 d2 -1543043832 returning 1654267165
d1 111223333 d2 111223334 returning -1
d1 111223333 d2 111223333 returning 0
readPerson: ssn-111223334 name-Shirish Rai, dob-dec 23 1974
d1 111223334 d2 -1543043832 returning 1654267166
d1 111223334 d2 111223334 returning 0
readPerson: ssn-111443335 name-Roland Hendel, dob-feb 13 1973
d1 111443335 d2 -1543043832 returning 1654487167
d1 111443335 d2 111223334 returning 220001
d1 111443335 d2 111443335 returning 0
```

Notice that the integers are being interpreted correctly, and the function is returning the correct result.

■**Note** Don't forget to remove the byte swap (htonl) in the getPKey method before trying out the Btree comparison callback; otherwise, you'll notice an incorrect integer comparison.

Alignment Issues

To improve memory access performance, most modern operating systems read or write multiple bytes of data during every access. Most 32-bit architectures read or write 4 bytes, or a *word*, at a time, even when not all 4 bytes are required for an operation. This optimization can result in subtle bugs if the data isn't aligned on the word boundary. Since relational databases are aware of the database schema, they can make the necessary adjustments to take care of alignment issues. In Berkeley DB, the application has to handle the alignment. To understand the problems that can arise, let's take a look at an example. I've assumed that the database environment has been initialized before. Suppose you have to store the structure shown in Listing 6-21 as the key in a database.

Listing 6-21. *A Structure to Demonstrate Data-Alignment Issues*

```
struct DataAlign
{
    int a;
    char b;
    int c;
};
```

Now insert a record with an instance of this structure as the key, as shown in Listing 6-22.

Listing 6-22. *Inserting an Instance of the DataAlign Structure*

```
Db miscDb(&dbenv, 0);
miscDb.open(NULL, "Misc_Db", NULL, DB_BTREE,
            DB_CREATE | DB_THREAD, S_IRUSR|S_IWUSR);

DataAlign d;
d.a = 1;
d.b = (char)2;
d.c = 3;

char *dataStr = "Data alignment test";

Dbt key((void*)&d, sizeof(d));
Dbt data((void*)dataStr, strlen(dataStr) + 1);
miscDb.put(NULL, &key, &data, 0);
```

Now try to read this record using the code shown in Listing 6-23.

Listing 6-23. *Reading the DataAlign Structure Instance from the Database*

```
DataAlign d1;
d1.a = 1;
d1.b = (char)2;
d1.c = 3;

Dbt newKey((void*)&d1, sizeof(d1));
ACE_HEX_DUMP((LM_ERROR, (char*)(newKey.get_data()),
             newKey.get_size()));
Dbt value1;
value1.set_flags(DB_DBT_MALLOC);
int ret = miscDb.get(NULL, &newKey, &value1, 0);

if(ret == 0)
{
    std::string str = (char*)(value1.get_data());
    ACE_DEBUG((LM_ERROR, "get: %s\n", str.c_str()));
}
else
{
    ACE_DEBUG((LM_ERROR, "data not found\n"));
}
```

You'll see the following result:

```
hy@linux:~/ws/bdb_book/chap_6> ./misc
HEXDUMP 12 bytes
01 00 00 00 02 3d aa bf  03 00 00 00              .....=......
data not found
hy@linux:~/ws/bdb_book/chap_6>
```

The lookup fails because the structure isn't aligned. The actual storage for member b is 4 bytes, even though b is of type char and should be 1 byte long. The three unused bytes contain uninitialized junk values. The hex dump of the key you used for get shows some arbitrary data for member b where there should have been just 2. Let's do a dump on the table to see what actually got stored in the database:

```
hy@linux:~/ws/bdb_book/chap_6> db_dump misc_env/Misc_Db
VERSION=3
format=bytevalue
type=btree
db_pagesize=4096
HEADER=END
 010000000262edbf03000000
 4461746120616c69676e6d656e74207465737400
DATA=END
hy@linux:~/ws/bdb_book/chap_6>
```

You can see that the key contains some junk for the member b where there should have been just the single value of 02.

There are two ways to fix this problem. You can either pack the data in the key in such a way that the storage takes up only 1 byte for the member b, or you can initialize the unused bytes in the storage for member b to zeros. Listing 6-24 shows you how to initialize the structure to zeros before you insert the data.

Listing 6-24. *Proper Initialization of Structures with Alignment Issues*

```
DataAlign d;
memset(&d, 0, sizeof(d));
d.a = 1;
d.b = (char)2;
d.c = 3;
```

Listing 6-25 shows you how to initialize the structure, which is used to hold the read data, to zeros.

Listing 6-25. *Proper Initialization of the Structures Used for Reading a Record*

```
DataAlign d1;
memset(&d1, 0, sizeof(d1));
d1.a = 1;
d1.b = (char)2;
d1.c = 3;
Dbt newKey((void*)&d1, sizeof(d1));
```

You should see the following output:

```
hy@linux:~/ws/bdb_book/chap_6> ./misc
HEXDUMP 12 bytes
01 00 00 00 02 00 00 00   03 00 00 00          ............
get: Data alignment test
hy@linux:~/ws/bdb_book/chap_6>
```

The member b is showing up correctly as 2, and the record was found.

To pack data correctly in the structures, you can use DB_DBT_MALLOC, DB_DBT_REALLOC, and DB_DBT_USERMEM flags in the Dbt instances passed to the library. You can pay attention to alignment issues when you design your structs, as well. For example, if you declare the struct as shown in Listing 6-26, then a and b will be int-aligned, and no additional padding will be needed.

Listing 6-26. *Example of a Structure That Doesn't Have Alignment Issues*

```
struct DataAlign
{
    int a;
    int c;
    char b;
};
```

It's the introduction of a member in the middle with unusual alignment that requires the compiler to insert the padding. In general, it's good practice to zero out the key and data portions of your Dbt prior to use. It's also important to think about endian issues early, because you may need to restore the database you've created to a different architecture from the system on which you created it. Berkeley DB includes support for making the file metadata—everything that you use in the library—platform-portable. However, since you don't know anything about the contents of your records, you can't take care of alignment or byte-order issues inside your records.

Secondary Indices

Berkeley DB allows you to create multiple indices on a database. It's desirable to have multiple indices if the application needs to look up the entries using different keys. If only one index exists on the database and you want to look up an entry with a key different than the one used in the index, you'll have to search all the entries sequentially until you find the one you're looking for. For example, in the Person database, you used ssn as the key to store the records. If you want to look up the record of Roland Hendel, you would have to iterate through the entries until you found the record for Roland Hendel. However, if you have an additional index on the database that uses name as the key, you could go directly to the desired record. A secondary index can greatly improve the performance of a database if it's frequently accessed through a nonprimary key.

If you had to create a secondary index on name for the Person database in a relational database, we could write and execute a SQL statement like this:

```
CREATE INDEX Person_Name_Db ON Person(name);
```

Person_Name_Db is the name of the index, and name is the field in a Person record that would be used for the index. To create a secondary index in Berkeley DB, you'd have to do a little extra work.

Berkeley DB maintains a secondary index in a database of its own, which isn't very different from the main database. The library treats the secondary index like any other database. The only difference between a secondary index and a main database is that the entries in a secondary index always refer to entries in the main database with which it is associated. The entries in the secondary index are of the form "secondary key, primary key." They provide a mechanism to locate the primary database record through the secondary key. After the main database handle has been created, you can create a secondary database handle and associate it with the main database handle, as shown in Listing 6-27.

Listing 6-27. *Associating a Secondary Database Handle with the Primary Database*

```
Db *db = new Db(env, 0);
db->open(txn, "Person_Name_Db", NULL, DB_BTREE,
         DB_CREATE | DB_THREAD, S_IRUSR|S_IWUSR );
personDb->associate(txn, db, DbUtils::getSecKey, 0);
```

The db handle is the secondary database handle that is opened with the name Person_Name_Db and is associated with the personDB handle, which is the primary database handle.

■**Note**   I've used a convention for naming databases. All database names have a suffix _Db. The secondary indices start with the primary database name followed by the field/fields used as the secondary index. For example, Person_Db is a primary database, and Person_Name_Db is a secondary index on Person_Db that uses the name as the secondary key.

In the associate method, the second argument is the secondary database handle. The third argument is the function pointer to a callback, which returns the secondary key when provided the primary key and the value stored against the primary key. Listing 6-28 shows the definition of the callback.

Listing 6-28. *Implementation of the Secondary Callback*

```
325 int DbUtils::getSecKey(Db *secondary, const Dbt *pKey,
326         const Dbt *data, Dbt *secKey)
327 {
328     const char *dbName;
329     const char *fileName;
330     int ret = secondary->get_dbname(&fileName, &dbName);
331
332     Person p;
333     p.deserialize((char*)(data->get_data()));
334     size_t len = p.name_.length() + 1;
335     char *name = (char*)(malloc(len));
336     memcpy(name, p.name_.c_str(), len);
337
338     memset(secKey, 0, sizeof(Dbt));
339     secKey->set_data(name);
340     secKey->set_size(len);
341     secKey->set_flags(DB_DBT_APPMALLOC);
342     ACE_DEBUG((LM_ERROR, "getSecKey called for %s, sec key returned %s\n",
343             fileName, name));
344     return 0;
345 }
```

The arguments include the secondary database handle, the pointer to the primary key, the pointer to the primary database record, and the pointer to the secondary key. The secondary key has to be filled in by the method. The secondary key callback is expected to create the secondary key from the primary key-value pair. The secondary key could be a part of the value, or it could be something derived from the value and the primary key. In this case, it's a part of the value. Let's step through the method:

- **Lines 328–330**: Retrieve the database name from the Db handle. If you want to use the same callback for all the secondary indices (which is sometimes convenient), you can use the database name to execute different secondary key calculation routines.

- **Lines 332–333**: The library returns the primary key-value pair in the form of a byte array. Here you use the deserialize method to create the key and value structures from the array.

- **Lines 334–336**: Allocate a buffer to hold the secondary key and copy the key into it. You cannot simply return a pointer to the name_ field in the Person object you created by deserializing the byte array, because name_ is an instance of std::string, which gets deallocated at the end of the method. The secondary key you create here shouldn't be deleted until the library has used it to create the secondary index.

- **Lines 338–340**: You copy the pointer to the allocated key into the secondary key Dbt.

- **Line 341**: You set the DB_DBT_APPMALLOC flag to indicate to the library that the secondary key was allocated by the callback, so that the library can free the memory associated with the secondary key after it's done with the secondary key. You could have identified the name string within the data Dbt passed as an argument. In that case, a new allocation wouldn't have been necessary, and therefore, the flag wouldn't have been set.

- **Lines 342–343**: You can print out the database name and the returned secondary key for debugging purposes.

The first argument passed in the callback is the Db handle of the secondary index. It isn't required for constructing the secondary index itself, but you can use it to identify which index the callback was invoked on. It's possible to register a common callback routine for all your secondary indices. When the callback is invoked, you can construct the appropriate secondary key depending on the passed Db handle.

Once a secondary index has been associated with a primary database, all modifications done on the primary index are reflected on the secondary database automatically. For example, if a record is deleted from the primary table, the library deletes the corresponding entry in the secondary database automatically. All operations on the secondary database are similarly reflected on the primary database.

■**Note** The automatic secondary index management happens only in the context of the application that called associate, and only while it is running. There is nothing stored in the actual database that would allow a separate application, linked to the same database, to maintain the secondary index. Therefore, all applications that modify the database have to associate the secondary database independently. Also, you need to ensure that the secondary database is associated every time the application is restarted.

In a real-world application, the secondary index is often used more frequently than the primary index, because a secondary index is usually created on keys that are used heavily for lookups. Therefore, it's very important to facilitate easy creation and maintenance of the secondary indices within the database framework. Listing 6-29 shows how you can create and associate secondary indices as a part of the database setup you developed earlier in the chapter. First, you have to extend the DbDesc structure to store additional information about the secondary indices.

Listing 6-29. *Structure to Store Information About the Secondary Index*

```
typedef struct
{
    const char*    dbName;
    const char*    fileName;
    int            id;
    int            isSec;
    int            primaryId;
} DbDesc;
static const DbDesc dbDescArr[] =
{
```

```
    { "Person_Db", "person.txt", 1, FALSE 0 },
    { "Person_Name_Db", "", 2, TRUE, 1 }
};
```

You can see that two new fields have been added to the structure: isSec indicates whether the database is a secondary index, and primaryId stores the primary database ID if isSec is true.

Notice that the CSV initialization file for the Person_Name_Db database is empty. That's because a secondary database doesn't need to be populated. Instead, the library creates it automatically. Let's revisit the loadDb method. Listing 6-30 shows the loadDbs method with support for the secondary databases.

Listing 6-30. *The loadDbs Implementation Intializes Secondary Databases*

```
71 void DbUtils::loadDbs(DbEnv *env)
72 {
73     dbEnv_ = env;
74     for(int i=0; i < numDb; i++)
75     {
76         DbDesc dd = dbDescArr[i];
77         Db *db = new Db(env, 0);
78         DbTxn *txn;
79         try
80         {
81             env->txn_begin(NULL, &txn, 0);
82             db->set_pagesize(512);
84             db->open(txn, dd.dbName, NULL ,
85             DB_BTREE, DB_CREATE | DB_THREAD, S_IRUSR|S_IWUSR);
86             if(dd.isSec)
87             {
88                 DbMapIter it = dbMap_.find(dd.primaryId);
89                 if(it != dbMap_.end())
90                 {
91                     Db *primary = it->second;
92                     primary->associate(txn, db, DbUtils::getSecKey, 0);
93                 }
94                 else
95                 {
96                     ACE_DEBUG ((LM_ERROR, "unknonw primary db %d\n",
97                                 dd.primaryId));
98                     throw;
99                 }
100            }
101            txn->commit(0);
102            dbMap_[dd.id] = db;
103        }
104        catch(DbException &txn_ex)
105        {
106            txn->abort();
```

```
107            }
108        }
109        for(int i=0; i < numDb; i++)
110        {
111            DbDesc dd = dbDescArr[i];
112            if(!dd.isSec)
113                load(dd.fileName, dd.dbName, dd.id);
114        }
115 }
```

The only difference between this and the earlier version is the check in lines 86-100 to see if the database being loaded is a secondary index. If it is a secondary database, then you can look up primaryId in the handle map and associate the secondary handle with the primary handle. You do need to take care, however, to list all your secondary indices after the primary databases in the DbDesc array. Otherwise, the lookup for the primary database will fail. Also, notice that the load call in line 113 has been moved out to a separate loop, so that all secondary indices have been associated by the time you begin loading the entries. If you compile these changes and load the database again, you'll see the following results:

```
hy@linux:~/ws/bdb_book/chap_6> ./tds
readPerson: ssn-1 name-Manish Pandey, dob-jan 13 1971
getSecKey called for Person_Name_Db, sec key returned Manish Pandey
readPerson: ssn-111223334 name-Shirish Rai, dob-dec 23 1974
getSecKey called for Person_Name_Db, sec key returned Shirish Rai
readPerson: ssn-111443335 name-Roland Hendel, dob-feb 13 1973
getSecKey called for Person_Name_Db, sec key returned Roland Hendel
```

Notice that after every insert in the primary index, the getSecKey method is called. If you list the files in the environment directory, you'll see that a new file Person_Name_db has been created:

```
hy@linux:~/ws/bdb_book/chap_6/chap5_env> ls -al
total 423
drwxr-xr-x  2 hy users       320 2006-01-28 00:10 .
drwxr-xr-x  3 hy users       872 2006-01-28 00:09 ..
-rw-r--r--  1 hy users      1024 2006-01-28 00:10 Account_Db
-rw-r--r--  1 hy users      1024 2006-01-28 00:10 Bank_Db
-rw-r-----  1 hy users     24576 2006-01-28 00:10 __db.001
-rw-r-----  1 hy users    278528 2006-01-28 00:10 __db.002
-rw-r-----  1 hy users     98304 2006-01-28 00:10 __db.003
-rw-r-----  1 hy users    450560 2006-01-28 00:10 __db.004
-rw-r-----  1 hy users     16384 2006-01-28 00:10 __db.005
-rw-r-----  1 hy users  10485760 2006-01-28 00:10 log.0000000001
-rw-r--r--  1 hy users      1024 2006-01-28 00:10 Person_Db
-rw-r--r--  1 hy users      1024 2006-01-28 00:10 Person_Name_Db
```

If you dump the entries in Person_Name_Db, here's what you'll see:

```
hy@linux:~/ws/bdb_book/chap_6/chap5_env> db_dump Person_Name_Db
VERSION=3
format=bytevalue
type=btree
db_pagesize=512
HEADER=END
 4d616e6973683682050616e64657900
 00000001
 526f6c616e642048656e64656c00
 06a47d87
 53686972269736820520616900
 06a12226
DATA=END
```

The key is the secondary index returned by the getSecKey method, and the value is the primary key associated with the secondary index.

Database Operations

You're now ready to explore database operations in detail. You've already seen how the basic database operations are done in Berkeley DB. However, to design a fully functional database, you'll need a rich operations interface. Berkeley DB is very different from relational databases in this respect, because relational databases depend upon SQL to provide a rich interface for performing complex operations. Berkeley DB has the following basic operations:

- Db::get: For reading a key-value pair

- Db::pget: For reading a key-value pair using a secondary index

- Db::put: For inserting a key-value pair

- Db::del: For deleting a key-value pair

- Dbc::get: For reading multiple key-value pairs using a cursor

- Dbc::pget: For reading multiple key-value pairs through a secondary index using a cursor

- Dbc::put: For inserting a key-value pair using a cursor

- Dbc::del: For deleting a key-value pair using a cursor

- Db::join: For creating a cursor over a natural join

These operations are sufficient for maintaining a database; however, the challenge here is in making these operations available to the application through an easy-to-use interface. As you've seen so far, every operation requires quite a bit of processing before you can invoke the actual database methods. In this section, I'll show you how to integrate these operations in the framework you've developed so far so that most, if not all, processing can be hidden from the application.

One way to design convenient data-access methods is to enhance the wrapper class Person that you've developed for loading the database. Since the class already contains methods for serializing, deserializing, and extracting keys, all you need to add are some querying methods. For example, since you've created an index on the name field in the Person database, it would make sense to include querying methods that use the name index in addition to the ones that use the primary key. Listing 6-31 shows the list of querying methods that you can add.

Listing 6-31. *Query Methods Based on Secondary Indices*

```
//generic insert
void insert();

//methods using the primary key
void getBySSN(unsigned long ssn);
void delBySSN(unsigned long ssn);
void updateBySSN();

//methods using the name secondary index
DbIter getByName(std::string name);
void delByName(std::string name);
void updateByName();
```

The insert and updateBy methods don't take any arguments, since you can set the fields in the Person object before invoking these methods. The getByName method returns an iterator, because the name isn't the primary key, and multiple records can have the same name. I'll go over the iterator details in the "Cursors" section.

This set of methods is by no means comprehensive. You can have getBy, delBy, and updateBy methods for all possible combinations of the fields in the Person object—for example, getByNameAndSSN and getByDOBAndSSN. In a relational database, you can create any random query by using SQL without having to write code to support it. However, the SQL parsing, planning, and optimization imposes a significant overhead on all queries. In Berkeley DB, there is no such overhead, as all the queries that will be executed are known and compiled in advance. You build only as much infrastructure as the application will require.

You've already seen how the insert works in the previous loadDb example. Let's add the getBySSN and getByName methods to the Person class to understand how get works. Just like the dbPut method, which inserts records, we'll add the dbGet method in the base class DbEntry to read records, as Listing 6-32 shows.

Listing 6-32. *Implementation of the dbGet Method*

```
217 int DbEntry::dbGet(Db *db, Dbt *key, Dbt* data)
218 {
219     int ret = -1;
220     DbTxn *txn;
221     try
222     {
223         DbUtils::dbEnv_->txn_begin(NULL, &txn, 0);
224         ret = db->get(txn, key, data, 0);
```

```
225        if(ret)
226            DbUtils::dbEnv_->err(ret, "DbEntry::dbGet" );
227        txn->commit(0);
228    }
229    catch(DbException &txn_ex)
230    {
231        DbUtils::dbEnv_->err(txn_ex.get_errno(), "DbEntry::dbGet");
232        txn->abort();
233    }
234    return ret;
235 }
```

dbGet is very similar to dbPut. It's a wrapper around the Db::get method, which executes the method within a transaction and does some basic exception-handling. You could have done this within the getBySSN method, but it would've been repetitive, as you would have had to add the same code to the other getBy methods. Listing 6-33 shows how you can implement the getBySSN method.

Listing 6-33. *Implementation of getBySSN*

```
347 int Person::getBySSN(unsigned long ssn)
348 {
349     int ret = -1;
350     unsigned long ssnVal = htonl(ssn);
351     Dbt key;
352     Dbt data;
353     data.set_flags(DB_DBT_MALLOC);
354     key.set_data((void*)(&ssnVal));
355     key.set_size(sizeof(ssn));
356     ret = dbGet(DbUtils::getDbHandle(PERSON_DB), &key, &data);
357     if(ret == 0)
358         deserialize((char*)(data.get_data()));
359     return ret;
360
361 }
```

Let's go over the implementation of the getBySSN method:

- **Line 350**: You convert the passed ssn to the big-endian format, since you've stored all keys in the big-endian format.

- **Lines 351–352**: You set the DB_DBT_MALLOC flag in the data Dbt so that the library can allocate the space for the returned value.

- **Lines 354–355**: You prepare the key Dbt.

- **Line 356**: You retrieve the value stored against the passed ssn using the base class method dbGet.

- **Lines 358–359**: If you find the key call deserialize with the returned byte array. This fills in the member variables of the Person object with the values returned by dbGet.

You can now try to use the getBySSN method to look up a stored entry, as shown in Listing 6-34.

Listing 6-34. *Looking Up a Person Record Using the Primary Key*

```
Person p;
unsigned long ss = 111223334;
if( p.getBySSN(ss) == 0)
{
    ACE_DEBUG((LM_ERROR, "Found record for ssn %u: name %s dob %s \n",
            ss,
            p.getName().c_str(),
            p.getDOB().c_str()));
}
```

By adding this code in main or by writing a separate program, you can test out the getBySSN method. This piece of code is analogous to the following SQL statement:

```
SELECT * FROM Person WHERE ssn = 111223334;
```

When you run the test program, this is what you'll see:

```
Found record for ssn 111223334: name Shirish Rai dob dec 23 1974
```

Similarly, you can build a wrapper for the delete method in DbEntry, as shown in Listing 6-35.

Listing 6-35. *Implementation of dbDel*

```
217 void DbEntry::dbDel(Db *db, Dbt *key)
218 {
219     DbTxn *txn;
220     try
221     {
222         DbUtils::dbEnv_->txn_begin(NULL, &txn, 0);
223         int ret = db->del(txn, key, 0);
224         if(ret)
225             DbUtils::dbEnv_->err(ret, "DbEntry::dbDel" );
226         txn->commit(0);
227     }
228     catch(DbException &txn_ex)
229     {
230         DbUtils::dbEnv_->err(txn_ex.get_errno(), "DbEntry::dbDel");
231         txn->abort();
232     }
233 }
```

You can also build a higher-level delBySSN in the Person class, as shown in Listing 6-36.

Listing 6-36. *Implementation of delBySSN in Person*

```
381 void Person::delBySSN(unsigned long ssn)
382 {
383     int ret = -1;
384     unsigned long ssnVal = htonl(ssn);
385     Dbt key;
386     key.set_data((void*)(&ssnVal));
387     key.set_size(sizeof(ssn));
388     dbDel(DbUtils::getDbHandle(PERSON_DB), &key);
389 }
```

The application can use delBySSN to delete an entry, as shown in Listing 6-37.

Listing 6-37. *Using delBySSN*

```
Person p;
unsigned long ss = 111223334;
p.delBySSN(ss);
```

An update method isn't available in Berkeley DB, so you'll have to simulate an update by doing a get followed by a put, as shown in Listing 6-38.

Listing 6-38. *Updating a Record*

```
Person p;
unsigned long ss = 111223334;
if( p.getBySSN(ss) == 0)
{
    p.setDOB("jan 1 2001");
    p.insert();
}
```

However, this update has a problem. It's possible that after a thread has called getBySSN and before it gets a chance to call insert, another thread will update the record. To protect against such race conditions, you can wrap the two operations within a transaction, as shown in Listing 6-39.

Listing 6-39. *Protecting an Update Operation with a Transaction*

```
DbTxn *txn;
try
{
    DbUtils::dbEnv_->txn_begin(NULL, &txn, 0);
    Person p;
    unsigned long ss = 111223334;
```

```
        if( p.getBySSN(txn, ss) == 0)
        {
            p.setDOB("jan 1 2001");
            p.insert(txn);
            txn->commit(0);
        }
    }
    catch(DbException &txn_ex)
    {
        txn->abort();
    }
```

Notice that the `txn` pointer is being passed as an argument in the `insert` and `getBySSN` methods. Since the actual database operations, which require the transaction handle, are embedded with the `insert` and `getBySSN` methods, you need to pass the higher-level transaction as an argument. You need to modify the method declarations as shown in Listing 6-40.

Listing 6-40. *Adding a Transaction Handle to the Access Functions*

```
void insert(DbTxn *txn=NULL);
void getBySSN(unsigned long ssn, DbTxn *txn=NULL);
void delBySSN(unsigned long ssn, DbTxn *txn=NULL);
```

By doing this, you can take care of higher-level transactions if they're being used, but the `txn` pointer will be set to `NULL` by default. You'd also have to modify the implementation to use the passed transaction handle instead of starting a new transaction. Listing 6-41 shows the `getBySSN` method implementation with the transaction handle.

Listing 6-41. *Using the Transaction Handle in the Access Function Implementation*

```
int Person::getBySSN(unsigned long ssn, DbTxn* txn)
{
    int ret = -1;
    unsigned long ssnVal = htonl(ssn);
    Dbt key;
    Dbt data;
    data.set_flags(DB_DBT_MALLOC);
    key.set_data((void*)(&ssnVal));
    key.set_size(sizeof(ssn));
    ret = dbGet(DbUtils::getDbHandle(PERSON_DB), &key, &data, txn);
    if(ret == 0)
        deserialize((char*)(data.get_data()));
    return ret;
}
```

The transaction handle is passed down to the `dbGet` method, which you need to modify, as shown in Listing 6-42.

Listing 6-42. *Passing the Transaction Handle to the Base Class*

```
int DbEntry::dbGet(Db *db, Dbt *key, Dbt* data, DbTxn* t)
{
    int ret = -1;
    DbTxn *txn = t;
    try
    {
        if(t == NULL)
            DbUtils::dbEnv_->txn_begin(NULL, &txn, 0);
        ret = db->get(txn, key, data, 0);
        if(ret)
            DbUtils::dbEnv_->err(ret, "DbEntry::dbGet" );
        if(t == NULL)
            txn->commit(0);
    }
    catch(DbException &txn_ex)
    {
        DbUtils::dbEnv_->err(txn_ex.get_errno(), "DbEntry::dbGet");
        if(t == NULL)
            txn->abort();
        else
            throw;
    }
    return ret;
}
```

You can change the other methods similarly.

■Tip It's always a good idea to have an argument for passing a transaction handle in your application-level API. By having an argument, in your APIs, for passing the transaction handle you can provide the application the ability to have transactions which span multiple database operations. There is an additional benefit, you can create a child transaction from the passed transaction handle and retry individual operations, when a deadlock occurs, without aborting the parent transaction.

Cursors

The remaining operations in the list of operations available in Berkeley DB are cursor-based operations. A cursor is a position within a database. You can use it to fetch a set of entries from a database one at a time, just like an iterator fetches the values stored in a vector one at a time. A cursor provides the only mechanism to iterate through a set of entries when the keys against which they're stored are not known in advance. To initiate a cursor-based iteration, a cursor has to be set to any one of the following locations within a database:

- DB_FIRST: The cursor points to the first key-value pair in the database.

- DB_LAST: The cursor points to the last key-value pair in the database.

- DB_SET: The cursor points to a known key in the database. This is analogous to a key-based search on a database. This is useful when you want start iterating through the entries in a database starting from a particular location. Suppose you have an application which displays 10 records at a time, from a database, in a scrolled window. You would want to start the iteration from the last read record when the user clicks on the scroll bar. You can always start from the first record every time the user scrolls, but that would be quite inefficient.

- DB_SET_RANGE: This option is similar to DB_SET, except when used on Btree-based database, it returns the smallest key, which is greater than or equal to the supplied key. DB_SET_RANGE works differently for a Btree because the entries in a Btree are sorted, and the library can locate the next closest key if the given key isn't found. When used with the Hash, Queue, and Recno access methods, it behaves exactly like DB_SET.

■Note If the cursor hasn't yet been initialized and any of the NEXT flags (DB_NEXT, DB_NEXT_DUP, DB_NEXT_NODUP) are specified, then the cursor is positioned on the first entry. Similarly, if any of the PREV flags (DB_PREV, DB_PREV_DUP, DB_PREV_NODUP) are specified for an uninitialized cursor, then the cursor is positioned on the last entry.

Listing 6-43 shows how you can create a cursor and use it to fetch a key-value pair.

Listing 6-43. *Using a Cursor to Fetch a Record*

```
Dbc *cursor;
int ret = db_->cursor(txn_, &cursor, 0);
Dbt key;
Dbt value;
ret = cursor->get(&key, &value, DB_FIRST);
```

The code in Listing 6-43 creates a cursor over a database handle and fetches the first key-value pair stored in the database. To position the cursor to the last entry, set the DB_LAST flag in the get call. Listing 6-44 shows how you can iterate through the rest of the entries.

Listing 6-44. *Iterating Through a Table Using a Cursor*

```
while( (ret = cursor->get(&key, &value, DB_NEXT)) != DB_NOTFOUND)
{
    void *valueArr = value.get_data();
    void *keyArr = key.get_data();
}
```

You can also call cursor->get with the DB_NEXT flag without first calling it with DB_FIRST. If get is invoked for the first time on a cursor with the DB_NEXT flag, it is treated as DB_FIRST. Similarly, if it is called for the first time with DB_PREV, it is treated as DB_LAST. To iterate backward, you would call cursor->get with the DB_PREV flag until DB_NOTFOUND is returned. You can use DB_CURRENT to keep the cursor on its current position and read the key-value pair stored on the current location.

Duplicate Keys

If a cursor is created on a database that supports duplicates, DB_NEXT and DB_PREV will iterate through the duplicates. For example, if you have a database with the following keys

```
Andrew
Bill
David
David
Dinesh
Lee
Lee
Lee
Mark
```

and you intend to iterate through only the unique keys, like the following

```
Andrew
Bill
David
Dinesh
Lee
Mark
```

you should use DB_NEXT_NODUP instead of DB_NEXT in the get calls. If you want to iterate over only the duplicates, you can set the cursor on the first duplicate and then use the DB_NEXT_DUP flag, like this:

```
Const char *name = "Lee";
Dbt key ((void*)name, strlen(name) + 1);
Dbt value;
ret = cursor->get(&key, &value, DB_SET);
while( (ret = cursor->get(&key, &value, DB_NEXT_DUP)) != DB_NOTFOUND)
{
/* application logic*/
}
```

Locking in Cursors

A cursor acquires locks on all the entries that have been accessed through it. The locks are held until the cursor is closed. The library locks all the entries visited by the cursor to ensure that the cursor gets a consistent snapshot of the database. If the cursor is opened as a part of a transaction, the locks are acquired with the locker ID of the transaction. If no transaction handle is used to open the cursor, the locker ID of the database handle is used to acquire the locks, which means that the entire database will get locked until the cursor is closed.

■**Caution** If you're using a transactional data store, you should always open a cursor within a transaction; otherwise, the entire database will get locked until the cursor is closed, as is the case in a concurrent data store.

Be very careful when using cursors; otherwise, you might end up locking a large portion of the database. This not only increases the risk of a deadlock, but it also blocks other threads of control from updating the records. You should make sure that the cursors aren't kept open for long periods of time.

Long-Running Cursors

You can't always control the duration of a cursor. In some cases, cursors are required to be kept open for long periods of time. For example, a graphical user interface (GUI) displaying the contents of a database in a scrolling window would want to keep a database cursor open for a long time. In most such casess, however, you don't need to guarantee the consistency of the entries visited by the cursor. In the GUI example, it would be perfectly fine if other threads are allowed to modify the entries being displayed. To allow applications to use long-running cursors with less strict locking, several cursor modes are available. The last argument in the method for creating cursors is a flag that indicates how much isolation the cursor will have. The following values are possible:

- DB_READ_COMMITTED: In this mode, other threads can modify the entries already visited by the cursor. However, if the cursor goes back to a visited row, it will read only committed data. This is also known as *degree 2 isolation*.

- DB_READ_UNCOMMITTED: In this mode, the other threads aren't only allowed to modify the visited rows, but the cursor can read the modified data that hasn't been committed yet. This is known as *degree 1 isolation*. The advantage here is that the cursor reads will never block, thereby increasing the performance. However, you should use this mode with caution, as you can read partially modified, inconsistent records.

- 0: If none of the above flags are set, then the cursor is created with *degree 3 isolation*. This means that no other thread can modify the entries that the cursor has visited until it is closed. This mode is also called *repeatable reads*.

■**Note** Don't confuse the cursor's degree of isolation with the degree of isolation of the transaction within which the cursor is created. A degree 2 cursor can be used within a degree 3 transaction.

Cursors and Secondary Indices

When you create a cursor on a secondary index, the Dbc::get method returns the key from the secondary index and the value from the primary database, as shown in Listing 6-45.

Listing 6-45. *Using Dbc::get*

```
int ret = primary->associate(txn, secondary, envp, 0);
.
.
Dbc *cursor;
ret = secondary->cursor(txn_, &cursor, 0);
Dbt key;
Dbt value;
ret = cursor->get(&key, &value, DB_FIRST);
```

In Listing 6-45, the Dbc::get call returns the key from the secondary handle and the value from the primary handle. Usually, the primary key is also needed when retrieving an entry from a cursor on a secondary index. You can use the Dbc::pget method to retrieve the primary key using a secondary index cursor, as shown in Listing 6-46.

Listing 6-46. *Using Dbc::pget*

```
Dbt key;
Dbt value;
Dbt pkey
ret = cursor->pget(&key, &pkey, &value, DB_FIRST);
```

By using Dbc::pget, you can hide the fact that a secondary index was used to retrieve a record. The application-level API can always return the key-value pair from the primary database whether or not the cursor was created on the primary database.

Database Iterators

Cursor operations are quite cumbersome to use. The values returned by and used by the cursors are byte arrays. An application can use the cursor methods directly, but that will result in duplicate marshalling/unmarshalling code scattered all over the application logic. It would be nice if you could integrate the cursor operations with the data-access class that you developed earlier in the chapter. It would be nicer if, at the same time, you could have an iterator-like intuitive interface for traversing a database. Let's attempt to define a very basic iterator interface. To begin with, define a read iterator that only allows read operations using a cursor, as shown in Listing 6-47. Once you have that, you can easily add the delete, insert, and update operations.

Listing 6-47. *Declaration of the DbIter Class*

```
Class DbIter
{
    DbIter();
    ~DbIter();
```

```
    bool next();
    bool prev();
    void close();
    DbEntry& getEntry();
};
```

The next and prev methods move the cursor forward/backward and return a flag that indicates whether an entry was found at the position. The close method closes the cursor, and getEntry returns the entry stored at the cursor location. An application would use this interface like the one shown in Listing 6-48.

Listing 6-48. *Using DbIter*

```
DbIter iter;
while(iter.next())
    DbEntry e = iter.getEntry();
iter.close();
```

The interface looks simple and easy to use, but there's one problem. As you can see, the interface uses the DbEntry class, which is an abstract class for the concrete database classes, such as Person. How can you associate the iterator to a concrete class such as Person? You could pass the database id as an argument in the constructor, and the getEntry method could then instantiate the appropriate concrete class from the byte array retrieved from the database. However, that would result in a giant if-then-else statement within the method, which would keep on growing as you add new databases. There's nothing wrong with that, but it's not an elegant solution.

Another way to solve the problem is to make the DbIter class a template class. Then you don't need to know, within the DbIter class, which database you're iterating over. The template could possibly increase the size of the executable, but it will reduce the complexity of the code and will make it more maintainable. Listing 6-49 shows the templatized version of DbIter with some more members added.

Listing 6-49. *The DbIter Template*

```
141 template <class Entry>
142 class DbIter
143 {
144     public:
145         DbIter();
146         ~DbIter();
147
148         bool next();
149         bool prev();
150         Entry& getEntry() {return curr_;}
151         void close();
152
153     private:
154         void init(u_int32_t flag);
155         int get(u_int32_t flag);
```

```
156
157        Dbc *cursor_;
158        int state_;
159        Entry curr_;
160        Db *db_;
161        DbTxn *txn_;
162        bool done_;
163        bool closed_;
164        static const int INACTIVE = 0;
165        static const int ACTIVE = 1;
171 };
```

Let's go over the declaration of the DbIter class:

- **Line 154**: init initializes the object with a cursor.

- **Line 155**: get is a utility method that invokes Dbc:get. The public method uses this method internally.

- **Line 157**: cursor_ is the cursor object used by the iterator.

- **Line 158**: state_ holds the current state of the cursor. It could be INACTIVE or ACTIVE.

- **Line 159**: curr_ holds the entry read from the current position of the cursor.

- **Line 162**: done indicates whether the cursor has reached the end of the database.

- **Line 163**: closed indicates that the cursor for this iterator has been closed.

Listing 6-50 shows the implementation of the DbIter class.

Listing 6-50. *The DbIter Constructor*

```
168 template <class Entry>
169 DbIter<Entry>::DbIter():
170     state_(INACTIVE),
171     cursor_(NULL),
172     done_(false),
173     closed_(false)
174 {
175 }
```

You don't need to do anything in the constructor except for initializing the member variables. Listing 6-51 shows the implementation of the destructor.

Listing 6-51. *Destructor of DbIter*

```
177 template <class Entry>
178 DbIter<Entry>::~DbIter()
179 {
180     close();
181 }
```

The destructor invokes close so that if the DBIter object goes out of scope before the cursor is closed, no database locks will be leaked. The implementation of the init method is shown in Listing 6-52.

Listing 6-52. *DbIter Initialization*

```
183 template <class Entry>
184 void DbIter<Entry>::init(u_int32_t flag)
185 {
186     try
187     {
188         db_ = curr_.getDbHandle();
189         DbUtils::dbEnv_->txn_begin(NULL, &txn_, 0);
190         int ret = db_->cursor(txn_, &cursor_, flag);
191         state_ = ACTIVE;
192     }
193     catch(DbException& ex)
194     {
195         DbUtils::dbEnv_->err(ex.get_errno(), "DbIter::init");
196         txn_->abort();
197     }
198 }
```

Let's go over the initialization routine.

- **Line 188**: You first look up the Db handle using the getDbHandle method of DbEntry.

- **Line 189**: You create a transaction. (You can enhance the DbIter class to accept a transaction handle from outside.)

- **Line 190**: You create a cursor using the Db handle. Notice that you're creating a cursor with degree 3 isolation. (You can enhance DbIter to accept the mode of the cursor as an argument in the constructor.)

- **Line 191**: The state is set to ACTIVE, which indicates that the object is ready for business.

Note that you don't commit the transaction that you used to create the cursor. The transaction will be committed when the cursor is closed. Since all the operations performed using this cursor will be done under this transaction, you would not want to commit it before the cursor is closed. Listing 6-53 shows how you can close an instance of DbIter.

Listing 6-53. *Closing DbIter*

```
200 template <class Entry>
201 void  DbIter<Entry>::close()
202 {
203     if(closed_)
204         return;
205     try
206     {
```

```
207        cursor_->close();
208        txn_->commit(0);
209     }
210     catch(DbException& ex)
211     {
212        DbUtils::dbEnv_->err(ex.get_errno(), "DbIter::close");
213        txn_->abort();
214     }
215     closed_ = true;
216 }
```

The close method first closes the underlying cursor and then commits the transaction inside which the cursor was created. In the end, the closed flag is set to true. You can iterate through the entries in a database using DbIter::next or DbIter::prev. Listing 6-54 shows how you can implement these methods.

Listing 6-54. *Implementation of next and prev*

```
218 template <class Entry>
219 bool DbIter<Entry>::next()
220 {
221     if(state_ != ACTIVE)
222         init(0);
223     get(DB_NEXT);
224     return !done_;
225 }
226
227 template <class Entry>

228 bool DbIter<Entry>::prev()
229 {
230     if(state_ != ACTIVE)
231         init(0);
232     get(DB_PREV);
233     return !done_;
234 }
```

The next and prev methods are very similar, except for the flag that is passed in the get call. Let's look at the next method; the same discussion applies to prev:

- **Lines 221–222**: When a DbIter instance is used for the first time to do a next or prev, the state_ flag will be INACTIVE, and the init method will be invoked to initialize the underlying cursor.

- **Line 223**: The private method get is invoked with the DB_NEXT flag to perform the actual cursor operation.

- **Line 224**: The done flag is returned so that the caller can know whether the end of the database has been reached.

While iterating through the entries in a database using next or prev, you can use the get method to read a particular entry. Listing 6-55 shows how you can implement the get method.

Listing 6-55. *Implementing DbIter::get*

```
236 template <class Entry>
237 int DbIter<Entry>::get(u_int32_t flag)
238 {
239     Dbt key;
240     Dbt value;
241     int ret = -1;
242     if(closed_ || done_)
243         return ret;
244
245     ret = cursor_->get(&key, &value, flag);
246     if(ret == 0)
247     {
248         curr_.deserialize((char*)(value.get_data()));
249     }
250     else if(ret == DB_NOTFOUND)
251     {
252         done_ = true;
253         close();
254     }
255     else
256     {
257         DbUtils::dbEnv_->err(ret, "DbIter::get");
258     }
259     return ret;
260
261 }
```

The get method is the heart of the DbIter class. It performs the actual cursor operations on the database. Let's look at it in detail:

- **Lines 242–243**: The closed and done flags are checked to see if the cursor is still active. If it isn't, then no operation is performed on the cursor that could result in a crash.

- **Line 245**: The cursor is used to retrieve an entry from the database, and the flag passed as an argument to the method is passed in the Dbc::get method.

- **Line 248**: If a record is found, then deserialize is called on the returned data bytes, which will fill up the member variables in the Entry object.

- **Lines 252–253**: If the library returns DB_NOTFOUND, then the cursor is closed, and the done flag is set to true.

You can also add a user-friendly typedef to create a unique type for every database. Listing 6-56 shows how you can use the DbIter class in the application code.

Listing 6-56. *Using DbIter*

```
typedef DbIter<Person> PersonIter;
PersonIter iter;
while(iter.next())
{
    Person p = iter.getEntry();
    ACE_DEBUG((LM_ERROR, "Found record for ssn %u: name %s dob %s \n",
                        ss,
                        p.getName().c_str(),
                        p.getDOB().c_str()));

}
iter.close();
```

If you compile and run this sample application code on the Person database you created earlier, you'll see the following output:

```
hy@linux:~/ws/bdb_book/chap_6> ./tds
Found record for ssn 111223334: name Manish Pandey dob jan 13 1971
Found record for ssn 111223334: name Shirish Rai dob dec 23 1974
Found record for ssn 111223334: name Roland Hendel dob feb 13 1973
hy@linux:~/ws/bdb_book/chap_6>
```

As you can see, the DbIter class makes the cursor operations really simple. You can enhance it vastly to include Dbc::del, Dbc::put, and other features available in the Berkeley DB cursor API.

Equality Joins

Berkeley DB provides a facility to perform an equality join on secondary indices of a database. You can use it for efficiently evaluating the entries in the primary database, for which the secondary indices satisfy certain constraints. For example, suppose you had multiple entries in the Person database with the same name and date of birth, as shown in Listing 6-57.

Listing 6-57. *Database Entries with Duplicate Fields*

```
111223333,Manish Pandey,jan 13 1971
111223334,Shirish Rai,dec 23 1974
111443335,Roland Hendel,feb 13 1973
111443336,Roland Hendel,feb 13 1973
111443337,Roland Hendel,feb 13 1973
```

To find out all the entries where the name is Roland Hendel and the date of birth is feb 13 1973, the simplest thing to do would be to iterate through all the entries and look for the name and the date. However, full iteration can be very expensive if the database is huge. You can design a more efficient solution with the use of secondary indices. If you have two indices defined on the database—one on the name and the other on the date of birth—you could go straight to the desired name and the desired date of birth using the indices and then retrieve all the entries where the primary key is the same for both the indices. With this approach, you're iterating over only those entries where either the name is Roland Hendel or the date of birth is feb 13 1973, which is clearly more efficient than the full database scan. The equality join does the same thing. Let's see how you can use it programmatically. You can use the database access infrastructure you've developed so far. Listing 6-58 shows you how to define a method in the Person class.

Listing 6-58. *A Query That Uses the Equality Join*

```
void getByNameAndDob(std::string& name,
                     std::string dob, DbTxn* txn=NULL);
```

The intention here is to search for all the records that have the supplied name and date of birth and print them out. Listing 6-59 shows what the implementation using the equality join would look like.

Listing 6-59. *The Implementation of getByNameAndDob*

```
421 void Person::getByNameAndDob(std::string& name,
422          std::string dob, DbTxn* txn)
423 {
424     try
425     {
426
427         Dbt key;
428         Dbt value;
429
430         Dbc *nameCur = NULL;
431         Db *personNameDb = DbUtils::getDbHandle(PERSON_NAME_DB);
432         int ret = personNameDb->cursor(NULL, &nameCur, 0);
433         key.set_data((void*)(name.c_str()));
434         key.set_size(name.length() + 1);
435         ret = nameCur->get(&key, &value, DB_SET);
436         if(ret)
437         {
438             DbUtils::dbEnv_->err(ret, "Person::getByNameAndDob");
439             nameCur->close();
440             return;
441         }
442
443         Dbc *dobCur = NULL;
444         Db *personDobDb = DbUtils::getDbHandle(PERSON_DOB_DB);
445         ret = personDobDb->cursor(NULL, &dobCur, 0);
446         key.set_data((void*)dob.c_str());
447         key.set_size(dob.length() + 1);
448         ret = dobCur->get(&key, &value, DB_SET);
```

```
449        if(ret)
450        {
451            DbUtils::dbEnv_->err(ret, "Person::getByNameAndDob");
452            nameCur->close();
453            dobCur->close();
454            return;
455        }
456
457        Dbc *curArr[3];
458        curArr[0] = nameCur;
459        curArr[1] = dobCur;
460        curArr[2] = NULL;
461
462        Db *personDb = DbUtils::getDbHandle(PERSON_DB);
463        Dbc *joinCur;
464        ret = personDb->join(curArr, &joinCur, 0);
465        if(ret)
466        {
467            DbUtils::dbEnv_->err(ret, "Person::getByNameAndDob");
468            nameCur->close();
469            dobCur->close();
470            return;
471        }
472
473        while( (ret = joinCur->get(&key, &value, 0)) == 0)
474        {
475            Person p;
476            p.deserialize((char*)(value.get_data()));
477            ACE_DEBUG((LM_ERROR, "Found %s\n", p.toString().c_str()));
478        }
479        nameCur->close();
480        dobCur->close();
481        joinCur->close();
482    }
483    catch(DbException& ex)
484    {
485        DbUtils::dbEnv_->err(ex.get_errno(),"Person::getByNameAndDob");
486    }
487 }
```

Let's walk through the code:

- **Line 431**: You retrieve the database handle of the secondary index based on the name field.

- **Line 432**: You create a cursor on the index.

- **Lines 433–441**: You position the cursor using DB_SET to the name, passed in the argument, in the secondary index.

- **Lines 443–455**: Repeat the first three steps for the secondary index based on the dob field.

- **Lines 457–460**: You store the created cursors in an array. There's no limit on the number of cursors you can store in this array; therefore, any number of secondary index constraints can participate in the equality join.

- **Lines 462–471**: You create a join cursor using the primary database handle and the created cursor array.

- **Lines 473–478**: You retrieve the records from the join cursor until no more are found.

The code is pretty straightforward, though a bit cumbersome. However, once you've written it, you can use it as a generic function for querying records using the name and the dob constraints. Listing 6-60 shows how to use this method.

Listing 6-60. *Using getByNameAndDob*

```
Person joinTest;
std::string n = "Roland Hendel";
std::string dob = "feb 13 1973";
joinTest.getByNameAndDob(n, dob);
```

You'll see this output:

```
Found Name: Roland Hendel SSN: 111443335 DOB: feb 13 1973
Found Name: Roland Hendel SSN: 111443336 DOB: feb 13 1973
Found Name: Roland Hendel SSN: 111443337 DOB: feb 13 1973
```

It's possible to write a generic routine that can combine any number of secondary indices of a database for an equality join. However, it's up to you whether you want to write a single complex method or numerous simple methods. It is sometimes better to write a little bit of duplicate code rather than write totally generic yet complex code. Since your application won't be running queries using multiple indices on all the databases, there's no reason to build the functionality for every database. Remember, the biggest benefit that you get from Berkeley DB is that you can build exactly as much database support as you need.

In Listing 6-60, you simply printed the records to stdout. That won't be very useful in a real application. You would probably need to return the list of records back to the caller. To achieve that, you can either populate a vector and return it, or you can return an iterator based on the join cursor. You'll have to enhance the DbIter class for doing that so that it can work with a join cursor.

■**Tip** An equality join is an efficient but an often neglected way of evaluating multiple secondary index constraints. It's better than writing your own query routines that are based on full table scans.

Bulk Retrieval

Bulk retrieval allows you to read multiple records from the database in a single access. It can result in a significant performance improvement if you have an application that routinely reads a large number of consecutive database records. For example, if you have a database that stores log records and you need to display the logs in a GUI every time an operator has to inspect the logs, your application will always be reading a large number of consecutive records from the database. The use of bulk retrieval can vastly improve the performance of such applications.

Bulk retrieval results in performance improvement, because it reduces the number of API invocations for a set of record retrievals. The most expensive part of a database lookup is the potential disk I/O. Bulk retrieval doesn't necessarily reduce the frequency of disk I/O, which is affected more by the database page size and the size of the cache. Therefore, it's not a major tuning knob for the database, but it can still be quite useful for the type of applications described in this section.

Bulk retrieval is exposed in the API through a set of flags in the get method of the cursor interface:

- DB_MULTIPLE: When this flag is specified in Dbc::get, all entries having the same key can be retrieved with a single call.

- DB_MULTIPLE_KEY: This flag retrieves multiple key-data pairs in one call, which may or may not include records with duplicate keys.

Once you have the buffer, which contains multiple data items, from a Dbc::get call in a Dbt object, you can use one of the following interfaces to iterate through the records within your application code:

- MultipleDataIterator: Returns keys and values from the returned buffer one at a time

- MultipleKeyDataIterator: Returns one key-value pair at a time from the buffer

- MultipleRecnoDataIterator: Returns a key-value pair from the buffer, but the key is of the type db_recno_t

To understand the flags and the iterator interface better, let's walk through Listing 6-61, which retrieves data in bulk. Once again, you're using the infrastructure you've developed so far. This code adds another method called getBulk to the Person class.

Listing 6-61. *Implementation of getBulk*

```
489 void Person::getBulk()
491     try
492     {
493         //the 5K buffer that will be used for bulk retreival
494         int BULK_LEN = 5 * 1024;
495         char buff[BULK_LEN];
496         Dbt bulk;
497         bulk.set_data(buff);
498         bulk.set_ulen(BULK_LEN);
499         bulk.set_flags(DB_DBT_USERMEM);
```

```
500
501        //create a cursor on the database
502        Dbc *bulkCur;
503        Db *personDb = DbUtils::getDbHandle(PERSON_DB);
504        int ret = personDb->cursor(NULL, &bulkCur, 0);
505
506        //in a loop retrieve 5K worth of records at a time
507        while(true)
508        {
509            Dbt key;
510            ret = bulkCur->get(&key, &bulk,
511                    DB_MULTIPLE_KEY | DB_NEXT);
512            if(ret)
513            {
514                DbUtils::dbEnv_->err(ret,
515                        "getBulk:bulkCur:get");
516                break;
517            }
518            DbMultipleKeyDataIterator mIter(bulk);
519            Dbt d;
520            Dbt k;
521            Person p;
522            while( (mIter.next(k, d)) )
523            {
524                p.deserialize((char*)(d.get_data()));
525                ACE_DEBUG((LM_ERROR, "getBulk: %s\n",
526                        p.toString().c_str()));
527            }
528        }
529        bulkCur->close();
530    }
531    catch(DbException& ex)
532    {
533        DbUtils::dbEnv_->err(ex.get_errno(),
534                "Person::getBulk");
535    }
532 }
```

Let's go over the main portions of the getBulk routine:

- **Lines 494–496**: You declare a buffer of 5KB. Dbc::get will return as many records as will fit in this buffer without breaking any record. If the buffer isn't big enough to store even a single record, then Dbc::get will return a DB_BUFFER_SMALL error.

- **Lines 497–498**: You initialize a Dbt object with the buffer. Set the ulen flag in Dbt to indicate that the user has supplied the buffer to be used for Dbc::get.

- **Line 499**: You set the DB_DBT_USERMEM flag to indicate that the user is responsible for managing the Dbt memory.

- **Lines 501–504**: You create a cursor on the primary Person database. Bulk retrieval can be done on any database, primary or secondary.

- **Lines 507–517**: You do a Dbc::get on the cursor using the DB_MULTIPLEKEY flag in a loop until no more records are found. At the most, 5K worth of records will be returned in each iteration.

- **Line 518**: You declare a MultipleKeyDataIterator using the bulk Dbt populated by Dbc::get.

- **Lines 519–527**: You call next on MultipleKeyDataIterator to read all the records returned in the bulk object.

As you can see, the retrieved records are simply printed on stdout. In a real application, you might want to return a list or a vector of the Person object from the getBulk method. If you invoke this method like this

```
Person bulk;
bulk.getBulk();
```

you'll see an output like the following:

```
getBulk: Name: Manish Pandey SSN: 111223333 DOB: jan 13 1971
getBulk: Name: Shirish Rai SSN: 111223334 DOB: dec 23 1974
getBulk: Name: Roland Hendel SSN: 111443335 DOB: feb 13 1973
getBulk: Name: Roland Hendel SSN: 111443336 DOB: feb 13 1973
getBulk: Name: Roland Hendel SSN: 111443337 DOB: feb 13 1973
```

Notice that the getBulk method returns both duplicate and nonduplicate keys. If you want to get only the duplicate entries associated with the current key, you should use the DB_MULTIPLE flag in Dbc::get. Suppose that on line 518, where you declared MultipleKeyDataIterator, you use MultipleDataIterator instead, as shown in Listing 6-62.

Listing 6-62. *Using MultipleDataIterator*

```
518             DbMultipleDataIterator mIter(bulk);
519             Dbt d;
520             Dbt k;
521             Person p;
522             while( (mIter.next(d)) )
523             {
524                 p.deserialize((char*)(d.get_data()));
525                 ACE_DEBUG((LM_ERROR, "getBulk: %s\n",
526                             p.toString().c_str()));
527             }
```

You'll get the following output:

```
getBulk: Name:  SSN: 623026438 DOB: : id-3 nÄA=@Citi
getBulk: Name: Manish Pandey SSN: 111223333 DOB: jan 13 1971
getBulk: Name:  SSN: 639803654 DOB:
getBulk: Name: Shirish Rai SSN: 111223334 DOB: dec 23 1974
getBulk: Name:  SSN: 2273158150 DOB:
getBulk: Name: Roland Hendel SSN: 111443335 DOB: feb 13 1973
getBulk: Name:  SSN: 2289935366 DOB:
getBulk: Name: Roland Hendel SSN: 111443336 DOB: feb 13 1973
getBulk: Name:  SSN: 2306712582 DOB:
getBulk: Name: Roland Hendel SSN: 111443337 DOB: feb 13 1973
```

Every alternate entry looks like it's corrupted, but it's actually not corrupted. If you use MultipleDataIterator, the keys against which the entries are stored in the database are returned as a data Dbt along with the value Dbt one at a time. The garbage shows up in the output because you're trying to create a Person object out of the key Dbt returned by the iterator. This behavior isn't explicitly documented.

■**Tip** Bulk retrieval is another ignored feature that can result in significant performance improvement for certain kinds of applications. It improves performance by reducing the number of API invocations.

Summary

Berkeley DB provides many advanced access features that are exposed through flags in the generic access methods. These features can sometimes be difficult to understand and use. An easy-to-use wrapper interface, which makes these features available to the application through an intuitive API, makes it much easier to use these performance-enhancing features.

The absence of database schema interpretation within the Berkeley DB library makes it impossible for the library to detect and catch errors related to byte ordering and data alignment. The fact that an application-specific wrapper can easily catch such errors further underscores the need to have such a wrapper. As you've seen, it's not very difficult to implement such a wrapper, but it's equally important not to *over*-implement the wrapper. The wrapper should strictly stick to the needs of the application; otherwise, you'll lose the benefit of using Berkeley DB. A thick and complex wrapper will make your database infrastructure as unpredictable and as inefficient as a relational database.

In the next chapter, I'll show you how to develop some of the server-side components commonly needed for building a Berkeley–DB based database framework. I'll shift the focus from client-side interfaces to server-side components.

■■■

CHAPTER 7

A Real-World Data Store

Berkeley DB is a library; therefore, you cannot use by itself as a fully functional database system. You yourself have to take care of a number of details, such as threading, IPC, and process structure. The design of this supporting framework usually has a profound effect on the performance, stability, and scalability of the database solution built on top of Berkeley DB. The absence of a process structure in Berkeley DB makes it extremely flexible, allowing you to use it with almost any application architecture. However, there are certain restrictions in the way that you can create, use, and destroy the Berkeley DB environment. These restrictions drive the database framework design. I'll first discuss these restrictions and then explore the possible framework designs.

In the code examples you've seen up until now, not much attention has been paid to the architecture of the data store. Initially, you developed a primitive CDS, followed by a minimal TDS. In the last chapter, you learned how to develop client-side interfaces on top of Berkeley DB APIs. In this chapter, I'll go over the structure of the database framework and show you how to design a functioning system using Berkeley DB.

Constraints on Environment Usage

The Berkeley DB environment is used to make the database shareable among multiple processes and threads. In traditional relational databases, the sharing is provided by a central server, which creates, maintains, and shuts down the database resources. Processes that need to access the resources connect to the central server through sockets. This is a very clean and robust way of managing the resources, because they exist in a stand-alone address space. There is virtually no way for the client processes to corrupt the database.

However, this model also imposes a significant performance overhead, because every database access involves socket I/O and multiple process hops. To avoid this overhead, Berkeley DB shares the database resources through shared memory. All processes that need to access the database link to the common shared memory region. This approach results in significant improvement in performance, but at the same time, it increases the risk of database corruption by the client processes. If a process that has linked to the shared region crashes while it's operating on the database resources, the environment can become corrupted. This possibility of environment corruption imposes certain rules that the application processes have to follow while using Berkeley DB. Let's take a look at these rules:

- **The application should serialize environment creation**: No process or thread should be allowed to use the database environment unless it has been created, recovered, and verified. If multiple processes try environment creation at the same time, the library will serialize them, making it simpler for you.

- **The application should detect environment corruption**: Some mechanisms should be put in place to detect if an environment was not shut down gracefully, because an ungraceful shutdown can cause database corruption. If an environment gets corrupted, all the processes that are linking to it should stop using it until it has been re-created and recovered.

- **Environment shutdown should be single-threaded**: An environment handle should always be closed gracefully. The thread in charge of managing the environment should wait for all the threads to finish, close all the open database handles, and finally close the environment handle. This should be done synchronously from a single thread; otherwise, unwanted race conditions can occur where a thread may try to use a closed environment. There could be multiple processes attached to the same environment. When one process shuts down its database and environment handles, other processes are not affected.

- **Environment recovery should be single-threaded**: Despite the most careful design, unexpected crashes cannot be ruled out in any system. To handle an ungraceful shutdown, a single thread should run recovery on the failed environment and restore it to a known consistent state. During recovery, a new environment is created from the backing files and the transaction logs. Since the existing environment is removed during recovery, any operation on the original environment will fail and return an error. Recovery should never be performed by more than one thread at the same time.

These rules have to be followed in all application architectures designed around Berkeley DB. Let's look at the various types of application structures most commonly used and see how these rules can affect the architecture.

- **Single-threaded single process**: This is the simplest architecture possible; there is no sharing involved in this model. The single-threaded process first opens the environment and then shuts it down after it's done using the database. There is no need to enforce synchronization.

- **Multithreaded single process**: This is slightly more complicated, because you have to create the environment from one thread. When all the threads are done using the database, you have to close the environment and the database handles after ensuring that no other thread is using them.

- **Multithreaded multiple cooperating processes**: This is a complicated application structure to manage. The term *cooperating* here implies that all the processes using the environment are spawned or managed by a single controlling process, or a *controller*. The controller can spawn or kill any process. The presence of a controller makes a difference, because the controller can synchronize the environment creation, recovery, and shutdown. In addition, you can also use a controller as a container of all the initialization and configuration logic. This is the most common architecture used by Berkeley DB–based server applications.

- **Multithreaded multiple unrelated processes**: This is the most complex application structure to handle. There is no controlling entity, and processes can be created and killed randomly. If a process causes environment corruption, the other processes using the environment need to be informed somehow about the corruption so that they can stop using the environment until it is recovered. There's no easy way of doing that without a controller process. Most solutions that don't involve a controller process are prone to deadlocks.

In the next few sections, I'll go through each application structure and use a sample application to demonstrate how you can design the database framework for each one of them.

■**Note** In this chapter's code examples, I've used the Boost smart pointer library in addition to the ACE libraries. Both Boost and ACE are open source with no GPL restrictions. To obtain more information about Boost, you can visit `http://www.boost.org`. You can find more information about ACE at `http://www.cs.wustl.edu/~schmidt/ACE.html`.

A Single Process With One Thread

A single process with a single thread is the simplest possible structure. No synchronization issues are involved. When the process comes up, it creates an environment handle, recovers it, and verifies it. When it's done with the database, it closes all the database resources. I'll focus on the multithreaded single process; the single-threaded process is simply a special case of the more general discussion.

A Single Process With Multiple Threads

Let's start with environment creation. The main requirements for environment creation are that it should be recovered prior to being used in case the environment is in a corrupted state, and the recovery should be done by single thread. Technically, you need to run recovery only if the environment is corrupted. However, it's impossible for the application to know whether recovery is necessary. To get around this problem, the library expects the recovery to be run at startup whether or not the environment was corrupted earlier. It is harmless to run recovery even when it isn't required. If only one process is using the environment, all the threads in the process can easily share a single DbEnv handle. However, there are no restrictions on the number of DbEnv handles that you can create on an environment. To allow proper environment initialization and sharing of a single DbEnv handle, you can use the *singleton pattern*.

■**Note** The singleton design pattern ensures that a single instance of a singleton class is created only once within a process. That way, it is ensured that everyone accesses the same instance of the class.

Listing 7-1 shows you how you can utilize the singleton pattern. I'll continue to use the code we've developed so far, but I'll introduce modifications needed to accommodate the architectural restrictions discussed here. The biggest change is introduced in the DbUtils class, which you developed in Chapter 6 as a collection of utility methods. I'll make this class a singleton, where the single instance of the environment handle (and the single instance of each database handle) gets created. Let's take a look at the new class declaration.

Listing 7-1. *DbUtils with a Smart Pointer*

```
35 class DbUtils;
36 typedef boost::shared_ptr<DbUtils> DbUtils_SP;
37
38 class DbUtils
39 {
40     public:
41
42         ~DbUtils();
43         static void getStrVal(std::istream& instrm,
44                                   std::string& value);
45         void closeDbResources();
46         static int getSecKey(Db *secondary, const Dbt *pKey,
47                 const Dbt *data, Dbt *secKey);
48
49         Db* getDbHandle(int dbId);
50         static DbUtils_SP& getInstance();
51         static DbEnv* getEnv();
52         void loadDbs();
53
54     protected:
55         DbUtils();
56         DbUtils(const DbUtils&);
57         DbUtils& operator= (const DbUtils&);
58
59         void load(const char*file,
60                     const char* dbName, int id);
61
62         typedef std::map< int, Db* > DbMap;
63         typedef std::map< int, Db* >::iterator DbMapIter;
64
65         DbMap dbMap_;
66         DbEnv dbEnv_;
67         static bool isInitialized_;
68         static ACE_Recursive_Thread_Mutex initMutex_;
69
70         static DbUtils_SP singleton_;
69 };
```

Let's go over the new declaration of DbUtils:

- **Line 36**: You declare an alias for shared_ptr of the DbUtils class. shared_ptr is a class from the Boost memory management library, which implements the smart pointer concept with reference counting. shared_ptr is useful when an object is being used in multiple threads and no one thread is in charge of cleaning up the object once it is no longer in use. shared_ptr maintains a reference count of the object stored inside it. When the reference count becomes zero, it invokes the destructor of the object. Since shared_ptr itself is allocated on the stack, it gets deallocated automatically. The DbUtils instance is a perfect candidate to be stored in shared_ptr, because when the process is about to exit, the singleton instance of DbUtils will get cleaned up. This in turn cleans up the DbEnv handle.

- **Line 42**: The destructor is public to allow shared_ptr to clean up the instance.

- **Line 50**: The static public method returns the singleton shared_ptr instance of the DbUtils class.

- **Lines 55–57**: The default constructor, copy constructor, and the assignment operator are declared protected to disallow any other instance of the class.

- **Line 67**: A flag indicates if the singleton has already been instantiated.

- **Line 68**: A mutex protects the singleton creation. ACE_Recursive_Thread_Mutex is a recursive mutex, which the same thread can acquire multiple times. It's an easy way to prevent self-deadlocks.

- **Line 70**: The member variable singleton_ holds the static singleton instance of the DbUtils class.

You'll realize the power of the smart pointer concept when I go over the worker threads that use the DBUtils class. Apart from making the code clean, smart pointers virtually eliminate memory-management tasks from the application code.

Now let's look at the implementation of the DbUtils class, shown in Listing 7-2. You'll notice that all the code related to the environment creation, which was scattered in multiple classes earlier, has now been moved to the DbUtils class. I've listed only the portions that have changed from Chapter 6.

Listing 7-2. *New Implementation of getInstance in DbUtils*

```
DbUtils_SP& DbUtils::getInstance()
{
    ACE_Guard<ACE_Recursive_Thread_Mutex> guard(initMutex_);
    if(!isInitialized_)
    {
        singleton_.reset(new DbUtils());
        isInitialized_ = true;
    }
    return singleton_;
}
```

The getInstance method is the only method that the application code can use to get an instance of the DbUtils class, because the constructors and the assignment operator are declared protected. The method itself is very simple: it checks whether the singleton has already been initialized. If it hasn't, it creates the singleton and then returns shared_ptr inside which the newly created instance is stored. Once the pointer has been stored within shared_ptr by the reset method, you can use shared_ptr exactly like a pointer.

Another important thing to note here is the use of ACE_Guard for acquiring initMutex at the beginning of the method. Notice that the mutex is not being released at the end of the method. That's because ACE_Guard (which is stack-allocated) releases the mutex at the end when it is cleaned up automatically. If you were to use the mutex directly, the implementation would look like the code shown in Listing 7-3.

Listing 7-3. *The getInstance Implementation with a Mutex*

```
DbUtils_SP& DbUtils::getInstance()
{
    initMutex.acquire();
    if(!isInitialized_)
    {
        singleton_.reset(new DbUtils());
        isInitialized_ = true;
    }
    initMutex.release();
    return singleton_;
}
```

The problem with this code is that the mutex won't be released if, for instance, the reset method throws an exception. ACE_Guard, on the other hand, is guaranteed to be cleaned up no matter where the method returns from.

■**Note** Mutual exclusion is used here solely for the protection of the singleton creation from race conditions. It has no effect on the internal database locking.

Listing 7-4 shows how the constructor has been implemented.

Listing 7-4. *The DbUtils Constructor*

```
DbUtils::DbUtils():
    dbEnv_(0)
{
    try
    {
```

```
        const char *envhome = "./chap7_env";
        dbEnv_.set_errpfx("chap7_ex");
        dbEnv_.set_errcall(errCallback);
        dbEnv_.set_lk_detect(DB_LOCK_DEFAULT);
        dbEnv_.set_thread_count(16);
        u_int32_t envFlags =
            DB_CREATE | DB_INIT_MPOOL | DB_INIT_TXN |
            DB_INIT_LOG | DB_INIT_LOCK | DB_RECOVER | DB_THREAD;
        dbEnv_.open(envhome, envFlags, 0);
    }
    catch(DbException &dbex)
    {
        dbEnv_.err(dbex.get_errno(), "Db exception caught");
    }
    catch(...)
    {
        std::cout << "unknown exception caught" << std::endl;
    }
}
```

There's nothing new here. The environment creation that you did earlier in main has now been consolidated within the DbUtils class. This reorganization allows you to create the environment from any thread and not just from main.

In the destructor, the environment and the database handles are closed, as shown in Listing 7-5.

Listing 7-5. *The DbUtils Destructor*

```
DbUtils::~DbUtils()
{
    if(!isClosed_)
    {
        closeDbResources();
        isClosed_ = true;
    }
}
```

Listing 7-6 shows a shortcut for getting the environment handle.

Listing 7-6. *A Shortcut for Accessing the Environment Handle*

```
DbEnv* DbUtils::getEnv()
{
    return &(getInstance()->dbEnv_);
}
```

Listing 7-7 demonstrates how an application program would use the `DbUtils` class for managing the database resources.

Listing 7-7. *How to Use DbUtils*

```
 28 typedef boost::scoped_ptr<DbWorker> DbWorker_SP_;
114 int main(int argc, char **argv)
115 {
116     try
117     {
118         DbUtils_SP utils = DbUtils::getInstance();
119         utils->loadDbs();
120
121         DbWorker_SP w1(new DbWorker( WRITER, 1));
122         if(w1->activate((THR_NEW_LWP | THR_JOINABLE), 1) != 0)
123             ACE_DEBUG((LM_ERROR, "Could not launch w1\n"));
124
125         DbWorker_SP r1(new DbWorker( READER, 2));
126         if(r1->activate((THR_NEW_LWP | THR_JOINABLE), 1) != 0)
127             ACE_DEBUG((LM_ERROR, "Could not launch r1\n"));
128
129         ACE_Thread_Manager *tm =
130             ACE_Thread_Manager::instance();
131         tm->wait();
132     }
133     catch(DbException& dbex)
134     {
135         ACE_DEBUG((LM_ERROR,
136                     "caught DbException in main %d\n",
137                     dbex.get_errno()));
138     }
139     catch(...)
140     {
141         ACE_DEBUG((LM_ERROR, "unknown exception caught\n"));
142     }
143 }
```

Let's see how the sample program uses `DbUtils`:

- **Line 28**: `DbWorker_SP_` is a `typedef` for a `shared_ptr` of `DbWorker`. Just like you used a `shared_ptr` for the `DbUtils` instance, you store the `DbWorker` thread object within a `shared_ptr`.

- **Line 118**: You obtain the `DbUtils` instance using the `getInstance` method. Internally, that creates a `DbEnv` handle and runs recovery on the environment.

- **Line 119**: You create the database handles and load data in the databases.

- **Lines 121–127**: You create two worker threads that will use the database environment. One will perform read operations, and the other will perform both read and write operations. The first argument (READER or WRITER) in the DbWorker constructor indicates whether the worker thread will perform read operations or write operations.

- **Lines 129–131**: You get an instance of the default ACE_Thread_Manager and wait for the threads to finish. This is a shortcut for doing a wait on each thread individually.

This code fulfills all the requirements for opening and shutting down the database resources gracefully. Before any worker thread starts using the databases, you open the database environment and run recovery on it. When all the threads are done, you shut down the databases and close the environment. You don't see the code that does the shutdown, because it's hidden within the shared_ptr implementation. shared_ptr maintains a reference count of the stored pointer. When it becomes zero, it cleans up the pointer by invoking its destructor.

In this code example, the DbUtils instance is guaranteed to be around until the program ends because you created it in main. If the program receives an uncaught exception, the DbUtils destructor will get called when the stack-allocated shared_ptr destructs at the end of main. The same thing will happen with the DbWorker pointers. Since they're stored within shared_ptr objects, they're guaranteed to be cleaned up. If you remember, you had to delete all the DbWorker objects on your own in Chapter 5 because you didn't use shared_ptr then.

Handling an Ungraceful Exit

One of the main advantages of a client/server database is that the database resources are maintained in an independent address space, which is under the control of the server process. When a client application crashes or exits ungracefully, it doesn't affect the database. With Berkeley DB, however, that isn't the case, because multiple processes can link directly to the database. Berkeley DB provides a number of mechanisms to deal with ungraceful process exits, but it can be challenging for a beginner to understand them. I'll go over these techniques in the next few sections.

The code in the preceding section handles the initialization properly, but can it handle a situation in which one of the threads exits ungracefully without releasing the database resources? You can't force a thread to crash, but you can definitely exit a thread without releasing the resources. To do that, let's create a cursor on the Person table that you developed in Chapter 5 and use it in the reader thread to read records. From the writer thread, I'll update an entry in the Person table in an infinite loop. Let's examine the reader and writer implementations, as shown in Listing 7-8.

Listing 7-8. *The Implementation of runReader*

```
71 void DbWorker::runReader()
72 {
73     ACE_DEBUG((LM_ERROR,
74                 "(%t)DbWorker::runReader: thread id %t\n"));
75     PersonIter *iter = new PersonIter();
76     while (iter->next())
77     {
78         Person p = iter->getEntry();
```

```
79          ACE_DEBUG((LM_ERROR,
80                      "(%t)runReader:ssn %u: name %s dob %s\n",
81                      p.getSSN(),
82                      p.getName().c_str(),
83                      p.getDOB().c_str()));
84      }
85      delete iter;
86 }
```

This code creates a `PersonIter`, which you can use to go over all the records in the `Person` table. The iterator is then deleted. Notice in Listing 7-9 that the iterator is created on the heap, allowing you to exit the thread without invoking the destructor when you want to simulate an ungraceful exit.

Listing 7-9. *The Implementation of runWriter*

```
 88 void DbWorker::runWriter()
 89 {
 90     while(true)
 91     {
 92         Person p;
 93         unsigned long ss = 111223334;
 94         DbTxn *t;
 95         try
 96         {
 97             DbUtils::getEnv()->txn_begin(NULL, &t, 0);
 98             if( p.getBySSN(ss, t) == 0)
 99             {
100                 p.setDOB("jan 1 2001");
101                 p.insert(t);
102                 t->commit(0);
103                 ACE_DEBUG((LM_ERROR,
104                             "(%t)runWriter: insert done\n"));
105             }
106         }
107         catch(DbException& ex)
108         {
109             DbUtils::getEnv()->err(ex.get_errno(),
110                     "DbEntry::dbPut");
111             t->abort();
112         }
113         ACE_OS::sleep(1);
114     }
115 }
```

The writer reads a record from the `Person` table and updates it in an infinite loop. Let's keep the writer unchanged. You can see the output when you run the program in its current form:

```
(1084136368)runReader: thread id 1084136368
(1082035120)runWriter: insert done
(1084136368)runReader:ssn 111223333: name Manish Pandey dob jan 13 1971
(1084136368)runReader:ssn 111223334: name Shirish Rai dob jan 1 2001
(1084136368)runReader:ssn 111443335: name Roland Hendel dob feb 13 1973
(1084136368)runReader:ssn 111443336: name Roland Hendel dob feb 13 1973
(1084136368)runReader:ssn 111443337: name Roland Hendel dob feb 13 1973
(1082035120)runWriter: insert done
(1082035120)runWriter: insert done
(1082035120)runWriter: insert done
(1082035120)runWriter: insert done
```

The reader thread starts, followed by the writer. The reader then iterates through the database. The writer waits until the reader is done, because the iterator opens a DEGREE_2 isolation cursor. After the reader is done, the writer goes on with its infinite loop.

To simulate an ungraceful exit, let's remove the while loop in the reader so that it exits without iterating through the database until the end:

```
void DbWorker::runReader()
{
    ACE_OS::sleep(2);
    ACE_DEBUG((LM_ERROR,
                "(%t)runReader: thread id %t\n"));
    PersonIter *iter = new PersonIter();
    iter->next();
    Person p = iter->getEntry();
    ACE_DEBUG((LM_ERROR,
                "(%t)runReader:ssn %u: name %s dob %s\n",
                p.getSSN(),
                p.getName().c_str(),
                p.getDOB().c_str()));
}
```

If you had allocated PersonIter on the stack, you couldn't have prevented the destructor from being invoked. To simulate an ungraceful exit of the reader thread, you read the first entry from the cursor and then return it without closing or deleting the iterator. Let's see how the program behaves now:

```
(1082035120)runWriter: insert done
(1082035120)runWriter: insert done
(1084136368)runReader: thread id 1084136368
(1084136368)runReader:ssn 111223333: name Manish Pandey dob jan 13 1971

<the program hangs at this point>
```

The cursor holds a read lock on the entire database. This blocks the writer forever, because the reader thread exits without releasing it. At this point, the program can either release the locks held by the reader thread or it can exit and restart. On startup, the environment recovery will clear all the lock tables, and then the program can proceed. The only way to detect if a thread has exited without releasing the databases resources it acquired is by maintaining a log of database access by all threads. If a thread exits in the middle of a database operation, you would know that the resources held by it will never be released. Implementing such a scheme could be a lot of work because the thread accounting will have to interface with the lock management of Berkeley DB. In version 4.4.x, a new set of APIs was introduced to make it much easier to implement such a framework. The DbEnv::failchk method allows an application thread to verify that an abruptly exiting thread has not corrupted the database environment.

Using DbEnv::failchk

The application can use the DbEnv::failchk method to determine if the environment is in a consistent state. DbEnv::failchk works in conjunction with two other methods. Before discussing DbEnv::failchk, you need to understand the other two because it depends on them.

Using DbEnv::set_thread_id

DbEnv::set_thread_id is a new method added in version 4.4.x. You can use it to register a callback method that can return a unique ID for a given thread of control to the Berkeley DB library. When this method is called on a DbEnv handle, the library invokes the registered callback for every database operation, allowing it to maintain a list of active threads that have acquired database resources. Listing 7-10 shows you how to implement and register the set_thread_id callback for the application.

Listing 7-10. *The Implementation of the threadId Method*

```
void DbUtils::threadId(DbEnv *env,
                        pid_t *pid,
                        db_threadid_t *tid)
{
    ACE_thread_t id = ACE_Thread::self();
    *tid = id;
    ACE_DEBUG((LM_ERROR,
                "DbUtils::(%t) threadId: returning %u\n",
                id));
}
```

The callback returns the thread ID maintained by ACE. You may use any other means of obtaining the thread ID. The only requirement is that the IDs should be unique during the lifetime of the process. If the ID scheme that you're using reuses the thread IDs, then you may get incorrect results from DbEnv::failchk. If your platform doesn't allocate unique IDs, you can implement a thread identification scheme of your own. Once you've decided on the method for obtaining the thread IDs, you can register your callback like this:

```
dbEnv_.set_thread_id(DbUtils::threadId);
```

Now let's take a look at the other method.

Using DbEnv::set_isalive

DbEnv::set_isalive is another callback that you have to register using the environment handle before you can call DbEnv::failchk. Once DbEnv::set_thread_id has been registered, the library uses this method to check if all the threads that have acquired database resources are still active. Once again, the responsibility of finding out the status of a given thread is on you. Depending on the thread-identification system that you used in the DbEnv::set_thread_id callback, you should implement the DbEnv::set_isalive callback appropriately. I used the ACE-thread IDs, so I'll use ACE_Thread_Manager to determine if a particular thread is still active. Listing 7-11 shows how to do that. The callback should return 1 if the thread is still active; otherwise, it should return 0.

Listing 7-11. *Implementing isAlive*

```
86 int DbUtils::isAlive(DbEnv *env,
87                      pid_t pid,
88                      db_threadid_t tid)
89 {
90     if(mainThId_ == tid)
91     {
92         return 1;
93     }
94     ACE_Thread_Manager *tm = ACE_Thread_Manager::instance();
95     ACE_UINT32 state = 0;
96     ACE_thread_t id = tid;
97     int ret = tm->thr_state(id, state);
98     ACE_DEBUG((LM_ERROR,
99                 "DbUtils::isAlive: ret %d tid %u state %u\n",
100                ret, id, state));
101     if(ret == false ||
102        state == ACE_Thread_Manager::ACE_THR_CANCELLED ||
103        state == ACE_Thread_Manager::ACE_THR_TERMINATED)
104          return 0;
105     else
106          return 1;
107 }
```

Let's go over the code line by line:

- **Lines 90–93:** The default ACE_Thread_Manager doesn't manage the main thread. Since you're initializing the environment and the databases in the main thread, this code will always return true if the method is invoked for the main thread. The mainThId variable is initialized in main by calling utils->setMainThId(ACE_Thread::self()).

- **Lines 94–97:** Get an instance of the default ACE_Thread_Manager and get the status of the thread whose ID is stored in tid.

- **Lines 101–106**: If the thr_state method returns false, then ACE_Thread_Manager won't know about the thread. This means that the thread has already finished. If the state is reported as unknown, cancelled, or terminated, then you return 0. If the callback returns 1, you know that the thread is still active.

You now need to register these callbacks with the environment handle, as Listing 7-12 demonstrates. You can do that anytime during the life cycle of the handle, but it's recommended that you do it before any operations are done on the environment, so that the corruption detection framework is in place before you use the environment.

Listing 7-12. *Registering Callbacks Related to failchk*

```
123 DbUtils::DbUtils():
124     dbEnv_(0)
125 {
126     try
127     {
128         const char *envhome = "./chap7_env";
129         dbEnv_.set_errpfx("chap7_ex");
130         dbEnv_.set_errcall(errCallback);
131         dbEnv_.set_lk_detect(DB_LOCK_DEFAULT);
132         dbEnv_.set_thread_count(16);
133         u_int32_t envFlags =
134             DB_CREATE | DB_INIT_MPOOL | DB_INIT_TXN |
135             DB_INIT_LOG | DB_INIT_LOCK | DB_RECOVER |
136             DB_THREAD;
137         dbEnv_.open(envhome, envFlags, 0);
138         dbEnv_.set_thread_id(DbUtils::threadId);
139         dbEnv_.set_isalive(DbUtils::isAlive);
140     }
141     catch(DbException &dbex)
142     {
143         dbEnv_.err(dbex.get_errno(), "Db exception caught");
144     }
145     catch(...)
146     {
147         std::cout << "unknown exception caught" << std::endl;
148     }
149 }
```

Let's take a look at the code in detail:

- **Line 132**: set_thread_count sizes the thread control block within the library. It sets the maximum number of threads that you can use in the environment. You should set this number to anything greater than the estimated number of threads in your application.

- **Lines 138–139**: You register the thread_id and isalive callbacks with the environment handle.

You're now ready to use DbEnv::failchk to determine environment sanity, as shown in Listing 7-13. You can call this method as frequently as needed. Different applications may need to invoke this API at different frequencies, depending on how much overhead associated with the check they can tolerate. Since you're simulating a thread crash in the application code, you know exactly where to check for environment sanity—in the DbEntry::dbPut method, which the Person class uses to insert entries in the database.

Listing 7-13. *Using the failchk Routine*

```
372 void DbEntry::dbPut(Db *db, DbTxn* t)
373 {
374     serialize();
375
376     void *pkey = NULL;
377     int keyLen = 0;
378
379     getPKey(pkey, keyLen);
380
381     Dbt pkeyDbt(pkey, keyLen);
382     Dbt valueDbt(serializedData_, serializedLen_);
383
384     DbTxn *txn = t;
385     try
386     {
387         int state = DbUtils::getEnv()->failchk(0);
388         ACE_DEBUG((LM_ERROR,
389                 "DbEntry::dbPut: dbenv_failchk returned %d\n",
390                 state));
391         if(t == NULL)
391         if(t == NULL)
392             DbUtils::getEnv()->txn_begin(NULL, &txn, 0);
393         int ret = db->put(txn, &pkeyDbt, &valueDbt, 0);
394         if(ret)
395             DbUtils::getEnv()->err(ret, "DbEntry::dbPut" );
396         if(t == NULL)
397             txn->commit(0);
398     }
399     catch(DbException &txn_ex)
400     {
```

Just before starting, the transaction for Db::put DbEnv::failchk is invoked (on line 387). Similarly, you can instrument other database operations in the code. Let's see what difference the newly instrumented code makes for the simulated thread crash. If you can either resolve the hang in the writer or at least detect that the writer is going to hang forever, your efforts will be worthwhile:

```
-
-
DbUtils::(1082035120) threadId: returning 1082035120
DbUtils::(1082035120) threadId: returning 1082035120
DbUtils::(1082035120) threadId: returning 1082035120
DbUtils::(1082035120) threadId: returning 1082035120
(1082035120)runWriter: insert done
(1084136368)runReader: thread id 1084136368
DbUtils::(1084136368) threadId: returning 1084136368
DbUtils::(1084136368) threadId: returning 1084136368
DbUtils::(1084136368) threadId: returning 1084136368
-

-
DbUtils::(1084136368) threadId: returning 1084136368
(1084136368)runReader:ssn 111223333: name Manish Pandey dob jan 13 1971
DbUtils::(1082035120) threadId: returning 1082035120
DbUtils::(1082035120) threadId: returning 1082035120
-

-
DbUtils::(1084136368) threadId: returning 1084136368
(1084136368)runReader:ssn 111223333: name Manish Pandey dob jan 13 1971
(1084136368)runReader: finished
DbUtils::(1082035120) threadId: returning 1082035120
DbUtils::(1082035120) threadId: returning 1082035120
-

-
DbUtils::isAlive: ret 1 tid 1082035120 state 1
DbUtils::isAlive: ret 1 tid 1082035120 state 1
DbUtils::(1082035120) threadId: returning 1082035120
DbUtils::(1082035120) threadId: returning 1082035120
DbUtils::isAlive: ret 1 tid 1082035120 state 1
DbUtils::isAlive: ret 0 tid 1084136368 state 0
Aborting txn 0x8000000d: 0/1084136368
DbUtils::(1082035120) threadId: returning 1082035120
DbUtils::(1082035120) threadId: returning 1082035120
DbUtils::(1082035120) threadId: returning 1082035120
DbUtils::(1082035120) threadId: returning 1082035120
DbUtils::(1082035120) threadId: returning 1082035120
DbUtils::isAlive: ret 1 tid 1082035120 state 1
DbEntry::dbPut: dbenv_failchk returned 0
DbUtils::(1082035120) threadId: returning 1082035120
DbUtils::(1082035120) threadId: returning 1082035120
DbUtils::(1082035120) threadId: returning 1082035120
DbUtils::(1082035120) threadId: returning 1082035120
(1082035120)runWriter: insert done
DbUtils::(1082035120) threadId: returning 1082035120
```

```
DbUtils::(1082035120) threadId: returning 1082035120
-

-
```

In the program output, you can see that the writer thread started, followed by the reader. The reader exits after it reads the first record. After some time, you'll see the following line:

```
Aborting txn 0x8000000d: 0/1084136368
```

This is where the library detects that the reader thread is no longer active and aborts the cursor transaction started by it. Notice that the library invokes the isalive callback just before aborting the transaction to determine if the thread is active:

```
DbUtils::isAlive: ret 0 tid 1084136368 state 0
```

Finally, at the bottom you can see that the writer is able to proceed further, even though the reader thread exited without finishing its transaction:

```
(1082035120)runWriter: insert done
```

Not only were you able to detect that a thread ended abruptly, but you were also able to proceed despite unresolved transactions.

■**Note** The DbEnv::failcheck API is extremely powerful, because it combines the thread management of the application with the lock management of the library, and yet it is still completely independent of the threading framework that the application is using.

It may be inefficient to call DbEnv::failchk before every database operation, because as you can see, that can result in multiple method invocations. If this overhead becomes significant for the application, you can create a background thread that invokes this call after some fixed interval. This won't be as quick, in detecting an abnormal thread exit, as running failchk before every operation, but it still will detect a problem within a fixed amount of time. If you can further assume that failures are rare, then you can be pretty sure that you're not using a corrupted environment.

DbEnv::failchk may not be able to resolve the problem originating from all types of thread crashes. If the thread dies within a critical section, then DbEnv::failchk will either return DB_RECOVER or throw an exception. You'll see an output like this when that happens:

```
-
DbUtils::(1078930528) threadId: returning 1078930528
DbUtils::isAlive: ret 0 tid 1078930528 state 0
(1078930528) chap7_ex errMsg: Thread/process ➥
18446744072633444632/1078930528 failed: Thread died in Berkeley DB library
(1078930528) chap7_ex errMsg: DbEntry::dbPut: DB_RUNRECOVERY: ➥
Fatal error, run database recovery
-
-
```

A Note on DS, CDS, and TDS

The discussion so far and in the rest of the chapter assumes that you're using Berkeley DB as a TDS. However, this discussion applies, with minor modifications, to both CDS and DS applications as well. The main difference between a TDS and a CDS or a DS is that the latter two have no concept of recovery. Since CDS and DS don't support transactions and don't maintain a transaction log, they cannot run recovery. Whenever I talk about running recovery from here on out, you should replace the idea of recovery with that of *re-creating the database*. If the database gets corrupted in a CDS or DS, you can only remove it and re-create it.

Another point to note is that if you created the database environment without specifying a backing file, then the database will exist only while the application is running. Once the application exits or dies, you cannot recover the database, despite whether or not the database was configured as a TDS.

■Note TDS, CDS, and DS are policy decisions you make about the environment in your application. The actual database files are the same in each case, and in fact you can use them in DS, CDS, and TDS applications at different times.

Multiple Processes

Dealing with multiple threads sharing the environment within a single process was quite straightforward. Now let's turn our attention toward a more complex application configuration. Consider a case in which multiple multithreaded applications share a Berkeley DB environment. In the case of a single process, you were able to deal with thread crashes easily, because they were all inside one process. In one process, you can easily get the thread status and terminate and restart the threads if the environment gets corrupted. With multiple processes, however, it's difficult to synchronize and serialize database recovery and environment error detection. Multiple processes cases can fall into one of two categories:

- **A group of cooperating processes**: In this case, a common entity starts and destroys the processes. Usually such processes are also aware of each other and interact with each other. It is simpler to deal with environment corruptions here, because the infrastructure to deal with process crashes is already present.

- **A group of unrelated process**: This is the most difficult case to manage. No central entity can start or destroy processes. Usually the processes aren't even aware that other processes are sharing the environment. The biggest challenge in this case is that operating systems don't always allow you to control an unrelated process. You have to trust that the individual processes will detect and rectify environment corruptions without stepping on the toes of other processes.

It's easier to grasp the concepts and issues related to a topic if you have a concrete example to work with. Let's enhance the code example for the single process case to address these more generic and complex cases. I'll show you how to develop a test bed, like you did in the last section, which you can use first to simulate the problems you're trying to solve and then to develop solutions to solve them.

Groups of Cooperating Processes

The main characteristic of such applications is that a single entity controls all the processes sharing the environment. The controller process starts all the other processes and then waits for them to finish. It can restart the processes that happen to either crash or exit. Since the controller is the parent of all the other processes, it has the privilege to kill them if needed. The controller process can be a simple script or a sophisticated process manager.

You've already developed a single-process multithreaded application tds in the last section. Let's build a controller process that can start a number of tds processes. I've chosen to use the ACE_Process_Manager class to build the controller process.

The ACE_Process_Manager is a class in the ACE library that spawns and manages a group of processes. It allows you to register a callback that's guaranteed to be invoked when the process exits. Different operating systems handle process creation and destruction in different ways. For example, on UNIX, the parent process receives a SIGCHLD signal when a child process exits. Windows, however, has no concept of signals. ACE_Process_Manager hides these differences and provides a platform-independent interface. Another reason why I chose to use ACE here, as in many examples earlier, is that it has a well-designed object-oriented framework, which allows us to focus on the database rather than on building the framework.

The Watcher Class

Listing 7-14 shows the process controller, which I've named Watcher.

Listing 7-14. *Implementing Watcher*

```
22 class Watcher :
23     public ACE_Event_Handler
24 {
25     public:
26         Watcher();
27         ~Watcher();
```

```
28
29        void execProc(const char* cmdLine);
30
31        virtual int handle_exit(ACE_Process* proc);
32        ACE_Process_Manager *pm_;
33 };
```

Let's take a look at the declaration of the Watcher class in detail:

- **Line 23**: The Watcher class is derived from ACE_Event_Handler so that it can receive events, such as the death of a child process. ACE_Event_Handler is a general-purpose event-handling interface that works in conjunction with ACE_Reactor, which is a class encapsulating an event loop.

- **Line 29**: execProc is used to spawn a child process from Watcher.

- **Line 31**: handle_exit is a virtual function from ACE_Event_Handler. This method is invoked every time a child process exits. This is the place where you can perform all the tasks that you may want to execute on a child's exit. This process is of great importance, as you'll see.

- **Line 32**: pm_ stores the ACE_Process_Manager instance used for managing the child processes.

Before going over the implementation of Watcher, let's take a look at Listing 7-15, which shows main where Watcher and ACE_Process_Manager get used.

Listing 7-15. *Starting Watcher*

```
78 int main(int argc, char **argv)
79 {
94    Watcher w;
95    w.pm_ = ACE_Process_Manager::instance();
96    w.pm_->open(16, ACE_Reactor::instance());
97    w.execProc("./tds 2");
98    w.execProc("./tds 3");
99    w.execProc("./tds 4");
100   w.execProc("./tds 5");
101   ACE_Reactor::instance()->run_reactor_event_loop();
102 }
```

Here's a look at the code in detail:

- **Line 94**: Create an instance of Watcher.

- **Line 95**: Get the default ACE_Process_Manager instance.

- **Line 96**: Iinitialize the process manager with the default ACE_Reactor. This means that the process manager will work with the event loop of the default reactor.

- **Lines 97–100**: Launch multiple instances of tds. In a real application, you would launch different types of processes here. Since you're only creating a test bed, you're launching the same process multiple times. To help modify the behavior of tds slightly for different instances, you're passing an argument to tds.

- **Line 101**: Start the event loop of the default reactor.

The framework of the controller process is ready. Now you have a way to launch multiple processes and then wait for the events from the child processes. In a real application, the process launch would be driven through a configuration file so that the set of processes to be launched and their arguments could be modified without changing Watcher. You now have to add the following pieces to Watcher:

- **Berkeley DB environment initialization**: This allows the child processes not to worry about environment consistency.

- **Child process accounting**: Just as you kept a record of all the threads that were launched in the single-process case, here you have to account for every child process that was launched. Whenever a process exits, you need to execute DbEnv::failchk to see if the process released all the database resources.

- **Event handling**: You'll have to implement an event-handling routine in Watcher for handling child process exits.

Environment Initialization

To initialize the environment, you do the same thing as you did in the single-process case. First, you create the DbUtils instance and then load the databases; however, you have to register the thread_id and isalive callbacks separately for Watcher. You won't be able to use the callbacks you defined for the single-process case in DbUtils, because those aren't aware of the processes that are sharing the environment. It's possible to enhance the same callbacks to handle processes as well, but it's better to leave them alone and design a separate set of callbacks for Watcher. This way, you can keep the process accounting independent of the individual processes. In addition, you need to make sure that you don't load the default databases in every child process. Doing so would result in updated data being overwritten by the default database every time a child process loads the databases.

To ensure that you load the database only once, assign an ID to each process, including Watcher. In DbUtils, you can check the process ID before loading the default database. Listing 7-16 shows the new main method of the Watcher process.

Listing 7-16. *The Implementation of main in Watcher*

```
78 int main(int argc, char **argv)
79 {
80     DbUtils::processNumber_ = 1;
81     try
82     {
83         DbUtils_SP utils = DbUtils::getInstance();
84         utils->getEnv()->set_thread_id(Watcher::threadId);
85         utils->getEnv()->set_isalive(Watcher::isAlive);
```

```
86          utils->loadDbs();
87      }
88      catch(DbException &ex)
89      {
90          DbUtils::getEnv()->err(ex.get_errno(),
91                                  "error in main");
92      }
93      Watcher w;
94      w.pm_ = ACE_Process_Manager::instance();
95      w.pm_->open(16, ACE_Reactor::instance());
96      w.execProc("./tds 2");
97      w.execProc("./tds 3");
98      w.execProc("./tds 4");
99      w.execProc("./tds 5");
100     ACE_Reactor::instance()->run_reactor_event_loop();
101 }
```

Let's take a look at this code in detail:

- **Line 80**: You assign Watcher the process number 1. In DbUtils, you load the default database only if the process number is 1.

- **Line 83**: You get the DbUtils instance.

- **Line 84**: You register the thread_id callback as the Watcher::threadId method.

- **Line 85**: You register the isalive callback as the Watcher::isAlive method.

Child-Process Accounting

In order to implement the thread_id and isalive callbacks in the Watcher process, you first need to implement the child-process accounting. The basic concept in process accounting is the same as that of thread accounting in the single-process case. You need a way of remembering all the processes launched by Watcher. When a process exits, you need to make sure that it released all the database resources. In addition, you may need to restart the child process if it exited prematurely. The code shown in Listing 7-17 will help you achieve these goals.

Listing 7-17. *Data Structures for Holding Child Process Information*

```
struct ProcInfo
{
    ACE_Process_Options opts_;
    ACE_Process proc_;
};
typedef boost::shared_ptr< ProcInfo > ProcInfo_SP;
typedef std::map< pid_t, ProcInfo_SP > ProcMap;
typedef std::map< pid_t, ProcInfo_SP >::iterator ProcMapIter;
```

The ProcInfo structure stores the ACE_Process object and the ACE_Process_Options object associated with a child process. The ACE_Process object contains the state information of a process, which includes the exit status. The ACE_Process_Options object stores all the information required for launching a child process, such as its command-line arguments, its standard I/O handles, and so on. You're storing ACE_Process_Options to allow Watcher to relaunch a child process if it exits prematurely. ProcInfo_SP is a shared pointer for the ProcInfo class. The shared pointer ensures that the ProcInfo object gets cleaned up properly when it goes out of scope.

ProcMap is a map that stores a ProcInfo object against the process ID of a child process launched by Watcher. This allows you to efficiently look up a process ID to check if Watcher launched it. ProcMapIter is an iterator on the ProcMap.

Event Handling

You can register an ACE_Event_Handler with ACE_Process_Manager to ensure that whenever a child process exits, the handle_exit method of the event handler will be invoked. In the event handler, you can perform the check to see if the database environment is in a consistent state. Listing 7-18 shows the declaration of the Watcher class with the enhancements discussed so far.

Listing 7-18. *Handling Events in* Watcher

```
class Watcher :
    public ACE_Event_Handler
{
    public:
        Watcher();
        ~Watcher();

        void execProc(const char* cmdLine);

        virtual int handle_exit(ACE_Process* proc);
        static void threadId(DbEnv *env,
                            pid_t *pid,
                            db_threadid_t *tid);
        static int isAlive(DbEnv* env,
                        pid_t pid,
                        db_threadid_t tid);

        ACE_Process_Manager *pm_;
    private:
        void killAllChildren();
        static ProcMap pMap_;
};
```

Now let's take a look at the implementation of Watcher, as shown in Listing 7-19. The execProc method is used to spawn a child process.

Listing 7-19. *Spawning a Child Process*

```
14 void Watcher::execProc(const char* cmdLine)
15 {
16     ProcInfo_SP info;
17     info.reset(new ProcInfo);
18     info->opts_.command_line(cmdLine);
19     pid_t pid = pm_->spawn(&(info->proc_), info->opts_);
20     pm_->register_handler(this, pid);
21     pMap_[pid] = info;
22     ACE_DEBUG((LM_ERROR,
23                 "(%t)execProc: launched %s pid %d\n",
24                 cmdLine, pid));
25 }
```

Let's take a look at the details:

- **Line 17**: You create a `ProcInfo` object for the process to be spawned.

- **Line 18**: You set the options for the child in the `info` object.

- **Line 19**: You spawn the child process. The `spawn` method returns the process ID of the child.

- **Line 20**: You register `Watcher` as the event handler for the spawned child.

- **Line 22**: You insert the `ProcInfo` object against the process ID in the `ProcInfo` map.

Listing 7-20 shows the `handle_exit` method, which is the event handler that's invoked every time a child process exits.

Listing 7-20. *Handling Child Process Termination*

```
27 int Watcher::handle_exit(ACE_Process* proc)
28 {
29     ACE_DEBUG((LM_ERROR, "***** process %d exited ***** \n",
30                 proc->getpid()));
31     try
32     {
33         int state = DbUtils::getEnv()->failchk(0);
34         if(state != 0)
35         {
36             ACE_DEBUG((LM_ERROR,
37                 "handle_exit:dbenv_failchk returned %d\n",
38                 state));
39         }
40     }
```

```
41      catch(DbException &ex)
42      {
43          DbUtils::getEnv()->err(ex.get_errno(),
44                  "failchk returned err\n");
45          killAllChildren();
46          ACE_OS::exit(1);
47      }
48 }
```

In handle_exit, you just run DbEnv::failchk. If the environment is in a corrupted state, then you exit from Watcher after terminating all the children. Listing 7-21 shows the threadId method, which is similar to the threadId method of DbUtils.

Listing 7-21. *The Implementation of Watcher::threadId*

```
61 void Watcher::threadId(DbEnv *env,
62                          pid_t *pid,
63                          db_threadid_t *tid)
64 {
65      ACE_thread_t id = ACE_Thread::self();
66      *tid = id;
67      *pid = ACE_OS::getpid();
68      ACE_DEBUG((LM_ERROR, "Watcher::threadId %t pid %d\n",
69                          ACE_OS::getpid() ));
70 }
```

Note that threadId will only be called from the watcher process. Listing 7-22 shows the isAlive method, which is the heart of the corruption detection scheme.

Listing 7-22. *The Implementation of Watcher::isAlive*

```
72 int Watcher::isAlive(DbEnv* env,
73                      pid_t pid,
74                      db_threadid_t tid)
75 {
76      int ret = 0;
77      if(pid == ACE_OS::getpid())
78          return 1;
79      ProcMapIter it = pMap_.find(pid);
80      if(it != pMap_.end())
81      {
82          ret = (it->second)->proc_.running();
83      }
84      else
85          ret = 1;
```

```
86     ACE_DEBUG((LM_ERROR,
87                 "isAlive: returning %d for %d\n",
88                 ret, pid));
89     return ret;
90 }
```

Take a look at the important lines:

- **Lines 77–78:** If the isAlive method is invoked on the process ID of the watcher process, then isAlive returns true.

- **Lines 79–83:** If the method isn't invoked on the watcher process, then you try to find the process ID in the pMap_. If you find it there, then watcher invoked the process. isAlive returns the status of the process as found in the ACE_Process object.

- **Lines 84–85:** If the process ID isn't found in the map, the process manager knows nothing about the process. This can happen only if a process was spawned by the watcher, but it did not add an entry for it in the process map, which should never happen.

■**Note** In the single-process case, you neither set the pid argument in the thread_id callback, nor did you use it in the isalive callback, because you have to worry about only one process.

With this scheme, you need to take care of a situation in which the operating system recycles the process IDs. If a process ID is recycled to create a process spawned by watcher, then you need to update the process map, maintained by watcher, with the new ACE_Process object, and everything will work well. If an unrelated process is assigned a recycled ID and isAlive is invoked on the ID, then the isAlive method will return false, which will still be correct.

Listing 7-23 shows the killAllChildren method, which is used for terminating all the children. It's called either when an irrecoverable environment corruption is detected or when watcher is exiting. You should kill all the children when watcher dies; otherwise, watcher will lose track of the children it has spawned and result in wrong results from the isAlive method.

Listing 7-23. *The Implementation of killAllChildren*

```
16 void Watcher::killAllChildren()
17 {
18     ProcMapIter it = pMap_.begin();
19     for(; it != pMap_.end(); ++it)
20     {
21         pm_->terminate(it->first, SIGKILL);
22         ACE_DEBUG((LM_ERROR,
23                     "terminated %d\n", it->first));
24     }
25 }
```

I've used SIGKILL to terminate the children, because otherwise the children might attempt to use the environment that's most likely in a corrupted state and may hang forever. Let's now turn our attention to the tds process. You need to make some modifications there, too, to make it work for the multiple related-processes case.

Note ACE makes sure that SIGKILL works as you'd expect it to on both UNIX and Windows, one of the advantages of using ACE.

Modifications Needed in Child tds Processes

The biggest change that you need to make for the child tds processes is in the way you open the database environment. The child processes shouldn't be running recovery, as that's done exclusively by watcher, so you need to open the environment without the DB_RECOVER flag. Listing 7-24 shows what the new DbUtils constructor looks like.

Listing 7-24. *The DbUtils Constructor*

```
123 DbUtils::DbUtils():
124     dbEnv_(0)
125 {
126     try
127     {
128         const char *envhome = "./chap7_env";
129         dbEnv_.set_errpfx("chap7_ex");
130         dbEnv_.set_errcall(errCallback);
131         dbEnv_.set_lk_detect(DB_LOCK_DEFAULT);
132         dbEnv_.set_thread_count(16);
133         u_int32_t envFlags =
134             DB_INIT_MPOOL | DB_INIT_TXN |
135             DB_INIT_LOCK | DB_THREAD;
136         if(processNumber_ == 1)
137             envFlags |= DB_INIT_LOG | DB_RECOVER | DB_CREATE;
138         dbEnv_.open(envhome, envFlags, 0);
139         dbEnv_.set_thread_id(DbUtils::threadId);
140         dbEnv_.set_isalive(DbUtils::isAlive);
141     }
142     catch(DbException &dbex)
143     {
144         dbEnv_.err(dbex.get_errno(), "Db exception caught");
145     }
146     catch(...)
147     {
148         std::cout << "unknown exception caught" << std::endl;
149     }
150 }
```

Let's take a look at a few lines in particular:

- **Lines 133–137:** You check the process serial number. If it's a child process, then don't include the DB_INIT_LOG, DB_RECOVER, and DB_CREATE flags in the set of flags passed to DbEnv::open. These flags are needed to run recovery on the environment.

You need to make the other change in the main method of the tds process. Remember that you passed a command-line argument to the tds processes when you spawned them from the watcher. You need to use the argument to set the process serial number for each child process, as shown in Listing 7-25.

Listing 7-25. *The Implementation of tds main*

```
int main(int argc, char **argv)
{
    if (argc > 1)
    {
        DbUtils::processNumber_ = atoi(argv[1]);
        ACE_DEBUG((LM_ERROR,
                    "(%P:%t)tds:main: process number %d\n",
                    DbUtils::processNumber_));
    }
    else
    {
        ACE_DEBUG((LM_ERROR, "(%P:%t)tds:main: too few args\n"));
        return 1;
    }
-
-
```

Now you're ready to run the multiple related-processes case. As you did for the single-process case, you have to simulate a process crash to test the framework. You can force one of the child processes to exit without letting it close some of the open database resources, as Listing 7-26 shows.

Listing 7-26. *The Implementation of runReader*

```
void DbWorker::runReader()
{
    ACE_DEBUG((LM_ERROR,
                "(%P:%t)runReader started\n"));
    PersonIter *iter = new PersonIter();
```

```
    while(iter->next())
    {
        Person p = iter->getEntry();
        ACE_DEBUG((LM_ERROR,
                    "(%P:%t)runReader:ssn %u: name %s dob %s\n",
                    p.getSSN(),
                    p.getName().c_str(),
                    p.getDOB().c_str()));
        if(DbUtils::processNumber_ == 4)
            ACE_OS::exit(1);
    }
    iter->close();
    delete iter;
    ACE_DEBUG((LM_ERROR, "(%P:%t)runReader: finished\n"));
}
```

In the runReader method, you can exit from the process if the processNumber is 4 after reading just one record from the cursor on the Person database. Since you allocated the cursor on the heap and you're exiting without deleting the pointer to the cursor for process number 4, you've made sure that some database resources will definitely be leaked.

Let's run the watcher process to see how it behaves:

```
-
-
-
(32463:1078930528)tds:main: process number 2
(1078930528)execProc: launched ./tds 2 pid 32463
loadDbs: going to load Dbs processNumber_ 2
(32463:1082035120)runWriter started
(32463:1084136368)runReader started
(32463:1082035120)runWriter: insert done
(32463:1084136368)runReader:ssn 111223333: name Manish Pandey dob jan 13 1971
(32463:1084136368)runReader:ssn 111223334: name Shirish Rai dob jan 1 2001
(32463:1084136368)runReader:ssn 111443335: name Roland Hendel dob feb 13 1973
(32463:1084136368)runReader:ssn 111443336: name Roland Hendel dob feb 13 1973
(32463:1084136368)runReader:ssn 111443337: name Roland Hendel dob feb 13 1973
(32463:1084136368)runReader: finished
(1078930528)execProc: launched ./tds 3 pid 32466
(32466:1078930528)tds:main: process number 3
loadDbs: going to load Dbs processNumber_ 3
(32466:1082035120)runWriter started
(32466:1084136368)runReader started
(32466:1082035120)runWriter: insert done
(32466:1084136368)runReader:ssn 111223333: name Manish Pandey dob jan 13 1971
(32466:1084136368)runReader:ssn 111223334: name Shirish Rai dob jan 1 2001
(32466:1084136368)runReader:ssn 111443335: name Roland Hendel dob feb 13 1973
(32466:1084136368)runReader:ssn 111443336: name Roland Hendel dob feb 13 1973
(32466:1084136368)runReader:ssn 111443337: name Roland Hendel dob feb 13 1973
```

```
(32466:1084136368)runReader: finished
(32463:1082035120)runWriter: insert done
(32469:1078930528)tds:main: process number 4
(1078930528)execProc: launched ./tds 4 pid 32469
loadDbs: going to load Dbs processNumber_ 4
(32469:1082035120)runWriter started
(32469:1084136368)runReader started
-
-
```

Initially, watcher loads the default databases. I haven't included that part of the output, because it's the same as in the single-process case. In the output just shown, you can see that the child processes 2 through 4 are launched. You can also see that the children start executing; notice the process ID prefixes for the children. First, the children start the reader thread and then the writer thread. Things seem to be humming along nicely. Let's see what happens next:

```
-
-
(32469:1082035120)runWriter: insert done
(32469:1084136368)runReader:ssn 111223333: name Manish Pandey dob jan 13 1971
(32472:1078930528)tds:main: process number 5
(1078930528)execProc: launched ./tds 5 pid 32472
***** process 32469 exited *****
isAlive: returning 1 for 32463
isAlive: returning 1 for 32466
isAlive: returning 1 for 32472
-
-
```

The reader thread of process number 4 (pid 32469) kicks in. It reads the first record from the Person database and exits the process. watcher detects that 32469 has exited. It immediately starts the diagnostics via the DbEnv::failchk command and starts invoking isAlive on all the threads that have invoked database operations:

```
-
-
isAlive: returning 1 for 32466
isAlive: returning 0 for 32469
Freeing locks for locker 0x74: 32469/1078930528
isAlive: returning 1 for 32463
isAlive: returning 1 for 32463
-
-
```

When it reaches 32469, the isAlive method returns false. Notice that for all other process IDs, it returns true. The failchk routine, knowing that 32469 is no longer running, frees up the locks held by it:

```
-

-

isAlive: returning 0 for 32469
Aborting txn 0x80000020: 32469/1084136368
isAlive: returning 1 for 32472
isAlive: returning 1 for 32463
isAlive: returning 1 for 32466
(32466:1082035120)runWriter: insert done
(32463:1082035120)runWriter: insert done
loadDbs: going to load Dbs processNumber_ 5
(32472:1082035120)runWriter started
(32472:1084136368)runReader started
(32472:1082035120)runWriter: insert done
(32472:1084136368)runReader:ssn 111223333: name Manish Pandey dob jan 13 1971
(32472:1084136368)runReader:ssn 111223334: name Shirish Rai dob jan 1 2001
(32472:1084136368)runReader:ssn 111443335: name Roland Hendel dob feb 13 1973
(32472:1084136368)runReader:ssn 111443336: name Roland Hendel dob feb 13 1973
(32472:1084136368)runReader:ssn 111443337: name Roland Hendel dob feb 13 1973
(32472:1084136368)runReader: finished
(32466:1082035120)runWriter: insert done
(32463:1082035120)runWriter: insert done
(32472:1082035120)runWriter: insert done
-

-
```

The cursor transaction left unresolved by 32469 is finally aborted. That gives the other threads a chance to continue, as you can see from the previous output.

You succeeded in detecting and rectifying an environment error by using DbEnv::failchk even when multiple processes were operating independently on the environment. However, that may not be the case every time a process dies in a real application. Some environment corruptions are irrecoverable. For example, when a process dies while it's in the middle of updating the transaction log, there's no way of fixing the corruption other than running recovery on the environment. When something like that happens, you'll notice a slightly different behavior from watcher. You might see something like the following:

```
-
-
***** process 30622 exited *****
isAlive: returning 1 for 30625
isAlive: returning 0 for 30622
(30615:1078930528) chap7_ex errMsg: Thread/process 30622/1082035120 failed: ➡
Thread died in Berkeley DB library
(30615:1078930528) chap7_ex errMsg: failchk returned err
: DB_RUNRECOVERY: Fatal error, run database recovery
terminated 30616
terminated 30619
terminated 30622
terminated 30625
DbUtils::closeDbResources
-
```

After a process (pid 30622) dies (or exits abruptly), the watcher tries to verify that environment consistency by running failchk. In this case, failchk isn't able to fix the side effects of the crash, so it throws an exception. (It will return a DB_RUNRECOVERY error if exceptions aren't enabled in the library.) watcher then kills all the children and exits. Whenever it's launched again, it will run recovery on the environment and restart all the children.

If a thread dies inside the Berkeley DB library, it may have been in the middle of an operation that was protected by something other than transactional locking. For example, when Berkeley DB needs to read a page from disk into the buffer cache, it allocates a buffer in shared memory, and it uses some short-term latching to protect that operation. There's no way to track those short-term latches so that they can be released. Even if they can be released, the library cannot ensure that the buffer cache is in a consistent state. As a rule, the library allows the application to assume that if a thread or process dies *outside* of the Berkeley DB library, then corruption didn't cross the boundary *into* Berkeley DB. But if the application dies in the library, the library assumes the worst and forces recovery.

■Note Once you've received DB_RUNRECOVERY from a database method, it's not safe to perform any database operations using the environment handle. You'll notice that the process usually hangs if an operation is performed after DB_RUNRECOVERY has been received. The only option you have at that point is to exit from the process.

Groups of Unrelated Processes

Now let's take a look at the most complex architecture for sharing a Berkeley DB environment. Certain applications comprise of a group of loosely coupled processes. The processes aren't started and controlled by a single controlling entity, like watcher in the previous section. Designing the database framework for such applications has a few challenges:

- **There's no controlling entity**: Even if you implement a `watcher` process that can detect environment corruption, you can't force the other processes to restart, because `watcher` may not have sufficient privileges to do that.

- **Running recovery is problematic**: While coming up, a process can't be sure that recovery has been performed on the environment; therefore, every process sharing the environment has to run recovery before using the environment. Running recovery can result in the removal of the existing shared memory region files of the environment, so it's not safe to run recovery while another process is using the environment.

There is no easy way of solving these issues. Any solution must take into consideration the specific design of the application. It is virtually impossible to design a framework that will work for all applications. I'll discuss certain techniques and guidelines that you can use to make it easy for you to design a custom solution for your application. Let's first look at the features that the library provides out of the box.

The `DB_REGISTER` Flag

`DB_REGISTER` is a flag (introduced in version 4.4.x) for configuring an environment for applications that include a group of multiple unrelated processes that have to share an environment. When this flag is set, the library, while opening the environment, checks whether another process has exited while holding a `DbEnv` handle on the same environment. If it finds that a process exited without releasing the `DbEnv` handle, then it checks if recovery needs to be run on the environment. If `DB_RECOVER` or `DB_RECOVER_FATAL` are also set, then the library automatically performs recovery before opening the environment. If these flags aren't set, then the `open` call returns with the `DB_RUNRECOVERY` error. If it finds that the environment is in a good state, the `DB_RECOVER` and `DB_RECOVER_FATAL` flags are ignored. You should note two things about this flag:

- **`DB_REGISTER` works accurately only if all the processes sharing the environment specify `DB_REGISTER` while opening the `DbEnv` handle**: The library comes to know about the other processes that are using the environment because during `DbEnv::open` (if this flag is set), the environment registers the process ID of the opening process. If a process didn't register its ID, then the other processes won't know about it and `DB_REGISTER` won't work correctly.

- **`DB_REGISTER` only registers `DbEnv` handles at the process level**: This means that if two threads within the same process create two separate `DbEnv` handles with `DB_REGISTER` set, the library will register the last handle and associate it with the process ID. If the handle that was created first corrupted the environment, the library won't detect it.

`DB_REGISTER` provides an easy way to check if a process exited without releasing the database handles and whether that resulted in environment corruption. It also eliminates unnecessary recovery. Basically, it makes it safe to specify `DB_RECOVER` or `DB_RECOVER_FATAL` in shared environments. To better understand its behavior, let's use `DB_RECOVER` in a shared environment and see what difference it makes.

Using `DB_REGISTER`

Once again, let's use the trusted `tds` example along with the `watcher` to simulate a group of unrelated processes that share the same database environment. You can keep most of the code as it was in the previous section, just comment out the `DbEnv::failchk` calls, because `DB_REGISTER` isn't compatible with DbEnv::failchk. It's recommended that you don't use both of them in the same program. Better still, let's make the example flexible enough to be used for trying out both DbEnv::failchk and DB_REGISTER by providing a command-line argument. Add a static flag in DbUtils called unrelated_ to indicate that you want to run the test bed as a group of unrelated processes. Listing 7-27 shows what you do in tds main.

Listing 7-27. *The Implementation of tds main - revisited*

```
int main(int argc, char **argv)
{
    if (argc >= 3)
    {
        DbUtils::processNumber_ = atoi(argv[1]);
        DbUtils::unrelated_ = atoi(argv[2]);
    }
-
-
-
```

Next, check the unrelated_ flag while setting the flags for DbEnv::open, as shown in Listing 7-28.

Listing 7-28. *The DbUtils Constructor Revisited*

```
125 DbUtils::DbUtils():
126     dbEnv_(0)
127 {
128     try
129     {
130         const char *envhome = "./chap7_env";
131         dbEnv_.set_errpfx("chap7_ex");
132         dbEnv_.set_errcall(errCallback);
133         dbEnv_.set_lk_detect(DB_LOCK_DEFAULT);
134         dbEnv_.set_thread_count(16);
135         u_int32_t envFlags =
136             DB_INIT_MPOOL | DB_INIT_TXN |
137             DB_INIT_LOCK | DB_THREAD;
138         if(unrelated_ == 1)
139         {
140             envFlags |= DB_INIT_LOG | DB_RECOVER |
141                         DB_CREATE |
142                         DB_REGISTER;
143         }
144         else if(processNumber_ == 1)
145         {
146             if(processNumber_ == 1)
147                 envFlags |= DB_INIT_LOG | DB_RECOVER |
148                             DB_CREATE;
```

```
149                    dbEnv_.set_thread_id(DbUtils::threadId);
150                    dbEnv_.set_isalive(DbUtils::isAlive);
151            }
152            dbEnv_.open(envhome, envFlags, 0);
153        }
154        catch(DbException &dbex)
155        {
156            dbEnv_.err(dbex.get_errno(), "Db exception caught");
157        }
158        catch(...)
159        {
160            std::cout << "unknown exception caught" << std::endl;
161        }
162 }
```

Let's take a look at some of these lines in detail:

- **Lines 138–142:** If the unrelated_ flag is set to 1, then set the DB_REGISTER flag.

- **Lines 144–150:** If the unrelated_ flag isn't set to 1, then register the thread_id and isalive callbacks. Also, set the DB_RECOVER flag only when the processNumber_ is 1.

Check the unrelated_ flag again when you run DbEnv::failchk, as Listing 7-29 shows.

Listing 7-29. *DbEntry::dbGet -revisited*

```
371 int DbEntry::dbGet(Db *db, Dbt *key, Dbt* data, DbTxn* t)
372 {
373     int ret = -1;
374     DbTxn *txn = t;
375     try
376     {
377         if(DbUtils::unrelated_ == 0)
378         {
379             int state = DbUtils::getEnv()->failchk(0);
380             if(state != 0)
381             {
382                 ACE_DEBUG((LM_ERROR,
383                 "DbEntry::dbGet: dbenv_failchk returned %d\n",
384                 state));
385                 ACE_OS::exit(1);
386             }
387         }
-
-
-
```

To simulate a group of unrelated processes, where no single entity has control over all the processes sharing the environment, let's make watcher not do anything when a child process exits. Listing 7-30 shows what the modified handle_exit method looks like.

Listing 7-30. *Watcher::handle_exit Revisited*

```
40 int Watcher::handle_exit(ACE_Process* proc)
41 {
42     ACE_DEBUG((LM_ERROR, "***** process %d exited ***** \n",
43                 proc->getpid()));
44     if(DbUtils::unrelated_ == 1)
45         return;
46     try
47     {
48         int state = DbUtils::getEnv()->failchk(0);
49         if(state != 0)
50         {
51             ACE_DEBUG((LM_ERROR,
52                 "handle_exit:dbenv_failchk returned %d\n",
53                 state));
54         }
55     }
56     catch(DbException &ex)
57     {
58         DbUtils::getEnv()->err(ex.get_errno(),
59                 "failchk returned err\n");
60         DbUtils::runRecovery_ = 1;
61         killAllChildren();
62         ACE_OS::exit(1);
63     }
64 }
```

Take a look at the details of a few of these lines:

- **Lines 44–45:** You simply return from the exit handler if you're simulating unrelated processes.

- **Lines 46–63:** If you're simulating a group of related processes, you keep doing what you did earlier.

Finally, you modify watcher main, as shown in Listing 7-31.

Listing 7-31. *watcher main - revisited*

```
97 int main(int argc, char **argv)
98 {
99     DbUtils::processNumber_ = 1;
100    DbUtils::unrelated_ = 1;
```

```
101    try
102    {
103        DbUtils_SP utils = DbUtils::getInstance();
104        utils->getEnv()->set_thread_id(Watcher::threadId);
105        utils->getEnv()->set_isalive(Watcher::isAlive);
106        utils->loadDbs();
107    }
108    catch(DbException &ex)
109    {
110        DbUtils::getEnv()->err(ex.get_errno(),
111                            "error in main");
112    }
113    Watcher w;
114    w.pm_ = ACE_Process_Manager::instance();
115    w.pm_->open(16, ACE_Reactor::instance());
116    w.execProc("./tds 4 1");
117    w.execProc("./tds 3 1");
118    w.execProc("./tds 5 1");
119    w.execProc("./tds 2 1");
120    ACE_Reactor::instance()->run_reactor_event_loop();
121 }
```

Here are the specifics on a few of the lines:

- **Line 100**: You set the unrelated_ flag to 1.

- **Lines 101–112**: You initialize the databases with the default data.

- **Lines 116–119**: You start the tds child processes with the unrelated_ argument set to 1.

Before using DB_REGISTER, let's see how the group of processes behaves without DB_REGISTER. Comment out the DB_REGISTER flag from DbEnv::open in DbUtils and start the watcher, as shown in Listing 7-32.

Listing 7-32. *Calling DbEnv::open Without DB_REGISTER*

```
-
-
138        if(unrelated_ == 1)
139        {
140            envFlags |= DB_INIT_LOG | DB_RECOVER |
141                    DB_CREATE;
142                // DB_REGISTER;
-
-
```

Here's what you'll see:

```
-
(9733:1078930528)tds:main: processNumber_ 4, unrelated_ 1
(1078930528)execProc: launched ./tds 4 1 pid 9733
loadDbs: going to load Dbs processNumber_ 4
(9733:1082035120)runWriter started
(9733:1084136368)runReader started
(9733:1082035120)runWriter: insert done
(9733:1084136368)runReader:ssn 111223333: name Manish Pandey dob jan 13 1971
(9736:1078930528)tds:main: processNumber_ 3, unrelated_ 1
(1078930528)execProc: launched ./tds 3 1 pid 9736
(9737:1078930528)tds:main: processNumber_ 5, unrelated_ 1
(1078930528)execProc: launched ./tds 5 1 pid 9737
(9738:1078930528)tds:main: processNumber_ 2, unrelated_ 1
(1078930528)execProc: launched ./tds 2 1 pid 9738
***** process 9733 exited *****
loadDbs: going to load Dbs processNumber_ 3
(9736:1082035120)runWriter started
(9736:1084136368)runReader started
-

-
(9736:1082035120)runWriter: insert done
(9736:1082035120)runWriter: insert done
(9736:1082035120) chap7_ex errMsg: PANIC: fatal region error detected; run recovery
(9736:1082035120) chap7_ex errMsg: DbEntry::dbPut: DB_RUNRECOVERY: ➥
Fatal error, run database recovery
***** process 9736 exited *****
loadDbs: going to load Dbs processNumber_ 5
(9737:1082035120)runWriter started
(9737:1084136368)runReader started
(9737:1082035120)runWriter: insert done
-

-
(9738:1084136368)runReader:ssn 111443336: name Roland Hendel dob feb 13 1973
(9738:1084136368)runReader:ssn 111443337: name Roland Hendel dob feb 13 1973
(9738:1084136368)runReader: finished
(9737:1082035120) chap7_ex errMsg: PANIC: fatal region error detected; run recovery
(9737:1082035120) chap7_ex errMsg: DbEntry::dbPut: DB_RUNRECOVERY: ➥
Fatal error, run database recovery
***** process 9737 exited *****
(9738:1082035120)runWriter: insert done
(9738:1082035120)runWriter: insert done
(9738:1082035120)runWriter: insert done
(9738:1082035120)runWriter: insert done
-

-
```

Notice that all the child processes exit except for the last one. You can also see that the library is returning a number of DB_RUNRECOVERY errors. This happens because when you launch the tds processes, each one performs recovery on the environment, unaware of other tds processes that are sharing the environment. During recovery, since the shared memory region of the environment is re-created, the exiting DbEnv handles in other processes return the DB_RUNRECOVERY error. Only the last tds process (ID 9738) survives and keeps running, because no one cleans up the environment underneath its DbEnv handle.

Now uncomment the DB_REGISTER flag to see what difference it makes:

```
-
-
(9637:1078930528)tds:main: processNumber_ 4, unrelated_ 1
(1078930528)execProc: launched ./tds 4 1 pid 9637
loadDbs: going to load Dbs processNumber_ 4
(9637:1082035120)runWriter started
(9637:1084136368)runReader started
(9637:1082035120)runWriter: insert done
(9637:1084136368)runReader:ssn 111223333: name Manish Pandey dob jan 13 1971
(9640:1078930528)tds:main: processNumber_ 3, unrelated_ 1
(1078930528)execProc: launched ./tds 3 1 pid 9640
(9641:1078930528)tds:main: processNumber_ 5, unrelated_ 1
(1078930528)execProc: launched ./tds 5 1 pid 9641
(1078930528)execProc: launched ./tds 2 1 pid 9642
***** process 9637 exited *****
(9642:1078930528)tds:main: processNumber_ 2, unrelated_ 1
loadDbs: going to load Dbs processNumber_ 5
(9641:1082035120)runWriter started
(9641:1084136368)runReader started
-
-
(9642:1084136368)runReader:ssn 111443336: name Roland Hendel dob feb 13 1973
(9642:1084136368)runReader:ssn 111443337: name Roland Hendel dob feb 13 1973
(9642:1084136368)runReader: finished
(9642:1082035120)runWriter: insert done
(9641:1082035120)runWriter: insert done
(9640:1082035120)runWriter: insert done
(9642:1082035120)runWriter: insert done
(9641:1082035120)runWriter: insert done
(9640:1082035120)runWriter: insert done
(9642:1082035120)runWriter: insert done
-
-
```

In this case, process 9637 exits because you forced it to exit from the reader thread (remember that you did that to simulate a process crash in the last section). The rest of the tds processes (9642, 9641, and 9640) keep running, without receiving DB_RUNRECOVERY errors from the library.

In conclusion, DB_REGISTER allows independent processes to share an environment without allowing them to step on each other's toes. This powerful tool can greatly simplify application design.

Database Configuration

In this section, I'll discuss the database server configurations commonly found in Berkeley DB–based applications. Relational databases mostly use the client/server configuration. Berkeley DB allows much more flexibility in this respect. Processes can link directly to the database environment or they can access the database through a stand-alone database server. It's even possible to have both direct linking and stand-alone server-based access in the same application. Let's look at some of the common features of each configuration.

Client/Server Configuration

Even though one of the main benefits of using Berkeley DB is that it eliminates the performance overhead associated with a stand-alone database server, it makes sense for certain applications to use Berkeley DB in the client/server configuration. If application processes link to the database environment directly, they're expected to restart when recovery is performed on the environment. In other words, every process that links to the database environment depends on every other process to run reliably. For certain applications, this may not be acceptable. Berkeley DB offers numerous other benefits to make it an attractive alternative despite being deployed in the client/server configuration. When deciding whether you should use this configuration, consider the topology, process relationships, performance, and complexity.

Topology

For applications distributed on multiple machines, the client/server configuration may be the only alternative available. If the application process using the database has to run on a machine that doesn't have the database, it cannot link to the database environment directly. It isn't possible to put the database files on remote filesystems such as NFS or AFS and access them locally from multiple machines. Since most remote filesystems don't allow remote files to be mapped into process memory, you can't use them to create the database environment. Even if a particular filesystem supports file mapping, there's usually no support for mutexes across remote filesystems. In effect, to support a database environment on a remote filesystem, the operating system must support coherent, distributed shared memory, which isn't supported by any commercial operating system.

Process Relationships

If the processes in your application are loosely coupled with each other, then you may want to use the client/server configuration. If a process linking to the database environment exits without releasing its database resources, the environment has to be recovered, as you saw in this chapter's code examples. Running recovery on an environment invalidates all the handles associated with the environment, which can cause all processes, holding the handles, to restart. If your application cannot tolerate such behavior, it should access the database through a stand-alone server.

Performance

If you're looking at response times of a couple of microseconds, then you shouldn't use the client/server model. A stand-alone database server imposes significant I/O and process context switch overheads to make sub-millisecond response times impossible. You should consider linking to the database environment directly if you want that kind of performance.

Complexity

Implementing a stand-alone database server can be a significant amount of work. In addition to the components that you built in the code examples, you have to build the following components:

- **Connection manager**: This handles the connectivity between the database server and the applications.

- **Thread manager**: On the database server, you'll have to create a thread pool for handling client requests.

- **Session manager**: This manages client sessions on the server.

- **Marshalling/unmarshalling**: To send a database request over a socket or some other form of IPC, you may have to implement marshalling and unmarshalling routines, unless you're using CORBA, Remote Method Invocation (RMI), or some other remote procedure call (RPC) framework.

Direct Linking

In the code examples, you linked directly to the database environment from the application processes. Direct linking delivers the best performance, because it eliminates the overhead of multiple process hops and socket I/O associated with a stand-alone server. However, it's also prone to process address space corruption. If a rogue process corrupts the common shared memory region of the environment, then all the processes linking to it will be affected.

There is no need to have a connection manager, a thread manager, or a session manager if all processes are linking directly to the database environment. All database operations happen within the context of application threads. You may have to implement some background threads or processes to perform backups, deadlock detections, and so on, but it will still be much easier than designing a stand-alone database server.

Hybrid Approach

In replicated environments, it's possible to have both direct linking as well as client/server-based access to the database. Applications dealing with a large amount of traffic can use this hybrid approach to distribute the load on multiple machines. Berkeley DB supports single-master multiple-clients replication. Application processes can link directly to the replicated read-only environments to read data and access the master environment through a stand-alone server for making updates. I'll discuss this approach in detail in the next chapter.

Summary

In this chapter, you learned how to design a functioning database framework using Berkeley DB. I showed you how to integrate Berkeley DB with various types of application structures. You learned how to recover from failures in shared environments by designing the application properly and using the features available in the library.

The material in this chapter lays the foundation for the next two chapters, in which you'll learn about database replication and distributed transactions. In the next chapter, I'll take up replication. Replication is an important feature of Berkeley DB. It is used for providing fault tolerance, high availability, and load distribution.

CHAPTER 8

■ ■ ■

Replication

Database replication is an important feature that you'll come across in a large number of mission-critical applications. Technically, replication involves the creation of one or more replicas of an existing environment. You can use it to provide fault tolerance, high availability, data distribution, backups, and load balancing.

You can replicate a database in a number of different ways. The way you implement replication in a database determines how you'll design the application that will use replication. This is especially true for Berkeley DB, because, as with its other features, you have to implement a big portion of the replication framework. In version 4.5.x of Berkeley DB, an easy-to-use wrapper interface called the *Replication Manager* has been added, making it simple to use and deploy replication. However, Replication Manager doesn't provide as much flexibility as the base replication API.

In this chapter, I'll first go over the basics of replication, and then I'll explain how replication is implemented in Berkeley DB. The focus in this discussion will be on the components that you have to develop. I'll show you how to extend the transactional data store example to do replication. Finally, I'll go over the Replication Manager interface, which provides a ready-made TCP/IP-based replication framework, and I'll show you how it simplifies the application layer.

What Is Database Replication?

In this section, I'll go over the replication concepts in general, without touching upon Berkeley DB. In the "Berkeley DB Replication Architecture" section, I'll discuss Berkeley DB replication in particular. As the name suggests, replication means creating an exact replica of an existing database. You can create a replica in numerous ways. In the simplest replication scheme, you can take a backup of the database and re-create the same database, using the backup, in a different location. Obviously, replicating the database in this manner can be quite inefficient and difficult to manage. The complexity and the effectiveness of a replication scheme depends on the following factors:

- **Frequency**: The more frequently the database is copied, the bigger the overhead it imposes on the database server. On the other hand, if the database is copied infrequently, then the replica won't be up to date. Some databases allow clients to sync up from other clients, thereby reducing the load on the master. Berkeley DB is one such database.

- **Granularity**: You can achieve replication at the database level, where each committed transaction is composed of a unit of change and is sent and applied to the replica. Such schemes are efficient, but it's difficult to make them application-aware to do more *intelligent* replication. You can also do replication at a logical level, where application-level operations are sent to the replica and rerun. Logical replication is application-specific and cannot be used for applications for which it wasn't designed.

- **Scope**: The scope determines what portion of a database gets replicated. A database can be fully replicated, or it can be partially replicated. Full replication is simpler to implement, but it can be wasteful, whereas partial replication is more complex to implement and maintain.

Apart from these aspects, you can also classify replication schemes by the number of masters that are allowed in a replicated environment. Let's take a look at the possible configurations.

Single-Master Replication

Single-master replication refers to the scheme where having a single database serves as the "source of truth." You then make one or more copies of that database. Figure 8-1 illustrates single-master replication.

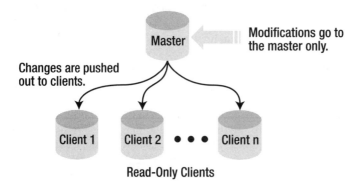

Figure 8-1. *Single-master replication*

There is only one master at any given time in single-master environments. All other nodes in the environment are *clients* of the master environment. Only the master can update the database, so you must write all the applications to update only the master database. Single-master architecture suffers from the limitation that all updates have to go through a single machine.

Multimaster Replication

Figure 8-2 shows the setup for multimaster replication. Unlike single-master replication, more than one node can update the database.

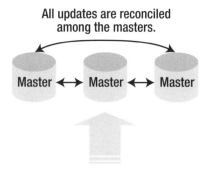

Figure 8-2. *Multimaster replication*

More than one master can reside in the environment. All masters can update the database at the same time. This scheme is complex to implement, because it has to work in situations where more than one master updates a record at the same time. Conflict resolution in such conditions can be difficult and error-prone.

Usually, multimaster systems know something about the semantics of the data they manage—for example, whether the data comes from an address book or an e-mail server—and they use that knowledge to help resolve conflicts in a way that makes sense. In multimaster systems, the distributed database *eventually* settles down into a consistent state. Conflicting updates may be made by more than two nodes and will need to propagate around and get resolved everywhere, which may happen at different times. Multimaster replication also allows multiple master nodes to share the load of database updates and reads.

Hybrid Master-Client Replication

Figure 8-3 shows yet another replication scheme in which clients can perceive some of the clients as masters, when in reality they're just clients.

In hybrid master-client replication, some clients behave as masters for other clients. The clients behaving as masters aren't able to make database updates, but they're allowed to relay the updates to other clients. This is still a single-master configuration, but the hybrid clients share the overhead of sending updates to the clients. This is quite useful in setting up hierarchical replication frameworks. If there is a large number of clients, the master can get overloaded with the task of keeping all the clients up to date, the hybrid scheme will reduce the load on the master.

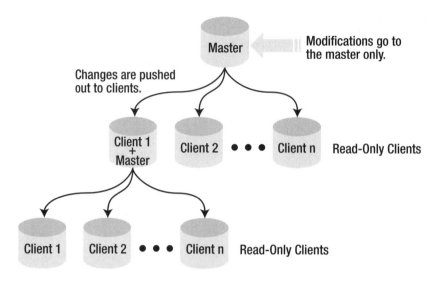

Figure 8-3. *Hybrid master-client replication*

Berkeley DB Replication Architecture

Berkeley DB supports single-master replication and hybrid master-client replication. There can be only one master and multiple clients at any given time. The master database can be used for both reads and updates/deletes, while the clients may be used for reads or may serve as hot standbys[1] for the master. In Berkeley DB, replication is done at the physical level, which means that the changes that happen to the physical storage due to modifications in the database are sent over to the replicas. The change log that is captured in the transaction logs constitutes the content that's exchanged between the master and the clients during replication, as shown in Figure 8-4.

Figure 8-4 shows a portion of the transaction log on the master. Two log records, LSN[1][1092829] and LSN[1][1092873], are shown from the log. When the master updates the clients, it sends the transaction log records to them. The clients then update their transaction logs with these records and apply them to the databases when a COMMIT record is encountered. The transaction logs maintained by Berkeley DB are tightly coupled with the underlying storage, so the replication too is strongly linked with the underlying storage mechanism. The physical structure and layout of the database on the clients must exactly match that of the master. This is assumed, and to some extent enforced, by the Berkeley DB replication APIs. A transaction-log record contains the database page number, the offset within that page where the modification starts, and the modified bytes—basically everything that is needed to make the exact same change on the replica.

---

1. A *hot standby* is a replication client that's always in sync with the master and can become a master immediately after the master fails.

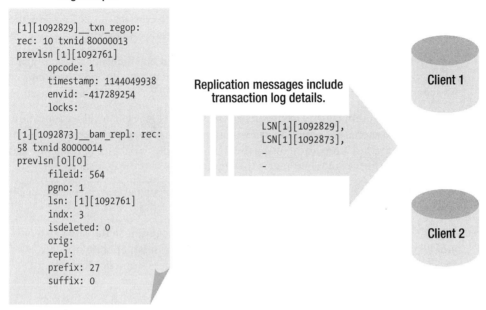

Figure 8-4. *Transaction log–based replication*

Berkeley DB's method of doing replication has two significant consequences:

- It isn't possible to do selective replication, because the sequential structure of the transaction log makes it impossible for a replica to skip unwanted logs.

- The endian-ness of the nodes participating in the replicated environment must be the same.

It is up for debate whether making replication based on the transaction logs is a good idea in view of these restrictions. The advantage of using the transaction logs for replication is that it makes it extremely fast and efficient, since no additional processing is required to drive replication. Also, when transaction logs are generated, they're shipped out to the clients. If the replication scheme were more intrusive, the library would have to analyze every modification and determine whether it should be applied to a particular client, thereby imposing a significant overhead. On the negative side, this scheme imposes a rather restrictive limitation that the entire database is replicated on every client. For applications that store large amounts of data in the database, replicating everything can be extremely inefficient.

Salient Features of Berkeley DB Replication

You need to be aware of the following key aspects of Berkeley DB replication, should you ever decide to use replication in your environment:

- **It supports master election**: If the master fails, then the existing clients can conduct an election to elect a new master.

- **It works with TDS**: Replication is based on transaction logs, so you should always configure the Berkeley DB environment as TDS if the application needs replication.

- **There's no restriction on the node location**: The nodes (or machines) participating in a replicated environment can be located on the same machine, on a different machine, or on a separate hardware partition in a Non-Uniform Memory Access (NUMA) system.

- **It gives the application control over synchronization**: Berkeley DB lets the application control how the clients are synchronized with the master. They can either synchronize in real time or at fixed intervals, allowing them the flexibility to balance consistency and performance in the way that best meets the requirements of the application.

- **It offers full database replication**: It isn't possible to replicate parts of the database; all clients receive a complete copy of the master database.

- **It has the same endian-ness on all nodes**: All nodes participating in the replicated environment have to be of the same endian-ness. This means it isn't possible to have a Sun-SPARC machine participating in an environment where some x86-based Linux machines are also present.

Berkeley DB provides only the core replication functionality. Replication framework components that cannot be implemented in a platform-agnostic manner aren't included in the library. The application is responsible for filling in the missing pieces.

Replication Framework Components

Some of the main components in the replication framework are left for you to implement. Berkeley DB has left out the components that depend heavily on the platform on which the application is running. Figure 8-5 shows the replicated database stack.

Figure 8-5 shows the layers within the database that participate in the execution of a database operation. The operation invoked by the application thread in the master environment goes through the access API and the transaction subsystem. You can invoke the replication callbacks in two different ways. If the master environment has been configured with the DB_TXN_NOSYNC flag, which means that the transaction logs aren't flushed to the local disk before the transaction is committed, then the replication callback will be invoked before the transaction is *committed* on the master. Once one or more clients acknowledge the receipt of the replication message, the transaction is committed on the master. On the other hand, if the master environment has been configured with the DB_TXN_SYNC flag (which is set by default), then the replication callback is invoked after the transaction log is flushed to the disk, and the transaction is marked as committed on the master. The replication subsystem invokes the communication callbacks, provided by the application, to deliver the details of the transaction to the clients. When a client receives the message, it forwards it to its replication subsystem, which in turn sends it to the transactional subsystem for final processing.The Berkeley DB replication framework has been carefully designed to allow you to take control of most of the performance hot spots in the stack. Additionally, as mentioned earlier, the framework also lets the application control the platform-dependent and application-dependent aspects. Let's examine these application-dependent aspects in detail.

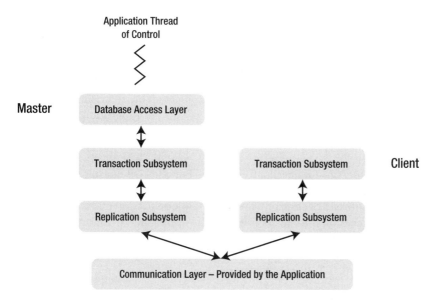

Figure 8-5. *The replication stack*

Communication Layer

As shown in Figure 8-5, the replication subsystem doesn't deliver the replication messages to the clients on its own. It simply invokes a previously registered callback, provided by the application, to send the messages. Current (4.5.x and above) Berkeley DB releases supply a default communication layer, so that if you need a simple TCP/IP-based transport, you can get started quickly. You can override or change this default implementation if the ready-made framework doesn't fulfill all the requirements. In the older versions (prior to 4.5.x), you had to implement the communication framework. Designing the communication framework can be a challenging task if you're not experienced in designing networking applications. Therefore, an easy-to-use default communication layer was included in version 4.5.x. The communication layer was left out of the older releases because it would've been very difficult, if not impossible, to provide all possible implementations in a single library. However, when Berkeley DB's engineering team noticed that developers used TCP/IP sockets to implement the layer in the majority of applications, it made a default TCP/IP-based implementation a part of version 4.5.x.

Node Management

In releases 4.5.x and later, the node-management functionality is available by default from the library if you're using the default TCP/IP-based communication framework. If you decide not to use the default framework, you'll have to handle the responsibility of maintaining a list of participating nodes. Node management includes monitoring the connections with the nodes and assigning replication priorities to the nodes (I'll discuss these priorities in detail in the section on elections).

Once again, the Berkeley DB designers could have implemented node management, but they left it out because it's impossible to guess the best management scheme for an application, for two reasons. First, the library doesn't know what kind of communication protocol the application is using, so it can't implement connection management. Second, the library has no visibility of the topology of the replicated environment. The environment could be static, where the number of nodes never changes, or it could be dynamic, where nodes can join or leave the environment. If the environment is dynamic, then node-management data structures have to be properly protected for thread safety. Providing thread safety in a static environment can result in unnecessary mutex-related overheads. Only the application has full visibility of these aspects, and that's why Berkeley DB leaves node management for the application to deal with.

Thread Management

If you're not using the default communication framework, Berkeley DB doesn't create any threads of its own. All database functions and replication operations are performed in the context of the application's thread of control. The actual implementation of the threading framework for the communication framework is left for the application to fill out. Only the application knows how many threads should be employed for delivering the replication messages and what kind of threading library will be best suited for the purpose. Of course, this doesn't apply if you're using the default TCP/IP implementation.

Security

The security of the communication framework is also left for the application to implement. The application determines how much security is needed for the node connections. If all the nodes are operating in a fairly secure private environment, then there's no need to encrypt, authenticate, and authorize the messages. For example, if you're replicating a database within a multislot chassis, you don't need to provide any security for the replicated environment as no replication message ever leaves the chassis. On the contrary, if an application has replicated nodes placed in geographically diverse locations and connected over the Internet, you definitely need some kind of security. However, if those nodes are connected over a VPN going over the public Internet, then you don't need to encrypt the messages. Therefore, it's impossible to implement a security scheme that you can apply to all applications, and that's why it has been left for the application to implement.

If you're using the default TCP/IP-based communication layer, then you don't have the option to use secure sockets.

Building the Replication Framework Using the Base API

In this section, you'll learn about the base replication API, which is what you'll use if you're not using the TCP/IP-based default communication framework. In the "Replication Manager Interface" section, I'll go over the default implementation as well. If you're interested in using that, you can skip this section. However, going over the base API will give you a good understanding of how the replication framework works in Berkeley DB. Even if you want to use the default communication framework, it still may be a good idea to read through this section.

You now have enough background information to start building the replication framework. You can build a simple framework relatively easily. The Berkeley DB source distribution contains one such implementation. If you have to use replication for a small, noncritical application, such an implementation will suffice.

▓**Note** You can find the replication example in the Berkeley DB source distribution under `examples_c/`
`ex_repquote`.

However, if you're thinking of using Berkeley DB replication for some other critical application, such as a router or a high-traffic web site, then you'll have to spend a lot of time designing the replication framework properly. One of the purposes of this chapter is to make you aware of the challenges so that you're better prepared when you actually get down to building the framework. Let's begin with the set of APIs that you'll be using to build the framework.

▓**Note** In the rest of this chapter, the terms *replicas*, *nodes*, or *sites* mean the same thing; they all refer to the Berkeley DB environments participating in replication. A replication framework involves three distinct components: the database environment (the term *replica* is suitable when talking about the environment), the communication layer (a networked entity is usually called a *node*), and the replication management framework, which deals with sites. It's natural to refer to the same entity with different names in different contexts, so I've used all three terms in this chapter.

Replication APIs

As you already know, the framework is divided into two parts—one that's included within the Berkeley DB library, and another that the application has to implement. Table 8-1 lists the APIs that allow you to configure the replication framework and hook in the portion provided by the application to the part available from the library. This table doesn't include the APIs for accessing the default TCP/IP-based communication framework. I'll go over those APIs later in the "Replication Manager Interface" section, which is devoted to the default communication framework.

Of the APIs listed in Table 8-1, the first four are the most important. You cannot write a replicated application without using these four APIs, unless you're using the default TCP/IP-based communication framework. The others are also useful but not absolutely necessary. One important thing missing from the API descriptions and the reference guide bundled with the source distribution is the sequence in which the application should invoke these APIs. You can figure that out either by trying out different sequences or by looking at the ex_repquote example online, but either ways it is a tedious process.

Table 8-1. *Base Replication APIs*

API	Description
DbEnv::rep_process_message	Used to pass on a message, received from a replica, to the library for processing the contents.
DbEnv::set_rep_transport	Used to configure the callback that the library will use when it has to send a message to a replica.
DbEnv::rep_start	Used to indicate to the library that the application is ready to handle replication messages and that the library can initiate replication.
DbEnv::rep_elect	Used to launch an election for selecting a master from among the known replicas.
DbEnv::rep_set_config	Used to modify the replication configuration. The library will use the default values if the application doesn't invoke this API.
DbEnv::set_rep_limit	Used to set the various types of limits in the replication framework.
DbEnv::rep_sync	Used to force the syncing of a replica that was instructed earlier to delay the sync (through the DB_REP_CONF_DELAYCLIENT flag in the rep_set_config method). This API is also used for managing the load on an overloaded master.
DbEnv::rep_stat	Used to gather replication-related statistics from the library.

Figure 8-6 shows the sequence in which the application should invoke the replication APIs.

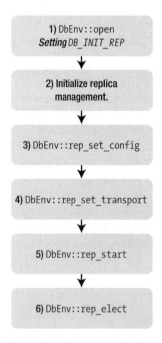

Figure 8-6. *Recommended sequence for invoking replication APIs*

When a new replica has to join a replication environment, it first opens the database environment with the DB_INIT_REP flag set to true. This flags allows the library to initialize in the replication mode. Without this flag, all subsequent invocations of replication APIs will result in runtime errors or exceptions.

Next, the application should set up the infrastructure for managing replicas, which includes setting up communication channels and creating the data structures for holding the state and connection information of the replicas. If you're using the default communication framework, then you don't need to do this. You can perform this step at anytime before DbEnv::rep_start is called. Basically, the replica management infrastructure should be ready before you start exchanging messages with the replicas.

Before calling DbEnv::rep_start, you also need to set the replication transport callback with the library (you don't need to do this if you're using the default communication framework). If you don't set this before calling rep_start, the library won't be able to respond to a message received from a replica. You set the transport by calling DbEnv::set_rep_transport. After setting the transport, you can call DbEnv::rep_start. This will bootstrap the replication process within the library. The library starts sending its information to all the known replicas. If the replica management and replication transport aren't available by this time, the library will fail to communicate with the replicas after rep_start.

The sequence of events laid out so far has to happen on every node that's participating in a replication environment. The nodes participating in replication are known as the *replication group*. When a node in the replication group is initializing, it doesn't know about the status of other nodes in the group. It doesn't even know who the master is and who the other clients are. It may become the master itself if configured as a possible master. Information about the other nodes is gathered during the election process.

At this point, you need to start the election process to find out the master node by calling DbEnv::rep_elect. If there is no known master among the known replicas, the rep_elect call will launch an election process (I'll go over the details of the election in a bit); otherwise, the master will respond to the rep_elect message from a new replica by sending information about itself.

After an election has completed on a node, it will know the state of the group, the identity of the master, and also which other nodes are present in the group. If the newly initialized node isn't the master, the master will inquire the new replica about its current state and then, depending on the replication configuration, will proceed to bring it up to speed with itself. If the newly initialized node becomes the master, it will start syncing up the remaining client nodes.

■**Note** If you're still using version 4.3.28 or older, you won't find the DbEnv::rep_set_config and DbEnv::rep_sync APIs, as these were added in version 4.4.x. It is always recommended that you use the latest released version if possible. New features and bug fixes are constantly being added to newer releases.

To allow you to fully grasp how replication works in Berkeley DB, I'll walk you through a working prototype that will replicate a sample database from one site to another. I'll continue to use the transactional data-store example used so far in the book. I'll revisit only those portions that have to be changed. The goal is to run two transactional data-store programs (called tds until now) either on the same machine or on different machines. (If you have access to two machines, just make sure that they have the same endian-ness.) You'll load the Person database on one of them and then replicate it to the other data store. You'll see that when replication is performed, the entire database gets re-created on the other data store. To distinguish between a replicated and nonreplicated data store, I've renamed the new version of the data store to rep_tds.

Opening the Environment

Let's reuse the DbUtils class that you developed in the earlier chapters to open the environment in the replicated mode. Since DbUtils is a singleton, it's guaranteed that the constructor will be called only once during the lifetime of the process. Also, since you stored a singleton instance in shared_ptr, the cleanup of the singleton is guaranteed when the process terminates. As shown in Listing 8-1, you open the environment with an additional flag to indicate to the library that you want the environment to be replicated.

Listing 8-1. *Opening the Environment in the Replicated Mode*

```
126 DbUtils::DbUtils():
127     dbEnv_(0)
128 {
129     try
130     {
131         std::string envhome = "./chap8_env";
132         std::stringstream ss;
133         ss << envhome;
134         ss << "_";
135         ss << repId_;
136
137         dbEnv_.set_errpfx("chap8_ex");
138         dbEnv_.set_errcall(errCallback);
139         dbEnv_.set_lk_detect(DB_LOCK_DEFAULT);
140         dbEnv_.set_thread_count(16);
141         u_int32_t envFlags =
142             DB_INIT_MPOOL | DB_INIT_TXN |
143             DB_INIT_LOCK | DB_THREAD |
144             DB_INIT_REP | DB_INIT_LOG |
145             DB_RECOVER | DB_CREATE;
146         dbEnv_.open(ss.str().c_str(), envFlags, 0);
147     }
148     catch(DbException &dbex)
149     {
150         dbEnv_.err(dbex.get_errno(), "Db exception caught");
151     }
152     catch(...)
153     {
154         std::cout << "unknown exception caught" << std::endl;
155     }
156 }
```

Let's look at the new constructor implementation. Most of the code is still the same as before, except for a few flags:

- **Line 131**: Change the name of the environment directory to indicate that it belongs to the code example in Chapter 8.

- **Lines 134–135**: Append the replica ID to the name of the environment. This helps you run multiple instances of the replicated data store from the same directory on the same machine. The replica ID is passed in as a command-line argument to the program, which I'll go over shortly.

- **Line 144**: Specify the DB_REP_INIT flag in DbEnv::open call. The library handles replicated and nonreplicated environments differently. You cannot use a DbEnv handle not opened with this flag to participate in replication; it will result in runtime errors or exceptions. Other flags stay as they were before.

You'll pass the replica ID as a command-line argument so that you can determine which replica is being started dynamically. Listing 8-2 shows the main method where you do this.

Listing 8-2. *Initializing Replication*

```
125 int main(int argc, char **argv)
126 {
127    if(argc < 2)
128    {
129        ACE_DEBUG((LM_ERROR, "insufficient arguments\n"));
130        return 0;
131    }
132    DbUtils::repId_ = atoi(argv[1]);
133    try
134    {
135        DbUtils_SP utils = DbUtils::getInstance();
136
137        RepMgr *repMgr = RepMgrSingleton::instance();
138        repMgr->beginRep(DbUtils::repId_);
139    }
140    catch(DbException& dbex)
141    {
142        ACE_DEBUG((LM_ERROR,
143                    "caught DbException in main %d\n",
144                    dbex.get_errno()));
145    }
146    catch(...)
147    {
148        ACE_DEBUG((LM_ERROR, "unknown exception caught\n"));
149    }
150 }
```

Let's take a look at some of the details of what you do in main:

- **Line 132**: Convert the replica ID to an integer and store it in the static variable DBUtils::repId_.

- **Line 137**: You get the singleton instance of the RepMgr class, which you'll design for managing the replication tasks. Notice that for RepMgr, you've used a ready-made singleton template from the ACE library. It provides all singleton properties out of the box. I'll go over the details when I discuss the RepMgr implementation in the "Implementing the Replication Manager" section.

- **Line 138**: Initialize RepMgr by invoking its beginRep method.

Notice that you don't call the DbUtils::loadDbs method as you did earlier in main. You'll call this method from the RepMgr::beginRep method after a master node has been elected from among the participating nodes. Remember that Berkeley DB supports only a single master in a replicated environment; therefore, if you try to load the databases on a client node, the library will throw runtime errors. Let's now proceed to node management.

Managing Nodes

Node management occupies a central place in the design of the replication framework. Node management includes keeping track of all the other nodes from each node in the replication group, connecting to the nodes, and maintaining the connectivity. The data structure used for storing this information should be very efficient and should be optimized for the most common operations. The routines that modify the data structure should also be properly protected to prevent corruption if the framework is multithreaded. You should take care not to make the protection too restrictive, as that can result in the serialization of all access to the structures, thereby reducing the throughput. Let's examine the usage of the node management data structure:

- **Insertions**: During the initialization of the replication framework, an attempt is made to connect to all the known nodes in order to bootstrap the replication process. A node may or may not know about every other node in advance. In order to allow the propagation of the node information throughout the replication group, when a node gets connected to a peer, the peer tells the connecting node about the nodes it is connected to. If those nodes aren't already known on the connecting node, you'll have to add them to the list of nodes.

- **Deletions**: If the nodes in the replication groups aren't changing, there won't be any deletions from the data structure. However, if new nodes can join and leave the group, you might have to delete the departed nodes to avoid consuming too much memory for node management.

- **Lookups**: In any type of environment, whether it's dynamic or static, a large number of lookups will definitely be performed on the data structure. Every time the library has to communicate with a peer, the connection information (or the connection itself) will be looked up from the data structure.

An associative container, such as std::map, can perform all these tasks quite efficiently. It performs much better than a vector or a linked list because all operations involve lookups based on identifiers.

Next, let's examine how you can protect access to the map in the presence of multiple threads. You can simply have a mutex, which every thread can be forced to acquire before it accesses the map. The problem with doing that is it forces all the threads to serialize. The ideal solution would be to allow multiple threads to access the map as long as all of them are reading the entries and allow exclusive access when a thread has to modify an entry. The ACE library provides a solution in the form of read/write locks on regular mutexes. Multiple read locks can be acquired simultaneously, while only one write lock can be acquired at any given time. Read/write locks are more expensive to acquire than a plain mutex; therefore, it's advisable to use them only if the read contention is much higher than the write contention. In this case, that is definitely true. The declarations shown in Listing 8-3 provide the necessary data structures for maintaining the node information.

Listing 8-3. *The Replica Class*

```
55 class Replica
56 {
57     public:
58         Replica(ACE_INET_Addr addr, int id, int priority);
59         ~Replica();
60
61     private:
62         int                 id_;
63         int                 priority_;
64         ACE_INET_Addr       addr_;
65         RepSession          *sess_;
66         DbLsn               sentLsn_;
67         DbLsn               retLsn_;
68         ACE_Recursive_Thread_Mutex mutex_;
69
70         friend class RepMgr;
71         friend class RepSession;
72 };
73
74 typedef boost::shared_ptr<Replica> Replica_SP;
75 typedef std::map< int, Replica_SP > RepMap;
76 typedef std::map< int, Replica_SP >::iterator RepMapIter;
```

Let's go over the class declaration in detail:

- **Line 55**: The Replica class stores the information needed to connect to a node. It also stores the connection when the connection to a node succeeds.

- **Line 58**: The constructor takes ACE_INET_Addr, a user-friendly wrapper around the IP address; the ID of the node; and the priority of the node.

- **Line 65**: RepSession is the class that encapsulates a connection between two nodes. In this example, you're using TCP connections. Therefore, RepSession contains a reference to the TCP socket connection between two nodes.

- **Lines 66–67**: The log sequence numbers (LSNs) monitor the progress of replication between the two nodes.

- **Line 68**: The mutex protects an instance of the Replica class. This is different than the mutex that you'll use for protecting the map that stores Replica instances.

- **Line 74**: Replica_SP is the typedef for the shared_ptr for the Replica class. You'll use shared_ptr to store the instances of Replica so that you don't have to bother about the proper cleanup of the instances when they go out of scope.

- **Line 75**: This map stores Replica instances. Notice that you're storing a shared_ptr containing the Replica instance instead of Replica directly in the map.

- **Line 76**: RepMapIter is the typedef for the map iterator.

Once you open the environment properly in the replicated mode and create the node management data structure, the next thing to do is connect to the nodes.

Designing the Communication Framework

You must consider two things when designing the communication framework using the base API:

- **Communication protocol**: You can use any protocol and transport for communication. It can be a connection-oriented protocol, such as TCP, a connectionless protocol, such as User Datagram Protocol (UDP), or some proprietary protocol. The library is designed to work with any protocol, as long as the communication framework conforms to the Berkeley DB API.

- **Connection topology**: You have to decide how the nodes are connected with each other. You can let every node connect with every other node, or you can let every node connect to a set of predetermined nodes.

Let's go over the choices available for each of these in a bit of detail.

Communication Protocol

Broadly speaking, all protocols can be divided into two groups: connection-oriented and connectionless. I chose this categorization because whether a protocol is connection-oriented or not affects the design of the communication framework the most.

Connection-Oriented Protocols

The advantage of using a connection-oriented protocol is that you don't need to devise an acknowledgement scheme to determine if a message is received properly by the recipient. A connection-oriented protocol such as TCP has a built-in mechanism to ensure that the messages sent over it are delivered reliably. To ensure that a replication message is actually received by a peer, some kind of acknowledgement mechanism is needed in the communication framework. This assurance comes built-in with a connection-oriented protocol. If replication is happening over a network that isn't very reliable, then it would make sense to use a connection-oriented protocol such as TCP for setting up the communication framework for replication.

The disadvantage of connection-oriented protocols is that they're usually heavyweight. Most such protocols tend to include elaborate support for dealing with network congestion, optimizations for packet size, transmission buffers, and so on, all of which can reduce the performance quite a bit.

When deciding whether to use a connection-oriented protocol, follow this rule of thumb: if you can afford to work with the latency associated with TCP, then go for TCP. It's not worth trying to devise an acknowledgement scheme of your own unless you absolutely cannot afford to have any extra overhead.

Connectionless Protocols

The advantage of using a connectionless protocol such as UDP is that it doesn't have overheads that are associated with protocols such as TCP. Connectionless protocols are very lightweight and can be used to build custom solutions for specific applications. If you know that your network is very reliable and you don't need an elaborate acknowledgement scheme to ensure the delivery of messages, then you can eliminate the acknowledgements entirely from your messaging framework.

The obvious disadvantage of connectionless protocols is that you have to build your own acknowledgement scheme if your application needs it. If you require tremendous performance from the replication framework that TCP cannot provide, then you have no other option than to use UDP. Follow this rule of thumb: if TCP is too slow for your needs, only then you should consider UDP.

Connection Topology

In addition to the connection protocol, you also need to decide which nodes should connect to which nodes while setting up the communication links for the replication framework. Figure 8-7 shows some connection topologies.

You can devise any arbitrary connection scheme that suits your application. The ones shown here are representative of how nodes are usually connected. Berkeley DB supports a single master and multiple clients in a replicated environment. Let's examine each topology. When a master crashes or loses network connectivity, the clients conduct an election among themselves to elect a new master.

In case B, all the nodes connect only to the master node. When the master is unreachable, the client nodes B, C, and D cannot communicate with each other, because they aren't interconnected. This can result in the network partition of the nodes. Each node will think that no other node is available and will become a master (if that is allowed by the replication configuration). This can be a dangerous situation, because when A comes back online, it will find three master nodes. This can result in the modifications that were done on two of the three masters being discarded. It's possible to create connections between B, C, and D on the fly when A dies, but even then, there will be a significant delay before a new master can be elected. Having all the nodes connect to a single master node isn't a good idea. In the best case, it can lead to a slow election of the master, and in the worst case, it can result in modifications being discarded. However, if the master doesn't crash, then this topology creates the minimum number of connections among the nodes.

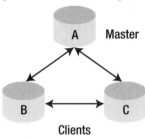

A) Every node connects to every other node.

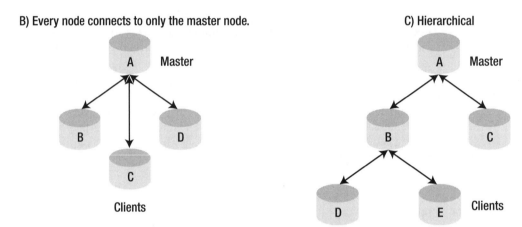

Figure 8-7. *Types of connection topologies in the replicated environment*

In case A, all the nodes connect to all the nodes. When the master dies, the remaining nodes, which are connected to each other, can elect a new master easily. The problem with this topology is that too many connections are being created. You have to create n(n-1) connections (where *n* is the number of nodes). If the number of nodes is large, then you end up wasting too many resources just for maintaining the connection, most of which may never be used.

In case C, a node hierarchy or a tree structure is used. Some client nodes connect to another client node without connecting directly to the master node. The advantage with this topology is that it reduces the load on the master node. If you have a large number of client nodes, then this may be a good topology to use. The disadvantage here is that if the intermediate master crashes, then all its children will get partitioned.

While designing the connection topology for your application, you should make sure that there are sufficient connections to prevent network partition when the master crashes, and at the same time, you should also make sure that you don't have too many connections. When the number of nodes is small, even if all nodes connect to all the other nodes, the overhead of maintaining the extra connections won't be very high. It becomes an issue when you have a large number of nodes. In this code example, I'll start with every node connecting to every other node and then you can make changes in the topology to work with a lesser number of connections.

▉**Note** A replication architecture that supports only a single master, like the one provided by Berkeley DB, requires that all nodes connect (directly or indirectly) to the master. The extra connections (other than the ones to the master) are needed only to allow the nonmaster nodes to conduct an election for the new master when the existing master crashes. However, after an election, when a new master gets elected, some of these extra connections may come in handy.

For the example, let's start with case A, in which all the nodes connect to all the other nodes, and then experiment with the other topologies. You'll provide the information about the other nodes to every node through a static list, such as the one shown in Listing 8-4.

Listing 8-4. *Data Structures for Storing Node Information*

```
struct RepInfo
{
    int             id;
    const char*     ip;
    unsigned short  port;
    int             priority;
};

static const RepInfo REP_INFO_ARR[] =
{
    {1, "127.0.0.1", 3000, 1},
    {2, "127.0.0.1", 4000, 2},
    {3, "127.0.0.1", 5000, 3},
};
static const int NUM_REPS = 3;
```

If you remember, you did something similar for providing a list of databases in the earlier code example in which you implemented a transactional data store. Since you're using a TCP socket for setting up the communication framework, you need to know the IP address and the port of every replica. In addition, you also specify an ID and a priority for every replica. You'll use unique global IDs for the replicas, though it isn't necessary to have global IDs. The priority is used during an election to elect a master. You use the static list REP_INFO_ARR to initialize the node information. You'll run all the replicas on the same machine, but they will listen on different ports. If you want to run your replicas on different machines, you should change this list accordingly.

Implementing the Communication Framework

Let's build the communication layer using TCP, so that you can stay focused on the discussion on replication rather than deal with the message-delivery issues you'd face if you were to use a connectionless protocol such as UDP. I'll try to keep the framework flexible enough so that you'll be able to replace the TCP-based implementation with a UDP-based implementation (or any other protocol).

Sockets API vs. ACE Library

You can use the Sockets API directly to implement the connections, since the Sockets API allows you to work with numerous protocol families through a common interface. However, if you're familiar with socket programming, you probably already know that writing a robust and portable networking application using the Sockets API can be challenging. Some of the problems that you encounter while using the Sockets API can include the following:[2]

- **Error-prone APIs**: For example, the Sockets API uses weakly typed integer or pointer types for socket handles, and there's no compile-time validation that a handle is being used correctly. For instance, the compiler can't detect that a passively listening handle is being passed to the send() or recv() function.

- **Overly complex APIs**: The Sockets API supports many communication families and modes of communication. Again, the compiler can offer no help in diagnosing improper use.

- **Nonportable and nonuniform APIs**: Despite its near ubiquity, the Sockets API is not completely portable. Furthermore, on many platforms, it is possible to mix Sockets-defined functions with OS system calls, such as read() and write(), but this is not portable to all platforms.

The ACE library once again comes to the rescue by providing a set of interfaces that you can easily configure for different types of communication protocols. The ACE interfaces enforce strong type checking while maintaining the flexibility, which results in cleaner and more robust code. In addition, ACE is extremely portable, relieving you of the headache of porting your application to different platforms.

■**Note** Even if you don't plan to use ACE for building your communication framework, it's instructive to see how much ACE IPC simplifies the IPC layer in an application. One of the reasons why I decided to use ACE for this code example is that it allows you to focus on replication without having to devote much effort to setting up the IPC layer.

ACE IPC Wrappers, ACE_Event_Handler, and ACE_Reactor

ACE provides the following interfaces or wrappers for implementing IPC:

- **Connector**: For the active side (or the client side) of the socket connection. The ACE_connector<> template provides this functionality.

- **Acceptor**: For the passive (or the server side) side of a socket connection. ACE_Acceptor <> provides this interface.

- **Service handler**: Encapsulates the connected session between the two entities on the two ends of a socket. ACE_Svc_Handler <> provides this interface.

---

2. Stephen D. Huston, James CE Johnson, Umar Syyid, *The ACE Programmer's Guide* (Boston, MA: Addison-Wesley Professional, 2003) p. 124.

Notice that all the interfaces are templates. These interfaces are generic in nature and can be used for any protocol or service that requires a connection to be set up. Being templates, their behavior can be easily modified by passing the appropriate template arguments, as you'll see when you use these templates for TCP sockets.

IP-based network communication conforms to the event-driven programming model, since you don't know in advance when and how much data is going to be available to be consumed. ACE provides a generic event-handling interface called the Reactor. The ACE_Reactor interface encapsulates an event-dispatching loop very much like the select (or poll) system call. The ACE IPC wrappers are tightly coupled with the ACE_Event_Handler interface. The ACE_Reactor waits in an infinite loop for events to happen. Events could be of any kind; here's a list of some of the common ones:

- **Input**: Received when there is something ready to be read from a file descriptor. The file descriptor can be for a socket, a pipe, and so on.

- **Output**: Received when there is some data to be written to a file descriptor.

- **Exit**: Indicates that a child process has finished executing.

- **Close**: Indicates that a file descriptor has been closed.

- **Signal**: Indicates that the process has received a signal.

- **Timer**: Received every time a timer expires.

The ACE_Reactor interface lets you handle these events by implementing a class that extends the ACE_Event_Handler interface.

In order to use this framework, you need to take care of events on both the active and passive side of the socket connection. To deal with the events during the connection establishment on the passive side, ACE provides a ready-made class called ACE_Acceptor. You can use ACE_Acceptor to listen for connections and spawn an instance of ACE_Svc_Handler to handle the events from the established session. To specify the class handling the session, you need to declare the acceptor like this:

```
typedef ACE_Acceptor< RepSession, ACE_SOCK_ACCEPTOR > RepListener;
```

You declare RepSession like this:

```
class RepSession:
    public ACE_Svc_Handler<ACE_SOCK_STREAM, ACE_MT_SYNCH>
```

On the client, the connection request is initiated by the ACE_Connector class, which returns an instance of ACE_Svc_Handler (in this case, an instance of RepSession) when the connection attempt is successful. Figure 8-8 shows how ACE_Acceptor, ACE_Connector, and ACE_Svc_Handler interact during the creation of a socket connection.

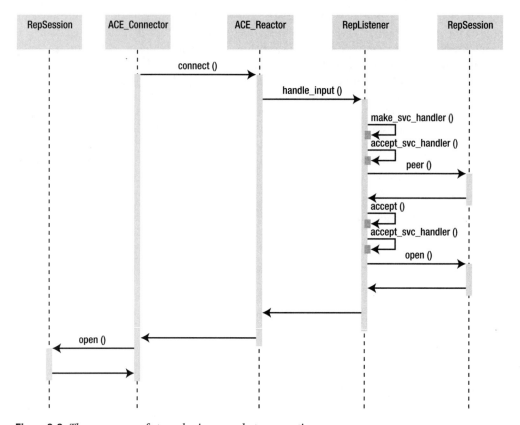

Figure 8-8. *The sequence of steps during a socket connection*

Let's define the ACE_Event_Handler class for handling the socket events. An instance of the RepSession class is created both on the server side and the client side of the socket when a connection is established, as you can see from Figure 8-8. Listing 8-5 shows the declaration of the RepSession class, which is derived from ACE_Svc_Handler.

Listing 8-5. *RepSession Class Declaration*

```
78 class RepSession:
79     public ACE_Svc_Handler<ACE_SOCK_STREAM, ACE_MT_SYNCH>
80 {
81     typedef ACE_Svc_Handler<ACE_SOCK_STREAM, ACE_MT_SYNCH>
82         super;
83
84 public:
85     RepSession();
86
87     virtual int open(void * = 0);
88     virtual int handle_input(ACE_HANDLE fd);
89     virtual int handle_output(ACE_HANDLE fd);
90     virtual int handle_close(ACE_HANDLE fd,
```

```
91                                  ACE_Reactor_Mask mask);
92      int envId_;
93 private:
94      ACE_Reactor_Notification_Strategy notifier_;
95
96      int processMsg(Dbt *control,
97                     Dbt *rec, int *envId,
98                     DbLsn *retLsn);
99 };
```

Let's take a look at the code in detail:

- **Line 79**: The RepSession class derives from the template ACE_Svc_Handler instead of directly from ACE_Event_Handler. ACE_Svc_Handler is derived from ACE_Event_Handler and ACE_Task_Base and is a specialized interface for handling the data exchange between connected peers. ACE_Event_Handler is, as you know, a generic event-handling interface. You used ACE_Task_Base in the previous chapters. It represents a thread and has an ACE_Message_Queue associated with it. The ACE_MT_SYNCH argument indicates that the derived class instance will be executing in a thread pool and will require synchronization.

- **Lines 81–82**: This typedef for the super class improves the readability of the code.

- **Line 87**: The open method is invoked by ACE_Acceptor (on the server side) and by ACE_Connector (on the client side) to register the handler for READ events in ACE_Reactor. The void * argument in this method is used by the invoker to pass a pointer to itself to ACE_Svc_Handler. You won't be using this for now.

- **Line 88**: This is the callback for handling a READ event on the socket file descriptor. The argument is of type ACE_HANDLE, which is a type-safe representation of a file descriptor.

- **Line 89**: This is the callback for handling WRITE events on a socket.

- **Line 90**: This is the callback for handling the close of a socket file descriptor. The mask indicates the event that triggered the handle_close callback.

- **Line 92**: envId_ is used to store the unique ID of the Replica with which this socket connection has been established. This ID is used by the library to identify a node and is assigned by the application.

- **Line 94**: ACE_Reactor_Notification_Strategy is used to configure ACE_Message_Queue, which is associated with ACE_Task_Base (remember RepSession is derived from ACE_Task_Base) to receive a notification whenever a message has been added to the message queue. By using the notification strategy, the WRITE operations on the socket can be made nonblocking.

By using the ACE_Svc_Handler interface, you make both reads and writes on the socket nonblocking. In addition, you also receive an event when the socket is closed. You could have used the Sockets API directly to implement the communication framework without using these complex-sounding classes and interfaces. The biggest problem in doing that is that it is virtually impossible to write nonblocking socket programs that are portable. To make the reads and writes nonblocking, you have to use something like select, which is not portable across platforms. You must be wondering why it's so important to make socket I/O nonblocking in the replication framework. Figure 8-9 shows the sequence of calls made during a typical operation on the database in a replicated environment.

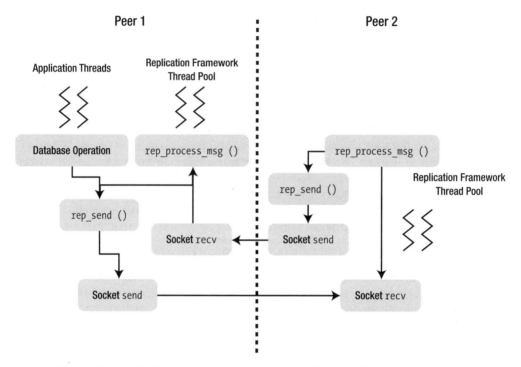

Figure 8-9. *Nested socket I/O invocations in the replication framework*

Let's examine the sequence of events:

1. An application thread invokes a Db operation Db::put or Db::del on Peer 1.

2. The library invokes the transport callback rep_send, which the replication framework provides.

3. The callback writes the replication message on the socket.

4. The replication framework on Peer 2 receives the message in the context of a thread in the framework thread pool.

5. The framework thread calls rep_process_message on the message.

6. The library internally figures out that in order to process the received message, it needs to send a message of its own to the sending Peer 1.

7. The library invokes the rep_send callback to send a new message to the Peer 1.

8. The original sending peer receives the new message and calls rep_process_message on it.

9. The library figures out that it in order to process the received message, it has to send another message to Peer 2. And the sequence repeats.

With this kind of a sequence, if you're doing blocking reads or writes on the sockets, you might end up in a situation where all the threads in the thread pools on both peers are blocked on sockets, and no thread is left to process the replication messages. Therefore, it's of the utmost importance that you never do blocking I/O on the socket connections.

Now let's move on to the central piece in the replication framework: the replication manager. This is the coordinator of all the activities for which the replication framework is responsible.

Implementing the Replication Manager

The replication manager is in charge of the following tasks:

- **Initializing the list of known nodes**: The replication framework has to be bootstrapped with a list of known nodes. It could be a static list read from a file or created dynamically.

- **Connecting to the nodes**: It's the responsibility of the replication manager to establish connections with all the known nodes in the replication group.

- **Polling the nodes to see if they remain connected**: If any node gets disconnected, the replication manager will connect to it again.

- **Providing the replication transport callback**: The replication manager implements the replication transport callback, which the library uses for sending replication messages to the peers.

Listing 8-6 shows the declaration for the replication manager RepMgr.

Listing 8-6. *Declaration of RepMgr*

```
 74 typedef boost::shared_ptr<Replica> Replica_SP;
 75 typedef std::map< int, Replica_SP > RepMap;
 76 typedef std::map< int, Replica_SP >::iterator RepMapIter;
 77
110 class RepMgr:
111     public ACE_Event_Handler
112 {
113     typedef ACE_Acceptor< RepSession, ACE_SOCK_ACCEPTOR >
114         RepListener;
115 public:
116     friend class
117         ACE_Singleton<RepMgr, ACE_Recursive_Thread_Mutex>;
118     int beginRep(int myId);
119     int addReplica(Replica& replica);
120     int send(const Dbt *cntl,
121             const Dbt *rec,
122             const DbLsn    *lsn,
123             int       eid,
```

```
124                 u_int32_t flags,
125             int msgId);
126     int connect(Replica_SP r);
127     virtual int
128         handle_timeout(const ACE_Time_Value &currTime,
129                             const void *act = 0);
130     int sendFirstMsg(int repId);
131     int startElec();
132     int setMaster(int envId);
133     int beginRole(int role);
134     bool isMaster();
135
136 private:
137     RepMgr();
138     ~RepMgr();
139
140     RepMap repMap_;
141     ACE_TP_Reactor        reactor_;
142     Replica_SP            myReplica_;
143     int                   myId_;
144     RepListener           listener_;
145     RepTask               tasks_;
146     ACE_RW_Thread_Mutex mapMutex_;
147     ACE_Recursive_Thread_Mutex masterMutex_;
148     int                   masterId_;
149     Dbt                   cData_;
150     friend class RepSession;
151 };
152
153 typedef ACE_Singleton<RepMgr, ACE_Recursive_Thread_Mutex>
154 RepMgrSingleton;
155
156 int repSend (DbEnv *env,
157         const Dbt *cnt,
158         const Dbt *rec,
159         const DbLsn *lsn,
160         int    eid,
161         u_int32_t flags);
```

Let's take a look at these lines in detail:

- **Lines 110–111:** RepMgr is derived from ACE_Event_Handler, because you need to use a timer to periodically check the connections to the nodes. Remember that you can use ACE_Reactor to generate timer events at fixed intervals; I'll show you soon how that's done.

- **Lines 113–114:** RepListener is declared here. I discussed its details in the previous section.

- **Lines 116–117**: `RepMgr` is a singleton. Here you use the `Singleton` template from ACE to make `RepMgr` a singleton class. You can access the singleton instance by using the `ACE_Singleton<>::instance` method after this declaration.

- **Line 118**: `beginRep` bootstraps the library to begin replicating. This is called after the communication framework is operational.

- **Line 119**: `addReplica` adds a new node to the list of nodes.

- **Line 120**: The replication transport callback uses `send` internally to write a replication message to a socket.

- **Line 126**: `connect` connects to a node.

- **Line 128**: `handle_timeout` is the callback that handles the time-out events created by `ACE_Reactor`.

- **Line 130**: `sendFirstMessage` is a non-Berkeley DB message that a node sends to a peer to identify itself. It's not always necessary, but for this code example it is. I'll discuss why this is later in this section.

- **Line 131**: `startElection` starts an election to elect the master node, as the name suggests.

- **Line 133**: Once an election is successful, `beginRole` is used to assume the role of either a master or a client.

- **Line 134**: This utility method finds out whether the node is a master.

- **Lines 137–138**: To make `RepMgr` a singleton, the constructor and the destructor are made private.

- **Line 140**: `RepMap` is of type `std::map` (declared on line 77). It is used to store instances of `Replica_SP`, which is a `shared_ptr` containing a pointer to an instance of the `Replica` class (declared on line 74).

- **Line 141**: This is the `ACE_Reactor` instance that I'll use for event handling. I'll use a special kind of reactor called `ACE_TP_Reactor`, where *TP* stands for *thread pool*. `ACE_TP_Reactor` has the capability to invoke the event handlers for various events in multiple threads concurrently. `ACE_TP_Reactor` can better utilize multi-CPU machines and can also improve the performance when numerous I/O operations are being performed in the event handlers.

- **Line 142**: This is the handle to the local `Replica_SP` instance; since it will be used very frequently, it makes sense to store it separately.

- **Line 143**: This is the replication ID of the local node. This isn't usually necessary, but since in this example you're using unique global replica Ids, you assign an ID to yourself.

- **Line 144**: This is the `RepListener` for the local node.

- **Line 145**: `RepTask` is a thread pool that you use for supplying threads to the `ACE_TP_Reactor`.

- **Line 146**: This is the mutex to protect the map containing `Replica` objects.

- **Lines 147–148**: Here you see the ID of the current master environment, and the mutex to protect its modification.

- **Line 149**: The opaque data gets sent to a new replica.

- **Lines 152–153**: Here's typedef for the RepMgr singleton.

- **Lines 155–160**: This is the replication transport callback. The library will invoke this method every time it has to send a message to another node.

Listing 8-7 shows how you declare the RepTask class, which you saw in RepMgr.

Listing 8-7. *Declaration of RepTask*

```
101 class RepTask:
102     public ACE_Task_Base
103 {
104     public:
105         RepTask();
106         ~RepTask();
107         virtual int svc();
108 };
```

RepTask is derived from ACE_Task_Base, which provides a thread pool implementation. The task to be performed by a thread in the pool is called from the svc() method. The main purpose of RepTask is to provide an implementation for the pure virtual method ACE_Task_Base::svc(). You use RepTask to provide threads for ACE_TP_Reactor. ACE_Reactor works in a single-threaded context. ACE_TP_Reactor is a multithreaded reactor implementation. When ACE_TP_Reactor receives an event, before it invokes an event handler routine it acquires an idle thread from the ACE_Task_Base thread pool and delegates the responsibility of listening for new events to that thread. It then continues with the event handling. This allows multiple events to be handled concurrently.

Replication Messages

Berkeley DB doesn't impose any restriction on the format of the replication messages that are exchanged among the replicas. All it requires is that the messages should somehow deliver a few data structures to the destination. This excerpt from Listing 8-6 shows the replication transport callback:

```
156 int repSend (DbEnv *env,
157             const Dbt *cnt,
158             const Dbt *rec,
159             const DbLsn *lsn,
160             int    eid,
161             u_int32_t flags);
```

Let's take a look at these lines in detail:

- **Line 156**: env is the environment handle with which this replication data is associated. In case the replication framework is handling replication for more than one environment, you can use this argument to locate the necessary resources.

- **Line 157**: cnt represents the control information for this message. The actual data contained in this structure isn't documented, but it contains information about the kind of data that is being sent across. This is a variable-length field (that's the reason it's of type Dbt) and is never empty.

- **Line 158**: rec contains the data being transported in the message. The actual contents of this structure are, once again, not documented, but it's generally used to ship the actual data stored in the database. This is also of variable length and may be empty for hand-shake messages.

- **Line 159**: lsn is the LSN of the record being shipped in this message. This is relevant only when the flags argument has the DB_REP_PERMANENT flag set to true. When the flag is true, the rec argument contains an actual data entry from the database.

- **Line 160**: eid is the environment ID of the destination node. If it's set to DB_EID_BROADCAST, then the message has to be sent to every node that is known to the local node.

- **Line 161**: The flags argument is used to indicate the nature of the replication message. Even though most of the replication messages originating from the library are opaque to the application, certain special messages (the ones that have to be handled in a special way by the framework) are exposed via this argument.

The library doesn't care if the communication framework is used for exchanging messages other than the ones generated by the library. It is sometimes necessary to have the nodes exchange a few (nonreplication) messages among themselves to bring the messaging framework into an operational state. To accommodate such messages, let's define a message structure that is slightly different from the one in the transport callback. Listing 8-8 shows how you declare the message header RepMsg.

Listing 8-8. *Declaration of RepMsg Structure*

```
struct RepMsg
{
    int         msgId;
    DB_LSN      lsn;
    u_int32_t   flags;
    int         envId;
    int         cntlLen;
    int         recLen;
};
```

In addition to the fields in the transport callback, you have the msgId field. This allows you to add your own messages to the protocol. The receiver always reads the RepMsg header from the socket. From the header, the receiver figures out the length of the cnt and the rec fields. For this example, you need only one message of your own in addition to the regular replication messages. You can have the following msgId values:

```
#define FIRST_MSG 1
#define REP_MSG 2
```

You can have other message types if you feel that you need more messages for administering your framework.

Replication Manager and Replication Message Classes

Let's now turn our attention to the implementation of the classes you've declared so far. I'll start with the methods in RepMgr, because that's where you can start and control every thing else. You looked at main previously. The RepMgr singleton instance is created from main, and then beginRep is invoked on it. Let's begin with the constructor, as shown in Listing 8-9. The constructor is private, since RepMgr is supposed to be a singleton.

Listing 8-9. *RepMgr Constructor*

```
RepMgr::RepMgr():
    masterId_(DB_EID_INVALID)
{
}
```

The constructor only sets the masterId_ to DB_EID_INVALID, which is a constant defined in the Berkeley DB library. It indicates that there is no known replication master. Listing 8-10 shows the implementation of the beginRep method, which starts the replication process.

Listing 8-10. *Implementation ofbeginRep*

```
68 int RepMgr::beginRep(int myId)
69 {
70     myId_ = myId;
71     ACE_Reactor r (&reactor_);
72     ACE_Reactor::instance(&r);
73
74     ACE_Reactor::instance()->schedule_timer(
75             this, 0, ACE_Time_Value::zero, 2);
76
77     tasks_.activate(THR_NEW_LWP | THR_JOINABLE, 2);
78
79     //configure replication
80     DbUtils_SP utils = DbUtils::getInstance();
81     DbEnv *env = utils->getEnv();
82     //Setup the communication framework
83     {
84         ACE_WRITE_GUARD_RETURN(ACE_RW_Thread_Mutex,
85                 g, mapMutex_, -1);
86         for(int i=0; i < NUM_REPS; i++)
```

```
87          {
88              RepInfo ri = REP_INFO_ARR[i];
89              Replica_SP replica;
90              ACE_INET_Addr addr(ri.port, ri.ip);
91              replica.reset(new Replica(addr,
92                          ri.id, ri.priority));
93              repMap_[ri.id] = replica;
94              if(ri.id == myId_)
95                  myReplica_ = replica;
96          }
97      }
98      cData_.set_data(&myId_);
99      cData_.set_size(sizeof(myId_));
100     if(listener_.open(myReplica_->addr_) == -1)
101     {
102         ACE_DEBUG((LM_ERROR,
103                 "(%t)beginRep: listener error on %s %d\n",
104                 myReplica_->addr_.get_host_addr(),
105                 myReplica_->addr_.get_port_number())));
106         return -1;
107     }
108     try
109     {
110         env->set_verbose(DB_VERB_REPLICATION, 1);
111         env->set_rep_transport(myId_, repSend);
112         env->rep_start(&cData_, DB_REP_CLIENT);
113         startElec();
114     }
115     catch(DbException& dbex)
116     {
117         env->err(dbex.get_errno(), "beginRep");
118     }
119     while(!utils->initDbDone_)
120     {
121         utils->loadDbs(isMaster() ? DB_REP_MASTER :
122                 DB_REP_CLIENT);
123         ACE_OS::sleep(1);
124         ACE_DEBUG((LM_ERROR, "waiting for Dbs to init\n"));
125     }
126
127     ACE_Thread_Manager *tm =
128         ACE_Thread_Manager::instance();
129     tm->wait();
130     return 0;
131 }
```

Let's take a look at these lines in detail:

- **Line 70**: The replication ID of the local node is passed from `main`, where it is retrieved from the command line.

- **Line 71**: This is the global `ACE_Reactor` instance to the one you declared in `RepMgr`. Remember that you're using a special kind of reactor—`ACE_TP_Reactor`. By calling the `ACE_Reactor::instance` method, the global `ACE_Reactor` will refer to the reactor.

- **Lines 74–75**: The `ACE_Reactor::schedule_timer` method instructs the reactor to create a timer event at fixed intervals. Here you create a timer event every two seconds. I'll discuss why that's needed in a little bit.

- **Line 77**: Start the `RepTask` thread loop. I'll go over the `svc` method of the class in a moment. In that method, you'll start the reactor event loop. You'll have two worker threads, as indicated by the second argument handling the reactor events.

- **Lines 80–81**: Get the environment handle from the `DbUtils` instance.

- **Line 84**: Acquire a write lock on `mapMutex_` so that you can start populating `repMap_` with the `Replica` instances.

- **Lines 86–96**: Iterate through `REP_INFO_ARR`, create a `Replica` instance for each entry in the list, and store it in `repMap_`. When you run into your own ID, you'll also store a reference in `myReplica_`.

- **Lines 98–99**: Populate the `cData_` with the ID of the local node. `cData_` is sent as a part of the first replication message sent by the library to a new replica. `cData_` plays an important role when a replica doesn't know in advance about all the other replicas.

- **Lines 98–105**: Invoke `open` on `RepListener` (derived from `ACE_Acceptor`), which causes a server socket to be created on the port assigned to the local node.

- **Line 110**: `DbEnv::set_verbose` enables verbose debug messages in the library. The first argument indicates the subsystem for which the messages have to be enabled. Here you enable it for replication. It's instructive to see what the library is doing under the hood by enabling this flag. It's also a valuable debugging tool. You shouldn't enable this flag in a production system, because it slows down the processing. You have to make sure that you compile the library with the `-enable-diagnostic` flag set to `true` to get the diagnostic messages.

- **Line 111**: Here you supply the replication transport callback to the library. In addition to the callback, you also supply the replication ID of the local environment.

- **Line 112**: Start every replica as a client. `DB_REP_CLIENT` is a constant defined in the library to represent a replication client.

- **Line 113**: Start an election to elect a master. It's possible that when this node joins a replicated environment, an elected master already exists. Even if that's the case, you can still call an election. Calling an election is harmless; it doesn't displace an existing master. If a master is known, the election will simply return the ID of the master.

- **Lines 119–125**: Until the databases are initialized, keep trying to load the databases. Unless the client syncs up with the master, the databases won't be available.

- **Lines 127–129**: Wait for the RepTask threads to exit. Since RepTask never exits, beginRep blocks here forever.

Before going on to the other RepMgr methods, let's look at RepTask::svc, as shown in Listing 8-11.

Listing 8-11. *Implementation of the svc Method in RepTask*

```
39 int RepTask::svc()
40 {
41     ACE_Reactor::instance()->run_reactor_event_loop();
42 }
```

ACE_Reactor::instance returns the global reactor instance when invoked without any argument. Earlier, you invoked the method with the ACE_TP_Reactor instance as the argument; that's when the global instance was set. Here you access that instance and start the event loop. Since you specified two threads in the activate method, the events received by the event loop will be handled concurrently in two threads. Listing 8-12 shows the time-out handler implementation in RepMgr.

Listing 8-12. *Time-Out Handler Implementation in RepMgr*

```
53 int RepMgr::handle_timeout(const ACE_Time_Value &currTime,
54                             const void *act)
55 {
56     ACE_READ_GUARD_RETURN(ACE_RW_Thread_Mutex,
57             g, mapMutex_, -1);
58     RepMapIter beg = repMap_.begin();
59     RepMapIter end = repMap_.end();
60     for(;beg != end; ++beg)
61     {
62         Replica_SP r = (*beg).second;
63         if(r->id_ != myId_ && r->sess_ == NULL)
64         {
65             connect(r);
66         }
67     }
68 }
```

RepMgr::handle_timeout handles the timer event generated by the reactor. You need a timer event to periodically check the status of the connections to the other nodes. You need to actively check the status of the peers from every node so that you can find out if a node has crashed as soon as possible. If you don't periodically check the status, you'll find out about the crashed nodes only when the master tries to send a replication message to the crashed node. That may not happen until the next database modification on the master.

There's nothing wrong with delaying the check until the next update, but it can slow down the syncing speed, since the node-management tasks will have to be carried out after every database update. When the timer expires—every two seconds, in this case—the reactor invokes handle_timeout. You iterate through the replica map repMap_ and check whether you have an active session with every node. If you don't have a session with a node, then you try to connect to it. When this method is called for the first time, you won't have any existing sessions. Therefore, you'll try connecting to every node, and that's how the connection framework comes into existence.

Let's look at the connect method, shown in Listing 8-13.

Listing 8-13. *Implementation of connect in RepMgr*

```
213 int RepMgr::connect(Replica_SP r)
214 {
215     ACE_WRITE_GUARD_RETURN(ACE_Recursive_Thread_Mutex,
216             g, r->mutex_ , -1);
217     ACE_DEBUG((LM_ERROR, "connect:: id %d  %s  %d\n",
218                 r->id_,
219                 r->addr_.get_host_addr(),
220                 r->addr_.get_port_number()));
221     ACE_Connector < RepSession, ACE_SOCK_CONNECTOR >
222         connector;
223     RepSession *s = NULL;
224     int res = connector.connect(s, r->addr_);
225
226     ACE_DEBUG((LM_ERROR, "connect::res is %d\n", res));
227     if(res == -1)
228     {
229         ACE_DEBUG((LM_ERROR,
230                     "(%t) error connecting to %s %d\n",
231                     r->addr_.get_host_addr(),
232                     r->addr_.get_port_number()));
233     }
234     else
235     {
236         //send the first message
237         r->sess_ = s;
238         sendFirstMsg(r->id_);
239     }
240     return res;
241 }
```

Let's delve into the code here:

- **Line 224**: You invoke connect on an ACE_Connector object. Notice that in the ACE_Connector declaration, the first argument is RepSession. This instructs ACE_Connector to create a RepSession instance when a connection is established with the peer. The connect method takes the address of the peer as an argument.

- **Line 237**: If the connection is successful, you store the RepSession instance in the Replica instance so that when a replication message has to be sent to this peer, the session can be used.

- **Line 238**: You send the first message to the peer. This message allows the peer to establish the identity of this node. If you were running the replicas from different machines, it would've been possible to establish the identity just by looking at the IP address of the connecting host. However, since you're running all replicas on the same machine, that's not possible. In either case, it's better to establish the identity of the connecting replicas explicitly.

If you revisit the sequence diagram (shown in Figure 8-8) of the connection setup, you'll see that when a connection gets established on the server side, a RepSession instance gets created. On the client side, you get back an instance of RepSession from the ACE_Connector::connect method. However, you don't do an active connect on the server, so you don't know when a RepSession instance got created. As such, there's no way to store the RepSession instance in the replica map, as you did after the ACE_Connector::connect call on the client. The RepSession::open callback comes in handy on the server. You won't know when the RepSession instance got created, but you'll know when the reactor invokes RepSession::open. Listing 8-14 shows how you can save the session in the replica map in the callback.

Listing 8-14. *Implementation of RepSession::open*

```
370 int RepSession::open(void *p)
371 {
372     if(super::open(p) == -1)
373         return -1;
374     this->notifier_.reactor(this->reactor());
375     this->msg_queue()->notification_strategy(
376             &this->notifier_);
377
378     //store the session in the map
379     RepMgr *mgr = RepMgrSingleton::instance();
380
381     ACE_INET_Addr remAddr;
382     int res = peer().get_remote_addr(remAddr);
383     ACE_DEBUG((LM_ERROR,
384             "(%t) open: connected to %s %d\n",
385             remAddr.get_host_addr(),
386             remAddr.get_port_number()));
387
388     ACE_READ_GUARD_RETURN(ACE_RW_Thread_Mutex,
389             g, mgr->mapMutex_, -1);
390     RepMapIter beg = mgr->repMap_.begin();
391     RepMapIter end = mgr->repMap_.end();
392     for(;beg != end; ++beg)
393     {
394         Replica_SP r = (*beg).second;
```

```
395            if( res == 0 && r->addr_ == remAddr)
396            {
397                envId_ = r->id_;
398                ACE_DEBUG((LM_ERROR, "(%t)connected to %d\n",
399                              r->id_));
400                r->sess_ = this;
401                break;
402            }
403        }
404    return 0;
405 }
```

If you don't define your own handler for the open event, then by default, the ACE library will register the newly created RepSession instance (or the ACE_Svc_Handler instance) as the handler for read events on the socket. Let's see what else you do in the handler:

- **Line 372**: You first call the default handler from the base class ACE_Svc_Handler so that the RepSession instance gets registered to handle read events.

- **Lines 374–375**: You set the notification strategy for the message queue associated with this ACE_Svc_Handler. With this set, the reactor will trigger a write every time a message is added to the queue.

- **Lines 381–382**: You retrieve the IP address of the peer.

- **Lines 390–403**: You locate the address (which includes the IP address and the port) of the peer in the replica map. If you find it, then you store the RepSession instance in the map. Note that you won't be able to find the address when open is invoked on the server side, because the port on the client side isn't going to be some random port. You'll see shortly how you identify a peer on the server side by using a special message. If, however, you're running the replicas on different machines, you could have used just the IP address rather than both the port and the IP address for identifying the peer.

I digressed a bit from the discussion on the methods in the RepMgr class, because it made sense to discuss the socket connection handling in one place. I'll come back to the remaining RepSession methods later on. So far, you've seen how to set up of the communication framework; now let's see how the messages are exchanged on the framework. As you already know, you have two types of messages: the regular replication message REP_MSG generated by the library, and the FIRST_MSG message that you created on your own. To send the two kinds of messages, you use a common fixed-sized header RepMsg. Listing 8-15 shows the transport callback that the library uses to send its messages.

Listing 8-15. *Implementation of the Replication send Callback*

```
609 int repSend(DbEnv *env,
610        const Dbt *cntl,
611        const Dbt *rec,
612        const DbLsn *lsn,
613        int    eid,
614        u_int32_t flags)
```

```
615 {
616     RepMgr *mgr = RepMgrSingleton::instance();
617     return mgr->send(cntl, rec, lsn, eid, flags, REP_MSG);
618 }
```

The callback invokes the send method defined in the RepMgr class with the msgId field set to REP_MSG. Similarly, the sendFirstMessage method invokes the send method, but with the msgId set to FIRST_MSG, as shown in Listing 8-16.

Listing 8-16. *Implementation of RepMgr::sendFirstMsg*

```
243 int RepMgr::sendFirstMsg(int repId)
244 {
245     send(NULL, NULL, NULL, repId, 0, FIRST_MSG);
246 }
```

Listing 8-17 shows how the RepMgr::send is defined.

Listing 8-17. *Implementation of the Internal send Method*

```
248 int RepMgr::send(const Dbt *cntl,
249                  const Dbt *rec,
250                  const DbLsn *lsn,
251                  int    eid,
252                  u_int32_t flags,
253                  int msgId)
254 {
255     //encode the message to be sent
256     RepMsg m;
257     int cntlLen = 0;
258     int recLen = 0;
259     memset(&m, 0, sizeof(m));
260     m.msgId = msgId;
261
262     if(msgId == FIRST_MSG)
263     {
264         m.envId = myId_;
265         m.cntlLen = 0;
266         m.recLen = 0;
267     }
268     else
269     {
270         if( flags & DB_REP_PERMANENT && lsn != NULL)
271         {
272             m.lsn.file = lsn->file;
273             m.lsn.offset = lsn->offset;
274         }
275         m.flags = flags;
```

```
276
277        if(cntl != NULL)
278            m.cntlLen = cntl->get_size();
279
280        if(rec != NULL)
281            m.recLen = rec->get_size();
282
283        cntlLen = m.cntlLen;
284        recLen = m.recLen;
285
286    }
287
288    int size = sizeof(m) + cntlLen + recLen;
289    ACE_DEBUG((LM_ERROR,
290    "(%t)send: msgId %d eid %d cntlLen %d, recLen %d\n",
291    msgId, eid, cntlLen, recLen));
292    char sendBuf[size];
293
294    char *offset = sendBuf;
295    memcpy(offset, &m, sizeof(m));
296    offset += sizeof(m);
297    if(cntl != NULL)
298    {
299        memcpy(offset, cntl->get_data(), m.cntlLen);
300        offset += m.cntlLen;
301    }
302    if(rec != NULL)
303    {
304        memcpy(offset, rec->get_data(), m.recLen);
305    }
306
307    //Create a message block to enqueue
308    ACE_Message_Block *mb =
309        new ACE_Message_Block(size);
310    std::memcpy(mb->wr_ptr(), sendBuf, size);
311    mb->wr_ptr(size);
312
313    ACE_READ_GUARD_RETURN(ACE_RW_Thread_Mutex,
314            g, mapMutex_, -1);
315    if(eid == DB_EID_BROADCAST)
316    {
```

```
317        RepMapIter beg = repMap_.begin();
318        RepMapIter end = repMap_.end();
319        for(; beg != end; ++beg)
320        {
321            Replica_SP r = (*beg).second;
322            if(r->id_ == myId_)
323                continue;
324            if(r->sess_ != NULL)
325            {
326                assert(r->sess_->msg_queue());
327                r->sess_->putq(mb->duplicate());
328                ACE_DEBUG((LM_ERROR,
329                    "repSend: added to send queue of %d\n",
330                    r->id_));
331            }
332            else
333            {
334                ACE_DEBUG((LM_ERROR,
335                    "repSend: no conn availbale for %d\n",
336                    r->id_));
337            }
338        }
339    }
340    else
341    {
342        RepMapIter it = repMap_.find(eid);
343        if(it != repMap_.end())
344        {
345            Replica_SP r = (*it).second;
346            if(r->sess_ != NULL)
347            {
348                r->sess_->putq(mb);
349                ACE_DEBUG((LM_ERROR,
350                    "repSend: added to send queue of %d\n",
351                    r->id_));
352            }
353            else
354            {
355                ACE_DEBUG((LM_ERROR,
356                    "repSend: no conn availbale for %d\n",
357                    eid));
358            }
359        }
360    }
361    return 0;
362 }
```

Let's take a look at the details:

- **Lines 256–260**: You prepare the message header RepMsg and assign the received msgId to the header.

- **Lines 262–267**: If it's the first message, then you set cntLen and recLen to 0 and set envId to the local node's replica ID. This message is used to communicate the local node's ID to the peer. Since you're running all replicas on the same machine, you cannot use the IP address to identify a replica; that's why you have to add this additional message in the protocol.

- **Lines 268–286**: If it's a replication message, then you set the cntlLen and recLen (if cntl and rec Dbts are not NULL) accordingly.

- **Lines 288–292**: You allocate a buffer big enough to hold the message header and variable-length rec and cntl.

- **Lines 294–305**: You copy the header, cntl, and rec into the buffer.

- **Lines 308–309**: ACE_Message_Block is a message buffer that the message queue uses. It's a variable-sized buffer with a read pointer and write pointer to help the application keep track of how much data has been read or written from or to the queue. It has been designed to read or write partial messages, so that you can use it easily for network I/O, where you rarely get to read or write entire messages in one shot.

- **Lines 310–311**: You copy the buffer you prepared earlier to the ACE_Message_Block instance, starting from the existing location of the write pointer and going up to the size of the buffer. In a newly created message block, both the read and write pointers point to the beginning of the block. You then update the write pointer to the new position.

- **Lines 315–339**: If the environment ID (eid) to which this message has to be sent is DB_EID_BROADCAST, then the message has to be sent to all known nodes. You iterate through the replica map for each node. If a RepSession instance exists for the node, then you add the message to the message queue of the session. You skip the entry associated with the local node. Note that you first call duplicate on the message before putting it on the queue. By calling duplicate, you increment the reference count of the message instance. One of the many useful features provided by ACE_Message_Block is reference counting. Every instance of ACE_Message_Block keeps a count of how many times it has been referenced and dereferenced (when a particular reference goes out of scope). When the reference count (incremented every time duplicate is called and decremented every time release is called on the message) of an instance becomes 0, it is cleaned up. If the message instance isn't being reference counted, then you either have to create new instances of it for every queue (so that each queue can clean up its copy when it's done with it) or somehow wait to clean it up until all the queues have processed the message. Creating individual copies for every queue can be very expensive if you're dealing with a large number of nodes. Designing a framework to wait for all the queues to use up the message can become quite complicated and error-prone. Therefore, reference counting is the best solution for this problem, and you get it for free with ACE_Message_Block.

- **Lines 340–360**: If the eid points to an individual node, then you look up the Replica instance associated with the node ID and put the message on its RepSession instance.

Note that you don't write the messages to the sockets from the send method but rather you simply add it to the message queue of the peer sessions. When a message is added to a queue, the reactor sends a notification to the session instance, since you enabled the notification strategy for the RepSession class. Therefore, you never block while writing to the socket. When you go through the RepSession::handle_output method (which is invoked when data is available to be written), you'll see that even there you never block on the socket.

Another point to note in the send method is the use of the ACE_READ_GUARD_RETURN macro for protecting the access to the replica map. ACE_READ_GUARD acquires a read lock on the specified mutex, which multiple threads can acquire concurrently. By acquiring a read lock on the mutex, you ensure that multiple threads can send messages to the peers concurrently. If you were to simply acquire the mutex, then all threads would be serialized while accessing the replica map, thereby creating an unnecessary bottleneck in the framework.

■**Tip** The key to writing a stable and scalable replication framework is nonblocking I/O and efficient message distribution. Common problems with message distribution include unnecessary duplication of messages, inefficient node lookups, and excessive locking of the structures.

To wrap up message sending in the replication framework, let's go over the last remaining piece, which is the RepSession::handle_output method. As Listing 8-18 shows, this method is invoked when the reactor generates a notification in response to an addition to the message queue of a RepSession or when the underlying socket is ready for writing.

Listing 8-18. *Output Handler Implementation in RepSession*

```
474 int RepSession::handle_output(ACE_HANDLE fd)
475 {
476     ACE_Message_Block *mb;
477     ACE_Time_Value noWait (ACE_OS::gettimeofday());
478     while(this->getq(mb, &noWait) != -1)
479     {
480         ssize_t sendCnt =
481             this->peer().send(mb->rd_ptr(), mb->length());
482         if(sendCnt == -1)
483             ACE_DEBUG((LM_ERROR,
484                         "(%t)rep id %d: output error\n",
485                         envId_));
486         else
487             mb->rd_ptr(ACE_static_cast(size_t, sendCnt));
488         if(mb->length() > 0)
489         {
490             ungetq(mb);
491             break;
492         }
493         ACE_DEBUG((LM_ERROR, "(%t)rep id %d: %d bytes sent\n",
```

```
494                        envId_, sendCnt));
495         mb->release();
496      }
497      if(this->msg_queue()->is_empty())
498          this->reactor()->cancel_wakeup(this,
499                  ACE_Event_Handler::WRITE_MASK);
500      else
501          this->reactor()->schedule_wakeup(this,
502                  ACE_Event_Handler::WRITE_MASK);
503      return 0;
504 }
```

Let's focus on some of the details:

- **Line 478:** While you have messages in the queue, you pick one message at a time to process it. The noWait argument indicates the time that you're willing to wait for a message to arrive if the queue is empty. Since it is set to an old timestamp, you never wait on the queue.

- **Lines 480–487:** You try to write the message to the socket using the send method on the peer. If you're able to write more than one byte, you update the read pointer of the message.

- **Lines 488–492:** If the message isn't written entirely to the socket, you put it back on the queue and break out of the while loop. Since you've already set the read pointer to the location in the queue up to which you've already written, you'll pick up from where you left off when the socket is ready to be written again.

- **Line 495:** If you reach this point, that means you were able to write the entire message on the socket, and you can now release the message. If the reference count reaches 0 after the release call, the message will be cleaned up.

- **Lines 497–502:** If the queue is emptied in the while –loop, then you don't want to be notified every time the socket is ready for writing. Instead, you wait until a new message is added to the queue. If the queue isn't emptied, then you want to know every time the socket is ready to be written.

As you can see, the handle_output method never blocks on the socket. The ACE_Reactor not only lets you handle the event through your event handlers, but it also lets you choose the events you want to listen for. Since you can enable or disable event-handler invocations, you can prevent unnecessary invocations depending on the need of the application.

You now know how a message gets written to the socket in a nonblocking manner. Let's see how the message is read on the other end of the socket. When the reactor on the other end of the socket detects that a message has arrived on a particular descriptor, it invokes the RepSession::handle_input method on the object registered to handle events for that descriptor. Listing 8-19 shows how you implement the handle_input method.

Listing 8-19. *Implementation of the Input Handler in RepSession*

```
408 int RepSession::handle_input(ACE_HANDLE fd)
409 {
410     ssize_t count = -1;
411     RepMsg m;
412     int res;
413
414     count = this->peer().recv_n(&m, sizeof(m));
415     if(count > 0)
416     {
417         if(m.msgId == FIRST_MSG)
418         {
419             envId_ = m.envId;
420             ACE_DEBUG((LM_ERROR,
421             "(%t)handle_input:received first msg from %d\n",
422             m.envId));
423             RepMgr *mgr = RepMgrSingleton::instance();
424             ACE_READ_GUARD_RETURN(ACE_RW_Thread_Mutex,
425                     g, mgr->mapMutex_, -1);
426             RepMapIter it = mgr->repMap_.find(m.envId);
427             if(it != mgr->repMap_.end())
428             {
429                 Replica_SP r = (*it).second;
430                 r->sess_ = this;
431                 ACE_DEBUG((LM_ERROR,
432                             "handle_input: added %d to map\n",
433                             m.envId));
434             }
435             res = 1;
436         }
437         else
438         {
439             char cntlBuf[m.cntlLen];
440             char recBuf[m.recLen];
441             ACE_DEBUG((LM_ERROR,
442         "(%t)handle_input: rep id %d:recLen %d cntlLen %d\n",
443             envId_, m.recLen, m.cntlLen));
444
445             if(m.cntlLen > 0)
446                 count = this->peer().recv_n(cntlBuf,
447                         m.cntlLen);
448             if(count > 0)
449             {
```

```
450                    if(m.recLen > 0)
451                        count = this->peer().recv_n(recBuf,
452                                    m.recLen);
453                    if(count > 0)
454                    {
455
456                        Dbt rec(recBuf, m.recLen);
457                        Dbt cntl(cntlBuf, m.cntlLen);
458                        DbLsn retLsn;
459                        res = processMsg(&cntl, &rec,
460                                &envId_, &retLsn);
461                        return 0;
462                    }
463                }
464            }
465        }
466        if(count == 0 || ACE_OS::last_error() != EWOULDBLOCK)
467        {
468            ACE_DEBUG((LM_ERROR,
469                "(%t)handle_input: rep id %d: conn closed\n",
470                envId_));
471            return -1;
472        }
473        return 0;
474 }
```

Let's take a look:

- **Line 414**: You read the message header from the socket, which is the size of the RepMsg structure.

- **Lines 417–436**: If the msgId in the header is FIRST_MSG, then you read envId from the message. If you received FIRST_MSG from a peer, you may not have the RepSession for the peer in the replica map. You look up envId in the map; if you find it, then you store the this pointer in the Replica instance.

- **Lines 437–440**: If the msgId is REP_MSG, then you read cntlLen and recLen from the header, so that you can retrieve the full message from the socket.

- **Lines 445–457**: You construct cntl Dbt and rec Dbt from the data read from the socket. rec Dbt may be empty for some messages.

- **Lines 459–460**: You call processMsg on the message sent by the peer.

- **Lines 467–473**: If you got an error while reading from the socket, which is not EWOULDBLOCK, then you return -1 to the reactor, which will close the socket. EWOULDBLOCK is returned when no more data is available to be read.

You must be wondering why in the handle_input method you don't take into consideration the partial reads from the socket, like you did for the partial writes in the handle_output method. The recv_n method actually does that for you. It ensures that you read exactly the number of bytes specified in the second argument. If those many bytes aren't available at the time, then it will return EWOULDBLOCK and you simply return back to the reactor. The reactor will invoke handle_input again when more data is available on the socket. In essence, you wait for the complete message to arrive without blocking on the socket, and that's exactly what you want.

■**Note** For the kind of messages that you're sending across to the peers with a fixed header and multiple variable-sized buffers in the body, it would be more efficient to use iovec structures in conjunction with recvv and sendv methods available from ACE. That would have prevented multiple reads and writes for retrieving a single message from the socket. However, to keep the discussion simple, I chose to use the recv_n and send_n methods.

The final method to consider in the communication framework is handle_close, as shown in Listing 8-20. You invoke this every time the reactor detects that a socket connection has terminated. You will need to perform some cleanup in this method.

Listing 8-20. *Implementation of the Close Handler in RepSession*

```
523 int RepSession::handle_close(ACE_HANDLE fd,
524                               ACE_Reactor_Mask mask)
525 {
526     ACE_DEBUG((LM_ERROR, "(%t)rep id %d:connection closed\n",
527                 envId_));
528     RepMgr *mgr = RepMgrSingleton::instance();
529     ACE_READ_GUARD_RETURN(ACE_RW_Thread_Mutex,
530             g, mgr->mapMutex_, -1);
531     RepMapIter it = mgr->repMap_.find(envId_);
532     if(envId_ != DB_EID_INVALID && it != mgr->repMap_.end())
533     {
534         Replica_SP r = (*it).second;
535         ACE_WRITE_GUARD_RETURN(ACE_Recursive_Thread_Mutex,
536                 g, r->mutex_ , -1);
537         r->sess_ = NULL;
538         ACE_DEBUG((LM_ERROR,
539                     "handle_close: sess for %d removed map\n",
540                     envId_));
541         if(envId_ == mgr->masterId_)
542         {
543             ACE_DEBUG((LM_ERROR,
544         "(%t)master disconnected, starting election\n"));
545             mgr->startElec();
546         }
547     }
548     return super::handle_close(fd, mask);
549 }
```

Let's delve into some of the details:

- **Lines 528–531**: You find the Replica instance associated with this session.

- **Line 537**: You set the session for the replica to NULL, since the connection to the replica has terminated.

- **Lines 541–546**: If the peer with whom this session was established is the master, then you start a new election. This is a crucial step, because if you don't launch a new election here, then a new master may not get elected. Note that losing the connection with the master is sufficient to launch a new election. The master may well be up and running, but if it cannot communicate with the rest of the nodes, it's as good as dead. When I discuss elections in the "Elections and Priorities" section, you'll see how you can control the election process.

- **Line 548**: You call handle_close of the base class so that the reactor can unregister the handler for the terminated connection.

You now have the communication framework ready. Now you can set up the rest of the framework to deal with the messages that are sent across the framework.

In the RepMgr::beginRep method discussed earlier, you invoked the RepMgr::beginRole method to bootstrap a node as a replication client. That is the entry point that causes everything else to start. Let's look at its implementation, as shown in Listing 8-21.

Listing 8-21. *Starting a Master or a Client*

```
203 int RepMgr::beginRole(int role)
204 {
205     DbUtils_SP utils = DbUtils::getInstance();
206     DbEnv *env = utils->getEnv();
207     try
208     {
209         ACE_WRITE_GUARD_RETURN(
210                 ACE_Recursive_Thread_Mutex,
211                 g, masterMutex_, -1);
212         env->rep_start(&cData_, role);
213         if(isMaster() && role != DB_REP_MASTER ||
214                 !isMaster() && role == DB_REP_MASTER ||
215                 !utils->initDbDone_)
216         {
217             utils->loadDbs(role);
218             ACE_DEBUG((LM_ERROR,"(%t) loaded Dbs\n"));
219         }
220     }
221     catch(DbException& dbex)
222     {
223         env->err(dbex.get_errno(), "beginRole");
224     }
225     ACE_DEBUG((LM_ERROR,"(%t) done beginRole\n"));
226 }
```

Here are the details:

- **Line 212**: You call `rep_start` on the environment handle. `cData_` points to arbitrary opaque data that the library will send to a node when it connects to it. It can be used to send any application-specific information to a newly connected node. You've stored the environment ID of the local node in `cData_`. When all the nodes don't know about all the other nodes, you can use `cData_` to pass connection information to the peers. The `role` argument in `rep_start` indicates whether the library should initialize replication as a master or as a client.

- **Lines 213–219**: You open the database handles here. Note that the `loadDbs` method now takes the replication role as an argument. If you remember, you load the default data into the databases inside `loadDbs`. You've shifted `loadDbs` from the `main` thread to here because you cannot update the databases unless you know whether the local node is a master. Therefore, you have to delay loading the databases until an election has been conducted and a master has been elected. The `role` argument is used in `loadDbs` to determine whether the default data should be loaded or not.

Elections and Priorities

To find out whether a node will be a master or a client, you need to conduct an election. Three main factors can affect an election:

- **Priority**: The bigger the priority of a node, the better chance that node has to win an election. A priority can either be 0 or a positive number. If a node has a priority of 0, then it can never win an election, even if it's the only node in existence. It's OK to assign the same priority to multiple nodes; the node that has the bigger LSN wins the election in that case.

- **Number of votes**: The number of votes needed to win an election affects the accuracy of an election. If you wait for all the nodes to vote in an election, then the election will be 100% accurate; there won't be any possibility that the wrong node has won an election. However, it's impractical to wait for all the nodes to vote. An election is usually triggered when a node (usually the master) crashes or becomes unreachable. If you decide to wait for all the nodes to respond, then you'll have to wait until the crashed node becomes operational. At this point, there won't be much of an advantage in having replication, because the application will be inoperational for the duration while the master is down. On the other hand, if you wait for too few nodes to vote in an election, then you can trigger race conditions, because then the wrong node could win an election. In most cases, it is best to wait for $n/2 + 1$ (where n is the number of nodes) votes before declaring a winner. However, this isn't true for certain cases; I'll visit those in a bit.

- **Largest LSN**: As you probably already know, the LSN measures how many transactions have been committed. The LSNs are incremented monotonically. The node with the maximum LSN, therefore, has the most committed transactions and is the preferred master. In an election, the largest LSN takes precedence over the assigned priorities. It is also used as a tiebreaker if two nodes get the same number of votes.

The `RepMgr::startElec` method runs an election. Listing 8-22 shows you how it is implemented.

Listing 8-22. *Running an Election*

```
162 int RepMgr::startElec()
163 {
164     DbUtils_SP utils = DbUtils::getInstance();
165     DbEnv *env = utils->getEnv();
166
167     int master = DB_EID_INVALID;
168     int priority;
169     int votes;
170     if(myId_ == 1)
171     {
172         priority = 100;
173         votes = 1;
174     }
175     else
176     {
177         priority = myReplica_->priority_;
178         votes = NUM_REPS/2 + 1;
179     }
180
181     while(master == DB_EID_INVALID)
182     {
183         try
184         {
185             env->rep_elect(NUM_REPS, votes,
186                             priority, 100, &master, 0);
187             ACE_DEBUG((LM_ERROR, "new master is %d\n",
188                                     master));
189             setMaster(master);
190             break;
191         }
192         catch(DbException& dbex)
193         {
194             env->err(dbex.get_errno(), "startElec");
195         }
196         ACE_DEBUG((LM_ERROR,
197             "startElec: unable to elect a master\n"));
198         ACE_OS::sleep(2);
199     }
200     return 0;
201 }
```

Have a look at some of the details of this code:

- **Line 167:** You initialize the master ID to DB_EID_INVALID, which is defined in the library to represent an invalid replica ID.

- **Lines 170–179**: In this example, you have three nodes with IDs 1, 2, and 3. You want the node with ID 1 to win the election, so you assign it the priority 100 and set the number of votes to 1. For all the other nodes, the priority is set to be the same as the ID, and the number of votes is set to n/2 + 1 (which evaluates to 2). With these settings, as soon as the node with ID 1 comes up, it immediately wins the election. All the other nodes have to win at least two votes to win an election. Note that this setup is equivalent to assigning a priority 0 to nodes 2 and 3, because they can never win an election.

- **Lines 181–199**: You call rep_elect until you get back an environment ID other than DB_EID_INVALID. The fourth argument in rep_elect is the amount of time in microseconds after which the library starts tallying votes for deciding the winner.

An election is conducted in two phases. In the first phase, all the nodes send out a message to every node known to them to ask them to participate in the election. The purpose of this phase is to find out how many nodes exist and will participate. The first phase ends either when the timeout (specified by the application through the rep_elect call) expires or when the library receives replies from nsites number of nodes (specified in the rep_elect call). In the second phase, each node that received a response from at least nvotes sites in the first phase votes for a site. The winner is declared on the basis of maximum votes. Since an election is restricted to a finite period, it's possible that no clear winner could be identified. When that happens, it's the responsibility of the application to run another election. That's the reason why, in the startElec function, you have to keep running election until a master is found.

Listing 8-23 shows the setMaster method that's called from line 189 in the starElec method in Listing 8-22.

Listing 8-23. *Setting the Master ID*

```
150 int RepMgr::setMaster(int envId)
151 {
152     ACE_WRITE_GUARD_RETURN(ACE_Recursive_Thread_Mutex,
153             g, masterMutex_, -1);
154     if(envId == myId_ && !isMaster())
155         beginRole(DB_REP_MASTER);
156     else
157         beginRole(DB_REP_CLIENT);
158     masterId_ = envId;
159     return 0;
160 }
```

This method is quite simple; it just invokes beginRep with the correct role. You could've done this in the startElec method also, but since you can sometimes find out about the master environment without running an election, you have to create a separate method. The startElec method is invoked on only one node, where it returns the ID of the master node when a master has been elected. So how do the other nodes comes to know that a master has been elected? The new master's ID is propagated to other nodes through a replication message, and the application comes to know about it when it processes the message using rep_process_message.

Replication Message Processing

All replication messages generated by the library are opaque to the application. The application either sends the messages to a peer or invokes rep_process_message to let the library handle them. However, since the application provides a significant part of the replication framework, it cannot be completely excluded from the processing. Whenever there's a situation in which the application has to take some action, the library returns a special return code from rep_process_message, allowing the application to finish the processing. Listing 8-24 shows these return codes.

Listing 8-24. *Processing a Replication Message*

```
551 int RepSession::processMsg(Dbt *control,
552         Dbt *rec, int *envId,
553         DbLsn *retLsn)
554 {
555     DbEnv *env = DbUtils::getEnv();
556     RepMgr *mgr = RepMgrSingleton::instance();
557     int res;
558     try
559     {
560         ACE_DEBUG((LM_ERROR, "processing msg from %d\n",
561                     *envId));
562         res = env->rep_process_message(control, rec,
563                 envId, retLsn);
564     }
565     catch(DbException& dbex)
566     {
567         env->err(dbex.get_errno(), "processMsg");
568         return -1;
569     }
570     switch(res)
571     {
572         case 0:
573             break;
574         case DB_REP_NEWSITE:
575             {
576                 int *repId = (int*)(rec->get_data());
577                 ACE_DEBUG((LM_ERROR,
578         "(%t)processMsg:received DB_REP_NEWSITE from %d\n",
579                 *repId));
580             }
581             break;
582         case DB_REP_HOLDELECTION:
583             mgr->startElec();
584             break;
```

```
585          case DB_REP_NEWMASTER:
586              mgr->setMaster(*envId);
587              ACE_DEBUG((LM_ERROR,
588                          "(%t) New master is %d\n",
589                          *envId));
590              break;
591          case DB_REP_ISPERM:
592              ACE_DEBUG((LM_ERROR,
593                "(%t)ISPERM returned for LSN[%d %d]\n",
594                retLsn->file, retLsn->offset));
595              break;
596          case DB_REP_NOTPERM:
597              ACE_DEBUG((LM_ERROR,
598                "(%t)NOTPERM returned for LSN[%d %d]\n",
599                retLsn->file, retLsn->offset));
600              break;
601          case DB_REP_DUPMASTER:
602              ACE_DEBUG((LM_ERROR,
603      "(%t)DUPMASTER received, launching election\n"));
604              mgr->beginRole(DB_REP_CLIENT);
605              mgr->startElec();
606              break;
607          case DB_REP_IGNORE:
608              ACE_DEBUG((LM_ERROR,
609                  "(%t)REP_IGNORE received\n"));
610              break;
611          case DB_REP_JOIN_FAILURE:
612              ACE_DEBUG((LM_ERROR,
613                  "(%t)JOIN_FAILURE received\n"));
614              break;
615          case DB_REP_STARTUPDONE:
616              ACE_DEBUG((LM_ERROR,
617                  "(%t)STARTUPDONE received\n"));
618              break;
619          default:
620              ACE_DEBUG((LM_ERROR,
621                "processMsg: unknown return code %d\n",
622                          res));
623              break;
624      }
625      return 0;
626 }
```

Let's go over each value returned by rep_process_message:

- DB_REP_NEWSITE: When a new node joins the environment by connecting to an existing node, the information is propagated to all other nodes whether or not the new node actually connects to them. In the example, if every node connects only to node 1 (rather than to every node), then node 1 will communicate with node 2 when node 3 connects to node 1. A node can use this return code to discover other nodes in the environment if it doesn't know about them in advance. This is a useful feature for dynamic environments where the number of nodes isn't fixed.

- DB_REP_NEWMASTER: This return code tells the application that a new master was elected. On a node where rep_elect wasn't called, this is how it comes to know that a new master was elected. When DB_REP_NEWMASTER is received by a node, it's the responsibility of the application layer to reconfigure the node in the correct role if the status of the node was changed. For example, if a node was running as a client and through this return code it was informed that it won the election, it should call rep_start with the role set to DB_REP_MASTER. This is done in the setMaster method.

- DB_REP_ISPERM: The library returns this code when it's successfully able to apply an update, sent in the message tagged with the flag DB_REP_PERMANENT, permanently. The word *permanently* may mean writing to the disk if the environment is so configured. Replication messages that contain data to be written to the database are sent with the DB_REP_PERMANENT flag. It's possible that the receiving environment isn't able to apply the change to the local environment due to an out-of-order delivery of the message or irreconcilable differences between the sending and receiving environments. However, if nothing of the sort happens, the library will return DB_REP_ISPERM. With this return code, the library also returns the LSN that it tried to apply to the local environment. The application can use the returned LSN to measure the progress of replication sync-up on the receiving node. The sending node can also use the returned LSN to determine if the changes being sent to the client are getting applied successfully. If the application requires that the clients be synced up every time a transaction is committed on the master, the master should wait for the clients to report an LSN with the DB_REP_ISPERM return code, which is greater than or equal to the one the master sent with the DB_REP_PERMANENT flag. Since the LSNs are generated sequentially, and since the library guarantees that it has successfully applied all the smaller LSNs if it reports DB_REP_ISPERM for a certain LSN, then a particular application thread on the master can assume that its LSN was applied successfully if the client reports DB_REP_ISPERM for a bigger LSN. DB_REP_ISPERM may not be returned for every LSN applied to the local environment. Sometimes, due to an out-of-order message, an LSN may arrive before it should have arrived. Later on, when all the missing LSNs are received, the library reports DB_REP_ISPERM only for the maximum LSN that it was able to apply successfully.

- DB_REP_NOTPERM: The library returns this code for a DB_REP_PERMANENT message if it was successfully processed the library but the change wasn't made permanent. That may happen if an LSN arrives out of order or if the local environment encountered a transaction that conflicts with an older transaction. The library returns the maximum LSN for which DB_REP_NOTPERM was reported.

- DB_REP_DUPMASTER: When the library detects that there are two or more masters in the group, it returns this error code to all the masters. When a master receives this error, it should reconfigure the environment as a client through DbEnv::rep_start with DB_REP_CLIENT as the role, and then it should call an election.

- DB_REP_IGNORE: The library returns this error code when the replication message cannot be processed, because it is irrelevant to the current state of the local environment. The application doesn't have to take any action on this. This feature was added in version 4.4.x.

- DB_REP_JOIN_FAILURE: When a new node joins a replication group, it tries to sync up its local environment with the latest state on the master. If the client tries to join with an existing local environment that was never (or not for a long time) a part of the replication environment, then it will have LSNs that clash with those on the master. The library tries to roll back the conflicting LSNs from the client environment, but if there is no similarity between the two environments, then every transaction on the client could be thrown out. When the differences in the environment are irreconcilable, then the library returns the DB_REP_JOIN_FAILURE error. The application then has to decide how to resolve the problem. It can either decide to not join the environment at all or it can clean up the existing environment by joining the replicated environment again. This return code was added in version 4.4.x.

- DB_REP_STARTUPDONE: When a new node joins a replicated environment, the master records the difference between latest LSN on the client and itself. This difference indicates the amount of sync-up that the client has to do to *catch up* with the master. When the client reaches that LSN, the library returns DB_REP_STARTUPDONE to the application. The application can use this return code to let the application threads start querying the database. Note that if new updates are being made on the master while the client it syncing up, the client may never be able to catch up with respect to the new updates. However, when the client catches up with the state that existed when it joined the environment, it may be a good time to let the application threads start using the environment. Because of the way LSNs are generated, it's impossible to determine whether the startup was done on the client if new transactions aren't happening on the master. Therefore, you shouldn't depend on this return code on the client to determine if it has caught up. A better way to determine sync-up is to find out the next expected LSN on the master when the client joins and then check the next expected LSN on the client periodically to see if it has exceeded the LSN recorded on the master. To do something like this, you would need to add another message of your own to the communication protocol. The next expected LSN is available from DbEnv::rep_stat method.

■Note The `rep_process_message` method may return values other than the ones listed. The values listed here are only the ones returned by the library. System errors such as "File not found," "Permission Denied," and so on may not be caught by the library and may be passed through to the application. Handling all possible error conditions within the library and returning database-specific error codes isn't always possible. You may have to do some investigative work to troubleshoot such errors. If you find that the library doesn't handle a valid error condition, you should report that to Oracle support at `https://metalink.oracle.com/`. They might add a new error code in the next upcoming release.

Opening Databases in a Replicated Environment

One final thing that you need to do before trying out the replication framework, that you've built, is to change the way databases are opened. You've been opening the databases in the `DbUtils::loadDbs` method. Listing 8-25 shows how you have to change that method to work in a replicated environment.

Listing 8-25. *loadDbs for a Replicated Environment*

```
187 void DbUtils::loadDbs(int role)
188 {
189     DbMapIter it = dbMap_.begin();
190     for(; it != dbMap_.end(); ++it)
191     {
192         Db *db = it->second;
193         db->close(0);
194     }
195     ACE_DEBUG((LM_ERROR,
196                 "loadDbs: closed existing handles \n"));
197
198     int dbFlags = DB_THREAD;
199     if(role == DB_REP_MASTER)
200         dbFlags |= DB_CREATE;
201     else if(role == DB_REP_CLIENT)
202         dbFlags |= DB_RDONLY;
203
204     bool opened = false;
205     for(int i=0; i < numDb; i++)
206     {
207         DbDesc dd = dbDescArr[i];
208         ACE_DEBUG((LM_ERROR,
209                     "(%t)opening %s\n",
210                     dd.dbName));
211         Db *db = new Db(&dbEnv_, 0);
212         DbTxn *txn;
213         opened = false;
214         while(!opened)
215         {
```

```
216              try
217              {
218                  dbEnv_.txn_begin(NULL, &txn, 0);
219                  db->set_pagesize(512);
220                  if(dd.isSec)
221                  {
222                      db->set_flags(DB_DUPSORT);
223                      db->open(txn, dd.dbName, NULL ,
224                              DB_BTREE, dbFlags, 0644);
225                      opened = true;
226                      DbMapIter it = dbMap_.find(dd.primaryId);
227                      if(it != dbMap_.end())
228                      {
229                          Db *primary = it->second;
230                          primary->associate(txn, db,
231                                  DbUtils::getSecKey, 0);
232                      }
233                      else
234                      {
235                          ACE_DEBUG((LM_ERROR,
236                                      "unknonw primary db %d\n",
237                                      dd.primaryId));
238                          throw;
239                      }
240                  }
241                  else
242                  {
243                      db->open(txn, dd.dbName, NULL ,
244                              DB_BTREE, dbFlags, 0644);
245                      opened = true;
246                  }
247                  txn->commit(0);
248                  dbMap_[dd.id] = db;
249              }
250          catch(DbException &txn_ex)
251          {
252              txn->abort();
253              dbEnv_.err(txn_ex.get_errno(), "loadDbs");
254          }
255          if(!opened)
256              ACE_OS::sleep(2);
257      }
258  }
259
260  if(role == DB_REP_MASTER)
261  {
262      ACE_DEBUG((LM_ERROR,
```

```
263                          "loadDbs: going to load default data \n"));
264           for(int i=0; i < numDb; i++)
265           {
266               DbDesc dd = dbDescArr[i];
267               if(!dd.isSec)
268                   load(dd.fileName, dd.dbName, dd.id);
269           }
270       }
271       if(opened)
272           initDbDone_ = true;
273 }
```

Databases in a replicated environment have to be reopened when the role of a node changes. When a node is running as a client, the databases are read-only; when the node is running as a master, there is no restriction. Let's see how you can achieve that. The following list details the key lines of code in the new version of DbUtils::loadDbs:

- **Lines 189–194**: First close all the open database handles. When you call loadDbs for the first time, you won't have any open handles; therefore, the map will be empty. Subsequent invocations will only be made when the role of a node changes.

- **Lines 198–200**: If this is the master node, then you specify DB_CREATE so that the database can be created if it doesn't already exist.

- **Lines 201–202**: If this is a client node, then you specify the DB_RDONLY flag. It isn't mandatory to open the databases on the client in read-only mode; the library will allow you to open them in read-write mode. This won't result in any inconsistency in the database, because the library will return an error (EACCES) if you try to modify the database on the client. However, it's still better to explicitly open the database on the client in read-only mode, because if the role of the node changes, then you can prevent the application from modifying the database during the syncing-up phase. You can reopen the databases in the read-write mode once you know that the environment has synced up. Versions later than 4.5.x do a pretty good job at preventing write access on a client. Versions older than 4.5.x did not prevent write access on clients during sync-up.

- **Lines 214–257**: If you get an exception while opening the databases, then retry until you can open the databases. Note that on the client, you haven't specified DB_CREATE. Therefore, until the databases are synced up from the master, you may not have the database files, if the client is syncing up for the first time on the client.

- **Lines 248–256**: You load the default database only if this is the master node.

The rest of the method is the same as before.

Running the Example Code

You have everything you need to run the replicated transactional data store. If you're going to run the replicas on the same machine, then you'll have to create three environment directories on the same machine, like this:

```
hy@linux:~/ws/from_svn/trunk/chap_8> mkdir chap8_env_1
hy@linux:~/ws/from_svn/trunk/chap_8> mkdir chap8_env_2
hy@linux:~/ws/from_svn/trunk/chap_8> mkdir chap8_env_3
```

To distinguish the replicas, you pass the replica ID as a command-line argument. To track the debug output from each replica, it would be better if you start them from separate windows. Let's start the first one and see what happens:

```
hy@linux:~/ws/from_svn/trunk/chap_8> ./rep_tds 1
connect:: id 2  127.0.0.1  4000
(1083095984)rep id -2:connection closed
connect::res is -1
(1083095984) error connecting to 127.0.0.1 4000
connect:: id 3  127.0.0.1  5000
(1083095984)rep id -2:connection closed
connect::res is -1
(1083095984) error connecting to 127.0.0.1 5000
(1078942816)send: msgId 2 eid -1 cntlLen 28, recLen 4
repSend: no conn availbale for 2
repSend: no conn availbale for 3
loadDbs: closed existing handles
loadDbs: going to load Dbs
(1078942816) loaded Dbs
(1078942816) done beginRole
(14795:1078942816) chap8_ex errMsg: DB_ENV->rep_elect:WARNING: ➡
nvotes (1) is sub-majority with nsites (3)
(1078942816)send: msgId 2 eid -1 cntlLen 28, recLen 20
repSend: no conn availbale for 2
repSend: no conn availbale for 3
new master is 1
(1078942816)send: msgId 2 eid -1 cntlLen 28, recLen 0
repSend: no conn availbale for 2
repSend: no conn availbale for 3
-
-
```

First, the communication framework is set up. Attempts are made to establish connections with replicas 2 and 3, but they fail because you haven't started them yet. Next, an attempt is made to send a message to environment ID -1 (which is DB_EID_BROADCAST). This happens when you call rep_start in the code. Since you are not connected to any other replicas, the send fails. After calling rep_start, you call loadDbs and then call an election. The library returns a warning when you start the election:

```
DB_ENV->rep_elect:WARNING: nvotes (1) is sub-majority with nsites (3)
```

For replica 1, you've set the nvotes parameter to 1, while nsites is set to 3. The library prints this warning, because 1 is less than nsites/2 + 1, and the election result may not be reliable. However, since you want to make replica 1 the master, you're fine. After the election, you'll see multiple messages like this one:

```
(1078942816)send: msgId 2 eid -1 cntlLen 28, recLen 20
```

The library sends these messages to the peers to conduct the election. You'll see that the application finds the new master after this:

```
new master is 1
```

Let's now start replica 2 and observe what happens for replica 2:

```
connect:: id 1  127.0.0.1  3000
(1083095984) open: connected to 127.0.0.1 3000
(1083095984)OPEN:: connected to 1
connect::res is 0
(1083095984)send: msgId 1 eid 1 cntlLen 0, recLen 0
repSend: added to send queue of 1
connect:: id 3  127.0.0.1  5000
(1083095984)rep id -2:connection closed
connect::res is -1
(1083095984) error connecting to 127.0.0.1 5000
(1083095984)rep id 1: 28 bytes sent
(1078942816)send: msgId 2 eid -1 cntlLen 28, recLen 4
repSend: added to send queue of 1
repSend: no conn availbale for 3
loadDbs: closed existing handles
loadDbs: going to load Dbs
(1078942816) loaded Dbs
(1078942816) done beginRole
(1083095984)rep id 1: 60 bytes sent
(1085197232)handle_input: rep id 1:recLen 4 cntlLen 28
processing msg from 1
(1078942816)send: msgId 2 eid -1 cntlLen 28, recLen 20
repSend: added to send queue of 1
repSend: no conn availbale for 3
 (1085197232)rep id 1: 56 bytes sent
```

```
(1085197232)handle_input: rep id 1:recLen 0 cntlLen 28
processing msg from 1
(1083095984)rep id 1: 76 bytes sent
new master is 1
(1085197232)send: msgId 2 eid 1 cntlLen 28, recLen 0
(1083095984)rep id 1: 56 bytes sent
repSend: added to send queue of 1
(1078942816)send: msgId 2 eid -1 cntlLen 28, recLen 0
repSend: added to send queue of 1
repSend: no conn availbale for 3
(1078942816) done beginRole
(1083095984)rep id 1: 56 bytes sent
(1085197232)send: msgId 2 eid -1 cntlLen 28, recLen 0
repSend: added to send queue of 1
repSend: no conn available for 3
(1085197232) done beginRole
(1085197232) New master is 1
(1083095984)rep id 1: 56 bytes sent
(1085197232)handle_input: rep id 1:recLen 0 cntlLen 28
processing msg from 1
(1083095984)handle_input: rep id 1:recLen 24 cntlLen 28
processing msg from 1
(1085197232)handle_input: rep id 1:recLen 44 cntlLen 28
processing msg from 1
connect:: id 3  127.0.0.1  5000
(1083095984)rep id -2:connection closed
connect::res is -1
(1083095984) error connecting to 127.0.0.1 5000
(1085197232)ISPERM returned for LSN[1 64]
(1083095984)handle_input: rep id 1:recLen 36 cntlLen 28
processing msg from 1
-

-
processing msg from 1
(1083095984)handle_input: rep id 1:recLen 32 cntlLen 28
processing msg from 1
(1083095984)ISPERM returned for LSN[1 7656]
(1085197232)handle_input: rep id 1:recLen 4 cntlLen 28
processing msg from 1
(1083095984)handle_input: rep id 1:recLen 4 cntlLen 28
-

-
```

You'll notice that when replica 2 comes up, it immediately gets connected to replica 1 and starts exchanging messages with it. When replica 1 came up, no other node was available:

```
-
(1083095984)rep id 1: 60 bytes sent
(1085197232)handle_input: rep id 1:recLen 4 cntlLen 28
processing msg from 1
-
```

The message exchange continues, and replica 1 informs replica 2 that a master exists. Once the master is identified, the sync-up process starts. You'll see messages like the following:

```
-
processing msg from 1
(1083095984)handle_input: rep id 1:recLen 32 cntlLen 28
processing msg from 1
(1083095984)ISPERM returned for LSN[1 7656]
-
```

The ISPERM return code indicates that the library received a permanent record. The master sends permanent records when the client expresses the desire to sync up to the master. This goes on until the client syncs up. Let's look at what happens on replica 1 after replica 2 comes up:

```
-
-
(1085197232) error connecting to 127.0.0.1 5000
(1083095984) open: connected to 127.0.0.1 3384
(1085197232)handle_input:OPEN::received first msg from 2
handle_input: added 2 to map
(1085197232)handle_input: rep id 2:recLen 4 cntlLen 28
processing msg from 2
(1085197232)send: msgId 2 eid -1 cntlLen 28, recLen 4
repSend: added to send queue of 2
repSend: no conn available for 3
(1085197232)send: msgId 2 eid -1 cntlLen 28, recLen 0
repSend: added to send queue of 2
repSend: no conn available for 3
(1085197232)processMsg:received DB_REP_NEWSITE from 2
(1083095984)rep id 2: 60 bytes sent
(1083095984)rep id 2: 56 bytes sent
(1083095984)handle_input: rep id 2:recLen 20 cntlLen 28
processing msg from 2
(1085197232)handle_input: rep id 2:recLen 0 cntlLen 28
processing msg from 2
(1085197232)send: msgId 2 eid -1 cntlLen 28, recLen 0
repSend: added to send queue of 2
```

```
repSend: no conn available for 3
(1083095984)rep id 2: 56 bytes sent
(1083095984)handle_input: rep id 2:recLen 0 cntlLen 28
processing msg from 2
(1083095984)send: msgId 2 eid 2 cntlLen 28, recLen 24
repSend: added to send queue of 2
-
-
(1085197232)rep id 2: 80 bytes sent
(1085197232)rep id 2: 100 bytes sent
(1085197232)rep id 2: 92 bytes sent
(1085197232)rep id 2: 94 bytes sent
(1085197232)rep id 2: 622 bytes sent
-
-
```

Replica 2 receives a connection from replica 1. It also receives the DB_REP_NEWSITE from the rep_process_message. Since replica 1 already knows about replica 2, this isn't very useful, but the library informs the application about the new site anyway.

You know that the client and the master are exchanging messages, but you still don't know what's happening as a result of it. Remember that you open the databases on the client without the DB_CREATE flag, and you don't load the default databases on the clients. Therefore, the databases cannot get created on replica 2 unless they're synced up from the master. Let's look at the environment directory of replica 2 after the message exchange stops:

```
hy@linux:~/ws/from_svn/trunk/chap_8/chap8_env_2> ls -al
total 10820
drwxr-xr-x  2 hy users       440 2006-05-16 00:12 .
drwxr-xr-x  8 hy users      1456 2006-05-16 00:30 ..
-rw-r--r--  1 hy users      1024 2006-05-16 00:12 Account_Db
-rw-r--r--  1 hy users      1024 2006-05-16 00:12 Bank_Db
-rw-r-----  1 hy users     24576 2006-05-16 00:12 __db.001
-rw-r-----  1 hy users    278528 2006-05-16 00:12 __db.002
-rw-r-----  1 hy users    270336 2006-05-16 00:12 __db.003
-rw-r-----  1 hy users   1146880 2006-05-16 00:12 __db.004
-rw-r-----  1 hy users    352256 2006-05-16 00:12 __db.005
-rw-r-----  1 hy users     16384 2006-05-16 00:12 __db.006
-rw-r-----  1 hy users      8192 2006-05-16 00:12 __db.rep.db
-rw-------  1 hy users         4 2006-05-16 00:12 __db.rep.egen
-rw-r-----  1 hy users  10485760 2006-05-16 00:12 log.0000000001
-rw-r--r--  1 hy users      1024 2006-05-16 00:12 Person_Db
-rw-r--r--  1 hy users      1024 2006-05-16 00:12 Person_Dob_Db
-rw-r--r--  1 hy users      1024 2006-05-16 00:12 Person_Name_Db
hy@linux:~/ws/from_svn/trunk/chap_8/chap8_env_2>
```

The database files indeed got created! It looks like replication may be working. However, just because you see all the data files doesn't mean that the client has actually received all the data from the master. Of course, you can do a db_dump on all the databases and compare the entries with those on the master, but that's impractical if you have a large amount of data in the databases. The library should report DB_REP_STARTUPDONE when the client has caught up with the master, but as I've mentioned, that isn't returned unless new transactions have been committed after the sync-up started. You can find out about the progress of replication from the db_stat utility with the -r option. You should first run it for the master environment to find the next expected LSN:

```
hy@linux:~/ws/from_svn/trunk/chap_8/chap8_env_1> db_stat -r
Environment configured as a replication master
1/7700   Next LSN to be used
0/0      Not waiting for any missed log records
0        Next page number expected.
0        Not waiting for any missed pages.
0        Number of duplicate master conditions detected.
1        Current environment ID
100      Current environment priority
2        Current generation number
3        Current election generation number
0        Number of duplicate log records received
0        Number of log records currently queued
0        Maximum number of log records ever queued at once
0        Total number of log records queued
-
-
```

The master expects the next LSN to be 1/7700. Note that db_stat also reports the role of the node in the first line. Now run db_stat for the client:

```
hy@linux:~/ws/from_svn/trunk/chap_8/chap8_env_2> db_stat -r
Environment configured as a replication client
1/7700   Next LSN expected
0/0      Not waiting for any missed log records
0        Next page number expected.
0        Not waiting for any missed pages.
0        Number of duplicate master conditions detected.
2        Current environment ID
2        Current environment priority
2        Current generation number
3        Current election generation number
0        Number of duplicate log records received
0        Number of log records currently queued
-
-
```

You can see that the client reports the same next LSN: 1/7700. This means that the client and the master have indeed synced up.

Experimenting with the Code Example

Replication is such a vast topic that it isn't possible to discuss every possible configuration in a single chapter. The code example that you've developed provides a good test bed where you can try out various replication configurations. You might want to try out some of these exercises:

- Add more replicas by adding more entries in REP_INFO_ARR. This will help you understand how well the framework scales when you increase the number of replicas.

- Modify the connection topology so that not every node connects to every other, and then experiment with killing one or more replicas. You can modify the beginRep method so that every node only connects to one of the nodes when the communication framework is being initialized.

- Try out different priorities for each node and see how that affects the elections.

- Try different values for the nvotes, timeout, and nsite parameters in rep_elect.

- Use the cdata parameter in the rep_start method and the rep_process_message method to pass more information about a node, so that the nodes can connect to each other even when they don't have prior information about each other. That is how nodes connect in dynamic replication groups.

- Kill the master and see if a client assumes the master role. If that doesn't happen, investigate why it didn't happen. Perhaps the node priorities or nvotes and nsite values weren't set correctly to let a client become a master.

- Run the replicas on different machines, and observe how the network affects replication. Try out different types of network outages to see if the replicas are still able to discover each other.

- Add an acknowledgement mechanism in the RepMsgr::send method so that for every message with the DB_REP_PERMANENT flag, the application thread has to wait until the peer returns DB_REP_ISPERM for an LSN bigger or equal to the LSN associated with the message.

Network Partitions

A *network partition* happens when a replication group gets divided into two or more disjointed groups due to a lack of network connectivity. Figure 8-10 shows a replication group of seven nodes.

Node B is the master, and the rest of the nodes are clients. Due to a network problem, node E loses connectivity with node B, which results in nodes E, F, and G forming a replication group of their own. Nodes E, F, and G think that they're the only nodes left in the group, and they end up electing another master, E. However, nodes A, B, C, and D think that E, F, and G are no longer available. Network partitions can be nasty, because if both B and E modify the databases while the partition exists, then you end up with conflicts in the database. When connectivity is restored between the two groups, updates on one of the masters will have to be thrown away.

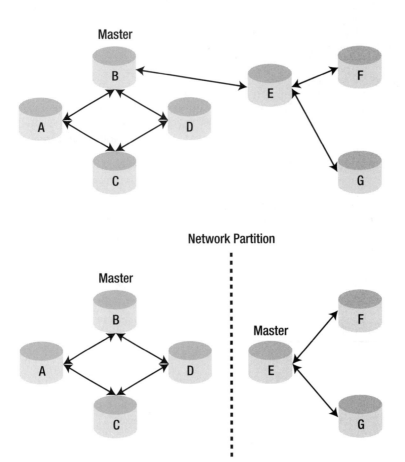

Figure 8-10. *Network partition of a replication group*

Recovering from a Network Partition

Berkeley DB allows replication groups to recover from network partitions. When the partitioned groups regain connectivity, the library detects that there are two masters. It returns DB_REP_DUPMASTER to the two master nodes. When that happens, the masters should reconfigure themselves as clients using rep_start with the role set to DB_REP_CLIENT, and then they should hold an election. The library will try to reconcile the databases on the two masters. If too many updates happen during the partition, then reconciliation may not be possible. The library will return a DB_REP_JOINFAILURE error if reconciliation fails. The application has to intervene in that case by cleaning up the databases on one of the masters.

Preventing Network Partitions

Partitions happen when sites aren't interconnected sufficiently. If every node connects to every other node, partitions will happen rarely. However, with a large number of nodes, connecting all nodes to all other nodes may not be possible. Another way to prevent a partition is to always conduct elections with the nvotes parameter set to n/2 + 1 (where *n* is the number of nodes). That will ensure that only one master will exist in the group with more than half the nodes.

The Degenerate Case

In some fault-tolerant systems, there are only two nodes in the replication group. With only two nodes, it's impossible to enforce the n/2 + 1 rule for elections, because then the failover would never happen. When the client loses connection with the master, if you conduct an election with nvotes set to n/2 + 1 (which evaluates to 2), then the client will never be able to win an election and take over as the master. For two-node systems, you have to decide, based on the needs of the application, when to declare the client as the master. You can follow these steps to allow the client to take over as the master:

1. Start an election with nvotes set to n/2 + 1.

2. If the election fails, keep running elections with n/2 + 1 until an application-defined time-out expires or the master can be contacted. That basically allows the client to "search" for the master for some amount of time.

3. If the master cannot be reached, then set nvotes to 1 and run the final election. This allows the client to assume the master role.

It's possible that the master didn't actually crash when the client took over as the master, but instead was just unreachable due to a network error. In this case, you'll end up with a network partition and will have to recover from that using the procedure described earlier.

Transactional Guarantees

In Berkeley DB, the granularity of replication is the transaction. Whenever a transaction is committed in the master environment, the library invokes the replication transport callback to deliver the update information to all the clients. The callback is executed in the context of the application thread that made the modification. The application thread, therefore, waits until the callback returns. The callback should return a nonzero value if either the delivery fails or a client is unable to apply the message permanently to its environment. If the callback returns an error (a nonzero value), the library will try to flush the transaction logs to the disk if the environment hasn't been configured for synchronous flushing of the transaction logs (by setting the DB_TXN_NOSYNC flag). The rationale behind this behavior is that if the client isn't able to apply the transaction permanently, then it should at least be made permanent on the master, so that the transaction isn't lost if the master fails. However, if the master isn't configured with DB_TXN_NOSYNC, then the return code from the callback will be ignored, because then the transactions will be flushed synchronously by default.

A common misunderstanding about the return value from the callback method is that if the callback returns a nonzero value, then the library will undo or roll back the transaction on the master. The transaction on the master is *never* rolled back, whether or not the client was able to apply the transaction. The replication callback is invoked only after the transaction has been committed in the master environment. There is no concept of a two-phase commit during replication, where a transaction is first prepared and then committed after all the clients have committed it. There is very little you can do if replication fails on the client. You have only the following options:

- **Block the application thread until the client can actually apply the transaction**: The associated LSN can identify the transaction. If the client reports that it was able to permanently apply an LSN greater than or equal to the one associated with the transaction, then you can assume the transaction was made permanent on the client. By blocking the thread, you can also trigger some kind of throttling mechanism in the application so that no new updates are made until the problem with the client is resolved.

- **Verify that another client was able to make the transaction permanent**: This way, you at least have one copy safe somewhere other than the master environment.

- **Start diagnostic procedures on the client that couldn't apply the transaction**: Maybe report the problem to the monitoring application, if that's available. It's possible that the disk might be full on the client or that its environment may be completely out of sync.

It's up to the application to determine when these corrective procedures should kick in. This could happen when a specified number of clients report an error or when any one client reports a problem. If you want to build a replicated application that's highly redundant, then you should ensure that a number of clients make the transactions permanent before returning from the callback. Usually, though, even if one client is successful in making the transaction permanent, you can safely return success from the callback.

Replication Manager Interface

In release 4.5.x, a new easy-to-use replication manager interface, called repmgr, was added to the replication API. The rationale behind the addition of this interface was that since a vast majority of application developers implement the replication framework using TCP/IP sockets, even though the library allows them to use just about any protocol and any communication transport, why not make a TCP/IP-based implementation a part of the library. As you must have realized, if you didn't skip directly to this section, building the replication manager using the base replication API isn't a trivial task. The repmgr interface will save you a lot of effort if you can live with a TCP/IP-based implementation, but it doesn't provide the kind of flexibility available in the base API. I'll go over the limitations a bit later in this section, but first let's take a look at the interface.

The repmgr interface provides the three components needed for implementing a replicated database using Berkeley DB: the communication framework, the node-management framework, and the threading framework. Table 8-2 describes the repmgr API. The difficult-to-build components needed for setting up the replication framework are available ready-made from the interface. All that you need to do is tell repmgr the IP addresses of the nodes present in the replicated group and start replicating. That's pretty much it. In reality, you'll need to tune the interface a little bit, but that's nothing compared to what you have to go through when using the base API.

Table 8-2. *The repmgr API*

API	Description
DbEnv::repmgr_set_local_site	The application uses this method to provide the local IP address and the local port information to the library.
DbEnv::repmgr_add_remote_site	The application uses this method to provide the IP addresses and ports of the other nodes to the library.
DbEnv::repmgr_set_ack_policy	The application uses this method to configure the replication-message acknowledgement policy.
DbEnv::repmgr_start	The application uses this method to start the replication manager.
DbEnv::repmgr_site_list	The application uses this method to retrieve the list of nodes and their status.
DbEnv::set_rep_limit	The application uses this method to set the various types of limits in the replication framework.

Notice that the set_rep_limit method is also present in the base API. Both the base API and the repmgr API use this method to set the limits of various replication parameters. Other than this method, the two APIs are completely independent of each other. Internally, the repmgr interface uses the base API methods. Listing 8-26 shows you how to retrofit the code example you developed earlier with the repmgr API.

Listing 8-26. *Using the Default Communication Framework*

```
28 int main(int argc, char **argv)
29 {
30     if(argc < 2)
31     {
32         ACE_DEBUG((LM_ERROR,
33                     "Insufficient arguments\n"));
34         exit(0);
35     }
36     DbUtils::repId_ = atoi(argv[1]);
37     try
38     {
39         DbUtils_SP utils = DbUtils::getInstance();
40         DbEnv *env = utils->getEnv();
41         RepInfo ri = REP_INFO_ARR[repId_];
42         env->rep_set_priority(ri.priority);
43         env->repmgr_set_local_site(ri.ip, ri.port, 0);
44         for(int i = 0; i < NUM_REP; i++)
45         {
46             RepInfo ri = REP_INFO_ARR[i];
47             if(ri.id != repId_)
48                 env->repmgr_set_remote_site(env,
```

```
49                                       ri.ip, ri.port, 0);
50          }
51          env->repmgr_set_ack_policy(DB_REPMGR_ACKS_ALL);
52          env->repmgr_start(2, DB_REP_ELECTION);
53      }
54      catch(DbException& dbex)
55      {
56          ACE_DEBUG((LM_ERROR,
57                      "caught DbException in main %d\n",
58                      dbex.get_errno()));
59      }
60      catch(...)
61      {
62          ACE_DEBUG((LM_ERROR, "unknown exception caught\n"));
63      }
64 }
```

Listing 8-26 shows a modified version of the tds.cc file. Earlier, you used the main in this file to launch the replication framework you developed yourself. The code in Listing 8-26 is all that you need to run a fully functional TCP/IP-based replication framework. Let's go over the new implementation:

- **Line 41**: You can continue to use REP_INFO_ARR that you created earlier to store the node information statically. You use the repId passed as an argument to locate the IP address and port information of the local node.

- **Line 42**: You set the priority of the local node. The purpose here is the same as in the base API.

- **Line 43**: You set the IP address and port information of the local node.

- **Lines 44–50**: You iterate through REP_INFO_ARR and add all nodes, except for the local node, as remote nodes.

- **Line 51**: You set the acknowledgement policy for the replication messages. The acknowledgement policy tells the library how many acknowledgements it should wait for before returning the control from the send callback. I'll discuss the other available options a bit later.

- **Line 52**: repmgr is started. The repmgr_start method takes two arguments. The first argument is the number of threads that repmgr will use internally. The second argument indicates the initial role of the local node. I'll discuss this method in detail later in this section.

Even a simple interface such as repmgr has to be tuned. You can never escape tuning, can you? Now let's go over the tunable parameters of the repmgr interface.

Tunable Parameters

As you can see from Listing 8-26, two methods require tunable parameters: repmgr_set_ack_policy and repmgr_start. Let's go over these methods in detail.

repmgr_set_ack_policy

This method takes just one argument, which specifies how a node waits for replication message acknowledgements from other nodes. Earlier in the chapter, I discussed in detail how acknowledgements are used to ensure the transactional guarantee of a replicated environment. The method allows you to select the right acknowledgement model for the application. Let's look at the available options (quoted here from the Berkeley DB API reference):

- DB_REPMGR_ACKS_ALL: The master should wait until all replication clients have acknowledged each permanent replication message.

- DB_REPMGR_ACKS_ALL_PEERS: The master should wait until all electable peers have acknowledged each permanent replication message (where *electable peer* means a client capable of being subsequently elected master of the replication group).

- DB_REPMGR_ACKS_NONE: The master should not wait for any client replication message acknowledgments.

- DB_REPMGR_ACKS_ONE: The master should wait until at least one client site has acknowledged each permanent replication message.

- DB_REPMGR_ACKS_ONE_PEER: The master should wait until at least one electable peer has acknowledged each permanent replication message (where *electable peer* means a client capable of being subsequently elected master of the replication group).

- DB_REPMGR_ACKS_QUORUM: The master should wait until it has received acknowledgements from the minimum number of electable peers sufficient to ensure that the effect of the permanent record remains durable if an election is held (where *electable peer* means a client capable of being subsequently elected master of the replication group). This is the default acknowledgement policy.

This is a pretty comprehensive list that can satisfy almost any application requirement. The only limitation is that the acknowledgement policy has to be the same on all the nodes in a replication group. Applications usually don't require a different acknowledgement policy on different nodes. The only reason why you may want a different policy on different nodes is if you have machines of varying reliability in your replication group. Then you may want to wait for more acknowledgements on less reliable nodes.

repmgr_start

This method has two tunable parameters: the number of threads, and the role of the node. The parameter for the number of threads lets you configure the number of threads that the repmgr interface will use to process replication messages. Note that the total number of threads used by the interface will be more than the number you set here, because a few threads are created by default for carrying out other repmgr tasks. There is no formula for finding out the right number of threads for your application. Having more threads will help if the database updates that are getting replicated are happening in different parts of the database, so that they don't block each other.

The flags argument in the method is used to indicate the initial role of a node when replication is initialized. The available options are listed here (quoted from the Berkeley DB API reference).

- DB_REP_MASTER: Start as a master site, and do not call an election. Note there must never be more than a single master in any replication group, and only one site at a time should ever be started with the DB_REP_MASTER flag specified.

- DB_REP_CLIENT: Start as a client site, and do not call for an election.

- DB_REP_ELECTION: Start as a client, and call for an election if no master is found.

- DB_REP_FULL_ELECTION: Run a single special election on startup, where a master will only be confirmed if all members of the replication group vote. Subsequent elections will revert to only requiring a simple majority to elect a new master.

As I've mentioned earlier in the chapter, usually the best option is to start every node as a client and run an election to find the node with the most current database, if your environment has more than one node that can become a master. If you have only one node that runs as the master all the time, then there is no point in running an election.

Limitations

Interface design is an exercise in trade-offs. In other words, there is no free lunch. The simplicity provided by the repmgr interface comes at the cost of reduced flexibility. Following are the main limitations of the repmgr interface.

- **No security**: The TCP/IP-based communication framework is built using an unencrypted Sockets API. If you don't want your replication messages to be snooped upon, you will have to either write your own Secure Sockets Layer (SSL)-based communication framework or run the replication traffic over an encrypted tunnel, such as a virtual private network (VPN).

- **POSIX threads**: The interface uses POSIX threads internally. While POSIX is the most widely used and the most widely supported threading standard, many applications use customized threading libraries. In the era of multicore CPUs, applications sometimes have to be built on customized threading frameworks, which can eek out the maximum performance.

- **The interface isn't exposed**: You could overcome the previous two limitations to a certain extent if the repmgr interface allowed you to access internal repmgr data structures and connection mechanisms.

- **No event notifications**: There's no way in the current API to register for receiving repmgr events such as "A new node was added," or "A node got disconnected." It's possible to query for the node status from the application code using repmgr_site_list, but this poll-based mechanism can be resource-intensive if the application needs real-time status information.

However, none of these limitations are serious. The main purpose of the new interface is to let a majority of users have a quick way to build and deploy replicated solutions. In that respect, the new interface delivers what it was supposed to deliver. Applications that need more sophisticated solutions can always the base API.

Summary

Replication is an extremely important feature of Berkeley DB. It lets you build fault tolerance, load balancing, and high availability into the application. Even though replication is available in most of the commercial database solutions, replication features available in Berkeley DB are unique. As with most of the other Berkeley DB features, the application layer can customize and configure the replication subsystem to a very high degree. The replication functionality in Berkeley DB has been designed so that it can work on any operating system, use any communication protocol, employ any kind of threading and synchronization model, and still offer a common code base for all solutions. That kind of flexibility is unprecedented in any other database solution.

The extreme flexibility comes at a price. The application has to provide many critical pieces of the replication framework. The application design and development effort in the case of Berkeley DB can be much bigger than that of an application using some other database if the TCP/IP-based default communication layer isn't used. For applications in which performance cannot be compromised at any cost, there aren't too many alternatives available other than Berkeley DB.

In the next chapter, I'll discuss distributed transactions, including some common applications of distributed transactions and replication. In many cases, the problem at hand can be solved by both distributed transactions and replication. I'll discuss such problems in particular and lay down some guidelines that will help you decide whether you should use replication or distributed transactions.

CHAPTER 9

Distributed Transactions and Data-Distribution Strategies

Adistributed transaction (XA) system allows different databases, and even different database engines, to participate in a single global transaction. As a result, you can update an employee record in DB2, update user preferences in Berkeley DB, and update payroll information in Oracle, all as part of a single, global distributed transaction.

This chapter will first discuss distributed transactions. You'll learn how to build a simple global transaction manager (GTM) and use it to execute transactions across multiple Berkeley DB environments. I'll then compare database replication with distributed transactions. Replication creates exact copies of databases, and as such, it is conceptually very different from XA. However, in a number of applications, it isn't necessarily apparent whether replication or XA would be the best option for distributing the data. I'll contrast the two approaches in several sections in the chapter. Finally, I'll analyze a few case studies that will help you understand the trade-offs involved in the two approaches.

Distributed Transactions

Traditionally, distributed transactions have been used to keep data in multiple independent databases logically consistent. For example, for organizational and control reasons, a company's IT department might keep track of user accounts, and the finance department might keep track of payroll. The two departments might be using different databases to do their jobs. When a new hire comes on board, both databases will have to be updated. Ideally, both databases should be updated as a part of a single transaction, because that guarantees that all employees will have user accounts and that the only people with user accounts are employees. In addition to the traditional use case, distributed transactions may also be needed for achieving one of these goals:

- **Fault tolerance**: Fault tolerance helps to avoid service disruption due to software or hardware failure. Distributing the database to a standby machine can allow a standby system to become active if the primary fails. You can achieve this through replication, but some applications need a way to roll back a transaction if replication fails. If that's the case, XA is the only alternative.

- **Load balancing**: Load balancing allows multiple machines to distribute the load of an overloaded system. By distributing the database to multiple servers, the load can be shared among them. This is commonly done by partitioning the data. For example, by putting employees whose names begin with A-M on server 1, and employees whose names begin with N-Z on server 2. Updates that need to touch both halves of the alphabet naturally need a distributed transaction.

- **Distributed deployment**: With the widespread use of outsourcing and global delivery models, the modern corporation is no longer a monolithic entity. It is quite common for a company to have databases and applications spread across multiple locations. In order to support such deployment scenarios, applications have to be designed in such a way that they can be deployed in distributed branch offices while still being managed from a centralized location. Distributed deployment is ultimately a data-distribution problem, and in most cases, it can only be solved with XA.

There two ways of achieving database distribution in Berkeley DB. You can either replicate the database or use distributed transactions. I've already discussed replication in the previous chapter. Now let's go over distributed transactions.

Properties of Distributed Transactions

As the name suggests, a distributed transaction is a transaction that spans multiple database instances (or *environments*, in Berkeley DB terminology). The database instances can be of the same or different types, and they may be running on the same or different machines. A transactional database, as you know, must provide the ACID properties. A distributed transactional system must provide the same. You can achieve ACIDity in a stand-alone database environment by writing a transaction log to the persistent store before *committing* a transaction. In a distributed transaction, you not only have to persist the transaction log, but you have to persist it in all the participating environments before the transaction can be marked as committed.

Let's think for a moment how you can do this. You have to ensure that all the participating environments have written the transaction log to the persistent store. To do this, you'll have to ask each environment to write the transaction log to the disk and then wait for each to report the status. If each is able to write the record to the disk successfully, then you can mark the transaction as committed. This would work if the write operation were to succeed in all the environments.

However, consider what would happen if the write operation failed in one or more environments. You would end up in a situation in which some environments have the transaction committed (as the transaction log is already written to the disk) and the rest have it aborted (as the transaction log could not be written to the disk). If you look at individual environments, you'll see that they're all consistent, but the overall distributed environment ends up being inconsistent. Clearly the trick of writing a log of the transaction to the disk, which works so well in a stand-alone environment, isn't good enough for a distributed environment.

Two-Phase Commit

It's evident that you need an intermediate stage between the *committed* and the *aborted* states to reliably commit a transaction simultaneously in multiple environments. A technique called the *two-phase commit* commits a transaction in two steps rather than just one, as demonstrated in Figure 9-1.

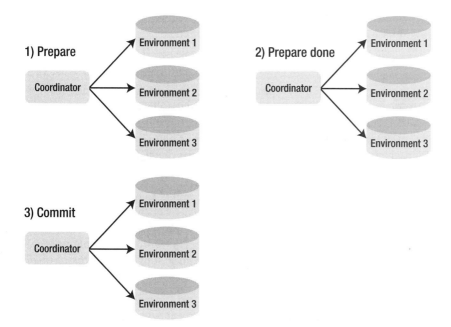

Figure 9-1. *Steps in a two-phase commit*

A two-phase commit requires an entity, called a *transaction monitor*, which is independent of the database environments participating in the distributed transaction. The coordinator first sends a *prepare* message to the participating environments. When an environment prepares a transaction, it actually writes a special log record called *prepare* to its transaction log. By writing the prepare message, the system guarantees that it will be able to commit subsequently. It's illegal for a participating database engine to ask to abort a prepared transaction, though the transaction monitor can require that if one of the participating engines is unable to prepare.

Note The difference between a prepared and a committed transaction is that the changes made to the database as a result of the prepared transaction aren't visible to the users of the database, whereas a committed change is visible.

The coordinator then waits for the participants to report back the results of the prepare command. If every one prepares the transaction successfully, the coordinator tells everyone to *commit*; otherwise, it asks everyone to *abort* the transaction. If the prepare fails on one or more environments, then the transaction is aborted everywhere. The additional intermediate state provided by the two-phase commit makes all the difference. The prepared state is permanent, like a committed transaction, but it's not visible to the outside world, allowing it to be rolled back safely if the commit fails. Most distributed transaction technologies are variants of the two-phase commit. The concept behind the two-phase commit is simple, but it's often difficult to implement it correctly. Not only is there an additional state to take care of, but there are also numerous variants that are difficult to quantify and handle correctly. The following are some of the common problems associated with distributed transactions:

- **Time-outs**: A two-phase commit is a synchronous protocol. The participating database engines, or *resource managers* (RMs), as they're called in the XA terminology, must all report back success or failure on the prepare step before the transaction monitor moves to the commit step. However, the RMs can all prepare in parallel and can all commit in parallel. If a particular environment doesn't report the progress due to a crash or a network problem, the entire system can hang. Therefore, the coordinator must apply reasonable time-outs for each step. Setting proper time-outs can be difficult, because there is no way to figure out the best time out value, other than by trial and error.

- **Deadlocks**: It's difficult to do deadlock detection and resolution in distributed transactions, because there is no central lock manager that can detect conflicts. You can build a central lock manager into the coordinator, but that can make it complicated. You can prevent deadlocks by acquiring locks according to a predefined order, but that might not always be possible. Usually, the GTM uses time-outs to abort long-running distributed transactions. This breaks deadlocks, but may also abort transactions that are making progress but are just slow.

- **Single point of failure**: The coordinator is the single point of failure. If the coordinator crashes, then the entire system will come to a halt until the coordinator can resume its activities. Therefore, the coordinator must be robust.

A good implementation of a distributed transaction framework is application-specific. It is practically impossible to design a framework that works well for all applications.

Distributed Transactions in Berkeley DB

Just like many other components, such as threading and IPC, which need to be customized for different applications and different platforms, the distributed transaction framework has been implemented minimally within Berkeley DB. The portions of the framework that require intimate knowledge of the application's environment have been left for the application developer to implement. Let's look at the components that Berkeley DB provides:

- **Prepare semantics**: A transaction within Berkeley DB can be *prepared* for commit in the context of a distributed transaction. You can use the DbTxn::prepare method to prepare a transaction.

- **Recover semantics**: When a database environment that participated in a distributed transaction crashes, it can use DbEnv::recover to get a list of prepared but uncommitted transactions present in the environment.

That's pretty much it. Using the terminology of the XA world, Berkeley DB is able to participate in a distributed transaction as a resource manager. Berkeley DB doesn't provide any of the other components needed to run distributed transactions. DbTxn::prepare and DbEnv::recover calls are all that's needed on a single resource manager. However, one main component that's missing is the coordinator. Let's see what a coordinator, or the GTM, has to do.

Managing the Global Transaction ID Namespace

In a database environment, local as well as global (or distributed) transactions may be taking place. Since you first have to prepare global transactions before you can commit them, and then you have to handle them differently during recovery, you need a way to distinguish them from local transactions. In addition, the IDs of the global transactions have to be unique across all the environments participating in the distributed transactions, because the GTM has to report the state of each global transaction during recovery. It's difficult to manage and generate these IDs from participating environments, because they usually don't communicate with each other. The GTM is the central coordinating entity that initiates, coordinates, and manages all the global transactions; therefore, it's the natural place for generating and managing the global transaction namespace.

Berkeley DB restricts the size of the *global IDs* (GIDs or XIDs) to 128 bytes, which is defined by the constant DB_XIDDATASIZE. There is no restriction on how the IDs are allocated. A GTM may choose to simply start from ID 1, and for each successive transaction, it can increment the ID by 1. Or, it can be more sophisticated and have the GID somehow indicate the environment IDs of the participating environments so that when an environment is recovering from a crash, the GTM can efficiently look up the transaction states from its database. A simple application that has to do just a few distributed transactions during its lifetime doesn't need to care too much about how the GIDs are allocated as long as they're unique. On the other hand, for an application that has to perform millions of distributed transactions, the GTM should divide the GID namespace such that it's easy to index the GIDs according to environment IDs, timestamps, and so on. The GTM should also have access to a database to store the GIDs. Because the GID namespace management is so application-specific, Berkeley DB leaves it to the application developer to implement.

■**Note** For high-volume applications, proper GID namespace management can be critical to the throughput of the system. You should take care to ensure the efficient lookup of GIDs based on various attributes such as environment IDs, timestamps, and so on. Preferably, the GID namespace should include these attributes.

It's possible for a database environment to participate in distributed transactions controlled by more than one GTM. If an environment receives distributed transactions from more than one GTM, then the GIDs should be unique across all the GTMs. While designing the GID namespace, you should consider the possibility of having multiple GTMs. If you cannot say for sure that your application will never have more than one GTM, you should reserve a portion of the namespace for the GTM ID.

The GTM can use Berkeley DB tables (or databases) to store the GIDs and Berkeley DB sequences to generate the GIDs. Of course, the allocation of an XID in the GTM should not be a part of the global distributed transaction. Instead, it should happen transactionally, but outside (and before) the global transaction. Keeping the XID allocation independent of the global transaction ensures the XID associated with a failed global transaction will not be reused. Reusing the XID of a failed global transaction can cause confusion on the RMs. In the code example, I'll use Berkeley DB for both executing the distributed transactions and storing the GTM data. In addition, all database instances participating in the global transaction framework are going to be Berkeley DB instances.

Note The XA example you'll develop in this chapter assumes that all the participating RMs are Berkeley DB environments. However, the concepts discussed here are not exclusive to Berkeley DB—they apply to all XA systems. When a non–Berkeley DB RM is participating in an XA system, you should replace the term *environment* with *database instance*.

Communicating with Participating Environments

The database environments participating in the distributed transactions can be present on the same machine as the GTM or on different machines. If they're all on the same machine, then communication channels aren't necessarily required, because the GTM can link with all participating environments directly and perform the required operations. If the environments reside on different machines, then the GTM has to set up the communication channels with the remote environments. Once the channels are set up, the GTM also has to monitor them and reestablish them if they fail. The issues involved in connection are similar to the ones you saw for replication. In fact, you can use the framework you developed for replication with minor modifications for distributed transactions.

Maintaining the State of Each Distributed Transaction

The GTM has to keep track of all the distributed transactions in existence at any given time. Specifically, it has to perform the following tasks for every distributed transaction:

- **Maintain a list of all the distributed transactions**: The GTM has to keep track of all distributed transactions in a persistent store. Persistent storage is needed in order to recover unresolved transactions after a GTM crash.

- **Maintain a list of all the database environments participating in each individual distributed transaction and the state of the transaction in those environments**: The GTM needs the individual environment state to determine whether the transaction should be committed or aborted. The per-environment state should be stored in the persistent storage. The environment records the states of the transactions in the individual environments; therefore, it isn't necessary to keep that information in the GTM.

- **Maintain the latest state of each transaction**: The possible states include

    - Pre-prepare

    - Preparing

    - Committing

    - Aborting

    - Done

I'll go over the significance of each state while going through the code example. You should always store this information in persistent storage, because if the GTM crashes, it will need this information to resolve the active transactions when it comes back up.

- **Clean up, or *forget*, the old transactions that all the participating environments have applied**: This is an optional task. There is nothing wrong in storing all historical transaction states, it's just not very useful.

Recovering from the Failure of a Participating Environment

The primary duty of the GTM is to coordinate transaction state among participating environments. It can recover the local transactions by consulting the transaction log, but the fate of a distributed transaction depends on how the rest of the participating RMs process the transaction. Even if the crashed environment is able to successfully prepare the transaction locally, it may have been aborted in another environment, in which case the crashed environment, when it comes up again, will have to ask the GTM about the final fate of the transaction. Let's walk through the procedure of recovering a local environment:

1. The GTM recovers the local environment by specifying the DB_RECOVER flag in the DbEnv::open call or by executing the db_recover utility with the -e option. Any in-progress distributed transactions that haven't yet been prepared will be rolled back by the local recovery. The GTM will have to be notified of any rolled-back global transaction so that the transaction can be aborted on the other participating environments.

2. The GTM then issues DbEnv::txn_recover to the local environment to recover the list of prepared but not committed (or aborted) distributed transactions from the local environment. It should resolve the unresolved transactions according to Table 9-1.

Table 9-1. *Resolution of Prepared Transactions in the Local Environment*

Transaction State in the GTM	Action Taken in the Local Environment
Committing	Commit.
Aborting	Abort.
Preparing	Wait for the GTM to report the final outcome.

Table 9-1 lists the actions needed in the local environment to resolve the prepared transactions. You might ask why you're committing a transaction in the local environment if the GTM reports the state as *committing*. The GTM records the state as *committing* only after all the local environments have prepared the transaction. This means that the transaction will ultimately get committed in all the environments and can be safely committed. The same argument applies for the state *aborting*. If the GTM reports the state as *preparing*, then the local environment can only wait until the fate of the transaction is known by the GTM.

Local Environment Recovery with Multiple GTMs

With multiple GTMs, the recovery process is more complicated. The main problem with multiple GTMs is that the local environment has no idea which distributed transaction belongs to which GTM. The transaction GID may have that information encoded in it, but it's opaque to the local environment. It's up to the requesting GTM to identify the transaction it owns. The DbEnv::txn_recover method returns the requested number of unresolved transactions to the calling GTM, which then can invoke DbEnv::txn_discard on the transactions that it doesn't own. The GTM has to invoke the DbEnv::txn_recover calls in a loop to exhaust the list of unresolved transactions. Let's go through an example to understand the problem with this interface.

When a local environment, which is associated with multiple GTMs, comes up after a crash, it is possible that all GTMs issue the DbEnv::txn_recover command at the same time. Suppose there are 100 unresolved transactions in a local environment and 2 GTMs, and they both invoke DbEnv::txn_recover at the same time, requesting 50 transactions. The first GTM will correctly receive the first 50 transactions; it will go through the list to see which ones belong to it, process them, and invoke DbEnv::txn_discard on the remaining ones. The second GTM will receive the last 50, since the local environment has no idea that the second DbEnv::txn_recover call came from a different GTM. Therefore, the second GTM will never receive the unresolved transactions that it owns in the first batch of 50. Similarly, when the first GTM comes back to retrieve the remaining transactions, it will find that there are no remaining transactions, and it will never be able to resolve the transactions it owns from the second batch of 50.

To overcome this problem, an individual GTM should retrieve all of its unresolved transactions in a single call. It should always request a large enough number of transactions to receive all unresolved transaction in a single call. In addition, the DbEnv::txn_recover calls from different GTMs should be serialized by the database process managing the local environment to prevent interleaving.

Recovery from a GTM Crash

The GTM is the single point of failure in a distributed environment. (You could use replication to a hot standby for fault tolerance, but you can never guarantee 100% availability.) Therefore, the GTM should be extremely robust and should be resistant to failures. However, you cannot prevent all failures just by designing a piece of software properly. Natural calamities, hardware failures, power failures, and other such failures can still cause a process to crash. When a GTM restarts after a crash, it should follow these steps to recover itself to a known good state:

1. Recover the local GTM environment using DB_RECOVER in the DbEnv::open call or by using the db_recover utility with the –e option.

2. Iterate through the database that stores the distributed transaction states and resolve all the transactions according to Table 9-2.

Table 9-2. *Resolution of Transactions After a GTM Crash*

State Found in the GTM	Command Executed on Local Environments
Committing	Commit on all local environments.
Aborting	Abort on all local environments.
Preparing	Wait for all local environments to report the result of prepare. If even one environment reports an error, abort the transaction everywhere; otherwise, commit it everywhere.
Pre-Prepare	Abort on all local environments.

Table 9-2 shows how the GTM should resolve the transactions while it's recovering from a crash. You'll recognize the first three states from the discussion on local environment recovery. This table features a new state called *Pre-Prepare*. This is the state of the transaction before the application is ready to start committing. Such transactions should always be aborted during GTM recovery. This state indicates that the application that started the distributed transaction, wasn't able to fully apply the changes intended for the transaction when the GTM crashed, therefore nothing could be said about the status of the transaction and as a result it should be aborted.

Building a Global Transaction Manager

A GTM is a complex piece of software. It takes years to design and implement a general-purpose GTM. Companies such as BEA, IBM, and HP, who have successful GTM products, have invested huge amounts of money and resources to perfect their solutions. It's impossible to discuss all the aspects of GTM design within the scope of this chapter. However, the complexity associated with building distributed transaction frameworks shouldn't discourage you from experimenting with distributed transactions. Many data-distribution problems can be solved elegantly by distributed transactions.

Berkeley DB is unique in the sense that it provides all the support needed to participate as an RM in an XA system while leaving the actual implementation of how an RA communicates and integrates with a GTM up to you. Berkeley DB allows you to tailor a GTM solution, which is good enough and sophisticated enough to solve the problem at hand. In this section, you'll build a simple GTM and use it to execute distributed transactions across multiple Berkeley DB environments. It's important to note that XA was designed, and mostly used, to support heterogeneous distributed databases. I'll be using only Berkeley DB–based RAs to make the code example simple. This exercise will help you understand distributed transactions better and will also provide a test bed for you to try out solutions for your own applications.

Assumptions

As mentioned earlier, building a general-purpose GTM is difficult, so I've limited the scope of the simple GTM. I've made the following assumptions:

- All participating environments reside on the same machine, and the GTM links to all participating environments directly. This implies that you don't have to build and manage the communication channels between the GTM and the local environments.

- There is only one GTM in the environment. This assumption will greatly simplify the recovery routines.

Code Organization

You'll get to reuse the code developed in the previous chapters to execute transactions in a stand-alone environment. You'll have to modify portions of it to work with multiple environments. Here are the main classes that you'll write:

- GTM: Implements the GTM.

- LocalTxnMgr: Encapsulates the distributed transaction functions for the local environment.

- GTxn: Encapsulates a distributed transaction.

- DbEntry: The base class for a database entry. You developed this class in the earlier chapters. The Berkeley DB database operations are performed here.

- GTxnEntry: Encapsulates an entry in the state table of the GTM

- Person: You developed this class in the previous chapters. You'll use it to demonstrate a distributed transaction.

Now let's go over the code.

GTM

The GTM class is in charge of opening the GTM environment, opening the local environments, initializing the GID sequence, and other such tasks. Listing 9-1 shows the declaration for the class.

Listing 9-1. *Declaration of the GTM Class*

```
105 class GTM
106 {
107     public:
108         friend class
109             ACE_Singleton<GTM, ACE_Recursive_Thread_Mutex>;
110
111         int openLocalEnvs();
112     private:
113         GTM();
114         ~GTM();
115
116         void close();
117         int openGTMDb();
118         int openSequence();
119         int getNextSeq();
```

```
120         int getNextGid(u_int8_t *gid);
121
122         EnvMap envMap_;
123         DbEnv gtmEnv_;
124         Db *gtmDb_;
125         DbSequence *seqDb_;
126         db_seq_t nextSeq_;
127         static u_int32_t gid_;
128         friend class GTxn;
129         friend class GTxnEntry;
130 };
131 typedef ACE_Singleton<GTM, ACE_Recursive_Thread_Mutex>
132 GTMSingleton;
```

Let's go over this code in detail:

- **Lines 108–109**: Assuming that you'll have only one GTM in the environment, you make the GTM class a singleton. This makes it easier to access the GTM handle within the code.

- **Line 111**: You use GTM::openLocalEnvs to initialize the database environments that will participate in the distributed transactions. Since you're assuming that the GTM will link directly to the local environments, you have this method here. By having direct access to the local environments, you're able to eliminate the need to set up communication channels with the local environments. You would have to replace this method with something like GTM::connectToLocalEnvs if you were to have your local environments on remote machines. You could've created a more generic base that you could use to derive more specific classes for connecting to local environments on the local machine and remote machines. But let's keep things simple rather than generic.

- **Lines 113–114**: Since GTM is a singleton, its constructor and destructor are private.

- **Line 116**: The GTM resources are closed in this method.

- **Line 117**: This method opens the GTM database, which will hold the states of active distributed transactions.

- **Line 118**: Open the sequence that you'll use to generate the GIDs for the distributed transactions.

- **Line 119**: This method retrieves the next sequence number.

- **Line 120**: This method retrieves the next GID.

- **Line 122**: This map contains the participating local environment handles.

- **Line 123**: This is the handle to GTM's database environment.

- **Line 124**: This is the handle to the GTM's transaction state database.

- **Line 125**: This is the handle to the sequence database.

- **Line 126**: This is the next generated sequence.

- **Lines 131–132**: This is a typedef for accessing the singleton instance of GTM.

Before going over the implementation of GTM, let's see how the local database environments are configured. You can use a static array to populate the details of the local environments, as shown in Listing 9-2. You've used the technique in previous chapters to bootstrap the code examples. In a real application, the static array will probably be replaced by a configuration file or an event handler that receives events from a configuration server.

Listing 9-2. *Structure to Hold the Environment Information*

```
struct EnvInfo
{
    int envId;
    const char *envDir;
};

static const EnvInfo ENV_INFO_ARR[] =
{
    {1, "env_1"},
    {2, "env_2"},
    {3, "env_3"}
};
```

The EnvInfo structure contains the environment ID and the directory where the environment is located. You're creating three local environments. You can also define a utility method to open an environment, as shown in Listing 9-3, which you'll use for opening the local environments as well as the GTM environment. A side effect of this implementation choice is that all three environments are configured identically. That's not necessary in practice. Each is an independent RM, so you can configure it differently—for example, different cache sizes, lock spaces, and so on.

Listing 9-3. *Utility Method to Open an Environment*

```
static int openEnv(const char *envDir, DbEnv& env);

int openEnv(const char *envDir,
        DbEnv& env)
{
    try
    {
        env.set_errpfx(envDir);
        env.set_errcall(errCallback);
        env.set_lk_detect(DB_LOCK_DEFAULT);
```

```
        u_int32_t envFlags =
            DB_INIT_MPOOL | DB_INIT_TXN |
            DB_INIT_LOCK | DB_THREAD |
            DB_INIT_LOG | DB_RECOVER |
            DB_CREATE;
        env.open(envDir, envFlags, 0);
    }
    catch(DbException &dbex)
    {
        ACE_DEBUG((LM_ERROR,
                    "Error opening env %s : %d\n",
                    envDir, dbex.get_errno()));
        throw;
    }
    return 0;
}
```

You must be quite familiar with this code by now. Nothing fancy is being done here. The location of the environment directory is passed to the openEnv method, which creates a transactional environment and returns the opened handle.

You're ready to look at the implementation of the GTM class. In the GTM::openLocalEnvs method, as shown in Listing 9-4, the environment IDs found in ENV_INFO_ARR are opened.

Listing 9-4. *Opening the Local Environments*

```
83 int GTM::openLocalEnvs()
84 {
85     for(int i=0; i < numEnvs_ ; i++)
86     {
87         LocalTxnMgr_sp localMgr;
88         localMgr.reset(new LocalTxnMgr(ENV_INFO_ARR[i].envDir,
89                     ENV_INFO_ARR[i].envId));
90         envMap_[ENV_INFO_ARR[i].envId] = localMgr;
91     }
92     return 0;
93 }
```

Let's take a look at a few lines in detail:

- **Lines 87–89**: You populate the LocalTxnMgr shared pointer with an instance of LocalTxnMgr using the information found in ENV_INFO_ARR. You use a shared pointer to store the LocalTxnMgr instance to avoid memory leaks when the handle goes out of scope without being cleaned up.

- **Line 90**: You save the local environment handle in envMap_.

Listing 9-5 shows how you implement the constructor, which is private.

Listing 9-5. *GTM Constructor*

```
GTM::GTM():
    gtmEnv_(0)
{
    try
    {
        openEnv("gtm_env", gtmEnv_);
        openGTMDb();
        openSequence();
    }
    catch(DbException &dbex)
    {
        ACE_DEBUG((LM_ERROR,
                    "Error opening GTM %d\n",
                    dbex.get_errno()));
    }
}
```

You open the database environment for GTM, followed by the state and the sequence databases.

■**Note** The environment directory names for the GTM and the local environments (in the ENV_INO_ARR array) aren't absolute paths. Therefore, the environment will be created in the current directory from where the program is launched. I chose to use a relative path to avoid any dependence on the directory structure. However, you should use an absolute path to make the environment locations independent of the launch directory.

Listing 9-6 shows the destructor for GTM.

Listing 9-6. *GTM Destructor*

```
GTM::~GTM()
{
    close();
}

void GTM::close()
{
    try
    {
        gtmDb_->close(0);
        gtmEnv_.close(0);
    }
```

```
      catch(...)
      {
          ACE_DEBUG((LM_ERROR,
                      "error closing GTM\n"));
      }
  }
```

The destructor, which is private, calls the GTM::close method. In GTM::close, you simply close the database and the environment handles. Notice that you don't close the sequence database, because the sequence database is physically located in the same database as GTM's transaction state database. Listing 9-7 shows how you open the state database.

Listing 9-7. *Opening the GTM Database*

```
 95 int GTM::openGTMDb()
 96 {
 97     gtmDb_ = new Db(&gtmEnv_, 0);
 98     DbTxn *txn;
 99     try
100     {
101         gtmEnv_.txn_begin(NULL, &txn, 0);
102         gtmDb_->open(txn, "GTM_Db", NULL,
103                 DB_BTREE, DB_CREATE | DB_THREAD, S_IRUSR | S_IWUSR;
104         txn->commit(0);
105     }
106     catch(DbException &dbex)
107     {
108         txn->abort();
109         gtmEnv_.err(dbex.get_errno(), "GTM::openGTMDb");
110         throw;
111     }
112     return 0;
113 }
```

Let's focus on a couple of sections in this function:

- **Line 97**: You create a database handle within the GTM environment.

- **Lines 99–111**: You open the database associated with the file GTM_db within a transaction.

The GTM::openSequence method is used to open the sequence database and initialize the sequence, if it isn't already initialized. You can use the sequence database to generate a unique sequence number for every new distributed transaction, as shown in Listing 9-8. The code in this method looks pretty involved for doing something as simple as generating a sequence. I've used a new Berkeley DB feature (added in version 4.4.x) to generate the sequence. Berkeley DB sequences are persistent and can be made thread-safe and transactionally protected. It's worth writing the extra code when you're getting so many useful features out of it.

Listing 9-8. *Opening the GTM Sequence Database*

```
115 int GTM::openSequence()
116 {
117     DbTxn *txn = NULL;
118     int err = 0;
119     bool retry = true;
120     bool create = false;
121     u_int32_t flags = DB_EXCL | DB_THREAD;
122
123     seqDb_ = new DbSequence(gtmDb_, 0);
124     std::string seqKey = "XID Sequence";
125     Dbt key(((void*)seqKey.c_str()), seqKey.size());
126
127     while(retry == true)
128     {
129         try
130         {
131             if(create)
132             {
133                 ACE_DEBUG((LM_ERROR,
134                             "Sequence not yet initialized\n"));
135                 seqDb_->initial_value(1000000);
136             }
137             gtmEnv_.txn_begin(NULL, &txn, 0);
138             seqDb_->set_flags(DB_SEQ_INC | DB_SEQ_WRAP);
139             seqDb_->open(txn, &key, flags);
140             txn->commit(0);
141             retry = false;
142         }
143         catch(DbException &dbex)
144         {
145             txn->abort();
146             err = dbex.get_errno();
147             gtmEnv_.err(dbex.get_errno(),
148                     "GTM::openSequence");
149             if(err != DB_NOTFOUND)
150                 throw;
151             flags |= DB_CREATE;
152             create = true;
153             retry = true;
154         }
155     }
156     return 0;
157 }
```

Have a look at these lines in detail:

- **Lines 119–120**: This flag indicates whether you need to try opening the sequence database once more. When you open the database for the first time, you have to open it with the DB_CREATE flag. The DbSequence class is, for some reason, not smart like the Db or the DbEnv classes, where you can specify the DB_CREATE flag even when the database or the environment aren't being opened for the first time. The Db and the DbEnv classes are smart to figure out that the database or the environment already exist and don't need to be created. If you get an error while opening the sequence without the DB_CREATE flag, you retry with the DB_CREATE flag set to true.

- **Line 121**: These flags are used for opening the sequence database. Note that you don't set DB_CREATE initially.

- **Line 123**: You create a sequence database using the gtmDb_ handle. The sequence facility in Berkeley DB allows you to create a sequence in any existing database. Since you're using the sequences generated by the sequence database for creating transaction GIDs that will be stored in gtmDb_, you can store the sequence in the same database.

- **Line 124**: Every sequence is associated with a key that lets you create multiple sequences in the same database. You name the sequence XID_Sequence. In Berkeley DB, the global transaction IDs are referred to as either GIDs or XIDs. The acronym XID comes from the XA standard, which is the most widely supported open standard used for implementing distributed transaction frameworks. Berkeley DB is XA-compliant.

- **Line 125**: You initialize a Dbt instance with the sequence key.

- **Line 127**: You keep trying until the retry flag is set.

- **Lines 131–136**: If the create flag is set, then you set the initial value of the sequence. This step is optional. If you don't set the initial value, the sequence will start from 1.

- **Line 138**: You configure the sequence database to create a sequence that increases monotonically and that wraps once it hits the maximum possible value. All sequences are 64-bit numbers; therefore, it will take an enormous number of distributed transactions to cause the sequence to wrap. However, you should handle the sequence wraps if possible.

- **Lines 149–150**: If the library returns an error that isn't DB_NOTFOUND, then rethrow the exception, because you'll know that the problem encountered isn't because the sequence was never initialized, but is instead due to something else.

- **Lines 151–153**: If the sequence was never created, add the DB_CREATE flag to the Db::open flags and retry.

You can use the GTM::getNextSequence method to generate the next sequence from the sequence database, as shown in Listing 9-9.

Listing 9-9. *Generating the Next Sequence*

```
159 int GTM::getNextSeq()
160 {
161     int ret = -1;
162     DbTxn *txn = NULL;
163     try
164     {
165         gtmEnv_.txn_begin(NULL, &txn, 0);
166         seqDb_->get(txn, 1, &nextSeq_, 0);
167         txn->commit(0);
168         ret = 0;
169     }
170     catch(DbException &dbex)
171     {
172         txn->abort();
173         gtmEnv_.err(dbex.get_errno(),
174                 "GTM::getNextSeq");
175     }
176     return ret;
177 }
```

The getNextSeq method is quite simple. It calls DbSequence::get on the sequence database to retrieve the next sequence number. Note that you do this operation within a self-contained transaction. If you want to associate some other database operations with the generation of the next sequence number for your distributed transactions, you should pass a transaction handle as an argument to this method. Listing 9-10 shows the function for generating the next GID.

Listing 9-10. *Generating the Next GID*

```
179 int GTM::getNextGid(u_int8_t *gid)
180 {
181     GTxnEntry entry;
182     getNextSeq();
183     memset(gid, 0, DB_XIDDATASIZE);
184     memcpy(gid, &nextSeq_, sizeof(nextSeq_));
185     return 0;
186 }
```

In the GTM::getNextGid method, you convert the generated sequence into a GID. You simply copy the 64-bit sequence into the first 64 bits of the 128-byte GID. You're not creating a more sophisticated namespace within the GID address space, more you're building a simple XA system using a single GTM. For some complex applications, you would have to include more information related to the GTM, participating environments, time of creation, location, and so on into the GID namespace to correctly identify a transaction.

LocalTxnMgr

The LocalTxnMgr class encapsulates a local environment that is participating in a distributed transaction. According to one of the assumptions, the local environments run on the same machine, and the GTM can access the local environment directly. All operations pertaining to a local environment are contained in this class. Listing 9-11 shows the code for the LocalTxnMgr class.

Listing 9-11. *Declaration for LocalTxnMgr*

```
55 class LocalTxnMgr
56 {
57     public:
58         LocalTxnMgr(const char* envDir, int envId);
59         ~LocalTxnMgr();
60
61         int addGTxn(u_int8_t *xid);
62         LocalTxnHndls_sp getLocalTxnHandles(u_int8_t *xid);
63         int processTxn(u_int8_t *xid, TXN_ACTION action );
64     private:
65         void close();
66         int openDbs();
67         int recoverGTxn();
68
69         DbEnv env_;
70         int envId_;
71         TxnMap txnMap_;
72         Db *personDb_;
73
74         friend class GTM;
75         friend class GTxn;
76 };
77
78 typedef boost::shared_ptr<LocalTxnMgr> LocalTxnMgr_sp;
79
80 typedef std::map< int, LocalTxnMgr_sp > EnvMap;
81 typedef std::map< int, LocalTxnMgr_sp >::iterator EnvMapIter;
```

Let's go over the important sections of this listing:

- **Line 58**: The constructor takes the environment ID and the environment directory as arguments. These are specified through ENV_INFO_ARR.

- **Line 61**: You use addGTxn to associate a local environment with a distributed transaction.

- **Line 62**: You use getLocalTxnHandles to access the transaction handles in the local environment. You need these while executing a distributed transaction in a local environment.

- **Line 63**: You use the processTxn method when a local environment has to process a distributed transaction.

- **Line 65**: You use this method to close the local environment.

- **Line 66**: You use this method to open the databases in the local environment.

- **Line 67**: You use recoverGTxn to recover prepared but unresolved distributed transactions when a local environment is being recovered after a crash.

- **Line 69**: This is the local environment handle.

- **Line 70**: This is the ID of the local environment, as known by the GTM.

- **Line 71**: The local environment has to associate a distributed transaction with a local transaction so that it can be committed, aborted, prepared, and so on when the GTM performs analogous operations on the distributed transaction.

- **Line 72**: You use the Person database handle to demonstrate a distributed transaction.

- **Line 78**: You use this typedef for the shared pointer for the LocalTxnMgr pointer.

- **Lines 80–81**: This map (and its iterator) associates an environment ID with a LocalTxnMgr instance. The GTM uses this map to access local environments through their IDs.

Listing 9-12 shows how you implement LocalTxnMgr, starting with the constructor.

Listing 9-12. *LocalTxnMgr Constructor*

```
188 LocalTxnMgr::LocalTxnMgr(const char *envDir, int id):
189     env_(0),
190     envId_(id)
191 {
192     ACE_DEBUG((LM_ERROR, "opening env %d\n", id));
193     openEnv(envDir, env_);
194     ACE_DEBUG((LM_ERROR,
195                 "recovering global txns for env %d\n", id));
196     recoverGTxn();
197     openDbs();
198 }
```

Let's take a look at a couple of important lines:

- **Line 193**: Use the static utility method, introduced earlier, to open the environment handle to the local environment. The environment is opened with the DB_RECOVER flag set, which ensures that all the local transactions are resolved properly.

- **Line 196**: After recovering the local environment, you recover the prepared but not yet resolved distributed transactions.

The destructor is pretty simple; it just calls the close method. In close, you close the Person database and the environment handle, as shown in Listing 9-13.

Listing 9-13. *Destructor of* LocalTxnMgr

```
200 LocalTxnMgr::~LocalTxnMgr()
201 {
202     close();
203 }
204
205 void LocalTxnMgr::close()
206 {
207     try
208     {
209         personDb_->close(0);
210         env_.close(0);
211     }
212     catch(...)
213     {
214         ACE_DEBUG((LM_ERROR,
215                     "error closing LocalTxnMgr\n"));
216     }
217 }
```

You use the openDbs method to open all the databases that will be used in the local environment. In a typical XA application you will find different databases in different participating environments. For this example, however, you have the same database in all the local environments. It just saves some lines of code. The purpose of demonstrating a distributed transaction is served equally well with the same database in all the local environments. Having said that, there can be legitimate use cases where the same set of databases is present in all environments in an XA system. Usually, when you'd like an identical update to happen in identical environments, you'd use replication. However, replication doesn't allow a transaction to be rolled back on the master if replication failed to deliver the update to the replicas, which is exactly the behavior required in certain cases. If you use XA instead of replication, the transactions can be rolled back if a particular node doesn't receive the update. Also, replication only allows one node at a time to act as the master, which can make updates, whereas any node can update the database with XA. The biggest drawback with XA is that it's much slower than replication. Listing 9-14 shows the openDbs method.

Listing 9-14. *Opening the Databases in an RM*

```
218 int LocalTxnMgr::openDbs()
219 {
220     personDb_ = new Db(&env_, 0);
221     DbTxn *txn;
222     try
223     {
224         env_.txn_begin(NULL, &txn, 0);
225         personDb_->open(txn, "Person_Db", NULL,
226                 DB_BTREE, DB_CREATE | DB_THREAD, 0644);
227         txn->commit(0);
```

```
228    }
229    catch(DbException &dbex)
230    {
231        txn->abort();
232        env_.err(dbex.get_errno(), "LocalTxnMgr::openDbs");
233        throw;
234    }
235    return 0;
236 }
```

Listing 9-14 shows a very simple method to open a database—nothing unusual here. You can probably now write this piece of code in your sleep. Listing 9-15 shows the addGTxn method.

Listing 9-15. *Adding a Global Transaction*

```
238 int LocalTxnMgr::addGTxn(u_int8_t *xid)
239 {
240    DbTxn *txn;
241    env_.txn_begin(NULL, &txn, 0);
242    txnMap_[xid] = txn;
243    return 0;
244 }
```

The txnMap_ map is populated by this method. Every time a new distributed transaction is started, its GID is added to the map. An RM uses this map when a distributed transaction is committed, aborted, or prepared for performing the analogous operation on the associated local transaction. Listing 9-16 shows the getLocalTxnHandles method.

Listing 9-16. *Retrieving Local Transaction Handles*

```
246 LocalTxnHndls_sp
247 LocalTxnMgr::getLocalTxnHandles(u_int8_t *xid)
248 {
249    LocalTxnHndls_sp handles;
250    handles.reset(new LocalTxnHndls);
251    handles->db = personDb_;
252    handles->txn = NULL;
253    TxnMapIter it = txnMap_.find(xid);
254    if(it != txnMap_.end())
255    {
256        handles->txn = it->second;
257        handles->env = &env_;
258        handles->envId = envId_;
259    }
260    return handles;
261 }
```

You use the getLocalTxnHandles method to access the transaction handle in the local environment when a database entry is being updated in the context of the distributed transaction. You use the GID of the distributed transaction to look up txnMap_ to retrieve the local transaction handle. Listing 9-17 shows the processTxn method.

Listing 9-17. *Processing a Global Transaction in an RM*

```
263 int LocalTxnMgr::processTxn(u_int8_t *xid, TXN_ACTION action)
264 {
265     int ret = -1;
266     TxnMapIter it = txnMap_.find(xid);
267     if(it != txnMap_.end())
268     {
269         DbTxn *txn = it->second;
270         try
271         {
272             switch(action)
273             {
274                 case PREPARE:
275                     ret = txn->prepare(xid);
276                     break;
277                 case COMMIT:
278                     ret = txn->commit(0);
279                     break;
280                 case ABORT:
281                     ret = txn->abort();
282                     break;
283                 default:
284                     break;
285             }
286         }
287         catch(DbException& ex)
288         {
289             txn->abort();
290             env_.err(ex.get_errno(),
291                     "LocalTxnMgr::processTxn");
292         }
293     }
294     return ret;
295 }
```

You use the processTxn method to apply an analogous operation on the local transaction when a distributed transaction is being processed. Let's go over the important sections in this method:

- **Line 266**: You look up the GID (or the XID) of the distributed transaction in txnMap_ to find the local transaction associated with the GID.

- **Lines 272–285**: The local transaction is processed accordingly, as the distributed transaction is processed.

- **Lines 287–292**: If the operation fails, then the local operation is aborted and an error is returned.

The recoverGTxn method is the heart of the distributed transaction-recovery mechanism. Listing 9-18 shows how a distributed transaction is recovered from a crash.

Listing 9-18. *Recovering a Global Transaction*

```
297 int LocalTxnMgr::recoverGTxn()
298 {
299     int res;
300     int askedCount = 5;
301     long retCount = 0;
302     DbPreplist prepList[askedCount];
303     u_int32_t flags = DB_FIRST;
305
306     do
307     {
308         try
309         {
310             res = env_.txn_recover(prepList,
311                     askedCount, &retCount, flags);
312             for(int i=0; i < retCount; i++)
313             {
314                 GTxnEntry entry;
315                 entry.getByXid(prepList[i].gid, NULL);
316                 ACE_DEBUG((LM_ERROR, "resolving\n"));
317                 ACE_HEX_DUMP((LM_ERROR,
318                         (const char*)(prepList[i].gid),
319                         DB_XIDDATASIZE));
320                 TxnStatus status = entry.getStatus();
321                 ACE_DEBUG((LM_ERROR, "txn status is %d\n",
322                         status));
323                 switch(status)
324                 {
325                     case COMMITTING:
326                         (prepList[i].txn)->commit(0);
327                         ACE_DEBUG((LM_ERROR,
328                                 "txn commited\n"));
```

```
329                           break;
330                     default:
331                         (prepList[i].txn)->abort();
332                         ACE_DEBUG((LM_ERROR,
333                                     "txn aborted\n"));
334                         break;
335                 }
336             }
337             flags = DB_NEXT;
338         }
339         catch(DbException& ex)
340         {
341             env_.err(ex.get_errno(),
342                     "LocalTxnMgr::recoverGTxn");
343         }
344     } while(retCount >= askedCount)
345     return res;
346 }
```

You use the DbEnv::txn_recover method to retrieve the list of prepared but unresolved transactions from the failed environment. The number of transactions can be huge, so Berkeley DB provides a DbCursor-like interface for retrieving them in batches. The library doesn't provide any method to read the total number of unresolved transactions, so you have to call DbEnv::txn_recover in a loop until you reach the end of the list. Let's take a look at some of these lines of code in detail:

- **Lines 301–302**: The unresolved transactions are returned in DbPrepList. The library returns only the requested number of transactions at a time, even if it finds more. If it finds less transactions than requested, then the list won't be fully populated. The library fills in retCount, indicating the actual number of transactions returned. The DbPredList structure contains the GID of the unresolved transaction and the DbTxn handle associated with the transaction.

- **Line 303**: This flag indicates that you're invoking DbEnv::txn_recover for the first time. You'll change it to DB_NEXT after the first invocation.

- **Line 306**: You keep calling DbEnv::txn_recover until you get a list that has less elements than requested. When you get a smaller list, you know that no more transactions are left.

- **Lines 314–315**: GTxnEntry represents an entry in the GTM's transaction state database. You use it to read an entry from the database given the GID of the transaction. The getByXid method populates a GTxnEntry instance from the database. The GTxnEntry instance operates on the GTM's database environment.

- **Line 320**: The state of the transaction is retrieved from the GTxnEntry instance and is used to process the transaction appropriately.

- **Lines 323–335**: You commit the transaction if the state is committing; for all other states, you abort the transaction. As shown in Table 9-1, for a transaction showing up as preparing, the local environment should wait until the GTM is able to resolve the transaction. That isn't applicable here, because the GTM and the local environments are running in the same address space. If a local environment is being recovered after a crash, it implies that the GTM also crashed along with the local environment and therefore cannot resolve any transactions until all local environments have been recovered. If you wait here, you'll end up waiting forever.

GTxn

The GTxn class represents a distributed transaction. It acts as the repository for all the information related to a distributed transaction until it is either committed or aborted. Listing 9-19 shows its declaration.

Listing 9-19. *Declaration of GTxn*

```
83 typedef std::list<int> GTxnEnvList;
84 typedef std::list<int>::iterator GTxnEnvListIter;
85 class GTxn
86 {
87     public:
88         GTxn();
89         int begin();
90         int addEnv(int envId);
91         int commit();
92         int abort();
93         int getLocalHandles(LocalHandles& handles);
94     private:
95         u_int8_t    xid_[128];
96         GTxnEnvList envList_;
97         GTxnEntry_sp   gTxnEntry_;
98         bool        begin_;
99         int processTxn(TXN_ACTION action);
100 };
```

Let's go over the details of the GTxn class declaration:

- **Lines 83–84**: You declare a list (and its iterator) containing the local environment IDs that are participating in a distributed transaction.

- **Line 89**: By invoking GTxn::begin, an application indicates that the operations performed on the local environments will constitute a distributed transaction, analogous to DbEnv::txn_begin.

- **Line 90**: The application uses GTxn::addEnv to add a local environment as a participant in a distributed transaction.

- **Lines 91–92**: You'll use the commit and abort methods to commit and abort a distributed transaction.

- **Line 93**: You'll use GTxn::getLocalHandles to retrieve the DbTxn handles from the local environments participating in the distributed transaction. You can do this because the local environments are running in the same process as the GTM and the application.

- **Line 95**: The GID (or the XID) associated with the distributed transaction is represented by the GTxn instance.

- **Line 96**: The envList_ list contains the environment IDs of the participating local environments. The GTxn::addEnv method populates this list.

- **Line 97**: The GTxnEntry instance corresponds to this GTxn instance. You use this instance to update the current state of the distributed transaction in the database.

- **Line 98**: This flag indicates that GTxn::begin has been invoked on the distributed transaction. Once this is set, no new environments can be added.

- **Line 99**: The processTxn private method processes the various stages of the distributed transaction.

Now I'll show you the implementation of GTxn one method at a time. Listing 9-20 shows the GTxn constructor.

Listing 9-20. *GTxn Constructor*

```
348 GTxn::GTxn():
349     begin_(false)
350 {
351     GTM *gtm = GTMSingleton::instance();
352     gtm->getNextGid(xid_);
353     gTxnEntry_.reset(new GTxnEntry(xid_));
354 }
```

In the constructor, you retrieve the next GID from the GTM. You use that GID to initialize the GTxnEntry entry for the distributed transaction. Listing 9-21 shows the implementation of the addEnv method.

Listing 9-21. *Adding an Environment to a Global Transaction*

```
356 int GTxn::addEnv(int envId)
357 {
358     if(begin_)
359         throw std::exception();
360
361     int ret = -1;
362     GTM *gtm = GTMSingleton::instance();
363     EnvMapIter it = (gtm->envMap_).find(envId);
```

```
364    if(it != (gtm->envMap_).end())
365    {
366        LocalTxnMgr_sp mgr = it->second;
367        ACE_DEBUG((LM_ERROR,
368                    "GTxn::addEnv: found env %@ for %d\n",
369                    &mgr->env_, envId));
370        mgr->addGTxn(xid_);
371        envList_.push_back(envId);
372        ret = 0;
373    }
374    return ret;
375 }
```

You use GTxn::addEnv to associate a local environment with a distributed transaction. All environments associated with a distributed transaction will participate in the prepare-commit-abort cycle. Let's look at the important lines in the begin method:

- **Lines 358–359**: Once GTxn::begin has been called on a distributed transaction, you don't allow new environments to be added to the list of local environments. You have to do this, because for this code example, you're handling the operations performed on the local environments under the covers. If the individual operations are performed by the application directly on the local environments, then you won't need to do this because the application would keep track of all the local environments that have to be involved.

- **Lines 363–373**: You find the LocalTxnMgr instance for the passed ID and add the GID to its map of distributed transactions.

Listing 9-22 shows the method getLocalHandles.

Listing 9-22. *Retrieving the Local Transaction Handles for a Global Transaction*

```
382 int GTxn::getLocalHandles(LocalHandles& handles)
383 {
384     GTM *gtm = GTMSingleton::instance();
385     GTxnEnvListIter beg = envList_.begin();
386     GTxnEnvListIter end = envList_.end();
387     for(; beg != end; ++beg)
388     {
389         int envId = (*beg);
390         EnvMapIter it = (gtm->envMap_).find(envId);
391         if(it != (gtm->envMap_).end())
392         {
393             handles.push_back(
394                     (it->second)->getLocalTxnHandles(xid_));
395         }
396     }
397     return 0;
398 }
```

You use the GTxn::getLocalHandles utility method to get all the local transaction handles associated with a distributed transaction. You use the local environment map in the GTM to look up all the local environment IDs associated with this distributed transaction, and then you retrieve the associated local DbTxn handles from the looked-up environment handles. Listing 9-23 shows the commit method of GTxn.

Listing 9-23. *Committing a Global Transaction*

```
400 int GTxn::commit()
401 {
402     gTxnEntry_->update(PRE_PREPARE);
403     int result = processTxn(PREPARE);
404     if(result)
405     {
406         abort();
407         std::cout << "txn aborted" << std::endl;
408         return -1;
409     }
410     gTxnEntry_->update(COMMITTING);
411     result = processTxn(COMMIT);
412     std::cout << "txn committed" << std::endl;
413     if(!result)
414     {
415         gTxnEntry_->update(DONE);
416     }
417     return 0;
418 }
```

GTxn::commit is where the action happens. When an application is ready to commit a distributed transaction, the two-phase commit is started. Let's see how it's done:

- **Line 402**: You set the state of the distributed transaction as PRE_PREPARE in the GTM database.

- **Line 403**: You call PREPARE on all the participating local environments. The processTxn method invokes DbTxn::txn_prepare on individual environments.

- **Lines 404–409**: If processTxn returns a nonzero value, DbTxn::txn_prepare must have failed on one of the local environments. In that case, you abort the distributed transaction by calling abort on all local transactions.

- **Line 410**: If DbTxn::txn_prepare succeeds on all environments, then set the state of the distributed transaction to COMMITTING.

- **Line 411**: Commit the local transactions.

- **Lines 413–416**: If all the local transactions are committed, then you're done, and you set the state to DONE. You could have deleted the state record from the GTM database at this point.

Listing 9-24 shows the processTxn method.

Listing 9-24. *Processing a Global Transaction*

```
430 int GTxn::processTxn(TXN_ACTION action)
431 {
432     int result = -1;
433
434     GTM *gtm = GTMSingleton::instance();
435     GTxnEnvListIter beg = envList_.begin();
436     GTxnEnvListIter end = envList_.end();
437     for(; beg != end; ++beg)
438     {
439         int envId = (*beg);
445         EnvMapIter it = (gtm->envMap_).find(envId);
446         if(it != (gtm->envMap_).end())
447         {
448             result = (it->second)->processTxn(xid_, action);
449             if(result)
450                 return result;
451         }
452     }
453     return result;
454 }
```

The GTxn::processTxn method goes through the list of environments associated with the distributed transactions and invokes LocalTxnMgr::processTxn. If any environment fails to apply the intended action on the local transaction, the method will return an error. Listing 9-25 shows the abort method.

Listing 9-25. *Aborting a Global Transaction*

```
420 int GTxn::abort()
421 {
422     gTxnEntry_->update(ABORTING);
423     int result = processTxn(ABORT);
424     if(!result)
425     {
426         gTxnEntry_->update(DONE);
427     }
```

The GTxn::abort method is just a shortcut for invoking GTxn::processTxn with the action set to ABORT.

GTxnEntry

GTxnEntry encapsulates an entry for a distributed transaction in the GTM database. GTxnEntry is derived from the DbEntry class, which you developed in the earlier chapters. DbEntry encapsulates all the Berkeley DB database operations and has not been changed much from its original version. Listing 9-26 shows the declaration of the GTxnEntry class.

Listing 9-26. *Declaration of GTxnEntry*

```
59 class GTxnEntry : public DbEntry
60 {
61     public:
62         GTxnEntry();
63         GTxnEntry(u_int8_t *xid);
64         void setStatus(TxnStatus status)
65         {status_ = status;}
66
67         TxnStatus getStatus()
68         {return status_;}
69
70         int deserialize(char *buf);
71         int getByXid(u_int8_t *xid, DbTxn *txn);
72         int update(TxnStatus status);
73     protected:
74         char* serialize();
75         void getPKey(void*& key, int& length);
76         std::string toString();
77     private:
78         u_int8_t    xid_[128];
79         TxnStatus    status_;
80 };
81 typedef boost::shared_ptr<GTxnEntry> GTxnEntry_sp;
```

GTxnEntry contains methods that allow access to the distributed transaction state entries in the GTM database. Let's look at the main methods:

- **Line 63**: This constructor takes the GID of a distributed transaction.

- **Line 70**: deserialize is a virtual method in DbEntry that you use for decoding members of the GTxnEntry instance from the binary data retrieved from the database.

- **Line 71**: You use getByXid to retrieve an entry from the GTM database given its GID.

- **Line 78**: You use the xid_ key in the GTM database.

- **Line 79**: The value stored against the xid_ is the state of the distributed transaction.

The implementation of these methods is similar to the other database access classes that you developed earlier based on DbEntry. There is, however, a small change. Let's look at the constructors, as shown in Listing 9-27, to understand what it is.

Listing 9-27. *Constructors of GTxnEntry*

```
GTxnEntry::GTxnEntry()
{
    GTM *gtm = GTMSingleton::instance();
    setEnv(&(gtm->gtmEnv_));
    memset(xid_, 0, DB_XIDDATASIZE);
}


GTxnEntry::GTxnEntry(u_int8_t *xid):
    status_(PRE_PREPARE)
{
    GTM *gtm = GTMSingleton::instance();
    setEnv(&(gtm->gtmEnv_));
    memcpy(xid_, xid, DB_XIDDATASIZE);
}
```

You'll notice that the setEnv method is being called in both the constructors to explicitly set the environment to the GTM's environment. In earlier chapters, you retrieved the environment handle from the static singleton instance of the DbUtils class. Here you cannot do that, because you have multiple database environments within the same process space. You need to specify the environment for each data access class. Listing 9-28 shows the marshalling and unmarshalling routines of GTxnEntry.

Listing 9-28. *Marshalling and Unmarshalling a GTxnEntry*

```
int GTxnEntry::deserialize(char *buf)
{
    char *tmpBuf = buf;
    int totalLen = 0;
    int elemLen = 0;

    elemLen = sizeof(status_);
    status_ = *((TxnStatus *)tmpBuf);

    std::cout << "status is " << status_ << std::endl;
    return 0;
}

char* GTxnEntry::serialize()
{
    memset (serializedData_, 0, 2048);

    char *buf= serializedData_;

    int elemLen = 0;
    int totalLen = 0;
```

```
    elemLen = sizeof(u_int32_t);
    memcpy(buf, &status_, elemLen);
    totalLen += elemLen;
    buf += elemLen;

    serializedLen_ = totalLen;
    return serializedData_;
}
```

There is no change in the GTxn::serialize and GTxn::deserialize methods. These methods are used for marshalling and unmarshalling the binary data to and from the database. Listing 9-29 shows the getByXid method.

Listing 9-29. *Implementation of getByXid*

```
int GTxnEntry::getByXid(u_int8_t *xid, DbTxn *txn)
{
    int ret = -1;
    Dbt key;
    Dbt data;
    data.set_flags(DB_DBT_MALLOC);
    key.set_data((void*)(xid));
    key.set_size(DB_XIDDATASIZE);
    GTM *gtm = GTMSingleton::instance();
    ret = dbGet(gtm->gtmDb_, &key, &data, txn);
    if(ret == 0)
        deserialize((char*)(data.get_data()));
    return ret;
}
```

Notice that the database handle is retrieved from the GTM singleton. In the previous chapters, you invoked the getDbHandle method to retrieve the handle from a static array, which stored all the database handles present in the only database environment. You need to be more specific here, because you have multiple environments. If you were running the local environments in individual processes, you could have used the old classes without any change. Listing 9-30 shows the update method.

Listing 9-30. *Implementation of the update Method*

```
int GTxnEntry::update(TxnStatus status)
{
    status_ = status;
    GTM *gtm = GTMSingleton::instance();
    dbPut(gtm->gtmDb_, NULL, true);
}
```

Similarly, you specifically set the database handle for the GTxnEntry::update method.

Person

The Person class in the earlier chapters had numerous methods to query, delete, update, and insert a Person entry using various fields in the Person class. Here you implement only the insert method to demonstrate a distributed transaction. Listing 9-31 shows the trimmed-down declaration.

Listing 9-31. *Declaration of the Person Class*

```
 83 class Person : public DbEntry
 84 {
 85     public:
 86         Person();
 87         Person(unsigned long ssn,
 88                 std::string name, std::string dob);
 89         int deserialize(char *buf);
 90         void insert(GTxn* txn);
 91     protected:
 92         char* serialize();
 93         void getPKey(void*& key, int& length);
 94         std::string toString();
 95     private:
 96         unsigned long      ssn_;
 97         unsigned long      ssnReversed_;
 98         std::string        name_;
 99         std::string        dob_;
100 };
```

The insert method is different from what it used to be in the previous chapters. Listing 9-32 shows how you implement it.

Listing 9-32. *Implementation of insert*

```
void Person::insert(GTxn* gTxn)
{
    LocalHandles handles;
    gTxn->getLocalHandles(handles);
    LocalHandlesIter beg = handles.begin();
    for(; beg != handles.end(); ++beg)
    {
        setEnv((*beg)->env);
        ACE_DEBUG((LM_ERROR, "Person::insert: env is %@\n",
                    (*beg)->env));
        dbPut((*beg)->db, (*beg)->txn);
    }
}
```

You look up all the local transaction handles associated with the distributed transaction and insert the Person entry in each environment. The assumption being made here is that you want to make the same insert in all the local environments within the context of the distributed transaction. Berkeley DB imposes no such restriction—you could have inserted totally different Person entries or, for that matter, entries in totally different tables within the same transaction. However, I've made this assumption to keep things simple.

If your local environments were located in independent processes, then you'd have to invoke a remote call to perform the insert operations. The remote invocation could have been in the form of an RPC call or a CORBA call of whatever you may have had at your disposal. I won't discuss the details of communicating with the remote environments here.

Finally, let's take a look at the application program, shown in Listing 9-33, that creates a distributed transaction using the framework that you developed.

Listing 9-33. *The main Method*

```
 1 #include "gtm.h"
 2
 3 int main(int argc, char **argv)
 4 {
 5     try
 6     {
 7         GTM *gtm = GTMSingleton::instance();
 8         gtm->openLocalEnvs();
 9
10         GTxn gTxn;
11         gTxn.addEnv(1);
12         gTxn.addEnv(2);
13         gTxn.begin();
14         Person p(123456789, "First Global Txn",
15                 "May 21 2006");
16         p.insert(&gTxn);
17         gTxn.commit();
18
19         GTxn gTxn1;
20         gTxn1.addEnv(1);
21         gTxn1.addEnv(2);
22         gTxn1.begin();
23         Person p1(223456789, "Second Global Txn",
24                 "May 22 2006");
25         p1.insert(&gTxn1);
26         gTxn1.commit();
27
28     }
29     catch(DbException& dbex)
30     {
31         ACE_DEBUG((LM_ERROR,
32                     "caught DbException in main %d\n",
33                     dbex.get_errno()));
34     }
```

```
35      catch(...)
36      {
37          ACE_DEBUG((LM_ERROR, "unknown exception caught\n"));
38      }
39 }
```

Let's take a look at these lines in detail:

- **Lines 7–8**: You create the GTM singleton instance and open the local database environments.

- **Line 10**: You create a distributed transaction.

- **Lines 11–12**: You add environments 1 and 2 to the distributed transaction.

- **Line 13**: You start the distributed transaction.

- **Lines 14–16**: You create an instance of the Person class and insert it using the distributed transaction handle.

- **Line 17**: You commit the distributed transaction.

- **Lines 19–26**: You create and commit another distributed transaction.

Running the GTM

Now you're ready to try out the GTM implementation. Let's find out how it works. When you execute the application for the first time, here's what you'll see:

```
hy@linux:~/ws/from_svn/trunk/chap_9> ./gtm
(32648:1078942816) gtm_env errMsg: GTM::openSequence: DB_NOTFOUND: ➥
No matching key/data pair found
Sequence not yet initialied
opening env 1
recovering global txns for env 1
opening env 2
recovering global txns for env 2
opening env 3
recovering global txns for env 3
creating new distributed Txn
next seq is 1000000
GTxn::addEnv: added env ID 1
GTxn::addEnv: added env ID 2
Person::insert: env ID is 1
Person::insert: env ID is 2
txn committed
creating new distributed Txn
next seq is 1000001
GTxn::addEnv: added env ID 1
GTxn::addEnv: added env ID 2
```

```
Person::insert: env ID is 1
Person::insert: env ID is 2
txn committed
```

Since you're running the GTM for the first time, the sequence database is not found. That's why you see the error from the library in the beginning. Next, you open the three local environ- ments, as specified by ENV_INFO_ARR, and the distributed transactions are recovered. Since this is the first run, no unresolved transactions are found in any environment. All environments are now open for business. You then create the first distributed transaction. A new sequence number, 1000000, is generated from the sequence database, and environments 1 and 2 are associated with the transaction ID. Then Person::insert is called, which internally inserts the entry in environments 1 and 2. Finally, the global transaction is committed. The same sequence is repeated for the second transaction.

You saw the distributed transaction got committed; now how do you make sure that the global transaction can be recovered when a local environment fails? Let's try to simulate a crash. Listing 9-34 shows how you can force the application to exit after the transaction is prepared in one environment but not on the other.

Listing 9-34. *Simulating a Crash During Global Transaction Processing*

```
int GTxn::processTxn(TXN_ACTION action)
{
    int result = -1;

    GTM *gtm = GTMSingleton::instance();
    GTxnEnvListIter beg = envList_.begin();
    GTxnEnvListIter end = envList_.end();
    for(; beg != end; ++beg)
    {
        int envId = (*beg);
        if(gtm->nextSeq_ == 1000005 && envId == 2)
        {
            exit(0);
        }
        EnvMapIter it = (gtm->envMap_).find(envId);
        if(it != (gtm->envMap_).end())
        {
            result = (it->second)->processTxn(xid_, action);
            if(result)
                return result;
        }
    }
    return result;
```

In the GTxn::processTxn method, you exit from the process if the sequence number is 1000005 and the environment ID is 2. This will leave the transaction 1000005 prepared in envi- ronment 1 and unprepared in environment 2. You should expect this transaction to be aborted when the application restarts. Let's see what happens:

```
hy@linux:~/ws/from_svn/trunk/chap_9> ./gtm
opening env 1
recovering global txns for env 1
opening env 2
recovering global txns for env 2
opening env 3
recovering global txns for env 3
creating new distributed Txn
next seq is 1000004
GTxn::addEnv: added env ID 1
GTxn::addEnv: added env ID 2
Person::insert: env ID is 1
Person::insert: env ID is 2
txn committed
creating new distributed Txn
next seq is 1000005
GTxn::addEnv: added env ID 1
GTxn::addEnv: added env ID 2
Person::insert: env ID is 1
Person::insert: env ID is 2
terminate called after throwing an instance of 'DbException'
  what():  DbEnv::stream_error: Invalid argument
Aborted (core dumped)
```

As expected, the process crashes when you try to prepare transaction 1000005. Now let's run the program again:

```
hy@linux:~/ws/from_svn/trunk/chap_9> ./gtm
opening env 1
recovering global txns for env 1
status is 0
resolving
HEXDUMP 128 bytes
45 42 0f 00 00 00 00 00  00 00 00 00 00 00 00 00    EB..............
00 00 00 00 00 00 00 00  00 00 00 00 00 00 00 00    ................
00 00 00 00 00 00 00 00  00 00 00 00 00 00 00 00    ................
00 00 00 00 00 00 00 00  00 00 00 00 00 00 00 00    ................
00 00 00 00 00 00 00 00  00 00 00 00 00 00 00 00    ................
00 00 00 00 00 00 00 00  00 00 00 00 00 00 00 00    ................
00 00 00 00 00 00 00 00  00 00 00 00 00 00 00 00    ................
00 00 00 00 00 00 00 00  00 00 00 00 00 00 00 00    ................
txn status is 0
txn aborted
opening env 2
recovering global txns for env 2
```

```
opening env 3
recovering global txns for env 3
creating new distributed Txn
next seq is 1000006
GTxn::addEnv: added env ID 1
GTxn::addEnv: added env ID 2
Person::insert: env ID is 1
Person::insert: env ID is 2
txn committed
creating new distributed Txn
next seq is 1000007
GTxn::addEnv: added env ID 1
GTxn::addEnv: added env ID 2
Person::insert: env ID is 1
Person::insert: env ID is 2
txn committed
```

When environment 1 is being recovered, it runs into the unresolved transaction 1000005. The status of the transaction is queried in the GTM and is found to be 0, which is PRE_PREPARE. Since the transaction was not successfully prepared, it is aborted. You see the same thing happening in environment 2, because the transaction was never prepared in that environment. The local transaction that got started when the record was inserted was cleaned up during the local recovery of the environment.

Disclaimer

The GTM you implement in this chapter isn't designed to be used in any serious application. You'll notice numerous design issues with it. First of all, you haven't protected the sensitive regions with mutexes; therefore, you cannot use it in multithreaded environments. Second, you've assumed that the same record is inserted in all the environments as a part of the distributed transaction. The application code has no control over what operations get performed on the local environments. A more robust design should give that control to the application code, so that the application can decide what operations are performed in the local environments as a part of a distributed transaction. Third, you've assumed that all environments are colocated in the same process. Finally, you've assumed that there is only one GTM. You could get away from devising a GID namespace management scheme because of that assumption.

Any assumption about the requirements of an application would have been incorrect, so I decided to make assumptions that would greatly simplify the example code and at the same time demonstrate the basic concept behind distributed transactions.

Data-Distribution Strategies

You are now acquainted with two techniques that you can use to distribute the data stored in a Berkeley DB environment to another Berkeley DB environment. One is replication, and the other is distributed transactions. Data distribution may be needed in an application for numerous reasons, and in many cases, it isn't obvious which of these techniques you should employ. In some cases, you can solve the problem either by replication or distributed transactions, while in others cases there is a clear advantage to using one of the techniques. There are also some cases in which you have to use both replication and distributed transactions. I'll discuss one case study for each of these cases.

Fault Tolerance

Good design alone cannot ensure that an application won't crash at a critical juncture. In any working system, there are too many "moving parts" that can fail. Apart from the application, the operating system, computer hardware, power supply, or any of a number of other things can fail. It's impossible to ensure that each and every component needed to operate a system will never fail. To provide reliability in an unreliable environment, computer systems usually resort to redundancy. If you have two systems, both of which can perform the desired operations in an identical manner, then the probability of both of them failing at the same time is smaller than the probability of one system failing. In order to perform all operations in an identical manner, the redundant systems need to share the state information. If the state information is stored in a database, then you can use either replication or distributed transactions to keep the redundant systems in sync. Figure 9-2 shows the components within a redundant system with two redundant nodes. In most software systems, there are three points of failure that are most likely to fail.

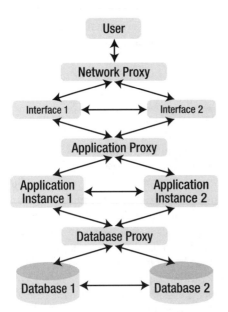

Figure 9-2. *Anatomy of a redundant system*

Network Failure

Network failure is one of the most common failures. A network failure may happen due to routing problems, hardware problems, or driver issues. To overcome network failure, most redundant systems use a network proxy. The basic idea behind a network proxy is to expose a virtual address to the users that is mapped to one of the physical addresses at any given time. If one of the physical network interfaces fails, then the proxy maps the virtual interface to the available interface, thereby ensuring that the users are always able to connect to one of the physical interfaces unless both interfaces fail at the same time. You can implement the network proxies by using broadcast protocols such as Virtual Router Redundancy Protocol (VRRP) or Common Address Redundancy Protocol (UCARP) or by using hardware load balancers.

When a network failure happens, the incoming user requests can get routed to a network interface different from the one they were going to before the failure. The application layer behind the network proxy should be capable of rerouting the requests.

Application Failure

Application failure can happen for numerous reasons, such as process crashes, operating system crashes, and hardware failures. An application process can fail even if it doesn't crash. Different applications have different ways of defining failure. For certain real-time applications, the process is considered to have failed even if the response time of a process deteriorates beyond a certain limit. Other applications may have a more relaxed definition of failure. Most applications work around such failures by running redundant process instances on independent machines and monitoring the processes through a monitoring process. The monitoring process *pings* the process instances periodically. If any process instance doesn't reply as expected, then it registers the other healthy process instance as the available instance in the application proxy.

Since an application instance can fail, it's difficult to ensure that when the network failure happens, the application instance corresponding to the destination network interface will be in a healthy state and ready to accept incoming requests. The application proxy ensures that the incoming requests get routed to the healthy application instance.

Database Failure

Like the other layers, a database may fail for multiple reasons. For example, it will stop accepting requests if the disk fills up and the database is unable to write transaction logs. The database process also might crash because of a bug in the code or because of memory corruption. When a database instance fails, the database proxy ensures that the database requests originating from the application instances get routed to the functioning database instance. Database failover is much more complex to handle than either network or application failure, because the databases on both nodes have to be in sync to allow seamless failover.

Databases on the two redundant nodes may be kept in sync either by replicating the database from one node to the other or by executing distributed transactions on both nodes for every database update. There are pros and cons to both approaches. Depending on the needs of the application, you can decide on which one to use. Let's look at the two options.

Replication

You can use replication to provide database redundancy. One of the nodes can either be designated or elected as the database master. All database updates have to be routed to the master instance. Both instances can handle the read-only queries. If a client node fails, all queries get routed to the master node by the database proxy. If the master node fails, then the client (or one of the client nodes) gets elected as the master and starts receiving all database requests.

Berkeley DB replication allows only single-master replication. Therefore, the application layer in a redundant system has to send the database updates to the node where the database master resides. Single-master replication makes a database proxy essential for a redundant system. Let's look at the pros and cons of using replication.

Advantages There are numerous advantages to using replication to provide fault tolerance:

- **Asynchronous**: One of the biggest advantages of using replication is that you can configure it to be asynchronous. For systems that require extremely quick database access in addition to fault tolerance, replication may be the only viable option. There is a possibility of data loss when replication is done asynchronously, but you can minimize that by carefully designing the acknowledgement scheme between the replicated nodes.

- **Nonblocking**: A distributed transaction cannot be committed unless it is committed on all the participating environments. Therefore, if one of the participating nodes crashes, transaction processing will come to halt. Replication has no such limitation. The library invokes the replication transport callback only after a transaction has been committed in the local environment. Therefore, failure of a replica doesn't stop transaction processing on the master.

- **Fast**: Since you can configure replication to be asynchronous and nonblocking, it can be much faster than XA. Also, replication doesn't require a GTM, so there's one less overhead to worry about.

- **Provides automatic elections**: When a master crashes in a replicated environment, one of the clients can be elected as the new master. When the original master comes back up, it can join the replicated environment as a client and receive from the new master all the transactions it missed while it was down. The election mechanism allows a node to fail and come back up without losing any database updates and without stopping transaction processing.

Disadvantages Some disadvantages to using replication to provide fault tolerance also exist:

- **Single master**: There can be only one master in a replicated environment, so all updates have to go to a single node. In applications where a large percentage of database operations involve updates, this limitation can lead to a performance bottleneck.

- **No transactional guarantee**: If an application requires a transaction guarantee, such as, any database update cannot not be committed unless it is committed on every node, then you cannot use replication. In replication, all transactions get committed in the master environment, whether or not they can be applied to the client nodes, so you cannot provide a transactional guarantee in a replicated environment. You should use distributed transactions in such cases.

- **Requires database proxy**: The application layer always has to send the update requests to the replication master, because updates can happen only on the master. Because of this limitation, it is essential to build a database proxy to allow the application processes to connect to the correct database instance. The application design becomes complicated because of the database proxy.

Distributed Transactions

You can set up the two (or more, depending on the kind of redundant configuration) database instances so that all updates are performed as distributed transactions. All update requests go through a GTM, which performs a distributed transaction involving both database instances. Figure 9-3 shows a redundant system that uses distributed transactions instead of replication.

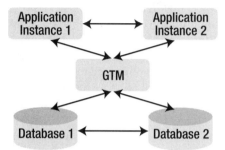

Figure 9-3. *Using GTM in a redundant system*

The database proxy is replaced by a GTM. All updates are performed on both database instances. If the update fails on one instance, the transaction won't be committed. The main advantage of this configuration is that the updates can be routed to any database. It is, in effect, a multimaster setup. The application layer doesn't need to go through a database proxy to figure out where the update request should be sent. Let's go through the pros and cons of this approach.

Advantages Here are the advantages to using XA to provide fault tolerance:

- **Multimaster setup**: In XA, the updates can be handled on both nodes. You don't need to set up a database proxy.

- **Transactional guarantees**: Distributed transactions ensure that when a transaction is committed, it is committed on all participating environments. If one of the database instances fails, you can be sure that the other database instance will have all the updates. There is no possibility of data loss.

Disadvantages Using XA for fault tolerance has some disadvantages as well:

- **Multiple single points of failure**: This setup has multiple single points of failure. Since all updates have to go through the GTM, it is a single point of failure. If the GTM fails, then the transaction processing will stop until it comes back up. In addition to the GTM, the individual database instances are also single points of failure because a distributed transaction cannot be committed unless all participating environments are up and running. When a database instance crashes, the transaction processing stops until that instance is brought online.

- **Need for a GTM**: Building a robust GTM can be a challenging task. Since this configuration requires a GTM, it is difficult to implement.

Deciding Between Replication and Distributed Transactions

The main purpose of having redundancy built into a system is to avoid single points of failure. Because the use of distributed transactions introduces another single point of failure to the system, XA is almost never used to provide fault tolerance. Replication is the hands-down favorite of designers for implementing fault tolerance.

However, certain applications cannot tolerate even a slight possibility of data loss during failover. In a replicated environment, the clients are always *slightly* behind the master. The possibility that some of the most recent transactions committed on the master might not show up on the clients is always there. Therefore, when a master fails, there is always a *slight* chance that when one of the clients becomes a master, the new master may not have some of the previously committed transactions. Certain critical applications, such as ones used in the banking industry, cannot afford to take the *slight* chance of missing a committed transaction, because that might mean missing a transaction worth thousands of dollars. For such applications, using distributed transactions is the only solution.

When distributed transactions are absolutely necessary, you have to work around the drawbacks associated with them. You can make the GTM fault-tolerant by running two instances of the GTM and replicating the GTM database on a backup node, which takes over if the active GTM instance fails. The single points of failure associated with database instances cannot be eliminated. You can only manage the downtime so that the failed database instance can be brought online as quickly as possible.

Load Balancing

Applications that traditionally were run on desktops are now being transformed into web-based applications that users can access online with a general-purpose browser. Even inherently desktop-bound applications such as word processors are now being offered as web-based services. This paradigm shift makes it easier for users to access these applications over the Internet cheaply, but it's also changing the way applications are designed. Applications designed to be deployed over the Internet have to take into consideration scalability issues, as potentially thousands of users could be using the application at any given time. This is not to say that only web-based applications have to be scalable, but rather that the Web is driving the need to build scalable solutions.

To be scalable, an application has to be designed carefully to avoid any performance bottlenecks. However, no matter how nicely it has been designed, it won't be able to scale forever. At some point, it will hit a limit after which it won't be able to handle more load. When the system hits the limit, you can use one of two ways to make it handle more load. You can either replace your machine with a more expensive one that can handle more load, or you can introduce another cheap machine and share the load. There are two problems with the first approach. First, it will cost you a lot more money than the second approach, and second, the expensive hardware will ultimately run out of steam as the load increases. The only permanent solution to the scalability problem is to share the load among multiple machines.

In order to share the load on multiple machines, the database should be available on all machines. It's possible to let all the processes running on load-sharing machines point to the same database, but then the database would become a bottleneck. You can either replicate the database to the machines, or you can use a GTM to execute distributed transactions on multiple machines. Let's evaluate the two approaches.

Replication

You can share the database among the load-sharing nodes by setting up replication among the nodes. Figure 9-4 shows a typical load-balancing setup that uses replication to make the database available on the nodes.

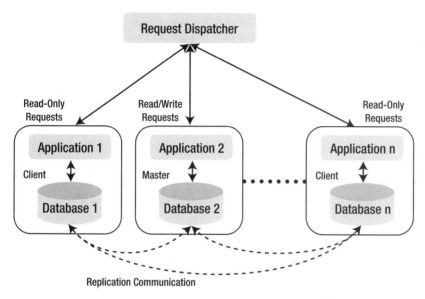

Figure 9-4. *Using replication for load balancing*

Since Berkeley DB allows only single-master replication, the update requests can be handled only at the master node. All the client nodes can handle only read-only requests. If a client node has to make an update, it will have to route that request to the master node. When the master node fails, one of the client nodes gets elected as the master. Here are the advantages to this approach:

- **Simpler to implement**: A solution based on replication is simpler to implement compared to a solution based on distributed transactions.

- **Fault tolerance**: With replication, fault tolerance comes for free. You can use the election mechanism available in Berkeley DB replication to elect a new master if the master node fails.

- **Scalable**: Berkeley DB replication can easily support hundreds of client nodes without putting too much load on the master node. It also supports various load-handling features such as delayed sync-up and cascading replication hierarchies, which further improve replication efficiency.

This approach also has some serious disadvantages; let's see what they are:

- **Single master**: Since Berkeley DB replication allows only single-master replication, you still have to handle all update requests at a single node. If the access pattern of the application involves mostly database updates rather than reads, then this approach won't result in load-sharing among the nodes. The master node will become a bottleneck.

- **Database proxy**: All client nodes have to forward the update requests to the master node; therefore, replication requires a database proxy that you can use to locate the master node from the client nodes. This can complicate the design of the application. It's possible to avoid the proxy by designating a single node as the master node so that the master node is known to every client node, but then the election mechanism wouldn't be used to provide fault tolerance to the application.

- **All data on all nodes**: Berkeley DB supports only full database replication. It isn't possible to replicate different sections of the database to different clients. If the database in question is huge, then all the clients will end up replicating tremendous amounts of data, most of which won't be needed most of the time.

Distributed Transactions

In XA, a database can be shared among the nodes by using distributed transactions. Figure 9-5 shows a load-balanced configuration that employs distributed transactions for sharing the database on multiple nodes.

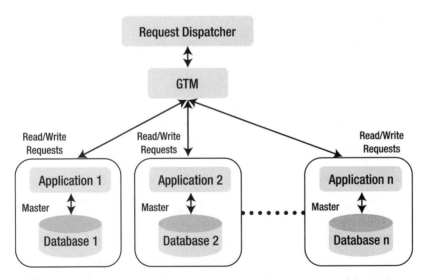

Figure 9-5. *Using distributed transactions for load balancing*

All database updates go through the GTM, which updates all participating nodes using distributed transactions. All nodes in this case can handle read/write operations. Here are the advantages to this approach:

- **Database proxy not required**: In this architecture, the load-sharing nodes don't need a database proxy to determine which node is the master node. All database updates go through the GTM.

- **Transactional guarantees**: When a distributed transaction is committed, the local transactions in all participating environments are guaranteed to be committed. If you need load balancing for critical applications, then this is the approach to choose.

- **Database address space can be split**: For large databases, it's possible to logically split the database among the load-sharing nodes with this approach.

The main drawbacks of this approach include the following:

- **Requires a GTM**: Once again, in an XA-based approach, a GTM is required, which can be hard to build.

- **Single point of failure**: The GTM, as well as the individual nodes, are single points of failure. If any one of those fails, the entire system won't be able to function anymore. You have to do extra work to ensure that a standby GTM is in place that can take over if the GTM fails.

- **Not scalable**: This architecture doesn't scale well for a large number of nodes. Since two-phase commit (used in distributed transactions) is a synchronous protocol, adding too many nodes to the load-balanced pool can significantly reduce the performance of the GTM.

For applications that have to deal with a tremendous amount of load and also have to operate on huge databases, none of the approaches discussed here will work. The problem with replication is that all nodes will end up with a large amount of data. It may not be feasible to load a large database on each load-sharing node. Most of the node resources will end up being wasted in maintaining the database. The problem with using distributed transactions is that you cannot use them with a large number of load-sharing nodes because of the synchronous nature of two-phase commits. It's possible to use both distributed transactions and replication in a single solution to provide load sharing and data division.

The Hybrid Approach

Web sites that have millions of customer accounts and handle hundreds of thousands of user requests every hour have to deal with a huge database and heavy load at the same time. Such applications are perfect candidates to apply a combination of replication and distributed transactions to solve the problem. However, not many applications use Berkeley DB in this manner. You can use distributed transactions to split a large database address space into smaller manageable address spaces. Once you've split the database, you can replicate it to multiple load-sharing nodes to handle the traffic. Figure 9-6 shows a load-balancing setup that uses both distributed transactions and replication to achieve load sharing.

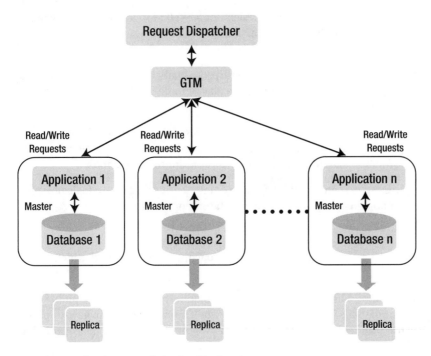

Figure 9-6. *Hybrid approach for load balancing*

The GTM in this setup has to provide an additional service. Now that the database address space has been split, not every database instance can handle all queries. The GTM has to maintain a mapping between the database regions and the database instances and route the queries to the correct database instance.

You may be wondering why you even need a GTM if you have independent database environments. You can have a simple routing component that looks up a mapping table to find out the database instance for every incoming request and routes the query to that instance. If the databases have nothing in common, then you can eliminate the GTM. However, that's rarely the case; databases can never be split like that. For example, consider a database for a web site that provides web-based e-mail to its subscribers. The database would have the following categories of information:

- **Subscriber information**: It would include information about the usernames, passwords, addresses, and profiles for each subscriber. This is biggest section in the database.

- **E-mail filtering rules**: It would need rules to filter out spam, viruses, and so on.

- **Advertisements**: It would include context-sensitive advertisements that would be displayed on users' screens.

As opposed to other information that's more or less static, the subscriber information keeps growing as new subscribers start using the service. When the web-site infrastructure has to scale to handle increased traffic as new users sign up, it would be desirable to split the database so that a node in the load-sharing pool can handle a set of users. For example, if you have

300,000 users and 3 machines to deploy to, you could divide the address space into three nodes, as shown in Figure 9-7.

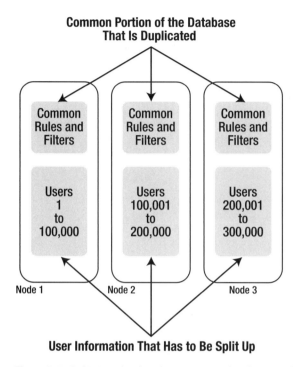

Figure 9-7. *Splitting the database among the three nodes*

You can easily route the queries to nodes 1, 2, and 3 depending on the user ID of the incoming request. However, to be able to process the requests, you would need to access the common information in the database, which includes the e-mail filtering rules and the advertisement information. You could argue that if the common information is small enough, it can be duplicated on the three nodes. That's a perfectly valid argument, but there's a catch. Suppose you have to update the e-mail filtering rules; how would you update the rules on three independent databases? You can't just update them one after the other independently, because if one of the nodes crashes while the update is going on, you'll end up with a situation where some nodes have the update and others don't. You would need a two-phase commit to ensure that either all the nodes get updated or none of them get updated. Therefore, you cannot get rid of the GTM even if you split the database end to end.

Summary

Through the DbTxn::prepare and DbEnv::txn_recover APIs, Berkeley DB provides all the support needed to build a participating RM in an XA system. You can use Berkeley DB as a GTM database, and you can also use it to work with an XA-compliant transaction manager. However, Berkeley DB doesn't provide a GTM implementation. In this chapter, you learned how to build a basic GTM. Distributed transactions can be complex to manage and difficult to troubleshoot.

However, in certain cases, you can solve the problem correctly only through the use of distributed transactions. Distributed transactions should not be disregarded as a possible solution just because of their complexity. Berkeley DB allows you to implement just the right distributed transactions–based solution for your application. It's possible to use Berkeley DB to build small and simple solutions based on distributed transactions.

In the next chapter, you'll learn how to use the database utilities that Berkeley DB provides. Database tuning and troubleshooting can be greatly simplified through proper utilization of these ready-made tools, which you should learn to exploit to their full potential.

CHAPTER 10

■ ■ ■

Berkeley DB Utilities

Berkeley DB allows you to implement administrative tasks such as backups, checkpoints, and log archival as a part of your application. Once you implement these tasks and tune the database properly, it requires no *outside* administration and tuning. However, during the development phase, you still need troubleshooting and tuning tools that aren't a part of the application. Berkeley DB comes packaged with some useful utilities that you can use for that purpose. Having a good understanding of these utilities and the information they provide can significantly reduce the amount of time you spend troubleshooting your Berkeley DB–based application. I'll go over the usage of the utilities and discuss the sitations in which each utility is useful.

Introduction to the Utilities

Berkeley DB utilities provide a way of performing administrative tasks on the database without having to write code. Almost all functions that the utilities perform can be accomplished programmatically. However, you often want to try out something quickly, and you don't want to spend hours writing throwaway code. You can use a Berkeley DB utility, if one is available for what you want to do. You'll use some utilities more than others while developing your application. Table 10-1 lists the utilities in the order of their usefulness, according to my experiences.

Depending on the requirements of your application, your interpretation of the most useful utilities may differ from the order shown in Table 10-1. Most applications usually perform a number of the listed functions programmatically; therefore, you'll find that you never have to use some of the utilities listed. However, you should still be familiar with the information provided by these utilities, because sometimes when you're looking for certain information to help you debug your application, you may not be aware that you can get it easily from one of the utilities. I recommend that you run these utilities against your Berkeley DB environment; you will come to learn a lot about your application. Let's go over each one of these utilities so you can learn how to use them. But first, you should understand some aspects that are common to all the utilities.

Table 10-1. *List of Berkeley DB Utilities*

Utility Name	Description
db_stat	Displays the statistics of various subsystems in the Berkeley DB environment
db_recover	Recovers a Berkeley DB environment
db_dump	Dumps the contents of a database
db_load	Loads data into a database
db_checkpoint	Creates a database checkpoint
db_deadlock	Runs deadlock detection on an environment
db_printlog	Prints the contents of the transaction log
db_archive	Performs database archival functions
db_hotbackup	Performs a hot backup of the data files and the transaction logs
db_verify	Verifies the consistency of a database

DB_HOME Environment Variable

All Berkeley DB utilities are sensitive to the DB_HOME environment variable. If DB_HOME is set in the shell from where the utility is run, then the Berkeley DB environment residing in the directory pointed to by the environment variable will be used for executing the utility. If DB_HOME is not set, then the current working directory will be used for the execution.

■**Tip** If your application has to deal with multiple environments, then it's better not to set DB_HOME while using the utilities. This way, you can avoid situations where you might expect the utility to be running against the current working directory but it is actually running against the directory in DB_HOME.

The Common Options

The following options are supported by almost all of the utilities, and they perform the same function wherever they're supported. Instead of grouping them under each utility, I've explained them here separately.

-h

You can use the -h option to specify the environment home directory. Even if DB_HOME is set, you can use the -h option to override it. If neither DB_HOME nor -h is specified, then the environment residing in the current working directory will be used.

-v

You can use -v to execute the utility in the verbose mode. Detailed execution messages are dumped on stdout when this option is specified. This option is not supported by db_stat, db_printlog, db_load, and db_dump, as these utilities return verbose information by default.

-P

If you used DbEnv::set_encrypt to enable encryption in the environment, then you can use -P to specify the password that the utility will use to decrypt the environment files. The password must be the same as the one set using DbEnv::set_encrypt. berkeley_db_svc doesn't support this option.

-N

When you specify this option, the utility doesn't try to acquire mutexes while traversing the environment data structures. This tool is useful for debugging corrupted environments. When a process crashes while holding a mutex on the critical section of the environment shared memory region, you cannot use it until recovery is performed. Running recovery basically destroys the existing environment and creates a new one, thereby destroying all the clues that point to the problem. With this option, you can look around the environment without destroying it.

-V

All Berkeley DB utilities support the -V option. When executed with this option, every utility prints the version number of the Berkeley DB library with which it is linked and then exits. No matter which utility you run with the -V option, you'll get the same output, as you can see from these results:

```
hy@linux:~/ws/bdb_book/chap_5/chap5_env> db_stat -V
Sleepycat Software: Berkeley DB 4.5.20: (September 20, 2006)
hy@linux:~/ws/bdb_book/chap_5/chap5_env> db_printlog -V
Sleepycat Software: Berkeley DB 4.5.20: (September 20, 2006)
```

This option isn't as trivial as it looks. When you're dealing with multiple library versions, this option can be extremely useful. If there is a mismatch between the library version that you used to create the Berkeley DB environment and the library version that's linked with the utility, you'll see strange errors such as the following:

```
hy@linux:~/ws/bdb_book/chap_5_old/chap5_env> db_stat -CA
db_stat: DB_ENV->open: Invalid argument
```

The db_stat output, shown here, is a result of running db_stat linked with version 4.4.20 against an environment created with version 4.3.28. If you run into such errors, the first thing to check is the library version. Starting from version 4.5.20, all Berkeley DB utilities can detect the version mismatch and report a proper error.

■**Note** When run with the -V option, the Berkeley DB utilities report the library version number they're linking to without opening the database environment. Therefore, they don't fail due to a version mismatch.

---

db_stat

db_stat is the single most important utility provided by Berkeley DB. It is also widely regarded as the most confusing. It reports a great deal of valuable information, but it takes practice and patience to understand the output. db_stat reports various types of database environment statistics, hence the name db_stat. The database environment consists of various subsystems; each subsystem maintains numerous statistical parameters pertaining to the usage of the subsystem. db_stat makes these parameters available through different command-line options. Table 10-2 shows the main options in the db_stat utility.

Table 10-2. *Main Options Available in db_stat*

Option Name	Subsystem
-C	Detailed internal information about the locking subsystem; useful for debugging.
-c	Statistics for the locking subsystem.
-l	Logging subsystem statistics.
-M	Detailed internal information about the database memory pool or the cache.
-m	Database cache statistics.
-R	Detailed internal information about the replication subsystem.
-r	Quick replication subsystem statistics.
-d	Statistics for a particular database file. If the file contains multiple databases, this option will report the statistics for the database that contains information about the databases stored in the file.
-s	Used in conjunction with the -d option. If a file contains multiple databases, then the file name will be specified through the -d option, and the database name will be specified through the -s option.
-t	Displays information about the transactional subsystem.
-e	Statistics related to the entire environment; an aggregate of statistics from all subsystems.

You'll use db_stat quite a lot while debugging your application. Let's go over the statistics for the various subsystems.

Locking Subsystem

The -C and the -c options show the locking subsystem information. The -c option provides a summary of the main locking parameters without going into too many details. Let's see what it provides:

```
hy@linux:~/ws/from_svn/trunk/chap_7/chap7_env> db_stat -c
34        Last allocated locker ID
0x7fffffff      Current maximum unused locker ID
9         Number of lock modes
1000      Maximum number of locks possible
1000      Maximum number of lockers possible
1000      Maximum number of lock objects possible
5         Number of current locks
9         Maximum number of locks at any one time
14        Number of current lockers
17        Maximum number of lockers at any one time
5         Number of current lock objects
8         Maximum number of lock objects at any one time
166       Total number of locks requested
161       Total number of locks released
0         Total number of locks upgraded
7         Total number of locks downgraded
1         Lock requests not available due to conflicts, for which we waited
0         Lock requests not available due to conflicts, for which we did not wait
0         Number of deadlocks
0         Lock timeout value
0         Number of locks that have timed out
0         Transaction timeout value
0         Number of transactions that have timed out
344KB     The size of the lock region
0         The number of region locks that required waiting (0%)
```

This information is useful for two things: for sizing the locking subsystem, and for measuring the performance of the locking subsystem.

Sizing the Locking Subsystem

The locking subsystem maintains the lock information in fixed-sized lock tables located in the shared memory region of the database environment. The output of db_stat -c can determine the size of the lock table. The following values are relevant to the size information:

- `Maximum number of lockers possible`: Reports the maximum number of locker entries that currently can be stored at a time in the lock table. The default value is 1000. You can change it by calling `DbEnv::set_lk_max_lockers` prior to calling `DbEnv::open` or by adding the line `set_lk_max_locker <desired number>` in the `DB_CONFIG` file.

- `Maximum number of locks possible`: Reports the maximum number of locks that can be allocated at any given time in the lock table. The default value is 1000, which you can change by invoking `DbEnv::set_lk_max_locks` prior to calling `DbEnv::open` or by adding `set_lk_max_locks <desired number>` in the `DB_CONFIG` file.

- `Maximum number of lock objects possible`: Shows the maximum number of objects that can be locked in the system at any given time. The default value of this too is 1000. You can modify it by calling `DbEnv::set_lk_max_objects` before calling `DbEnv::open` or by specifying `set_lk_max_objects <desired value>` in the `DB_CONFIG` file.

- `The size of the lock region`: Shows the size allocated in the shared memory region for the lock table.

- `Lock timeout value`: Indicates the maximum duration (assuming deadlock detection is running frequently enough) for which a lock will be kept in the lock table. Under certain circumstances, it's possible that a bigger time-out may result in more entries in the lock table, because the locks will take longer to time-out and will stay in the lock table for longer periods.

The easiest way to determine the best values for these parameters is to run your application under the maximum amount of stress that you think the system will be subjected to, and then run `db_stat -c` to see the actual number of locks, lockers, and lock objects used by the system. Next, set the maximum limits to twice the actual values. By doing that, you can be reasonably sure that you won't exceed the limit for any of these parameters, even under stress.

When the system runs out of space in the lock table, you'll get an `ENOMEM` error from all database operations that require a lock. If you compiled the library with the `--enable-debug` flag, then the library will also print out a more specific diagnostic message indicating which one of these three parameters exceeded the limit. When you see a Berkeley DB call return an `ENOMEM` error, you'll know that it's time to run `db_stat -c`.

■**Tip** The Berkeley DB APIs return the `ENOMEM` error either when the system is running low on resources (such as the memory or the disk space) or when the internal data structures used for running the database haven't been sized properly. One such data structure is the lock table; you can obtain the sizing information about it by running `db_stat -c`.

Measuring the Performance of the Locking Subsystem

You can determine how well the locking subsystem is performing by looking at the following values reported by `db_stat -c`:

- Maximum number of locks at any one time: The maximum number of simultaneous locks that the library allocates. If this number is more than half the Maximum number of locks possible, then you should increase the maximum possible locks, because it's likely that you'll exceed the limit soon. Similarly, you should check the Maximum number of lockers at any one time and the Maximum number of lock objects at any one time values to see if you've sized the lock table adequately.

- Number of deadlocks: Indicates the number of lock requests resulting in deadlocks. When the library determines that a lock request can result in a deadlock, it evicts one of the lockers immediately without waiting for its lock to time-out. Too many deadlocks point to either problems in the application logic, which is causing too much contention, or wrong database page size, which may be causing too many pages to be locked up during database operations. (For more details, see the discussion on deadlocks in Chapter 5.)

- Number of locks that have timed out: Indicates the locks that timed out. If too many time-outs are reported, then you probably should increase the lock time-out value, because the lockers aren't getting enough time to do their work.

Most of the other values reported by db_stat -c are used only occasionally, but it's good to know about them in case you run into a tricky problem that requires some extra information.

Detailed Information on the Locking Subsystem

Let's take a look at the -C option. The output from this option shows the contents of the lock table. I've found it quite useful for debugging leaked (acquired but never released) locks, lost (neither committed nor aborted) transactions, and leaked (opened but never closed) database handles. To fully utilize the information, you should print out the transaction IDs and locker IDs from your code. The -C option has a number of sub options, as you can see in Table 10-3.

Table 10-3. *The Suboptions in db_stat -C*

Suboption Name	Description
A	Displays information from all suboptions
c	Shows the lock-conflict matrix
l	Displays the information on lockers
o	Displays lock-object information
p	Displays the locking subsystem parameters

When suboption A is specified, it shows the information from all the other suboptions in one shot. The other suboptions show a single portion of the lock table. Let's run db_stat with each of these suboptions to understand what information you get out of them.

Lock-Conflict Matrix

You can see the lock-conflict matrix by running db_stat -Cc. Here's what you'll see when you run the command:

```
hy@linux:~/ws/from_svn/trunk/chap_7/chap7_env> db_stat -Cc
=-=-=-=-=-=-=-=-=-=-=-=-=-=-=-=-=-=-=-=-=-=-=
Lock REGINFO information:
Lock      Region type
5         Region ID
__db.005          Region name
0x4030e000        Original region address
0x4030e000        Region address
0x40363f40        Region primary address
0         Region maximum allocation
0         Region allocated
REGION_JOIN_OK    Region flags
=-=-=-=-=-=-=-=-=-=-=-=-=-=-=-=-=-=-=-=-=-=-=
Lock conflict matrix:
0        0        0        0        0        0        0        0        0
0        0        1        0        1        0        1        0        1
0        1        1        1        1        1        1        1        1
0        0        0        0        0        0        0        0        0
0        1        1        0        0        0        0        1        1
0        0        1        0        0        0        0        0        1
0        1        1        0        0        0        0        1        1
0        0        1        0        1        0        1        0        0
0        1        1        0        1        1        1        0        1
```

In the first section, you can see some information about the shared memory region where the lock table is stored. This isn't of much use to you if you're just using Berkeley DB, but it can be useful if you're troubleshooting some problem within the library. The second portion of the output shows the lock-conflict matrix, which the library uses to resolve deadlocks. The rows in the matrix represent the locks that are held, and the columns represent the locks that are requested. The number 1 indicates that the requested lock cannot be granted, and 0 indicates that it can be granted. The lock matrix shown here is the actual matrix that the library uses; it's slightly different from the one that is available (to be manipulated) from the locking API DbEnv::set_lk_conflicts. You have only six lock modes available from the API, whereas here you have nine available lock modes. If you poke around the source code to find out the modes, you'll see a matrix that looks like this:

```
More informative Lock conflict matrix:
        N    R    W    WT   IW   IR   RIW  DR   WW
N       0    0    0    0    0    0    0    0    0
R       0    0    1    0    1    0    1    0    1
W       0    1    1    1    1    1    1    1    1
WT      0    0    0    0    0    0    0    0    0
IW      0    1    1    0    0    0    0    1    1
IR      0    0    1    0    0    0    0    0    1
RIW     0    1    1    0    0    0    0    1    1
DR      0    0    1    0    1    0    1    0    0
WW      0    1    1    0    1    1    1    0    1
```

Table 10-4 explains what the lock-node acronyms represent in the previous results.

Table 10-4. *Explanation of the Lock-Mode Acronyms in the Lock-Conflict Matrix*

Lock-Mode Acronym	Description
N	Lock not granted
R	Read lock
W	Write lock
WT	Lock wait
IW	Intention to write
IR	Intention to read
RIW	Read with intention to write
DR	Dirty read
WW	Was write

Berkeley DB allows you to modify the lock matrix by using the locking API. However, you don't want to do that unless you're implementing a database of your own or implementing a locking framework using Berkeley DB's Lock API.

Locker Information

The current entries in the lockers table are displayed when you run db_stat -Cl:

```
hy@linux:~/ws/from_svn/trunk/chap_7/chap7_env> db_stat -Cl
=-=-=-=-=-=-=-=-=-=-=-=-=-=-=-=-=-=-=-=-=-=-=-=
Lock REGINFO information:
Lock    Region type
5       Region ID
__db.005        Region name
```

```
0x4030e000        Original region address
0x4030e000        Region address
0x40363f40        Region primary address
0          Region maximum allocation
0          Region allocated
REGION_JOIN_OK  Region flags
=-=-=-=-=-=-=-=-=-=-=-=-=-=-=-=-=-=-=-=-=-=
Locks grouped by lockers:
Locker  Mode       Count Status  ---------------- Object --------------
      10 dd=15 locks held 1    write locks 0    pid/thread 9738/1078930528
      10 READ         1 HELD    Person_Db                 handle       0
      11 dd=14 locks held 0    write locks 0    pid/thread 9738/1078930528
      12 dd=13 locks held 1    write locks 0    pid/thread 9738/1078930528
      12 READ         1 HELD    Account_Db                handle       0
      13 dd=12 locks held 0    write locks 0    pid/thread 9738/1078930528
      14 dd=11 locks held 1    write locks 0    pid/thread 9738/1078930528
      14 READ         1 HELD    Bank_Db                   handle       0
      15 dd=10 locks held 0    write locks 0    pid/thread 9738/1078930528
      16 dd= 9 locks held 1    write locks 0    pid/thread 9738/1078930528
      16 READ         1 HELD    Person_Name_Db            handle       0
      18 dd= 8 locks held 1    write locks 0    pid/thread 9738/1078930528
      18 READ         1 HELD    Person_Dob_Db             handle       0
      1a dd= 6 locks held 0    write locks 0    pid/thread 9738/1082035120
      1b dd= 5 locks held 0    write locks 0    pid/thread 9738/1082035120
      1c dd= 4 locks held 0    write locks 0    pid/thread 9738/1082035120
      1d dd= 3 locks held 0    write locks 0    pid/thread 9738/1082035120
      1e dd= 2 locks held 0    write locks 0    pid/thread 9738/1082035120
      1f dd= 1 locks held 0    write locks 0    pid/thread 9738/1082035120
8000000b dd= 0 locks held 4    write locks 3    pid/thread 19076/1082047408
8000000b WRITE         2 HELD    Person_Db                 page         1
8000000b WRITE         1 HELD    Person_Name_Db            page         1
8000000b WRITE         4 HELD    Person_Dob_Db             page         1
8000000b READ          1 HELD    Person_Db                 page         1
```

Here you can see the lock-region information in the beginning, which is identical to what was displayed when you ran db_stat -Cc. The region information is followed by a list of lockers currently present in the lock table. The list consists of information about the locker and the lock objects locked by the locker. For example, locker ID 10 belongs to thread 1078930528 in process 9738. Locker 10 currently holds a READ lock on the Db handle of the Person_Db database. You can also see that there are a number of lockers (1a, 1b, 1c, and so on) that don't hold any locks. These locker entries will ultimately be reused when new lockers have to be allocated.

■**Note** The process ID and the thread ID information will only be available in db_stat -Cl if you've used the DbEnv::set_thread_id method to set the IDs.

The locker IDs with large values are the ones that are owned by transactions. In the output, you can see that the locker ID 8000000b is owned by a transaction. This transaction holds four locks, out of which three are WRITE locks. The lock details indicate that the locks held by the transaction are page locks rather than handle locks.

In the output, take a look at the dd field, which indicates the deadlock detector ID assigned to the locker. You'll notice that sometimes when you run db_stat, the dd filed is 0 for all lockers. That happens when the no deadlocks are found in the system. When the first deadlock is detected, the lockers are assigned the IDs. The locker 8000000b shows a dd of 0, because it may have been started after the deadlock detector assigned the IDs.

Lock Object Information

You can obtain information about the lock objects by running db_stat -Co. It provides basically the same information as db_stat -Cl but in a different format:

```
hy@linux:~/ws/from_svn/trunk/chap_7/chap7_env> db_stat -Co
=-=-=-=-=-=-=-=-=-=-=-=-=-=-=-=-=-=-=-=-=-=-=-=
Lock REGINFO information:
Lock     Region type
5        Region ID
__db.005        Region name
0x4030e000      Original region address
0x4030e000      Region address
0x40363f40      Region primary address
0        Region maximum allocation
0        Region allocated
REGION_JOIN_OK  Region flags
=-=-=-=-=-=-=-=-=-=-=-=-=-=-=-=-=-=-=-=-=-=-=-=
Locks grouped by object:
Locker    Mode       Count Status ---------------- Object ---------------
8000000b READ          1 HELD    Person_Db             page       1
8000000b WRITE         2 HELD    Person_Db             page       1

      10 READ          1 HELD    Person_Db             handle     0

      12 READ          1 HELD    Account_Db            handle     0

      14 READ          1 HELD    Bank_Db               handle     0

8000000b WRITE         1 HELD    Person_Dob_Db         page       1

      16 READ          1 HELD    Person_Name_Db        handle     0

8000000b WRITE         1 HELD    Person_Name_Db        page       1

      18 READ          1 HELD    Person_Dob_Db         handle     0
```

As before, the locking region information is displayed first, and the lock objects are displayed next. The difference is that here the locks are arranged by the lock objects instead of the lockers. Also, notice that the lockers that don't hold any locks are missing from this display.

Locking Subsystem Parameters

By running db_stat -Cp, you can get information about the locking subsystem parameters:

```
hy@linux:~/ws/from_svn/trunk/chap_7/chap7_env> db_stat -Cp
=-=-=-=-=-=-=-=-=-=-=-=-=-=-=-=-=-=-=-=-=-=-=-=-=
Lock REGINFO information:
Lock      Region type
5         Region ID
__db.005        Region name
0x4030e000      Original region address
0x4030e000      Region address
0x40363f40      Region primary address
0         Region maximum allocation
0         Region allocated
REGION_JOIN_OK  Region flags
=-=-=-=-=-=-=-=-=-=-=-=-=-=-=-=-=-=-=-=-=-=-=-=-=
Lock region parameters:
46        Lock region region mutex [1/269 0% 21588/1076295360]
1031      locker table size
1031      object table size
343720    obj_off
335464    locker_off
0         need_dd
```

The important information in this output is the lock-region mutex. It shows the contention on the lock-region mutex. If that number gets high, then it means that you have too many threads trying to spend too much time in the database. When the lock table runs out of space, you can also check the current size of the table from this output.

Database Statistics

You can access database statistics by running db_stat -d. The information returned by this command is quite useful for tuning the database access method. Let's see what you get from this command:

```
hy@linux:~/ws/from_svn/trunk/chap_7/chap7_env> db_stat -d Person_Db
Sun Jun 11 17:55:32 2006        Local time
53162   Btree magic number
9       Btree version number
Little-endian   Byte order
        Flags
```

```
2        Minimum keys per-page
512      Underlying database page size
1        Number of levels in the tree
5        Number of unique keys in the tree
5        Number of data items in the tree
0        Number of tree internal pages
0        Number of bytes free in tree internal pages (0% ff)
1        Number of tree leaf pages
250      Number of bytes free in tree leaf pages (51% ff)
0        Number of tree duplicate pages
0        Number of bytes free in tree duplicate pages (0% ff)
0        Number of tree overflow pages
0        Number of bytes free in tree overflow pages (0% ff)
0        Number of empty pages
0        Number of pages on the free list
```

This command reports some basic information about the database, including the creation time, the access method, the byte order, the page size, and so on. It also reports some important tuning information.

Database Page Size

The database page size is reported by Underlying database page size. This is the quantum in which data is paged to and from the disk, and this is the minimum amount of data that is locked by a single lock. If you make the page size too small, then you'll do too much disk I/O that will slow down your application. If you make it too big, then the application will lose concurrency, because too much data will be locked up by every lock. You should look at the cache hit ratio (reported by db_stat -m) to assess whether your page size is too small. If your page size is too small—in other words, if most of your records don't fit into one page—then the cache hit ratio will be on the lower side (less than 80%). The smaller the page size, the more overflow records will be created, causing the cache hit ratio to reduce. You can determine whether the page size is too big by looking at the number of deadlocks (reported by db_stat -c). If you see too many deadlocks that you can't explain by the degree of concurrency in your application, then your database page size is probably too big.

When determining the correct page size, also consider the number of overflow pages. An overflow page is created when a record doesn't fit completely in a page. Overflow pages reduce the database performance tremendously, because some records might need multiple disk I/Os. If you see too many overflow pages, you should consider increasing the database page size.

Page-Fill Factor

The page-fill factor is the average percentage of used space on the database pages. If it's too low, then your database pages will be too sparsely populated, making locking and paging to and from the disk inefficient. A smaller fill factor also reduces cache heat. Since each page holds fewer records, there is a lower probability that the record you're looking for is in the cache. The fill factor is reported by Number of bytes free in tree leaf pages (the percentage is shown within brackets). A fill factor of less than 80% is considered to be bad. In the dump shown previously, the fill factor is just 51%. It's so low because you have only five records in the database that occupy only half a page. The fill factor is affected by the Db::set_bt_minkey for the BTree access method and the Db::set_h_ffactor for the Hash access method. By increasing the minimum number of keys that should be present on one page, you can increase the fill factor. The fill factor is also affected by the DB_REVSPLITOFF flag in the Db::set_flags method. If DB_REVSPLITOFF is set, then the pages won't be compacted when records are deleted from the database. When records are routinely added and deleted in a database, this flag will prevent excessive deadlocks, but it will also reduce the fill factor.

Logging Subsystem Statistics

Logging subsystem statistics is reported when you run the command db_stat -l:

```
hy@linux:~/ws/from_svn/trunk/chap_7/chap7_env> db_stat -l
0x40988 Log magic number
11      Log version number
32KB    Log record cache size
0       Log file mode
10Mb    Current log file size
57      Records entered into the log
3KB 683B        Log bytes written
0       Log bytes written since last checkpoint
18      Total log file I/O writes
0       Total log file I/O writes due to overflow
18      Total log file flushes
227     Total log file I/O reads
1       Current log file number
1146448 Current log file offset
1       On-disk log file number
1146448 On-disk log file offset
1       Maximum commits in a log flush
0       Minimum commits in a log flush
96KB    Log region size
0       The number of region locks that required waiting (0%)
```

This command reports some routine information about the transaction logs, including the current log file number, the current log file offset, and the total number of log bytes written to the disk. There is not much information here that you can use to tune the system. The only value you can use for tuning is the Log record cache size.

Transaction Log Cache

The log cache is used for holding the transaction logs before they're flushed to the stable storage. When in-memory logging is configured for the environment, the size of the largest transaction that your application is committing should always be less than the size of the log cache. By default, the size of this cache is 1MB for in-memory logging. If you try to commit a transaction bigger than 1MB, then your application will either hang or crash. The log cache cannot be paged in the in-memory configuration, so if any transaction doesn't fit in the cache, there isn't much the database can do about it. If you notice unexplained hangs or crashes in your application, make sure that you check the log cache size—perhaps some of your transactions are overflowing the cache.

When configured for on-disk logging, the cache size is set to 32KB by default. In the on-disk mode, the cache is flushed to the disk when it gets full, due to a long-running or a large transaction. Making the cache size bigger, when large or long-running transactions have to be run, improves the performance of the database.

Size of Transaction Logs

You can use the Current log file number and the Current log file size to find out the exact size of the transaction logs. If your log file size is too big, then you may not know just by looking at the transaction log file names how big the logs are. You can also find out how many logs have been flushed to the disk by looking at On-disk log file number and On-disk log file offset.

Cache Statistics

Cache statistics are reported by db_stat -m. The command displays the general cache statistics in the first section, followed by the statistics of the individual database caches:

```
hy@linux:~/ws/from_svn/trunk/chap_7/chap7_env> db_stat -m
257KB 868B      Total cache size
1         Number of caches
264KB     Pool individual cache size
0         Maximum memory-mapped file size
0         Maximum open file descriptors
0         Maximum sequential buffer writes
0         Sleep after writing maximum sequential buffers
0         Requested pages mapped into the process' address space
163       Requested pages found in the cache (95%)
8         Requested pages not found in the cache
0         Pages created in the cache
8         Pages read into the cache
4         Pages written from the cache to the backing file
0         Clean pages forced from the cache
0         Dirty pages forced from the cache
0         Dirty pages written by trickle-sync thread
8         Current total page count
8         Current clean page count
0         Current dirty page count
37        Number of hash buckets used for page location
179       Total number of times hash chains searched for a page
1         The longest hash chain searched for a page
163       Total number of hash chain entries checked for page
0         The number of hash bucket locks that required waiting (0%)
0         The maximum number of times any hash bucket lock was waited for
```

```
0        The number of region locks that required waiting (0%)
28       The number of page allocations
0        The number of hash buckets examined during allocations
0        The maximum number of hash buckets examined for an allocation
0        The number of pages examined during allocations
0        The max number of pages examined for an allocation
Pool File: Person_Db
512      Page size
0        Requested pages mapped into the process' address space
86       Requested pages found in the cache (97%)
2        Requested pages not found in the cache
0        Pages created in the cache
2        Pages read into the cache
2        Pages written from the cache to the backing file
```

This command reports some important tuning, as well as general information about the system. One of the most important tuning parameters is the size of the cache. This cache is used for storing the database pages in the shared memory region of the environment.

Cache Size

The size of the database cache is the biggest tuning knob at your disposal. You can improve the performance of your system significantly by setting the cache size correctly. It's set to 256KB by default. More often than not, this is too small. The bigger the cache size, the less disk I/O will be needed to service the database queries. The improvement in performance is directly proportional to the size of the cache, until the working set of records has not been paged into the memory. If the working set is too big to fit into the memory, then increasing the cache size doesn't have too much effect. However, there's no harm in allocating any spare memory in your system to the cache, if it will improve the performance.

The default cache size is set to be so small for historical reasons. Berkeley DB was originally written in 1991, when memory used to be quite expensive. At 64KB (the original default), you could fit 128 512-byte pages in the cache, and that was a lot at the time. The original default was set to be low to prevent any one application from hogging resources on what were often shared research machines.

Cache Hit Ratio

The cache hit ratio is defined as the percentage of requests that get serviced by the cache. The bigger the hit ratio, the lesser disk I/O needed to service the database queries. The cache hit ratio is reported under Requested pages found in the cache. If this value is small (less than 90%), you should think of increasing the cache size.

Transaction Statistics

db_stat -t displays some useful statistics about the transactional subsystem:

```
hy@linux:~/ws/bdb_book/chap_5/chap5_env> db_stat -t
1/17788 File/offset for last checkpoint LSN
Sat Jun 10 11:10:27 2006        Checkpoint timestamp
0x800079fe      Last transaction ID allocated
20      Maximum number of active transactions configured
5       Active transactions
5       Maximum active transactions
31230   Number of transactions begun
1       Number of transactions aborted
31224   Number of transactions committed
0       Number of transactions restored
16KB    Transaction region size
11      The number of region locks that required waiting (0%)
Active transactions:
        800079fa: pid/thread 21737/1084148656; begin LSN: file/offset 1/8146157
        800079fb: pid/thread 21737/1082047408; begin LSN: file/offset 0/0
        800079fc: pid/thread 21737/1090452400; begin LSN: file/offset 0/0
        800079fd: pid/thread 21737/1086249904; begin LSN: file/offset 0/0
        800079fe: pid/thread 21737/1088351152; begin LSN: file/offset 0/0
```

Take notice of a couple of important tuning parameters:

- `Maximum number of active transactions configured`: Determines how many transactions can be started simultaneously. After this limit is reached, any new invocation of `DbEnv::txn_begin` will return an error. Keeping this too small reduces the concurrency, whereas setting it too large results in a big portion of the environment cache being allocated to the transaction region. The child transactions are counted as independent transactions. You can change this value through the `DbEnv::set_tx_max` method. You should set this number high enough to handle all reasonably foreseeable transaction workloads in the application. It's often directly related to the number of concurrent threads or processes that the application plans to use.

- `Transaction region size`: Shows how big the transaction region is within the environment. If you modify the maximum number of active transactions, you'll notice that the transaction region size will change automatically. You cannot modify the transaction region size directly.

Apart from the tuning parameters, the `db_stat -t` command also shows the transactions that are currently active in the environment. In the previous output, you can see five active transactions and the thread IDs and process IDs associated with them. This information can be quite useful for debugging issues related to transactions, deadlocks, and time-outs when correlated with the output of `db_stat -l`.

Replication Statistics

Statistics on the replication subsystem are reported when you run `db_stat -r`. You'll see the following output when you run the command:

```
hy@linux:~/ws/from_svn/trunk/chap_8/chap8_env_1> db_stat -r
Environment configured as a replication master
1/13152 Next LSN to be used
0/0     Not waiting for any missed log records
0       Next page number expected.
0       Not waiting for any missed pages.
0       Number of duplicate master conditions detected.
1       Current environment ID
100     Current environment priority
4       Current generation number
5       Current election generation number
0       Number of duplicate log records received
0       Number of log records currently queued
0       Maximum number of log records ever queued at once
0       Total number of log records queued
0       Number of log records received and appended to the log
0       Number of log records missed and requested
1       Current master ID
0       Number of times the master has changed
1       Number of messages received with a bad generation number
6       Number of messages received and processed
0       Number of messages ignored due to pending recovery
0       Number of failed message sends
170     Number of messages sent
0       Number of new site messages received
3       Number of environments believed to be in the replication group
0       Transmission limited
0       Number of outdated conditions detected
0       Number of duplicate page records received
0       Number of page records received and added to databases
0       Number of page records missed and requested
Startup incomplete
0       Number of transactions applied
1       Number of elections held
1       Number of elections won
No election in progress
0.085991        Duration of last election (seconds)
0       Number of bulk buffer sends triggered by full buffer
0       Number of single records exceeding bulk buffer size
0       Number of records added to a bulk buffer
0       Number of bulk buffers sent
0       Number of re-request messages received
0       Number of request messages this client failed to process
0       Number of request messages received by this client
```

Replication statistics are quite useful in troubleshooting and tuning replication frameworks. Let's look at the troubleshooting information first:

- `Next LSN to be used`: This LSN indicates how far a replication client is with respect to the current master in terms of syncing up. If your replication framework isn't behaving as you expect, you can compare this LSN on the master with that of the client. If they aren't the same or close enough, you'll know that the sync-up isn't happening. You can also use this LSN to measure the progress of replication. If sync-up is proceeding without any problem, the client's LSN should continue to increase until it catches up with the master.

- `Number of duplicate master conditions detected`: When more than one master is detected in a replication group, this counter is incremented. Ideally, this counter should be 0. If you see too many duplicate master conditions, then there is a problem with your election parameters. Either the participating environments aren't waiting long enough to hear back from a sufficient number of nodes, or you have an intermittent network-partitioning problem.

- `Current election generation number`: This number is used in the election protocol to determine whether a node that thinks that it's the master is lagging behind other nodes in the group. It's possible that due to a network partition, the master node becomes unreachable for some nodes, which then elect a master among themselves. When the partition is gone, the master could be lagging compared to the other nodes. If the election generation number on the master is less than the other nodes, then the master is likely stuck in a network partition.

- `Number of log records currently queued`: If you see too many queued records, then there is a communication problem. The node is waiting to receive a missing log record, which is causing the subsequent records to queue up.

- `Current master ID`: This is the ID of the node that this node thinks is the master. It can be different from the actual master if the node isn't able to communicate with a sufficient number of nodes. If this ID is different on different nodes, then the nodes aren't communicating properly.

- `Number of times the master has changed`: If the master is changing too frequently, then the election parameters aren't being set properly. Common errors include not setting `numvotes` to `n/2 + 1` (where *n* is the total number of nodes) or setting the `timeout` too short in the `DbEnv::rep_elect` call.

- `Startup incomplete`: This is an indication that the client has not synced up to the master.

The main tuning parameters in the replication subsystem are the node priorities and the arguments passed to `DbEnv::rep_elect`. You use the node priorities to determine the winner of an election, among other things. The `numvotes` and `timeout` parameters in the `DbEnv::rep_elect` method determine how many node replies a node will wait for and for how long. You can use the `Duration of last election` reported here to see if the election process is waiting long enough for the nodes to reply. This number may be different from the time-out value you pass in `DbEnv::rep_elect`. Even though you may be passing a big time-out value, the election process may finish much earlier if a certain node is slow in responding. If you want to take the vote of the slow node into consideration, then you should increase `numvotes` and increase `timeout`.

db_recover

You can recover an environment using db_recover. Usually, you'll do environment recovery programmatically by specifying DB_RECOVER or DB_RECOVER_FATAL (for catastrophic recovery) in the DbEnv::open method. Sometimes, however, you might need to run recovery manually for troubleshooting some problem. In a production environment, you might not have the luxury of running a debug version of your application, and that could leave you with limited information in the event of a failure. With the db_recover utility, you can run recovery manually from the shell and troubleshoot problems with the environment. Table 10-5 shows the various options available in db_recover.

Table 10-5. *Options Available in db_recover*

Option Name	Option Description
-c	Performs catastrophic recovery
-e	Performs recovery without destroying the existing environment
-t	Performs recovery until the specified timestamp rather than to the most recent transaction

The different options allow you to run different types of recovery. Simple recovery is intended for simple application failures or system reboots when the database and log files survived across restarts. Catastrophic recovery is intended for recovery from either the log files or the database files, or both. Please see Chapter 5 for a detailed discussion on the various types of recovery.

Simple Recovery

The command db_recover, without any option, performs a simple recovery. In a simple recovery, the last checkpointed LSN (which is different from a checkpoint record) in the transaction log is looked up, and the environment is recovered until the most recent transaction found in the log. You'll see the following output when you run this command:

```
hy@linux:~/ws/from_svn/trunk/chap_7/chap7_env> db_recover -v
Finding last valid log LSN: file: 1 offset 1150271
Recovery starting from [1][1149697]
Recovery complete at Tue Jun 13 23:24:38 2006
Maximum transaction ID 8000000f Recovery checkpoint [1][1150271]
```

The output shows that the recovery is performed from the latest checkpointed LSN [1][1149697] until the most recent transaction and a recovery checkpoint are written to the log. You can do a simple recovery quickly and routinely while opening the environment. During recovery, all the existing environment files are cleaned up. Here's how an environment directory looks before running recovery:

```
hy@linux:~/ws/from_svn/trunk/chap_7/chap7_env> ls -l
total 4301
-rw-r--r--  1 hy users      1024 2006-03-04 13:18 Account_Db
-rw-r--r--  1 hy users      1024 2006-03-04 13:18 Bank_Db
-rw-r-----  1 hy users     24576 2006-06-13 23:54 __db.001
-rw-r-----  1 hy users    278528 2006-06-13 23:54 __db.002
-rw-r-----  1 hy users    270336 2006-06-13 23:54 __db.003
-rw-r-----  1 hy users     98304 2006-06-13 23:54 __db.004
-rw-r-----  1 hy users    352256 2006-06-13 23:54 __db.005
-rw-r-----  1 hy users     16384 2006-06-13 23:54 __db.006
-rw-r-----  1 hy users       175 2006-04-03 00:37 __db.register
-rw-r-----  1 hy users  10485760 2006-06-13 23:54 log.0000000001
-rw-r--r--  1 hy users      1024 2006-06-13 23:39 Person_Db
-rw-r--r--  1 hy users      1024 2006-06-13 23:39 Person_Dob_Db
-rw-r--r--  1 hy users      1024 2006-03-04 14:09 Person_Name_Db
```

After running recovery, you'll see something like this:

```
hy@linux:~/ws/from_svn/trunk/chap_7/chap7_env> ls -l
total 4253
-rw-r--r--  1 hy users      1024 2006-03-04 13:18 Account_Db
-rw-r--r--  1 hy users      1024 2006-03-04 13:18 Bank_Db
-rw-r-----  1 hy users       175 2006-04-03 00:37 __db.register
-rw-r-----  1 hy users  10485760 2006-06-13 23:55 log.0000000001
-rw-r--r--  1 hy users      1024 2006-06-13 23:55 Person_Db
-rw-r--r--  1 hy users      1024 2006-06-13 23:55 Person_Dob_Db
-rw-r--r--  1 hy users      1024 2006-03-04 14:09 Person_Name_Db
```

Notice that all the environment region files are gone. You won't see this happening when you run recovery programmatically, because the DbEnv::open method creates a new environment right after the recovery procedure destroys the existing environment.

Catastrophic Recovery

You need to perform catastrophic recovery either when you're restoring a backup or when some corruption exists in the data files prior to the last checkpointed LSN and cannot be fixed by a simple recovery. Catastrophic recovery starts the recovery process from the earliest transaction log found in the environment until the most recent log. Let's see what happens when you run catastrophic recovery on your environment instead of a simple recovery:

```
hy@linux:~/ws/from_svn/trunk/chap_7/chap7_env> db_recover -v -c
Finding last valid log LSN: file: 1 offset 1156877
Recovery starting from [1][28]
Recovery complete at Tue Jun 13 23:47:27 2006
Maximum transaction ID 8000030b Recovery checkpoint [1][1156877]
```

This time, the recovery starts from the first LSN—that is [1][28]—rather than the last checkpointed LSN. Catastrophic recovery can take a long time if you have a large amount of transaction logs sitting in your environment. However, this is the only sure way of fixing all corruptions and restoring a pristine state. Like the simple recovery, catastrophic recovery also removes the existing environment.

Preserving the Environment During Recovery

If you don't want to delete the existing environment during the recovery procedure, you can run db_recover -e. Here you can see the result of running this command:

```
hy@linux:~/ws/from_svn/trunk/chap_7/chap7_env> db_recover -v -e
Finding last valid log LSN: file: 1 offset 1162361
Recovery starting from [1][1159838]
Recovery complete at Wed Jun 14 00:02:00 2006
Maximum transaction ID 8000000f Recovery checkpoint [1][1162799]
hy@linux:~/ws/from_svn/trunk/chap_7/chap7_env> ls -l
total 4777
-rw-r--r--  1 hy users     1024 2006-03-04 13:18 Account_Db
-rw-r--r--  1 hy users     1024 2006-03-04 13:18 Bank_Db
-rw-r-----  1 hy users    24576 2006-06-14 00:02 __db.001
-rw-r-----  1 hy users   278528 2006-06-14 00:02 __db.002
-rw-r-----  1 hy users   270336 2006-06-14 00:02 __db.003
-rw-r-----  1 hy users    98304 2006-06-14 00:02 __db.004
-rw-r-----  1 hy users   352256 2006-06-14 00:02 __db.005
-rw-r-----  1 hy users    16384 2006-06-14 00:02 __db.006
-rw-r-----  1 hy users      175 2006-04-03 00:37 __db.register
-rw-r-----  1 hy users 10485760 2006-06-14 00:02 log.0000000001
-rw-r--r--  1 hy users     1024 2006-06-14 00:02 Person_Db
-rw-r--r--  1 hy users     1024 2006-06-14 00:02 Person_Dob_Db
-rw-r--r--  1 hy users     1024 2006-03-04 14:09 Person_Name_Db
```

You can see that the environment files are still present after the recovery has been done. You may want to use this option if you want to keep the existing environment around for further debugging. If environment corruption was the cause of the failure, -e may not work, and even if it does, it might not be a good idea, because it could cause your application to use corrupted data.

■**Caution** After running db_recover -e, the sizes of the various environment regions, such as the cache and logging region, will be set to the default values. If you're using this option, you should make sure that you have the correct region sizes specified in the DB_CONFIG file.

Recovering Up to a Timestamp

If you cannot recover your database up to the latest transaction log record due to corruption, then you can use db_recover -t to recover to a log record located just before the corruption. Another reason to do this is to undo an erroneous change to the database. For example, when a user deletes all the records in his address book erroneously, you may want to recover to the timestamp just before that happened. If you cannot recover the environment due to a corruption, then db_recover will report the LSN to the record that it couldn't recover. You can dump the transaction log to find out a timestamp just before the corrupted log record and recover to that timestamp. The db_printlog output listed here shows an excerpt of a sample transaction log:

```
hy@linux:~/ws/from_svn/trunk/chap_7/chap7_env>db_printlog
-
-
[1][1161281]__txn_regop: rec: 10 txnid 80000008 prevlsn [1][1161213]
        opcode: 1
        timestamp: 1150268510 (Wed Jun 14 00:01:50 2006, 200606140001.50)
        envid: -499431760
        locks:
-
-
hy@linux:~/ws/from_svn/trunk/chap_7/chap7_env> db_recover -v -t 200606140001.50
Finding last valid log LSN: file: 1 offset 1162891
Recovery starting from [1][11484]
Recovery complete at Wed Jun 14 00:15:37 2006
Maximum transaction ID 8000030b Recovery checkpoint [1][1162463]
```

Suppose you found a log record [1][1161213] just before the corrupted record by looking at the output of db_printlog. You can recover the environment until 200606140001.50 (which is the date Jun 14 00:01:50 2006 in the [[CC]YY]MMDDhhmm[.SS] format).

This option can be quite useful for troubleshooting issues related to hard-disk caches on cheap disks. On certain cheap Advanced Technology Attachment (ATA) hard disks, you'll find that even after a flush, the disk doesn't actually write everything to the disk. On systems using such disks, you might end up with corrupted environments that you can't recover, because entire database pages might be lost if the machine wasn't shut down gracefully. If you try to open such an environment using DB_RECOVER or DB_RECOVER_FATAL in DbEnv::open, you'll probably get the DB_PAGE_NOTFOUND error, because certain pages referred by the transaction log cannot be found on the disk. The library will ultimately return the DB_RUN_RECOVERY error, or if the corruption is bad enough, your application might just crash. In such a situation, you're supposed to restore a backup, but the problem with backups is that you can't take a backup after every transaction is committed. Even if you take a backup every hour (which might be quite aggressive for a busy system), you lose one hour's worth of committed data. It might make sense to invest in better storage technology if that's not acceptable.

Using db_recover, you can figure out until what point you can recover in the current corrupted environment. That allows you to recover to a more recent state than a restored backup, which might be quite old, depending on the frequency of your backups. That kind of control isn't available to you when you perform recovery programmatically by using DB_RECOVER. You can recover to a timestamp programmatically, but you would need to know the timestamp, so you probably would need to examine the log files manually.

db_dump

You can dump database contents using the db_dump utility. The dump generated by db_dump is in the binary format, because Berkeley DB doesn't understand the schema of the data being stored in the database. It's cumbersome to use db_dump to view the data structures stored in the database, because you have to parse its output to make any sense out of it. However, the db_dump has other uses—for example, you can use it as a verification and data-salvage tool.

Verification Tool

Even though the output from db_dump is in the binary format, you can still use it to quickly verify whether the database has the number of entries that were supposed to be in it. Let's see what the dumped output looks like:

```
hy@linux:~/ws/from_svn/trunk/chap_7/chap7_env> db_dump Person_Db
VERSION=3
format=bytevalue
type=btree
db_pagesize=512
HEADER=END
 06a12225
 2522a1064d616e6973682050616e646579006a616e2031332031393731300
 06a12226
 2622a106536869726967736820526169900 6a616e20312 03230303100
 06a47d87
 877da406526f6c616e642048656e64656c c0066656622031332031393733300
 06a47d88
 887da406526f6c616e642048656e64656c c0066656622031332031393733300
 06a47d89
 897da406526f6c616e642048656e64656c c0066656622031332031393733300
DATA=END
```

The data is dumped in hexadecimal representation of the binary data stored in the database. As you can see, it doesn't make too much sense. At the most, you can verify that the database contains the number of entries that you expect. After the line HEADER=END, the keys and the values are dumped on alternate lines. You can dump a slightly more readable format by using db_dump -p, which tries to convert the data into ASCII characters, but even this will be useful only if you have printable characters stored in the database. Here's an output of db_dump with the -p option:

```
hy@linux:~/ws/from_svn/trunk/chap_7/chap7_env> db_dump -p Person_Db
VERSION=3
format=print
type=btree
db_pagesize=512
HEADER=END
 \06\a1"%
%"\a1\06Manish Pandey\00jan 13 1971\00
 \06\a1"&
&"\a1\06Shirish Rai\00jan 1 2001\00
 \06\a4}\87
\87}\a4\06Roland Hendel\00feb 13 1973\00
 \06\a4}\88
\88}\a4\06Roland Hendel\00feb 13 1973\00
 \06\a4}\89
\89}\a4\06Roland Hendel\00feb 13 1973\00
DATA=END
```

You can obtain another useful output by running db_stat -da. Rather than a tuning or debugging tool, this is more of a visualization tool that helps you understand how records are stored in the database. This command shows not only the records found in a particular table, but also the actual layout of the records on the internal database pages. By looking at this output, you can understand better how page-level locking works. You can literally see which records are being locked when a page lock is acquired, what an overflow record is, and a lot of other difficult-to-understand concepts:

```
hy@linux:~/ws/bdb_book/chap_5/chap5_env> db_dump -da chap5_tds
In-memory DB structure:
btree: 0x90000 (open called, read-only)
bt_meta: 0 bt_root: 1
bt_minkey: 2
bt_compare: 0x4002beed bt_prefix: 0x4002bf8e
bt_lpgno: 0
=-=-=-=-=-=-=-=-=-=-=-=-=-=-=-=-=-=-=-=-=-=-=
page 0: btree metadata: LSN [1][9361919]: level 0
    magic: 0x53162
    version: 9
    pagesize: 512
    type: 9
    keys: 0 records: 0
    free list: 0
```

```
        last_pgno: 5178
        flags: 0
        uid: 67 68 9 0 5 3 0 0 27 f4 3 e4 61 3e 0 0 0 0 0 0
        minkey: 2
        root: 1
page 1: btree internal: LSN [1][8405455]: level 3 records: 0
        entries:    3 offset:   460
        [000]  500 count:    0 pgno: 3185 type: 1 len:    0
        [001]  480 count:    0 pgno: 3186 type: 1 len:    6 data: 1_19800
        [002]  460 count:    0 pgno: 4602 type: 1 len:    6 data: 1_30300
page 2: overflow: LSN [1][25548]: level 0
        prev:    3 next:   14 ref cnt:    1 len: 486 data: ➥
00000000000000000000000000000000000000000...
page 3: overflow: LSN [1][24918]: level 0
        prev:    4 next:    2 ref cnt:    1 len: 486 data: ➥
00000000000000000000000000000000000000000...
page 4: overflow: LSN [1][24288]: level 0
        prev:    5 next:    3 ref cnt:    1 len: 486 data: ➥
00000000000000000000000000000000000000000...
page 5: overflow: LSN [1][23658]: level 0
        prev:    6 next:    4 ref cnt:    1 len: 486 data: ➥
00000000000000000000000000000000000000000...
-
-
```

This output shows an overflow record. You can see the various database pages and data stored on the pages the LSNs associated with them.

Data Salvage

You can also use db_dump to salvage data from a corrupted database. Due to corruption, it may become impossible to read the entries in a database using the regular APIs. However, you still may be able to read certain entries if the corrupted portions are ignored. You can use db_dump -r and db_dump -R to do just that. The difference between the -r and the -R options is that -r tries to ignore the portions that are corrupted (for example, if the checksum of a page is wrong, then it will ignore that page), whereas -R dumps whatever it finds in the database whether or not it is corrupted. The output from -R is rarely useful unless you edit it manually to remove the inconsistencies.

■**Tip** Recovering data using these options can be extremely difficult and time-consuming. You shouldn't depend on these options for recovering your data. If you've lost all your backups and your data is too important to lose, only then you might want to try out these options; otherwise, it's not worth wasting your time.

db_load

You can use db_load to load data in a database without having to write a program to do that. This can be a convenient tool for creating a database to try out something quickly. However, the data that you load has to be in a specific format. It can be the output from the db_dump command, or it can be a list of key-value pairs in a text file. The text format is especially useful, because you can use it to load data generated by a non–Berkeley DB program. Let's see how you can create a Berkeley DB database using a text file containing database entries:

```
hy@linux:~/ws/from_svn/trunk/chap_7/chap7_env> cat data.txt
key 1
data 1
key 2
data 2
key 3
data 3
```

If you create a file called data.txt, which contains three key-value pairs, you can use that file to create a database. You can use the command shown here:

```
hy@linux:~/ws/from_svn/trunk/chap_7/chap7_env> db_load -f ./data.txt -T -t btree ➡
Loaded_Db
hy@linux:~/ws/from_svn/trunk/chap_7/chap7_env> db_dump -da Loaded_Db
In-memory DB structure:
btree: 0x90000 (open called, read-only)
bt_meta: 0 bt_root: 1
bt_minkey: 2
bt_compare: 0x4002beed bt_prefix: 0x4002bf8e
bt_lpgno: 0
=-=-=-=-=-=-=-=-=-=-=-=-=-=-=-=-=-=-=-=-=-=-=
page 0: btree metadata: LSN [0][1]: level 0
        magic: 0x53162
        version: 9
        pagesize: 4096
        type: 9
        keys: 0 records: 0
        free list: 0
        last_pgno: 1
        flags: 0
        uid: 10 ea 1 0 5 3 0 0 44 7b 2f 9a f5 58 0 0 0 0 0 0
        minkey: 2
        root: 1
```

```
page 1: btree leaf: LSN [1][38849]: level 1
        prev:      0 next:      0 entries:      6 offset: 4036
        [000] 4088 len:    5 data: key 1
        [001] 4076 len:    6 data: data 1
        [002] 4068 len:    5 data: key 2
        [003] 4056 len:    6 data: data 2
        [004] 4048 len:    5 data: key 3
        [005] 4036 len:    6 data: data 3
```

To create a database called Loaded_Db, you first load the text file using the db_load command with the -T option, which tells db_load that the file being loaded is a text file rather than an output from db_dump. Next, you dump the contents of the database to see what got stored in the database. As you can see, three database entries were created. The data loaded through the -T option is interpreted as an ASCII string; therefore, you cannot use it to load any random data structure.

You can also use db_load to added entries to an existing database. You can use the -n option to tell the utility whether you want to overwrite the existing entries against the key that you're adding.

db_checkpoint

db_checkpoint is the only Berkeley DB utility that runs as a daemon process by default. It provides the same functionality as DbEnv::txn_checkpoint. Most Berkeley DB–based applications perform checkpoints programmatically; however, in some cases, it may be desirable to run checkpoints from this utility. If a number of short-lived programs are using a common Berkeley DB environment and there's no watchdog process to monitor the environment, then you cannot run the checkpoints programmatically, unless of course you want to write a program just for performing checkpoints. You can use db_checkpoint in such applications to run checkpoints either at fixed intervals (using the -p option) or after a certain amount of data has been modified since the last checkpoint (using the -k option).

You can also use db_checkpoint for diagnostic purposes. If you run the utility with the -1 option, the utility will perform the checkpoint once and exit, without becoming a daemon process. Here's how you can run the utility with -1 option:

```
hy@linux:~/ws/from_svn/trunk/chap_7/chap7_env>db_checkpoint -1 -v
db_checkpoint: checkpoint begin: Sat Jul 21 17:32:58 2007

db_checkpoint: checkpoint complete: Sat Jul 21 17:32:59 2007
```

When you run db_checkpoint with the -v option, the starting and ending timestamps are printed; otherwise, no output is produced.

db_deadlock

db_deadlock allows you to run a deadlock detector on an environment. Deadlock detection is usually performed automatically in most Berkeley DB applications by setting the deadlock-detection policy through the DbEnv::set_lk_detect method. When you invoke this method, the library runs a deadlock-detector algorithm in the context of the application thread before a lock is about to be acquired. However, doing automatic deadlock detection may not be efficient if a large number of locks are acquired routinely, because the library will perform deadlock detection before every lock acquisition, whether or not a deadlock is present in the environment. If you don't want to do automatic detection, you can run the deadlock detector periodically either by calling DbEnv::lock_detect programmatically in a separate thread or by running the db_deadlock utility as a daemon process.

You shouldn't perform deadlock detection too frequently, because it will cause wasted CPU cycles, and you shouldn't perform it too infrequently, because it will result in threads waiting for locks that cannot be acquired (because they're in a deadlock). If you're unable to decide how frequently you should perform deadlock detection, let the library do it automatically by calling DbEnv::set_lk_detect. This will result in slightly less efficient deadlock detection, but at least the application threads won't be blocked unnecessarily. Here's how you run db_deadlock:

```
hy@linux:~/ws/from_svn/trunk/chap_7/chap7_env>db_deadlock
hy@linux:~/ws/from_svn/trunk/chap_7/chap7_env>
```

No deadlock is found in this environment, so there's no output.

db_printlog

db_printlog is a useful debugging tool that lets you look at the contents of the transaction log in a text format. While debugging tricky database problems, you may want to find out what operations are being performed. Sometimes even after adding copious log messages, you may not be able explain the observed behavior, because you may be focusing on the wrong part of your code or not looking at the right thread. By dumping the contents of the transaction log, you can see exactly what's happening in the environment, and you can get clues about the problem that you wouldn't otherwise get.

By default, db_printlog dumps all the transaction logs that are present in the environment, starting from the first record. Let's look at a sample output from db_printlog:

```
hy@linux:~/ws/from_svn/trunk/chap_7/chap7_env> db_printlog
[1][28]__db_debug: rec: 47 txnid 80000001 prevlsn [0][0]
    op:
    fileid: 0
    key:
    data:
    arg_flags: 0
```

```
[1][76]__fop_create: rec: 143 txnid 80000002 prevlsn [0][0]
    name: __db.1.1c0
    appname: 1
    mode: 644

[1][126]__fop_write: rec: 145 txnid 80000002 prevlsn [1][76]
    name: __db.1.1c0
    appname: 1
    pgsize: 512
    pageno: 0
    offset: 0
    page: 0 0 0 0 0x1 0 0 0 0 0 0 b10x5 0 0x9 0 0 0 0 0x2 0 0 0 0x9 0 0 0 0 0 0 ➡
  0x1 0 0 0 0 0 0 0 0 0 0 0 0 0 0 0 0 0 0 0 0 0xc3 0xde 0 0 0x5 0x3 0 0 0xe4 x0x1 ➡
  0x97 0x88 0x14 0 0 0 0 0 0 0 0 0 0 0x2 0 0 0 0 0 0 0  0 0 0 0x1 0 0 0 0 0 0 0 0 ➡
  0 0 0 0 0 0 0 0 0 0 0 0 0 0 0 0 0 0 0 0 0 0 0 0 0 0 0 0 0 0 0 0 0 0 0 0 0 0 0 0 ➡
  0 0 0 0 0 0 0 0 0 0 0 0 0 0 0 0 0 0 0 0 0 0 0 0 0 0 0 0 0 0 0 0 0 0 0 0 0 0 0 0 ➡
  0 0 0 0 0 0 0 0 0 0 0 0 0 0 0 0 0 0 0 0 0 0 0 0 0 0 0 0 0 0 0 0 0 0 0 0 0 0 0 0 ➡
  0 0 0 0 0 0 0 0 0 0 0 0 0 0 0 0 0 0 0 0 0 0 0 0 0 0 0 0 0 0 0 0 0 0 0 0 0 0 0 0 ➡
  0 0 0 0 0 0 0 0 0 0 0 0 0 0 0 0 0 0 0 0 0 0 0 0 0 0 0 0 0 0 0 0 0 0 0 0 0 0 0 0 ➡
  0 0 0 0 0 0 0 0 0 0 0 0 0 0 0 0 0 0 0 0 0 0 0 0 0 0 0 0 0 0 0 0 0 0 0 0 0 0 0 0 ➡
  0 0 0 0 0 0 0 0 0 0 0 0 0 0 0 0 0 0 0 0 0 0 0 0 0 0 0 0 0 0 0 0 0 0 0 0 0 0 0 0 ➡
  0 0 0 0 0 0 0 0 0 0 0 0 0 0 0 0 0 0 0 0 0 0 0 0 0 0 0 0 0 0 0 0 0 0 0 0 0 0
    flag: 1

[1][704]__fop_write: rec: 145 txnid 80000002 prevlsn [1][126]
    name: __db.1.1c0
    -
    -
```

Each record first shows the LSN associated with it. For example, the LSN of the first record is [1][28]. The LSN indicates the exact location of a particular record in the transaction log file. The first record is located at an offset of 28 bytes in the log file log.0000000001. After the LSN, you can see the description of the record. For example, the first record is of type __db_debug and has a record ID of 47. The descriptions and the IDs are internal representations of transaction log records, and they may change from release to release. After the description, you can see the transaction ID associated with the record. For the first record, it's 80000001. Finally, you can see the LSN of the previous record, which is [0][0]. You need the previous LSN to traverse the transaction log in the reverse order; reverse traversal is required for certain operations such as finding the last checkpoint record. You'll find some of the following record types useful in debugging:

- __dbreg_register: Indicates the opening of a database handle. You can see which databases were opened and in what order.

- __fop_create: Indicates the creation of a database page.

- __fop_write: Indicates a write operation on a database page.

- __txn_ckp: Indicates a checkpoint record. This record also shows the time at which the checkpoint was taken.

- __db_addrem: Indicates either a Db::put or a Db::del operation on a database.

- __bam_cdel: Indicates a Dbc::del operation on a Btree.

- __bam_adj: Indicates some shuffling of the data in a Btree.

Don't get too hung up on the exact meaning and purpose of these records. You should use this output just to get a rough idea of what's going on in the environment. For example, if you see a bunch of __db_addrem records in the log when you think you're not doing any inserts or deletes, then there is likely some other thread or process modifying the database that you're unaware of.

If the environment contains a large number of transaction logs, dumping all the records and looking through them to find the relevant information can be cumbersome. db_printlog provides a couple of useful options to dump only the records you might be interested in. By using the -r option, you can print the records in the reverse order. This output shows the output of db_printlog with the -r option:

```
hy@linux:~/ws/from_svn/trunk/chap_7/chap7_env> db_printlog -r
[1][11138]__txn_ckp: rec: 11 txnid 0 prevlsn [0][0]
    ckp_lsn: [1][10656]
    last_ckp: [0][0]
    timestamp: 1150663084 (Sun Jun 18 13:38:04 2006, 200606181338.04)
    envid: -1628935161
    rep_gen: 0

[1][11052]__dbreg_register: rec: 2 txnid 0 prevlsn [0][0]
    opcode: 1
    name: Person_Db0
    uid: 0xc3 0xde 0 0 0x5 0x3 0 0 0xe4 x0x1 0x97 0x88 0x14 0 0 0 0 0 0
    fileid: 0
    ftype: 0x1
    meta_pgno: 0
    id: 0x0

[1][10965]__dbreg_register: rec: 2 txnid 0 prevlsn [0][0]
    opcode: 1
    name: Account_Db0
    uid: 0xca 0xde 0 0 0x5 0x3 0 0 rH0xe9 0xb5 (0x9b 0x1 0 0 0 0 0
    fileid: 1
    ftype: 0x1
    meta_pgno: 0
    id: 0x0

-
-
```

The -r option is useful, because you're usually interested in the most recent activities. Other useful options are -b and -e. You can use -b to specify the starting LSN, and you can use -e to specify the ending LSN to the utility. When you specify these options, you can dump all the records between the starting and ending LSNs. The output of db_printlog for a specific LSN range is shown here:

```
hy@linux:~/ws/from_svn/trunk/chap_7/chap7_env> db_printlog -b 1/10790 -e 1/11052
[1][10790]__dbreg_register: rec: 2 txnid 0 prevlsn [0][0]
        opcode: 1
        name: Person_Name_Db0
        uid: >0xdf 0 0 0x5 0x3 0 0 0xf8 0xe 0xf5 0xa9 h0xa8 0x4 0 0 0 0 0
        fileid: 3
        ftype: 0x1
        meta_pgno: 0
        id: 0x0

[1][10881]__dbreg_register: rec: 2 txnid 0 prevlsn [0][0]
        opcode: 1
        name: Bank_Db0
        uid: 0xdd 0xde 0 0 0x5 0x3 0 0 T0xe3 0xf 0x95 0xc8 !0x3 0 0 0 0 0
        fileid: 2
        ftype: 0x1
        meta_pgno: 0
        id: 0x0

[1][10965]__dbreg_register: rec: 2 txnid 0 prevlsn [0][0]
        opcode: 1
        name: Account_Db0
        uid: 0xca 0xde 0 0 0x5 0x3 0 0 rH0xe9 0xb5 (0x9b 0x1 0 0 0 0 0
        fileid: 1
        ftype: 0x1
        meta_pgno: 0
        id: 0x0

[1][11052]__dbreg_register: rec: 2 txnid 0 prevlsn [0][0]
        opcode: 1
        name: Person_Db0
        uid: 0xc3 0xde 0 0 0x5 0x3 0 0 0xe4 x0x1 0x97 0x88 0x14 0 0 0 0 0 0
        fileid: 0
        ftype: 0x1
        meta_pgno: 0
        id: 0x0
```

One problem with using the -b and -e options is that you need to know a valid starting LSN and a valid ending LSN. The utility isn't smart enough to seek the closest valid LSN if you provide a bogus one. Sometimes you might have to run db_printlog -r first to find a valid LSN.

db_archive

db_archive is a tool for database archival and transaction log maintenance. It provides the same functionality as DbEnv::log_archive in the form of a command-line utility. When used with the -l option, it shows a list of the transaction log files in the environment, whether or not they're involved in any active transactions. The output of db_archive -l is shown here:

```
hy@linux:~/ws/from_svn/trunk/chap_7/chap7_env> db_archive -l
log.0000000001
```

You need this information to create a backup of the environment. If you run db_archive with the -d option, it will remove all the transaction log files that aren't referencing any active transaction. Once you take a backup, you can safely delete all unused log files. Unless you've taken a backup of all the log files, you shouldn't delete the logs if you want to be able to perform catastrophic recovery. When you use the -s option, you get a list of all the database files referenced in the environment:

```
hy@linux:~/ws/from_svn/trunk/chap_7/chap7_env> db_archive -s
Account_Db
Bank_Db
Person_Db
Person_Dob_Db
Person_Name_Db
```

You need this list to create a backup of the environment. To create a complete backup of an environment, you only need to back up the log files reported by db_archive -l and the database file reported by db_archive -s.

■Caution If you have any databases that were never opened during the lifetime of the existing environment, this command won't report them.

db_hotbackup

A hot backup can run on an operating environment. It acquires no locks, so it doesn't interfere with existing transactions, except for the fact that copying files around consumes some I/O and compute cycles. You can do everything that db_hotbackup does by using a combination of other utilities. The designers added this utility to Berkeley DB because there was great demand for a single utility that could be used to take a hot backup of a running system. Before the addition of this utility, taking a hot backup used to involve multiple steps, which the non-expert users used to find quite confusing. With this utility in place, you can easily create a hot backup without making any mistakes. Let's take a look at how this utility works. Start the transactional data store code example and try to perform a hot backup while it's running:

```
hy@linux:~/ws/bdb_book/chap_5/chap5_env> ls -al
total 27972
drwxr-xr-x  2 hy users       320 2006-06-18 16:56 .
drwxr-xr-x  7 hy users       680 2006-06-18 16:52 ..
-rw-r--r--  1 hy users   6057984 2006-06-18 16:56 chap5_tds
-rw-r-----  1 hy users     24576 2006-06-18 16:56 __db.001
-rw-r-----  1 hy users    278528 2006-06-18 16:56 __db.002
-rw-r-----  1 hy users    270336 2006-06-18 16:56 __db.003
-rw-r-----  1 hy users     98304 2006-06-18 16:56 __db.004
-rw-r-----  1 hy users    352256 2006-06-18 16:56 __db.005
-rw-r-----  1 hy users     16384 2006-06-18 16:56 __db.006
-rw-r-----  1 hy users  10485760 2006-06-18 16:56 log.0000000001
-rw-r-----  1 hy users  10485760 2006-06-18 16:56 log.0000000002
-rw-r-----  1 hy users  10485760 2006-06-18 16:56 log.0000000003
```

After the program has been running for a couple of minutes, you'll see the files listed in the chap5_env directory. Next, execute the db_hotbackup utility:

```
hy@linux:~/ws/bdb_book/chap_5/chap5_env> db_hotbackup -b ➥
/home/hy/ws/bdb_book/chap_5/hotbackup -h /home/hy/ws/bdb_book/chap_5/chap5_env/
hy@linux:~/ws/bdb_book/chap_5/chap5_env> cd ../hotbackup/
hy@linux:~/ws/bdb_book/chap_5/hotbackup> ls -al
total 17994
drwxr-xr-x  2 hy users       112 2006-06-18 16:56 .
drwxr-xr-x  7 hy users       680 2006-06-18 16:52 ..
-rw-------  1 hy users   7921152 2006-06-18 16:56 chap5_tds
-rw-------  1 hy users  10485760 2006-06-18 16:56 log.0000000003
```

You can see that the database file and the last log file have been copied, but the first two log files don't show up in the backup. Let's walk through the step that the utility performs to understand why you don't see all the logs from the environment in the backup:

1. Create the backup directory (specified with the -b option) if it doesn't already exist.

2. Copy the database files to the backup directory.

3. Copy the log files to the backup directory.

4. Perform catastrophic recovery on the backup.

5. Remove the unnecessary log files from the backup.

The utility cleans up the first two log files in the last step, because only the third log file must have contained references to active transactions. It would be better if you could avoid copying the first two logs to the backup, because the utility will remove them anyway. The -c option does just that. If you specify the -c option, the utility will first run a checkpoint and remove all unused log files, and then it will perform the backup procedure. This option can be extremely useful if your environment contains a large number of transaction logs. However, if you want to be extra careful and ensure that you don't lose the ability to perform a catastrophic recovery if the hot backup fails, you shouldn't use the -c option.

The -u option lets you update an existing hot backup. With the -u option, the first two steps in the list are omitted. You shouldn't perform any log file cleanup between any two hot backups if you're updating an existing backup, because when you specify the -u option, the database files won't be copied to the backup again. For catastrophic recovery to be successful, all transaction logs created since the last backup should be available.

db_verify

The db_verify utility provides the same functionality as the Db::verify method. With the db_verify utility, you can verify the integrity of all the databases contained in the specified file. db_verify, like Db::verify, doesn't acquire any locks on the database data structures while performing the verification. Therefore, you shouldn't use it on any database that's in use. You might notice that sometimes you cannot use Db::open to open a database that passes verification. This may happen if a thread of control exits without releasing the locks on the database resources. Because db_verify doesn't perform any locking, it won't notice that the database resources are inaccessible. Here is how you'd run db_verify:

```
hy@linux:~/ws/from_svn/trunk/chap_7/chap7_env>db_verify Person_Db
hy@linux:~/ws/from_svn/trunk/chap_7/chap7_env>
```

db_verify produced no output, because it was able to verify the integrity of Person_Db. If it hadn't, some errors would have printed out.

Summary

Berkeley DB utilities provide a powerful and easy way of performing various troubleshooting, tuning, and maintenance tasks on the Berkeley DB environment. If you know your way around these utilities, you can significantly reduce the time you spend developing and maintaining a Berkeley DB–based solution. These utilities provide a range of options, but only a small subset of those are useful to the application developer. Getting familiar with the most important utilities is neither difficult nor time-consuming.

I've now covered all the major aspects of Berkeley DB. In the next chapter, I'll shift gears. Instead of digging deeper into the details, I'll move in a horizontal direction and delve into the Berkeley DB Java API. The Java API provides the same functionality as the C++ API, but the format and the constructs are vastly different. You'll learn how to perform basic database operations using the Java API.

■ ■ ■

CHAPTER 11

Berkeley DB Java APIs

Berkeley DB provides two distinct database products for Java developers: one is the Java API written on top of the core Berkeley DB database—the topic of this book—and the other is the Berkeley DB Java Edition (JE). JE is a pure Java database designed to provide a persistence layer for Java objects. Databases created using JE can be used from a single JVM only. JE doesn't allow multiple JVMs or non-Java processes to share the databases. Unlike core Berkeley DB, JE does not support replication.

In this chapter, I'll go over the Berkeley DB Java APIs, but I won't discuss JE. The Berkeley DB core library is implemented in C; however, programming interfaces are available in a variety of languages, including C++, Java, Perl, and Python. Oracle officially supports some of these interfaces, which include the C++ and Java interfaces, while volunteers maintain others. I'll go over the Java APIs of the main database subsystems, and I'll highlight the differences and the similarities between the C++ and Java APIs. I'll also cover the Berkeley DB Collections API, which is similar to (but does not implement) the Java Collections API; it provides an easy-to-use layer on top of the base API.

Understanding the Two APIs

Berkeley DB actually supports two APIs for Java whose names are very similar. The term *Java API* refers to an API that is a thin layer on top of the C API. The *Java Collections API* is a higher-level, more abstract interface.

The Java API

As you already know, the Berkeley DB core library is implemented in C. It isn't difficult to see how the C++ API works with the core library, since it is relatively simple to create a C++ API around a C API. The C++ API is indeed a thin layer written on top of the C API. The Java API also is a thin layer on top of the C API, but the interaction is slightly more complicated, because the Java API has to operate within a JVM. The Java API uses the Java Native Interface (JNI) to invoke the C API methods. Figure 11-1 shows how Berkeley DB APIs interact with each other.

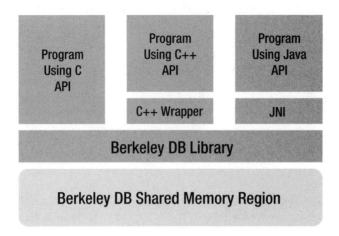

Figure 11-1. *Berkeley DB API relationships*

Architecturally, the C++ and the Java APIs aren't very different; they both interact with the Berkeley DB library through the native C API. When I go over the individual APIs, you'll notice that there is almost a one-to-one correspondence between the two sets of APIs. The C++ interfaces predate the Java interfaces, and the thinking of the designers of the C++ APIs heavily influenced the design of the Java interfaces. Some Java developers might find the Berkeley DB Java API a bit antiquated because of this. In Figure 11-1, you can see that programs using different APIs can share the same Berkeley DB environment. This is a powerful feature, because all the advantages associated with running the database within the process memory aren't lost, even when programs written in different languages are sharing the database.

■**Note** A Berkeley DB application cannot share databases with a Berkeley DB Java Edition application, because the file formats are different.

The Java Collections API

The Java Collections API is a higher-level API written on top of the basic Java API. The Java Collections API was originally written for the Berkeley DB Java Edition database, which is a completely different product. However, its interface was quite intuitive to Java programmers, so support for it was added to the Berkeley DB core product. The Berkeley DB engineering team follows a general philosophy of maintaining API parity between the Berkeley DB and Berkeley DB Java Edition products. However, this isn't always possible, because the Java product runs in a different framework and gets a richer set of services from the Java runtime than is available in C. In general, though, the designers try to design interfaces for each of the two products so that they can support them in both at least in principle. Figure 11-2 presents another perspective of the various Berkeley DB APIs and their relationships; you might remember this figure from Chapter 3.

The Java Collections API includes numerous design patterns that are routinely used in Java programming. I'll discuss both the basic Java API and the Java Collections API in this chapter.

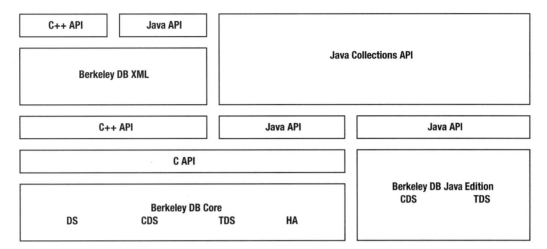

Figure 11-2. *Berkeley DB API relationships*

Berkeley DB Java API Packages

The Berkeley DB Java API consists of the following packages:

- com.sleepycat.db: Contains the core Berkeley DB functionality, which includes classes for the environment, database, transaction, cursor, sequence, and more.

- com.sleepycat.bind: Contains classes that you can use for defining the relationship (or the bindings) between the database entries and the application-level Java objects.

- com.sleepycat.bind.serial: Contains classes for the serial bindings. A serial binding is a type of binding that you can use to serialize Java objects for storing in the database.

- com.sleepycat.bind.tuple: Contains classes for tuple bindings. A tuple binding is a more efficient form of object serialization in which you can select which object members should be serialized and in what order.

- com.sleepycat.collections: Contains classes that provide data-access classes and interfaces based on the standard Java Collections API.

- com.sleepycat.util: Contains some utility classes that you'll rarely need to use.

If you're familiar with the Berkeley DB C (or C++) API, you'll easily be able to figure out how to use the classes in the com.sleepycat.db package. The other packages include classes that are unique to the Java API. The functionality contained in these packages cannot be included in the C or the C++ API because of the absence of certain features in these languages. Features such as serialization and reflection, which are available in Java, allow a lot more useful functionality to be provided through generic APIs.

Compiling and Using the Java API

To use the Berkeley DB Java API (which also includes the Berkeley DB Collections API), you must first compile the Berkeley DB distribution with the --enable-java flag:

```
hy@linux:~/sw/src/db-4.4.20/build_unix> ../dist/configure --enable-cxx ➡
--enable-debug --enable-diagnostics --enable-replication ➡
--prefix=/home/hy/sw/install/ --enable-java
```

After installing the new build, notice that you have a new JAR file, db.jar, in addition to a number of new libraries in the lib directory of your installation:

```
hy@linux:~/sw/install/lib> ls -al
-rwxr-xr-x  1 hy users  7235684 2006-06-21 10:40 libdb_java-4.4.so
-rw-r--r--  1 hy users      851 2006-06-21 10:40 libdb_java-4.4.la
-rw-r--r--  1 hy users  8519868 2006-06-21 10:41 libdb_cxx-4.4.a
-rw-r--r--  1 hy users  7649856 2006-06-21 10:41 libdb.a
-rw-r--r--  1 hy users  7649856 2006-06-21 10:41 libdb-4.4.a
-rw-r--r--  1 hy users  8021040 2006-06-21 10:41 libdb_java-4.4.a
-rw-r--r--  1 hy users  8519868 2006-06-21 10:41 libdb_cxx.a
lrwxrwxrwx  1 hy users       12 2006-06-21 10:41 libdb.so -> libdb-4.4.so
lrwxrwxrwx  1 hy users       17 2006-06-21 10:41 libdb_java.so -> libdb_java-4.4.so
lrwxrwxrwx  1 hy users       17 2006-06-21 10:41 libdb_java-4.so -> libdb_java-
4.4.so
lrwxrwxrwx  1 hy users       17 2006-06-21 10:41 ➡
libdb_java-4.4_g.so -> libdb_java-4.4.so
lrwxrwxrwx  1 hy users       16 2006-06-21 10:41 libdb_cxx.so -> libdb_cxx-4.4.so
lrwxrwxrwx  1 hy users       16 2006-06-21 10:41 libdb_cxx-4.so -> libdb_cxx-4.4.so
lrwxrwxrwx  1 hy users       12 2006-06-21 10:41 libdb-4.so -> libdb-4.4.so
-r--r--r--  1 hy users   206249 2006-06-21 10:41 db.jar
```

The libdb_java* files are the libraries used by the JNI to allow method invocations to cross the boundary between Java and C. In order to use the Java APIs, you have to add the lib directory to your LD_LIBRARY_PATH (which may already be there if you've been using the C++ or the C API in your programs) and the JAR file to your Java CLASSPATH.

The best way of learning an API is to work through a code example. Since you're already familiar with the Person database, let's build this chapter's example code for the Person database, but let's use the Java API this time. This will allow you to compare the Java implementation with the C++ implementation. You'll encounter these main classes during the course of this chapter:

- TDS.java: Contains the main method. It initializes and launches the remaining classes.

- JavaEnv.java: Contains the bulk of the code. It creates the environment and the databases. It also has the code for loading and dumping entries to and from the database.

- Person.java: Represents an entry in the Person database.

You'll need some other helper classes, which I'll introduce as you need them.

Opening the Environment

You use the com.sleepycat.db.Environment class to instantiate a database environment. You specify the environment configuration through the EnvironmentConfig class. Instead of using flags, as is the case with the C and C++ APIs, you use methods in EnvironmentConfig to configure the environment. Listing 11-1 shows an example.

Listing 11-1. *Creating an Environment*

```
package chap_11;
import com.sleepycat.db.Environment;
import com.sleepycat.db.EnvironmentConfig;
public class JavaEnv
{
    private EnvironmentConfig envConfig_ = null;
    private Environment env_ = null;
    private File envHome_ = new File("./chap11_env");

    private void createEnv() throws Exception
    {
        try
        {
            envConfig_ = new EnvironmentConfig();
            envConfig_.setErrorStream(System.err);
            envConfig_.setErrorPrefix("chap_11");
            envConfig_.setAllowCreate(true);
            envConfig_.setInitializeCache(true);
            envConfig_.setTransactional(true);
            envConfig_.setInitializeLocking(true);

            env_ = new Environment(envHome_, envConfig_);
        }
        catch(DatabaseException e)
        {
            System.err.println(
                    "createEnv: Database Exception caught " +
                    e.toString());
            throw e;
        }
        catch(Exception e)
        {
            System.err.println("createEnv: " + e.toString());
            throw e;
        }
    }
}
```

The setAllowCreate method is equivalent to the DB_CREATE flag, setInitializeCache corresponds to DB_INIT_MPOOL, and setTransactional corresponds to DB_INIT_TXN. Apart from these differences, the procedure of opening the environment is the same as it is in the C/C++ API. DatabaseException is the base class of all exceptions thrown by Berkeley DB.

■**Note** Even though it's more work to call an individual method for each flag in the environment configuration, it insulates the API from the internal flags. One of the problems with the C/C++ APIs is that if the flag names change from one version to another (which the Berkeley DB designers try hard not to do), then you'll have to change the application code as well. This isn't the case with the Java API, as the internal flags are not exposed.

Opening the Database

A database handle is represented by an instance of Database class. Like the environment, its configuration is specified through a separate class called DatabaseConfig. Listing 11-2 shows how you can create a database handle and use it to open the database.

Listing 11-2. *Opening a Database*

```java
import com.sleepycat.db.Database;
import com.sleepycat.db.DatabaseConfig;
.
.
public class JavaEnv
{
.
.
    private DatabaseConfig dbConfig_ = null;
    private Database personDb_ = null;
.
.
    private void createDbHandle() throws Exception
    {
        try
        {
            dbConfig_ = new DatabaseConfig();
            dbConfig_.setErrorStream(System.err);
            dbConfig_.setType(DatabaseType.BTREE);
            dbConfig_.setAllowCreate(true);
            dbConfig_.setTransactional(true);

            dbConfig_.setErrorPrefix("chap_11:PersonDb");
            personDb_ = env_.openDatabase(null, "Person_Db",
                    null, dbConfig_);
```

```
        }
        catch(DatabaseException e)
        {
            System.err.println(
                    "createDbHandle: Database Exception caught " +
                    e.toString());
            throw e;
        }
        catch(Exception e)
        {
            System.err.println("createDbHandle: " + e.toString());
            throw e;
        }

    }
```

Note that you don't create a Database instance directly; the openDatabase method returns it. By doing this, you associate the database with the environment. It's possible to create a database handle independent of the environment, like the following:

```
personDb_ = new Database("Person_Db", null, dbConfig_);
```

Now the database won't be associated with the environment. Instead, it will be created as an independent database in the current working directory. Such a database is useful only if you're going to use it from a single process and don't want to associate it with other databases and processes.

Creating Database Records

The Berkeley DB Java API uses the core Berkeley DB library for performing the database functions; as such, the database records created by the Java API are in the form of key-value pairs. Every database record has a key and a value. Both keys and values are arrays of bytes and are represented by the DatabaseEntry class in the API. The DatabaseEntry class is analogous to the Dbt class in the C++ API. Listing 11-3 shows the constructors of this class.

Listing 11-3. *DatabaseEntry Constructors*

```
DatabaseEntry()
DatabaseEntry(byte [] data)
DatabaseEntry(byte [] data, int offset, int size)
```

This class can work with only byte arrays, so if you want to use anything other than a byte array for either the key or the value, you'll have to first convert it to a byte array. Entities that might be used as the key or the value may include basic data types such as integers, strings, and longs, or complex types such as object instances. Converting basic types to byte arrays is unambiguous, but you can convert a complex type to a byte array in numerous ways. How an entity, which is not a byte array, is converted to a byte array is defined by the *binding* for the conversion. In order to better understand the various data bindings, let's look at the Person

record that you'll insert into the Person_Db database. Listing 11-4 shows the implementation of
the Person class.

Listing 11-4. *Creating Database Records*

```java
public class Person
{
    private Long ssn_;
    private String name_;
    private String dob_;

    public Person()
    {}

    public Person(Long ssn,
            String name,
            String dob)
    {
        ssn_ = ssn;
        name_ = name;
        dob_ = dob;
    }

    public void setSSN(Long ssn)
    {
        ssn_ = ssn;
    }

    public void setName(String name)
    {
        name_ = name;
    }

    public void setDOB(String dob)
    {
        dob_ = dob;
    }

    public Long getSSN()
    {
        return ssn_;
    }

    public String getName()
    {
        return name_;
    }
```

```
    public String getDOB()
    {
        return dob_;
    }

    public String toString()
    {
        return "Person: ssn = " + ssn_ + " name = " + name_
            + " dob = " + dob_;
    }
};
```

The Person record contains a person's SSN, name, and date of birth. The SSN is used as the key against which the record will be stored. For example, Listing 11-5 shows the key-value pair for a person named Manish Pandey.

Listing 11-5. *A Person Record*

```
//KEY
Long ssn = new Long(111223333);

//Value
Person manish= new Person(ssn, "Manish Pandey", "jan 13 1971");
```

In this example, you can easily convert the key (ssn) to a byte array to be stored in the Person_Db database. The value (manish) is not a primitive type, but rather is an object. You can convert it to a byte array by first implementing the Serializable interface in the Person class, as shown in Listing 11-6.

Listing 11-6. *Making Person Serializable*

```
public class Person implements Serializable
{
    private Long ssn_;
    private String name_;
    private String dob_;
.
.
```

You then invoke the writeObject method, as shown in Listing 11-7.

Listing 11-7. *Serializing a Person Object*

```
byte[1024] byteArray;
ByteArrayOutputStream bos = new ByteArrayOutputStream(byteArray);
ObjectOutputStream oos = new ObjectOutputStream(bos);
oos.writeObject(manish);
oos.close();
```

This approach is technically correct; you can serialize object instances using the Serializable interface for storage. However, this approach isn't very efficient. The default Java serialization includes the following information in a serialized object:

- **The Class member variable of the object**: This is a static variable common to all instances of the class.

- **The class signature**: This is also common to all the instances of the class.

- **Other entities**: The serialized values of all the nonstatic variables and references contained in the object are also included in the serialization of the object.

If you store multiple objects of the same class as entries in a database, you'll end up storing multiple copies of the information common (shown in the first two entries of the preceding list) to all the objects in the database. That not only wastes a lot of disk space, but it also slows down the database due to excessive disk I/O. The Berkeley DB bind APIs provide a more efficient mechanism for storing complex data types such as objects.

Binding Data Types in the Java API

The bind APIs provide an efficient way of converting simple and complex data types into byte arrays and vice versa. You can choose the best option from the following bind mechanisms available in the API:

- **Primitive binding**: Provides conversion for single-field primitive data types such as String, Integer, Boolean, and Long.

- **Serial binding**: Used for complex data types. It provides an efficient serialization mechanism of Java objects, which is optimized for database storage.

- **Custom or tuple binding**: Used for serializing complex data types. It allows you to implement custom serialization for Java objects.

Binding for Primitive Types

The bindings for converting primitive data types to byte arrays are defined in the com.sleepycat. bind.tuple package. You can use a specific binding class for your data type. For example, the key in the earlier example is a single-field value of type Long. You can convert it to a byte array, as shown in Listing 11-8.

Listing 11-8. *Using LongBinding*

```
DatabaseEntry key = new DatabaseEntry();
LongBinding.longToEntry(manish.getSSN(), key);
```

You can also use the getPrimitiveBinding method to select the proper binding class for your data type, as shown in Listing 11-9.

Listing 11-9. *Finding the Correct Binding Class*

```
DatabaseEntry key = new DatabaseEntry();
EntryBinding binding = TupleBinding.getPrimitiveBinding(Long.class);
binding.objectToEntry(manish.getSSN(), key);
```

Similarly, you can use the binding to extract a primitive data type from a byte array, as shown in Listing 11-10.

Listing 11-10. *Extracting Actual Data from Serialized Data*

```
Cursor cursor = null;
DatabaseEntry key = new DatabaseEntry();
DatabaseEntry data = new DatabaseEntry();

try
{
   txn = env_.beginTransaction(null, null);
   Long ssn = new Long();

   EntryBinding binding =
                TupleBinding.getPrimitiveBinding(Long.class);
   cursor = personDb_.openCursor(txn, null);
   while(cursor.getNext(key, data, LockMode.DEFAULT)
                        == OperationStatus.SUCCESS)
   {
       ssn = (Long)(binding.entryToObject(key));
       System.out.println("key: " + ssn);
   }
   cursor.close();
   cursor = null;
   txn.commit();
}
catch (DatabaseException e)
{
   if(cursor != null)
       cursor.close();
   txn.abort();
   System.err.println("addPersonEntries: " + e.toString());
   throw e;
}
```

This example shows how to retrieve a key-value pair from a database using a cursor. Here you only print out the key, but next you'll learn how to convert an object.

Serial Binding for Complex Types

Converting an object to a byte array and vice versa is more involved than converting a primitive type. As previously mentioned, you need to have information about the class—of which the object is an instance of—in order to convert a byte array to an object. The default Java serialization doesn't work well for database storage, because it includes the common class information with every serialized object. The serial binding for objects separates out the common class information from the member variable information and stores it in a separate repository, thereby saving space in the database. The common information about the classes is stored in a class catalog. You can use the StoredClassCatalog class to specify the database where the common information will be stored. In order to use the serial binding, you have to follow these steps:

1. Implement the Serializable interface in the class you want to store in the database.

2. Create a database to hold the class catalog.

3. Create a class catalog using the database handle.

4. Create the serial binding using the class catalog.

Listing 11-11 shows how to perform the tasks in this list.

Listing 11-11. *Using Serial Binding for Complex Types*

```
public class Person implements Serializable
{
    private Long ssn_;
    private String name_;
    private String dob_;
.
.
.
}


.
.

//Create a database to hold the common class information
classCatalogDb_ = env_.openDatabase(null,
                                    "ClassCatalog_Db", null, dbConfig_);

//Create a class catalog using the database handle
classCatalog_ = new StoredClassCatalog(classCatalogDb_);

//Instruct the binding to use the created catalog to hold the class
//information
EntryBinding binding = new SerialBinding(classCatalog_, Person.class);

//Store the Person object using the serial binding
Person manish
    = new Person(new Long(111223333), "Manish Pandey", "jan 13 1971");

DatabaseEntry key = new DatabaseEntry();
DatabaseEntry data = new DatabaseEntry();
```

```
LongBinding.longToEntry(manish.getSSN(), key);
binding.objectToEntry(manish, data);
personDb_.put(null, key, data);
```

Listing 11-12 shows how to deserialize an object.

Listing 11-12. *Deserializing an Object*

```
DatabaseEntry key = new DatabaseEntry();
DatabaseEntry data = new DatabaseEntry();

EntryBinding dataBinding =
            new SerialBinding(classCatalog_, Person.class);
EntryBinding keyBinding = TupleBinding.getPrimitiveBinding(Long.class

Person p = null;
Long ssn = null;

cursor = personDb_.openCursor(txn, null);
while(cursor.getNext(key, data, LockMode.DEFAULT)
                         == OperationStatus.SUCCESS)
{
    ssn = (Long)(keyBinding.entryToObject(key));
    p = (Person)(dataBinding.entryToObject(data));
    System.out.println("key: " + ssn + " value " + p);
}
```

Even though the serial binding is much more efficient than the default Java serialization, there is still a lot of room for improvement. The serial binding suffers from the following drawbacks:

- **Random ordering of the serialized member variables**: The member variables of the object being stored aren't serialized in any particular order. If the serial binding is being used for the keys, then you shouldn't expect the keys to be sorted correctly. The order of variable serialization in a complex key may change collation, which will affect the locality of reference and performance. A simple key doesn't have this problem.

- **Dumb serialization**: Even though the serial binding is smarter than the default Java serialization, it still cannot figure out if a particular member variable needs to be serialized. In most classes, some member variables don't need to be serialized. There is no way to ignore such members in the serial binding.

Custom tuple binding, which I'll discuss in the next section, overcomes these limitations.

Custom Tuple Binding for Complex Types

Tuple bindings are the ideal choice if you're concerned about the efficiency of the serialization/ deserialization routines and the proper sorting of the keys in the database. As mentioned in the previous section, serial binding doesn't address these issues. It is more work to implement tuple binding for a class, because you have to implement an extra class, the binding class that extends the TupleBinding class.

Once you have these classes, you can use the tuple binding, as shown in Listing 11-13. You implement an alternate Person class called Person1 to demonstrate tuple binding and allow you to compare the two bindings.

Listing 11-13. *An Alternate Person Class*

```
public class Person1
{
    private Long ssn_;
    private String name_;
    private String dob_;

    public Person1(Long ssn,
            String name,
            String dob)
    {
        ssn_ = ssn;
        name_ = name;
        dob_ = dob;
    }

    public Long getSSN()
    {
        return ssn_;
    }

    public String getName()
    {
        return name_;
    }

    public String getDOB()
    {
        return dob_;
    }

    public String toString()
    {
        return "PersonEnt: ssn = " + ssn_ + " name = " + name_
            + " dob = " + dob_;
    }
}
```

The new Person1 class is essentially the same as the Person class shown earlier, except that Person1 doesn't implement Serializable. Listing 11-14 shows you how the TupleBinding class is extended for Person1.

Listing 11-14. *Using TupleBinding*

```java
import com.sleepycat.bind.tuple.TupleBinding;
import com.sleepycat.bind.tuple.TupleInput;
import com.sleepycat.bind.tuple.TupleOutput;


public class PersonTupleBinding extends TupleBinding
{
    public void objectToEntry(Object o, TupleOutput out)
    {
        Person1 p = (Person1)o;
        out.writeLong(p.getSSN());
        out.writeString(p.getName());
        out.writeString(p.getDOB());
    }

    public Object entryToObject(TupleInput in)
    {
        Long ssn = in.readLong();
        String name = in.readString();
        String dob = in.readString();

        Person1 p = new Person1(ssn, name, dob);
        return p;
    }
}
```

You serialize the individual member variables to TupleOutput, which is analogous to the DataOutput interface; therefore, you don't need to implement Serializable for Person1.

■**Note** The order in which the members are written to TupleOutput should be the same as the order in which the members read out of TupleInput.

Once you have these two classes in place, you can use the tuple binding as shown in Listing 11-15.

Listing 11-15. *Using TupleBinding (Continued)*

```java
//Create a database to hold the common class information
classCatalogDb_ = env_.openDatabase(null,
                                    "ClassCatalog_Db", null, dbConfig_);
```

```
//Instruct the binding to use the created catalog to hold the class
//information
EntryBinding binding = new PersonTupleBinding();

//Store the Person object using the serial binding
Person manish
    = new Person(new Long(111223333), "Manish Pandey", "jan 13 1971");

DatabaseEntry key = new DatabaseEntry();
DatabaseEntry data = new DatabaseEntry();

LongBinding.longToEntry(manish.getSSN(), key);
binding.objectToEntry(manish, data);
personDb_.put(null, key, data);
```

Listing 11-16 shows you how to deserialize an object.

Listing 11-16. *Deserializing from TupleBinding*

```
DatabaseEntry key = new DatabaseEntry();
DatabaseEntry data = new DatabaseEntry();

EntryBinding dataBinding = new PersonTupleBinding();
EntryBinding keyBinding = TupleBinding.getPrimitiveBinding(Long.class

Person p = null;
Long ssn = null;

cursor = personDb_.openCursor(txn, null);
while(cursor.getNext(key, data, LockMode.DEFAULT)
                        == OperationStatus.SUCCESS)
{
    ssn = (Long)(keyBinding.entryToObject(key));
    p = (Person)(dataBinding.entryToObject(data));
    System.out.println("key: " + ssn + " value " + p);
}
```

Note that you don't use the StoredClassCatalog class while creating the binding, and you also don't open the catalog database. You have to use the StoredClassCatalog and the catalog database in the serial binding, because the Serializable interface requires the class information, which is stored in the catalog database.

Binding Data Types in the Collections API

The remaining bindings that I'll discuss are tightly coupled with the Berkeley DB Collections API. Before discussing those, let's first go over the Collections API briefly.

Java Stored Collections

The Berkeley DB Collections API is similar to the standard Java Collections API, but it doesn't conform strictly to the standard interface. A Berkeley DB collection class represents a database. When an operation is performed on the collection, a corresponding operation is executed on the underlying database. For example, if you add an entry to a StoredMap instance (a class derived from the standard Java Map), it is inserted into the database, which is represented by the instance. Similarly, if a map entry is read from the instance, it is actually read from the database. In order to support such operations on the database, the Stored Collections interface doesn't conform fully to the standard Java Collections contract. The main classes in the Stored Collections API include the following:

- StoredMap: Derived from the Map class. It represents a Map view of the database.

- StoredValueSet: Returned by Map.values(). You can use it to add or remove entries from the underlying database. It is useful for operating on the database when record keys are not known. If needed, it can be instantiated independent of StoreMap.

- StoredEntrySet: Represents a Set view of Map. Returned by Map.entrySet(). You cannot instantiate it directly.

- StoredList: Used mostly when the Recno, the Queue, or the Btree-Recnum access method is used. This class represents a sequential view of the database.

- StoredIterator: Implements the Iterator as well as the ListIterator interfaces for the stored collections, because certain ListIterator methods such as previous, hasPrevious, nextIndex, and previousIndex are useful for the stored collections.

In addition to the classes listed here, there are also StoredSortedMap, StoredSortedValueSet, and StoreSortedEntrySet. They implement the SortedMap and the SortedSet interfaces, respectively, and you can use them only if the keys in the database are ordered. This means that you can use them with the Btree and Queue access methods, but not with the Hash access method. Here are the main differences between the standard Java Collections and stored collections:

- **Support for duplicates**: The standard Java Collections interface doesn't support duplicates, whereas all stored collections support duplicates when the underlying database access method has been configured to support duplicates.

- **Support for the Collection.size method**: Since all stored collections either extend or implement standard Java Collection classes or interfaces, you can invoke the Collection.size method on them. However, the size method always throws the UnsupportedOperationException. It's difficult to accurately and efficiently estimate the total number of entries in a database without iterating over the database; therefore, stored collections don't support this operation.

- **Iterator behavior**: A standard Java Iterator is implicitly closed by the Java runtime when it goes out of scope. This isn't the case with StoredIterator. You always have to close it explicitly by calling the static StoredIterator.close() method.

Entity Binding

The bindings you've encountered so far have been based on independent key and value objects. However, it's more intuitive to deal with one application-level object that's mapped to a database entry. The application-level object contains both the key material and the value material. The entity binding allows you to have both the key and the value in a single object. You can use a single class to represent both the key and the value. Entity binding is more intuitive to use with the Collections API. You can use the Map.get call to get the entire entity in a single call from the database, and you can use Set.put to insert an entity into the database. Also, using entity binding makes it easier to handle a single class in the application code than to handle two classes for every database entry.

Just like the entry bindings, there are different types of entity bindings available in the Java API.

SerialSerialBinding

The most basic entity binding is SerialSerialBinding. It depends on the Serializable interface to convert an object to a byte array. As with the TupleBinding example you saw earlier, you have to implement the entity class along with the binding class before you can use the entity binding. Continuing with the Person class example, Listing 11-17 shows how you define the Person class for this binding.

Listing 11-17. *Implementation of Person Class to Be Used with SerialSerialBinding*

```java
public class Person
{
    private Long ssn_;
    private String name_;
    private String dob_;

    public Person()
    {}

    public Person(Long ssn,
            String name,
            String dob)
    {
        ssn_  = ssn;
        name_ = name;
        dob_  = dob;
    }

    public void setSSN(Long ssn)
    {
        ssn_  = ssn;
    }
```

```
    public void setName(String name)
    {
        name_ = name;
    }

    public void setDOB(String dob)
    {
        dob_ = dob;
    }

    public Long getSSN()
    {
        return ssn_;
    }

    public String getName()
    {
        return name_;
    }

    public String getDOB()
    {
        return dob_;
    }

    public String toString()
    {
        return "Person: ssn = " + ssn_ + " name = " + name_
            + " dob = " + dob_;
    }
}
```

Note that the Person class doesn't implement Serializable. It doesn't need to be Serializable, because this class won't be stored directly in the database. This class will be split into the key class, PersonKey, and the data class, PersonData, by the entity binding. Listing 11-18 shows you how to define those classes.

Listing 11-18. *PersonKey and PersonData Classes*

```
import java.io.Serializable;
public class PersonKey implements Serializable
{
    private Long ssn_;

    public PersonKey(Long ssn)
    {
        ssn_ = ssn;
    }
```

```java
    public final Long getSSN()
    {
        return ssn_;
    }

    public String toString()
    {
        return "(PersonKey: ssn = " + ssn_ + ")";
    }
}

import java.io.Serializable;

public class PersonData implements Serializable
{
    private String name_;
    private String dob_;

    public PersonData(String name, String dob)
    {
        name_ = name;
        dob_ = dob;
    }

    public final String getName()
    {
        return name_;
    }

    public final String getDOB()
    {
        return dob_;
    }

    public String toString()
    {
        return "(PersonData: name = " + name_ +
               " dob = " + dob_ + ")";
    }
}
```

Note that the PersonKey and the PersonData classes implement Serializable, since they will be stored in the database. The entity binding that you're going to use is called SerialSerialBinding, which implements the EntityBinding interface. This binding uses the Serializable interface to serialize the key and value objects, just like the SerialBinding class you saw earlier. Listing 11-19 shows the binding class.

Listing 11-19. *PersonBinding Class*

```
private static class PersonBinding extends SerialSerialBinding
{
    private PersonBinding(ClassCatalog catalog,
            Class keyClass, Class dataClass)
    {
        super(catalog, keyClass, dataClass);
    }

    public Object entryToObject(Object keyIn,
            Object dataIn)
    {
        PersonKey key = (PersonKey)keyIn;
        PersonData data = (PersonData) dataIn;
        return new Person(key.getSSN(), data.getName(),
                data.getDOB());
    }

    public Object objectToKey(Object o)
    {
        Person1 p = (Person1) o;
        return new PersonKey(p.getSSN());
    }

    public Object objectToData(Object o)
    {
        Person1 p = (Person1) o;
        return new PersonData(p.getName(), p.getDOB());
    }
}
```

The EntityBinding interface provides three methods—entryToObject, objectToEntry, and objectToData—to convert an entity object to a key-value pair and vice versa. Listing 11-20 shows you how to use this binding to store an entity object.

Listing 11-20. *Using the EntityBinding Interface*

```
SerialBinding personKeyBinding =
    new SerialBinding(classCatalog_, PersonKey.class);
EntityBinding personDataBinding =
    new PersonBinding(classCatalog_,
                        PersonKey.class, PersonData.class);
personMap_ = new StoredMap(personDb_, personKeyBinding,
                        personDataBinding, true);
```

```
personSet_ = (StoredValueSet)personMap_.values();
Person manish
  = new Person(new Long(111223333), "Manish Pandey", "jan 13 1971");
personSet_.add(manish1);
```

Listing 11-21 shows you how to retrieve an entity from the database.

Listing 11-21. *Reading Records That Were Stored Using the EntityBinding Interface*

```
Iterator i = personSet_.iterator();
try
{
    while(i.hasNext())
    {
        System.out.println(i.next().toString());
    }
}
finally
{
    StoredIterator.close(i);
}
```

SerialSerialBinding suffers from the same drawbacks as the serial entry binding. You cannot sort the keys, because you cannot control the order in which the member variables are serialized. In addition, the size of the serialized byte array is usually quite big, which results in wasted space in the database. Another entity binding, called TupleSerialBinding, addresses some of these issues.

TupleSerialBinding

TupleSerialBinding uses the tuple binding for the key and the serial binding for the value. You can sort the key in this binding, because the application can control the order in which members are serialized in the key byte array. You can use the same entity object, Person, which you defined for the SerialSerial binding. Listing 11-22 shows you how to implement the binding class.

Listing 11-22. *Person Class to Be Used with TupleSerialBinding*

```
    private static class PersonTupleSerialBinding
        extends TupleSerialBinding
    {
        private PersonTupleSerialBinding(ClassCatalog catalog,
                                          Class dataClass)
        {
            super(catalog, dataClass);
        }
```

```java
    public Object entryToObject(TupleInput keyIn, Object dataIn)
    {
        Long ssn = keyIn.readLong();
        PersonData data = (PersonData) dataIn;
        return new Person(ssn, data.getName(),
                data.getDOB());
    }

    public void objectToKey(Object o, TupleOutput to)
    {
        Person p = (Person) o;
        to.writeLong(p.getSSN());
    }

    public Object objectToData(Object o)
    {
        Person p = (Person)o;
        return new PersonData (p.getName(), p.getDOB());
    }
}
```

Note that the constructor for this binding requires only one class—the class that represents the data portion of the record—and not two. That's because you're using the tuple binding for the key, which you can extract from the entity object. As with the SerialSerial binding, you have three methods in this binding:

- entryToObject: For converting a database entry to a entity object

- objectToKey: For extracting the key byte array from an entity object

- objectToData: For extracting the PersonData object from the entity object

As Listing 11-23 shows, you can use TupleSerialBinding to insert an entity.

Listing 11-23. *Using the TupleSerialBinding Interface to Insert a Record*

```java
PersonKeyBinding keyBinding = new PersonKeyBinding();
PersonTupleSerialBinding personTupleSerialBinding =
    new PersonTupleSerialBinding(classCatalog_, Person.class);
personMap_= new StoredMap(personDb_, keyBinding,
                        personTupleSerialBinding, true);
personSet_= (StoredValueSet)personMap_.values();
Person manish
  = new Person(new Long(111223333), "Manish Pandey", "jan 13 1971");
personSet_.add(manish);
```

You can retrieve the entity in the same way as the SerialSerial binding, as shown in Listing 11-24.

Listing 11-24. *Reading Records That Were Stored Using the TupleSerialBinding Interface*

```
Iterator i = personSet_.iterator();
try
{
    while(i.hasNext())
    {
        System.out.println(i.next().toString());
    }
}
finally
{
    StoredIterator.close(i);
}
```

Serializable Entity Class

You must have noticed that you've defined the Person class multiple times. Initially, you used the Person class as the value in the serial entry binding. There you implemented the Serializable interface in the Person class, because you had to serialize the Person object so that it could be stored in the database. Then you used it as the entity class for the entity bindings. You didn't implement Serializable there, because the entity class isn't stored directly in the database.

You might have also noticed that you have redundant classes for the key and the value portions in the code examples of the entity bindings. All the information contained in the PersonKey and PersonData classes is available in the Person class. You couldn't use the Person object directly, because it contains both the key and value portions. If there is a way to not serialize the key while storing Person as the value, then you can eliminate the redundant classes. You can do this by making the Person class implement Serializable and declaring the member variables, which represent the key, as transient. When a member is declared as transient, then it is excluded from the serialized object, which in this case means that you'll get the same value as the serialized PersonData object when you serialize the Person object. Listing 11-25 shows you how to do that.

Listing 11-25. *Using transient to Exclude the Key from Serialization*

```
import java.io.Serializable;
public class Person implements Serializable
{
    transient private Long ssn_;
    private String name_;
    private String dob_;

    public Person()
    {}

    public Person(Long ssn,
            String name,
            String dob)
```

```
    {
        ssn_ = ssn;
        name_ = name;
        dob_ = dob;
    }

    public void setSSN(Long ssn)
    {
        ssn_ = ssn;
    }

    public void setName(String name)
    {
        name_ = name;
    }

    public void setDOB(String dob)
    {
        dob_ = dob;
    }

    public Long getSSN()
    {
        return ssn_;
    }

    public String getName()
    {
        return name_;
    }

    public String getDOB()
    {
        return dob_;
    }

    public String toString()
    {
        return "Person: ssn = " + ssn_ + " name = " + name_
            + " dob = " + dob_;
    }
}
```

You declare ssn_ as transient, because it's the only field that is used as the key. Listing 11-26 shows you how the binding class will look with this change.

Listing 11-26. *The Binding Class with the* transient *Key*

```
private static class PersonTupleSerialBinding extends
                                        TupleSerialBinding
{
    private PersonTupleSerialBinding(ClassCatalog catalog,
                                Class dataClass)
    {
        super(catalog, dataClass);
    }

    public Object entryToObject(TupleInput keyIn, Object dataIn)
    {
        Long ssn = keyIn.readLong();
        Person p = (Person) dataIn;
        p.setSSN(ssn);
        return p;
    }

    public void objectToKey(Object o, TupleOutput to)
    {
        Person p = (Person) o;
        to.writeLong(p.getSSN());
    }

    public Object objectToData(Object o)
    {
        return o;
    }
}
```

You have completely eliminated the redundant PersonKey and PersonData classes. It isn't essential to declare the key fields as transient. If they're not transient, then the value part of the database entries will also contain the key, which will waste some space but will be quite harmless otherwise. If the keys are big in size, then it makes sense to not include them in the values.

Transactions

The com.sleepycat.db.Transaction class encapsulates a database transaction. It is analogous to the DbTxn class in the C++ API. You cannot instantiate this class directly; you have to use the Environment.beginTransaction method to create an instance. Listing 11-27 demonstrates how to use this class.

Listing 11-27. *Creating a Transaction*

```
Transaction txn = null;
try
{
    txn = env_.beginTransaction(null, null);
    Person p = null;
    DatabaseEntry key = new DatabaseEntry();
    DatabaseEntry data = new DatabaseEntry();
    Person manish = new Person(new Long(111223333),
                              "Manish Pandey", "jan 13 1971");
    LongBinding.longToEntry(manish.getSSN(), key);
    binding.objectToEntry(manish, data);
    personDb_.put(null, key, data);

    txn.commit();
}
catch (DatabaseException e)
{
    txn.abort();
    System.err.println("addPersonEntries: " + e.toString());
    throw e;
}
```

Transactions and Stored Collections API

The Transaction object isn't used explicitly in the Berkeley DB Collections API. Transactions are executed through the com.sleepycat.Collections.TransactionRunner class. You can use the TransactionRunner.run() method to start a transaction. The operations to be performed within the transaction have to be specified through the TransactionWorker.doWork() method; therefore, the TransactionRunner and TransactionWorker classes work in conjunction. In addition to executing a transaction, TransactionRunner also performs the specified number of retries and handles exceptions. Listing 11-28 shows how to use TransactionWorker.

Listing 11-28. *Using TransactionWorker to Execute Transactions*

```
private class LoadDbs implements TransactionWorker
{
    public void doWork() throws Exception
    {
        javaEnv_.loadEntries(bindingType_);
    }
}
.
.
```

```
try
{
    TransactionRunner runner =
    new TransactionRunner(javaEnv_.getEnv());
    runner.setMaxRetries(3);
    runner.run(new DumpDbs());
}
catch(Exception e)
{
    System.err.println(
                "Exception caught while running transaction");
    e.printStackTrace();
}
.
.
.
```

The TransactionRunner instance runner executes the operations performed by LoadDbs, which implements the TransactionWorker interface within the context of a transaction. If the transaction encounters a DeadlockException (or some other exception that requires the application to retry the operation), then TransactionWorker will retry the operation three times, as specified by the setMaxRetries method.

The TransactionWorker interface has only one method, doWork, which you can use to specify the operations that TransactionRunner will perform within a single transaction. Once the TransactionRunner.run method is active in a thread, if the run method is invoked again, then the resulting transaction will become a nested transaction within the original transaction started by the first invocation of the run method. If the run method of the same TransactionRunner instance is invoked simultaneously from more than one thread, then a new transaction will be activated in each thread. Therefore, an invocation of the run method is coupled with the thread in which it is made.

■**Caution** Berkeley DB Java Edition, which is an independent product implemented purely in Java, currently doesn't support nested transactions. Since the Stored Collections API is supported by both Berkeley DB core and Berkeley DB JE, you should be careful not to use nested transactions if you plan to port your code from one product to the other.

Database Operations

You've already seen how to perform some database operations while going through the code examples of the bind APIs. You perform the basic operations in much the same way as you perform them using the C++ API. Database.get, Database.put, and Database.delete are the three basic, noncursor operations available. Apart from these basic operations, there are Database.putNoOverwrite and Database.putNoDupData, which aren't separate commands in the C++ API but are specified through the DB_NOOVERWRITE and DB_NODUPDATA flags.

Secondary Indices

A secondary index is a database that uses a key different than the primary key used to look up the key of a record in the primary database. For example, suppose you want to look up a Person record in the Person database not by the SSN, which is the primary key, but rather by the name of the person. You can either iterate through all the records in the database and look for the name you're interested in, or you can create a secondary database that's indexed on the name field of the Person records. The second option is much more efficient than the first one, especially if the database contains a large number of entries.

However, the secondary databases do have an overhead associated with them. In order to keep the secondary index consistent with the primary database, the library has to update the secondary indices every time an operation is performed on the primary database. The advantage provided by the secondary indices is usually greater than the disadvantage of having to manage additional databases. In order to create a secondary database using the Java API, you have to first implement a secondary key creator class, which can extract a secondary key when given a primary key and its value from the primary database. Listing 11-29 shows how to create a secondary index for a database.

Listing 11-29. *Creating a Secondary Index*

```
private static class PersonByNameKeyCreator
        extends TupleSerialKeyCreator
{
    private PersonByNameKeyCreator(ClassCatalog catalog,
                                   Class valueClass)
    {
        super(catalog, valueClass);
    }

    public boolean createSecondaryKey(TupleInput primaryKeyInput,
                                      Object valueInput,
                                      TupleOutput indexKeyOutput)
    {

        String name = primaryKeyInput.readString();
        indexKeyOutput.writeString(name);
        return true;
    }
}
```

Note that the createSecondaryKey method should return true in order for the library to maintain the secondary index properly. Using the primary key and the value stored against the key, the createSecondaryKey method returns the name in the Person record. Every time any record is added, updated, or deleted in the primary database, this method will be invoked to perform the corresponding operation in the secondary database. Listing 11-30 shows how you open the secondary database.

Listing 11-30. *Opening a Secondary Database*

```
SecondaryConfig secConfig = new SecondaryConfig();
secConfig.setTransactional(true);
secConfig.setAllowCreate(true);
secConfig.setType(DatabaseType.BTREE);
secConfig.setSortedDuplicates(true);
secConfig.setKeyCreator(new PersonByNameKeyCreator(classCatalogDb_,
                                                   Person.class));
SecondaryDatabase personByNameDb_ = null;
personByNameDb = env_.openSecondaryDatabase(null,
                                "PersonByNameDb",
                                null,_
                                personDb_,
                                secConfig);
```

You can use the `SecondaryConfig.setSortedDuplicates` method to configure the secondary databases to allow duplicates. You'll end up using this method often with secondary databases, because the secondary keys are usually not unique, which results in multiple records in the secondary database for every primary key. You can now use the secondary database to query `Person` records by name, as shown in Listing 11-31.

Listing 11-31. *Using a Secondary Database*

```
String name = "Manish Pandey";
DatabaseEntry secKey = new DatabaseEntry(name.getBytes("UTF-8"));
DatabaseEntry primaryKey = new DatabaseEntry();
DatabaseEntry value = new DatabaseEntry();
OperationStatus retVal = personByNameDb_.get(null, secKey,
                                primaryKey,
                                value,
                                LockMode.DEFAULT);
```

Complete Code Example

For someone who is learning how to use the Berkeley DB Java API, the `bind` API presents a challenge. This is especially true for programmers who are used to the C/C++ API and want to learn the Java API. Mastering the `bind` API is the key to mastering the Java API. The best way to understand the various bindings is to study and compare the code for various bindings to the same database record. Listing 11-33 does just that. You've seen how to use four different bindings (two entry bindings and two entity bindings) on the same set of `Person` records. You can execute the Java program, listed here, with one of the four bindings, which you can specify as a command-line option. Listing 11-32 shows the implemented bindings.

Listing 11-32. *The Binding Implemented in the Code Example*

```
public static final int SerialBinding = 1;
public static final int TupleBinding = 2;
public static final int EntityBinding = 3;
public static final int EntityTupleSerialBinding = 4;
```

You can execute the TDS.java program like this:

.
```
/home/hy/bdb_book/chap_11/> ./TDS 1
```
.
.
```
/home/hy/bdb_book/chap_11/> ./TDS 2
```
.
.
```
/home/hy/bdb_book/chap_11/> ./TDS 3
```
.

You can study the code for each binding and understand the differences between the various approaches. Listing 11-33 shows you how to use TransactionRunner and TransactionWorker, and it also shows you how to run a transaction directly using the Transaction class.

Listing 11-33 includes the following classes:

- TDS.java: This class contains the main method. It bootstraps the application and shuts it down.

- JavaEnv.java: This class creates the database environment and opens the databases. It contains the bulk of the logic, which includes most of the bind classes and the code for reading and dumping the databases using the various bindings.

- Person.java: This class is used as an entry in the Serial binding for storing the Person record and also as the Person entity for the TupleSerial bindings.

- Person1.java: This class is used to demonstrate the entity class in the SerialSerial binding.

- PersonData.java: This class is used as the value part in the SerialSerial binding.

- PersonKey.java: This class is used as the key part in the SerialSerial binding.

Listing 11-33. *Complete Listing of TDS.java*

```
package chap_11;
import com.sleepycat.collections.*;
import com.sleepycat.db.*;
public class TDS
{
    static JavaEnv javaEnv_ = null;
    static int bindingType_ = 0;
```

```java
    public TDS()
    {
        javaEnv_ = new JavaEnv();
    }

    private void startTDS(int bindingType)
    {
        bindingType_ = bindingType;
        try
        {
            TransactionRunner runner =
                new TransactionRunner(javaEnv_.getEnv());
            runner.run(new LoadDbs());
            runner.run(new DumpDbs());
        }
        catch(Exception e)
        {
            System.err.println(
                    "Exception caught while running transaction");
            e.printStackTrace();
        }
    }

    private class LoadDbs implements TransactionWorker
    {
        public void doWork() throws Exception
        {
            javaEnv_.loadEntries(bindingType_);
        }
    }

    private class DumpDbs implements TransactionWorker
    {
        public void doWork() throws Exception
        {
            javaEnv_.dumpEntries(bindingType_);
        }
    }

    public static void main(String args[])
    {
        int bindingType = Integer.parseInt(args[0]);
        TDS tds = new TDS();
        tds.startTDS(bindingType);
    }
}
```

```java
//JavaEnv.java
import java.io.*;
import java.util.*;
import com.sleepycat.db.*;
import com.sleepycat.collections.*;
import com.sleepycat.bind.serial.*;
import com.sleepycat.bind.tuple.*;
import com.sleepycat.bind.EntryBinding;
import com.sleepycat.bind.EntityBinding;

public class JavaEnv
{

    public static final int SerialBinding = 1;
    public static final int TupleBinding = 2;
    public static final int EntityBinding = 3;
    public static final int EntityTupleSerialBinding = 4;

    private Person manish
        = new Person(new Long(111223333), "Manish Pandey",
                    "jan 13 1971");
    private Person shirish
        = new Person(new Long(111223334), "Shirish Rai",
                    "dec 23 1974");
    private Person roland
        = new Person(new Long(111443335), "Roland Hendel",
                    "feb 13 1973");

    private Person1 manish1
        = new Person1(new Long(111223333), "Manish Pandey",
                    "jan 13 1971");
    private Person1 shirish1
        = new Person1(new Long(111223334), "Shirish Rai",
                    "dec 23 1974");
    private Person1 roland1
        = new Person1(new Long(111443335), "Roland Hendel",
                    "feb 13 1973");

    private EnvironmentConfig envConfig_ = null;
    private Environment env_ = null;
    private File envHome_ = new File("./chap11_env");

    private DatabaseConfig dbConfig_ = null;
    private Database personDb_ = null;
    private Database classCatalogDb_ = null;
    private StoredClassCatalog classCatalog_ = null;
```

```java
    private StoredMap personMap_ = null;
    private StoredValueSet personSet_ = null;

    Environment getEnv()
    {
        return env_;
    }

    private static class PersonBinding extends SerialSerialBinding
    {
        private PersonBinding(ClassCatalog catalog,
                Class keyClass, Class dataClass)
        {
            super(catalog, keyClass, dataClass);
        }

        public Object entryToObject(Object keyIn,
                Object dataIn)
        {
            PersonKey key = (PersonKey)keyIn;
            PersonData data = (PersonData) dataIn;
            return new Person(key.getSSN(), data.getName(),
                    data.getDOB());
        }

        public Object objectToKey(Object o)
        {
            Person1 p = (Person1) o;
            return new PersonKey(p.getSSN());
        }

        public Object objectToData(Object o)
        {
            Person1 p = (Person1) o;
            return new PersonData(p.getName(), p.getDOB());
        }
    }

    private static class PersonKeyBinding extends TupleBinding
    {
        private PersonKeyBinding()
        {}

        public Object entryToObject(TupleInput input)
        {
            Long ssn = input.readLong();
            return new PersonKey(ssn);
        }
```

```java
    public void objectToEntry(Object o, TupleOutput output)
    {
        PersonKey key = (PersonKey)o;
        output.writeLong(key.getSSN());
    }
}

private static class PersonTupleSerialBinding extends
                                        TupleSerialBinding
{
    private PersonTupleSerialBinding(ClassCatalog catalog,
                                Class dataClass)
    {
        super(catalog, dataClass);
    }

    public Object entryToObject(TupleInput keyIn, Object dataIn)
    {
        Long ssn = keyIn.readLong();
        Person p = (Person) dataIn;
        p.setSSN(ssn);
        return p;
    }

    public void objectToKey(Object o, TupleOutput to)
    {
        Person p = (Person) o;
        to.writeLong(p.getSSN());
    }

    public Object objectToData(Object o)
    {
        return o;
    }
}

private void createEnv() throws Exception
{
    try
    {

        envConfig_ = new EnvironmentConfig();
        envConfig_.setErrorStream(System.err);
        envConfig_.setErrorPrefix("chap_11");
        envConfig_.setAllowCreate(true);
        envConfig_.setInitializeCache(true);
        envConfig_.setTransactional(true);
        envConfig_.setInitializeLocking(true);
```

```java
            env_ = new Environment(envHome_, envConfig_);
        }
        catch(Exception e)
        {
            System.err.println("createEnv: " + e.toString());
            throw e;
        }
    }

    private void createDbHandle() throws Exception
    {
        try
        {
            dbConfig_ = new DatabaseConfig();
            dbConfig_.setErrorStream(System.err);
            dbConfig_.setType(DatabaseType.BTREE);
            dbConfig_.setAllowCreate(true);
            dbConfig_.setTransactional(true);

            dbConfig_.setErrorPrefix("chap_11:PersonDb");
            personDb_ = env_.openDatabase(null, "Person_Db",
                                          null, dbConfig_);

            classCatalogDb_ =
                env_.openDatabase(null, "ClassCatalog_Db",
                                  null, dbConfig_);
            classCatalog_ = new StoredClassCatalog(classCatalogDb_);
        }
        catch(Exception e)
        {
            System.err.println("createDbHandle: " + e.toString());
            throw e;
        }

    }

    private void addToPersonMap()
    {
        try
        {
            SerialBinding personKeyBinding =
                new SerialBinding(classCatalog_, PersonKey.class);

            EntityBinding personDataBinding =
                new PersonBinding(classCatalog_,
                        PersonKey.class, PersonData.class);
```

```
            personMap_ =
                new StoredMap(personDb_, personKeyBinding,
                        personDataBinding, true);

            personSet_ = (StoredValueSet)personMap_.values();

            personSet_.add(manish1);
            personSet_.add(shirish1);
            personSet_.add(roland1);
        }
        catch(Exception e)
        {
            System.err.println("addToPersonMap: " + e.toString());
        }
    }

    private void addToPersonMap1()
    {
        try
        {
            PersonKeyBinding keyBinding = new PersonKeyBinding();

            PersonTupleSerialBinding personTupleSerialBinding =
                new PersonTupleSerialBinding(classCatalog_,
                                              Person.class);
            personMap_ =
                new StoredMap(personDb_, keyBinding,
                        personTupleSerialBinding, true);
            personSet_ =
                (StoredValueSet)personMap_.values();
            personSet_.add(manish);
            personSet_.add(shirish);
            personSet_.add(roland);
        }
        catch(Exception e)
        {
            System.err.println("addToPersonMap1: " + e.toString());
        }
    }

    void loadEntries(int bindingType) throws Exception
    {
        EntryBinding binding = null;
        switch(bindingType)
        {
```

```
                case SerialBinding:
                    binding =
                        new SerialBinding(classCatalog_, Person.class);
                    addPersonEntries(binding);
                    break;
                case TupleBinding:
                    binding = new PersonTupleBinding();
                    addPersonEntries(binding);
                    break;
                case EntityBinding:
                    addToPersonMap();
                    break;
                case EntityTupleSerialBinding:
                    addToPersonMap1();
                    break;
                default:
                    System.out.println("Unknown binding");
                    break;
            }
    }

    private void addPersonEntries(EntryBinding binding)
                                        throws Exception
    {
        Transaction txn = null;
        try
        {
            txn = env_.beginTransaction(null, null);

            Person p = null;
            DatabaseEntry key = new DatabaseEntry();
            DatabaseEntry data = new DatabaseEntry();

            LongBinding.longToEntry(manish.getSSN(), key);
            binding.objectToEntry(manish, data);
            personDb_.put(null, key, data);

            LongBinding.longToEntry(shirish.getSSN(), key);
            binding.objectToEntry(shirish, data);
            personDb_.put(null, key, data);

            LongBinding.longToEntry(roland.getSSN(), key);
            binding.objectToEntry(roland, data);
            personDb_.put(null, key, data);
            txn.commit();
        }
```

```
        catch (DatabaseException e)
        {
            txn.abort();
            System.err.println("addPersonEntries: " + e.toString());
            throw e;
        }
}


void dumpEntries(int bindingType) throws Exception
{

    EntryBinding binding = null;
    switch(bindingType)
    {
        case SerialBinding:
            binding =
                new SerialBinding(classCatalog_,
                        Person.class);
            cursorPrint(binding);
            break;
        case TupleBinding:
            binding = new PersonTupleBinding();
            cursorPrint(binding);
            break;
        case EntityBinding:
        case EntityTupleSerialBinding:
            iteratorPrint();
            return;
        default:
            System.out.println("Unknown binding " + binding);
            return;
    }

}


private void cursorPrint(EntryBinding binding) throws Exception
{
    Transaction txn = null;
    Cursor cursor = null;
    DatabaseEntry key = new DatabaseEntry();
    DatabaseEntry data = new DatabaseEntry();

    try
    {
        txn = env_.beginTransaction(null, null);
        Person p = new Person();
```

```
            cursor = personDb_.openCursor(txn, null);
            while(cursor.getNext(key, data, LockMode.DEFAULT)
                    == OperationStatus.SUCCESS)
            {
                p = (Person)(binding.entryToObject(data));
                System.out.println("dumpEntries: " + p);
            }
            cursor.close();
            cursor = null;
            txn.commit();
        }
        catch (DatabaseException e)
        {
            if(cursor != null)
                cursor.close();
            txn.abort();
            System.err.println("addPersonEntries: " + e.toString());
            throw e;
        }
    }

    private void iteratorPrint() throws Exception
    {
        Iterator i = personSet_.iterator();
        try
        {
            while(i.hasNext())
            {
                System.out.println(i.next().toString());
            }
        }
        finally
        {
            StoredIterator.close(i);
        }
    }

    public JavaEnv()
    {
        try
        {
            createEnv();
            createDbHandle();
        }
```

```
        catch(DatabaseException e)
        {
            System.err.println("LoadDbs: " + e.toString());
        }
        catch(Exception e)
        {
            System.err.println("LoadDbs: non DB exception caught " +
                    e.toString());
        }
    }
}

//Person.java
import java.io.Serializable;
public class Person implements Serializable
{
    private Long ssn_;
    private String name_;
    private String dob_;

    public Person()
    {}

    public Person(Long ssn,
            String name,
            String dob)
    {
        ssn_  = ssn;
        name_ = name;
        dob_  = dob;
    }

    public void setSSN(Long ssn)
    {
        ssn_ = ssn;
    }

    public void setName(String name)
    {
        name_ = name;
    }

    public void setDOB(String dob)
    {
        dob_ = dob;
    }
```

```java
    public Long getSSN()
    {
        return ssn_;
    }

    public String getName()
    {
        return name_;
    }

    public String getDOB()
    {
        return dob_;
    }

    public String toString()
    {
        return "Person: ssn = " + ssn_ + " name = " + name_
            + " dob = " + dob_;
    }
}

//Person1.java
public class Person1
{
    private Long ssn_;
    private String name_;
    private String dob_;

    public Person1(Long ssn,
            String name,
            String dob)
    {
        ssn_ = ssn;
        name_ = name;
        dob_ = dob;
    }

    public Long getSSN()
    {
        return ssn_;
    }

    public String getName()
    {
        return name_;
    }
```

```java
    public String getDOB()
    {
        return dob_;
    }

    public String toString()
    {
        return "PersonEnt: ssn = " + ssn_ + " name = " + name_
            + " dob = " + dob_;
    }
}

//PersonKey.java
import java.io.Serializable;

public class PersonKey implements Serializable
{
    private Long ssn_;

    public PersonKey(Long ssn)
    {
        ssn_ = ssn;
    }

    public final Long getSSN()
    {
        return ssn_;
    }

    public String toString()
    {
        return "(PersonKey: ssn = " + ssn_ + ")";
    }
}

//PersonData.java
import java.io.Serializable;

public class PersonData implements Serializable
{
    private String name_;
    private String dob_;

    public PersonData(String name, String dob)
    {
        name_ = name;
        dob_ = dob;
    }
```

```
    public final String getName()
    {
        return name_;
    }

    public final String getDOB()
    {
        return dob_;
    }

    public String toString()
    {
        return "(PersonData: name = " + name_ +
                " dob = " + dob_ + ")";
    }
}
```

Summary

In this chapter, you learned how to use the Berkeley DB Java API. By leveraging Java language features such as reflection, collection, and serialization, you can use the Java API to present a much richer and more user-friendly interface when compared to the C++ API, even though the underlying database implementation is common for both APIs. In the next chapter, I'll present the Berkeley DB C API.

CHAPTER 12

Berkeley DB C API

Most of the older Berkeley DB applications were written using the C API, while a large percentage of the applications being written today use the C++ or the Java API. The C API doesn't have some of the higher-level constructs available in the C++ or the Java APIs. In that respect, the C API is primitive when compared to the other APIs. However, all other Berkeley DB APIs are wrappers around the C API. The Berkeley DB library itself has been implemented in C, and it even uses the C API methods internally. It is useful to understand how the lowest-level API works, even if you're not planning to use it in your application.

In this chapter, I'll go over the Berkeley DB C API. This chapter is meant for you to use as an introduction to the C API; it doesn't cover any topic in detail. For a detailed discussion on a specific topic, read one of the preceding chapters dedicated to the topic. You should refer to the C API reference manual[1] for detailed information about specific APIs.

Compiling and Installing the C API

The Berkeley DB `configure` script sets up the build environment to create the C API by default. The C API gets compiled even if you compile and install the C++ or the Java API, because all the other APIs use the C API. The compilation instructions are the same as those for other APIs. If you're building for a UNIX-like platform, run the commands in the following example from the `build_unix` directory in the root directory of the Berkeley DB distribution:

```
hy@linux:~/sw/src/db-4.4.20/build_unix> ../dist/configure --enable-debug ➥
--enable-diagnostics --prefix=/home/hy/sw/install/
hy@linux:~/sw/src/db-4.4.20/build_unix> make
.
.
.
hy@linux:~/sw/src/db-4.4.20/build_unix> make install
```

Make sure that you specify the `--prefix` as the location where you want the library to be installed, and not the one shown in the previous results. After you run `make` and `make install`, you see the following files in the `lib` directory of your installation location:

---

1. http://www.oracle.com/technology/documentation/berkeley-db/db/api_c/frame.html

```
hy@linux:~/sw/install/lib> ls -l
-rwxr-xr-x  1 hy users  7235684 2006-06-21 10:40 libdb_java-4.4.so
-rw-r--r--  1 hy users      851 2006-06-21 10:40 libdb_java-4.4.la
-rw-r--r--  1 hy users  7649856 2006-06-21 10:41 libdb.a
-rw-r--r--  1 hy users  7649856 2006-06-21 10:41 libdb-4.4.a
lrwxrwxrwx  1 hy users       12 2006-06-21 10:41 libdb.so -> libdb-4.4.so
lrwxrwxrwx  1 hy users       12 2006-06-21 10:41 libdb-4.so -> libdb-4.4.so
```

You'll find a static library (libdb-4.4.a) and a dynamic library (libdb-4.4.so). They're identical in functionality.

Basic Operations Using the C API

In this section, you'll learn how to use the C API to perform basic database operations. The underlying concepts and design issues related to using the C API are the same as those related to the C++ API, so I won't cover them here; refer to the previous chapters instead.

Opening the Environment

The database environment is represented by the DB_ENV structure in the C API. You have to initialize this structure in order to create an environment. Listing 12-1 shows how you can do that.

Listing 12-1. *Opening a Database Environment*

```
DB_ENV *env;
char *env_home = "./chap12_env";
int retval = db_env_create(&env, 0);
int envflags = DB_CREATE | DB_INIT_LOCK |
               DB_INIT_LOG | DB_INIT_MPOOL |
               DB_INIT_TXN | DB_RECOVER;

if(retval != 0)
{
    printf("Error creating DB_ENV handle: err: %d\n",
            retval);
    return -1;
}
env->set_errpfx(env, "chap_12_tds");
env->set_data_dir(env, ".");
retval = env->open(env, env_home, envflags, 0);
```

```
if(retval != 0)
{
    env->err(env, retval,
            "Error opening the environment");
    env->close(env, 0);
    return -1;
}
env->set_flags(env, DB_LOG_AUTOREMOVE);
env->set_cachesize(env, 5000000, 1);
return 0;
```

Follow these three steps to open an environment:

1. Initialize the environment handle.

2. Set the configuration parameters, which you have to specify before opening the environment.

3. Call open of the initialized DB_ENV handle.

Configuring the environment can be a bit confusing, because it involves tweaking a number of parameters, and there are numerous ways to tweak them. In addition, not all parameters can be specified everywhere. Some can only be specified before opening the environment, some have to be specified while opening the environment (in the open method) and the rest can be specified at any time during the lifetime of an environment handle. If multiple processes are opening an environment handle that points to the same environment, then all of them should specify the same configuration. You have to read the documentation carefully to determine when you can apply a particular configuration parameter.

One way you can avoid the confusion is by using the DB_CONFIG file. The DB_CONFIG file should be present in the environment home directory. You can use DB_CONFIG to specify any environment configuration flags or parameters other than the ones specified in the open method. Using the DB_CONFIG file helps you in three ways:

- **You can use the configuration parameters to change the configuration without changing the code**: If you don't use the DB_CONFIG file, any configuration change will require a code change and a recompilation. The library picks up the configuration from the DB_CONFIG file at runtime and overrides the existing configuration.

- **You don't need to worry about when to specify a particular configuration**: As mentioned earlier, you cannot specify all configuration parameters at all times. By using the DB_CONFIG file, you don't have to worry about that. The library picks up the necessary configuration parameter from the file when it needs it.

- **Configuration is uniform across all processes**: If multiple processes are sharing the environment, then you can enforce a common configuration by using the DB_CONFIG file. Without it, controlling the configuration settings can be challenging, especially if different programmers own and implement different processes.

You can use the DB_CONFIG file shown in Listing 12-2 for configuring the environment created in Listing 12-1.

Listing 12-2. *An Example of* DB_CONFIG

```
set_data_dir .
set_flag DB_LOG_AUTOREMOVE
set_cachesize 0 5000000 1
```

You can leave the configuration settings specified in the code as is, because the DB_CONFIG file silently overrides those settings.

Creating a Database Record

A Berkeley DB database is simple in structure. All records have two components: a key component and a value component. The key is indexed for fast lookup, and the value contains the data that is stored against the key. Both keys and values are of type DBT, which is an acronym for *DataBase Thang*. A DBT is a structure that stores a byte array. Listing 12-3 shows the structure as it is defined in db.h.

Listing 12-3. *The* DBT *Structure*

```
struct __DBT
{
    void      *data;    // pointer to key/data byte array
    u_int32_t size;     // length of the array
    u_int32_t ulen;     // length of user buffer
    u_int32_t dlen;     // get/put record length
    u_int32_t doff;     // get/put record offset
}
```

■**Note** For a detailed description of the fields in this structure, please refer to Chapter 4. In this chapter, I'll only use the data and size fields, which represent the location and the size of a byte array, respectively.

All records that you store in the database should be contiguous byte arrays. The application developer is responsible for data semantics. For example, if you're writing a data structure that contains pointers to the database, you'll have to flatten it out so that the library can write it safely to the disk.

Continuing to use the Person database example, let's store the structure, shown in Listing 12-4, as the value and the ssn field in the structure as the key.

Listing 12-4. *Structure to Hold the* Person *Record*

```
typedef struct
{
    int ssn;
    char dob[16];
    char name[64];
} person;
```

You can easily store a C structure in the database simply by type-casting it to a byte array. You'll see how to do that in the section "Simple Database Operations," later in the chapter.

Using Transactions

If your database environment is configured for transactions, then you can wrap database operations within transactions. Transactions provide the ACID properties to the database. (For more information about transactions and ACID properties, please refer to Chapter 5.) To enable transactions, open the environment with the flags, as shown in Listing 12-5.

Listing 12-5. *Opening an Environment with Support for Transactions*

```
int envflags = DB_CREATE | DB_INIT_LOCK |
               DB_INIT_LOG | DB_INIT_MPOOL |
               DB_INIT_TXN | DB_RECOVER;
retval = env->open(env, env_home, envflags, 0);
```

Except for DB_RECOVER and DB_CREATE, you need all of the flags shown in Listing 12-5 to create a transactional environment. When DB_RECOVER and DB_CREATE are specified, the library performs environment recovery before opening the environment. Recovery is needed if the database environment was not shut down cleanly the last time it was used. It's virtually impossible to guarantee a clean shutdown, so it's good practice to specify this flag while opening the environment. However, be careful not to open the environment using DB_CREATE from multiple threads at the same time, because DB_CREATE will destroy the existing environment. (For a detailed discussion on database recovery, please refer to Chapters 5 and 6.)

Continuing with transactions, Listing 12-6 shows how to create, abort, and commit a transaction.

Listing 12-6. *Using a Transaction*

```
//Creating a transaction
DB_TXN *txn;
retval = env->txn_begin(env, NULL, &txn, 0);
if(retval != 0)
{
    env->err(env, retval,
            "error in txn_begin");
    return -1;
}

//Aborting a transaction
retval = txn->abort(txn);
if(retval != 0)
{
    env->err(env, retval,
            "error while aborting transaction");
    return -1;
}
```

```
//Committing a transaction

retval = txn->commit(txn, 0);
if(retval != 0)
{
    env->err(env, retval,
            "error while committing transaction");
    return -1;
}
```

Opening the Database

Listing 12-7 shows you how to create a database handle. Like the environment handle, you first have to initialize a database handle before you can open it.

Listing 12-7. *Opening a Database*

```
int retval = 0;
DB *person_db;
//open the primary database

//Initialize the handle
retval = db_create(&person_db, env, 0);
if(retval != 0)
{
    env->err(env, retval,
            "Error creating DB handle");
    return -1;
}
//Set the specific error prefix for this handle
person_db->set_errpfx(person_db, "chap_12_tds:person_db");

person_db->set_flags(person_db,
                     DB_CHKSUM | DB_ENCRYPT);
//Protect the database handle creation with a transaction
//All subsequent operations using this handle will have to
// be performed within transactions
int dbflags = DB_CREATE | DB_AUTO_COMMIT;
retval = person_db->open(person_db, NULL, "person_db",
                         NULL, DB_BTREE, dbflags, 0);
if(retval != 0)
{
    //Use the handle-specific error prefix for logging the error
    person_db->err(person_db, retval,
                   "Error opening person_db");
    return -1;
}
```

There are numerous configuration parameters that you can specify for a database handle—some through the set_flags[2] method, and others through the flags argument in the open[3] method. You can specify a specific error message prefix for every database handle and then use the err method on the handle to log error messages, which is useful while debugging.

■**Note** You cannot specify database configuration through the DB_CONFIG file. Currently, you can use the DB_CONFIG file only for environment configuration.

Creating a Secondary Index

You can index a database on multiple keys. A database that is indexed on a nonprimary key is called a *secondary index*. A secondary index is useful if you're going to query the database frequently using a nonprimary key. The presence of a secondary index can significantly improve the lookup performance of such queries. For example, the primary key in the Person database is the SSN. If an application has to look up a Person record based on the name, then it will have to scan the entire database to find the relevant record. If you create a secondary index on the database keyed on the name, then the lookup can access the records directly using the name. Listing 12-8 shows how you can create a secondary index.

Listing 12-8. *Creating a Secondary Index*

```
DB *person_by_name_db;
retval = db_create(&person_by_name_db, env, 0);
if(retval != 0)
{
    env->err(env, retval,
            "Error creating DB handle");
    return -1;
}
person_by_name_db->set_errpfx(person_by_name_db,
        "chap_12_tds:person_by_name_db");
person_by_name_db->set_flags(person_by_name_db, DB_DUPSORT);

retval = person_by_name_db->open(person_by_name_db, NULL,
        "person_by_name_db", NULL, DB_BTREE, dbflags, 0);
if(retval != 0)
{
    person_by_name_db->err(person_by_name_db, retval,
                "Error opening person_db");
    return -1;
}
```

---

2. http://www.oracle.com/technology/documentation/berkeley-db/db/api_c/db_set_flags.html
3. http://www.oracle.com/technology/documentation/berkeley-db/db/api_c/db_open.html

```
retval = person_db->associate(person_db, NULL,
        person_by_name_db, get_sec_key, 0);
if(retval != 0)
{
    person_db->err(person_db, retval,
                    "Error associating person_by_name_db");
    return -1;
}
return 0;
```

You can open the secondary index just like a primary database, except that you have to associate it with the primary database handle using the associate method. The associate call provides a callback to the primary database handle. The callback returns the secondary key given the primary key and the corresponding value. You implicitly use the callback, get_sec_key, every time you add, delete, or modify a record to update the secondary index appropriately. Listing 12-9 shows how you can define the callback.

Listing 12-9. *Defining a Secondary Key Callback*

```
int get_sec_key(DB *db, const DBT *pkey,
    const DBT *pdata, DBT *skey)
{
    person *p = (person*)(pdata->data);
    skey->data = p->name;
    skey->size = sizeof(p->name);
    return 0;
}
```

The callback sets the pointer of the name field in the primary data DBT. The callback should return 0 if the secondary key creation is successful. A nonzero error code indicates an error.

■**Note** The secondary keys may not always be contained entirely within the primary key's key-value pair. The secondary key callback implementation is more involved for those cases. Please refer to Chapter 5 for a detailed discussion of the callback implementation.

Simple Database Operations

You now have all the components you need to load some records in the Person database and then read them from the database. Listing 12-10 shows a list of Person records that I'll use to show you how to perform some basic database operations.

Listing 12-10. *A List of Person Records*

```
person records[] =
{
    {111223333, "Manish Pandey", "jan 13 1971"},
    {111223334, "Shirish Rai", "dec 23 1974"},
    {111223335, "Roland Hendel", "feb 13 1973"}
};
int num_records = 3;
```

person_records is an array that holds three instances of the person structure. Let's see how to insert these instances in the Person database.

Inserting Records

Listing 12-11 shows how you can use the put method to insert the Person records in the Person database.

Listing 12-11. *Inserting a Record*

```
int i;
for(i=0; i < num_records; i++)
{
    person p = records[i];
    printf("inserting: ssn: %d, name: %s, dob: %s\n",
            p.ssn, p.name, p.dob);

    memset(&key, 0, sizeof(key));
    memset(&value, 0, sizeof(value));
    key.data = &(p.ssn);
    key.size = sizeof(int);

    value.data = &p;
    value.size = sizeof(person);

    retval = person_db->put(person_db, NULL,
            &key, &value, 0);
    switch(retval)
    {
        case 0:
            printf("put successful\n");
            continue;
        case DB_KEYEXIST:
            person_db->err(person_db, retval,
                    "%d already exists\n", records[i].ssn);
            break;
```

```
            default:
                person_db->err(person_db, retval,
                        "error while inserting %d error %d",
                        records[i].ssn, retval);
                break;
        }
    }
}
```

You initialize two DBT instances: one for the key, and the other for the value. The DBT value contains the pointer to the Person record, and the key points to the ssn field in the Person record. To store a C structure in the database, you can simply type-cast it to a void* (the type of the data field in the DBT structure). Direct type-casting, however, works only when the structure doesn't contain pointers to other structures or variables. If the structure contains pointers, then you have to create a contiguous buffer that can hold all the members, and you have to copy the members to it before storing it in the database. In other words, you have to *flatten out* the structure.

Deleting Records

To delete a record, you can use the del method shown in Listing 12-12. This time, you'll use a transaction.

Listing 12-12. *Deleting a Record*

```
int retval = 0;
DB_TXN *txn;
retval = env->txn_begin(env, NULL, &txn, 0);
if(retval != 0)
{
    env->err(env, retval,
            "error in delete_rec::txn_begin");
    return -1;
}
int ssn = 111223333;
DBT key;
memset(&key, 0, sizeof(key));
key.data = &ssn;
key.size = sizeof(ssn);

retval = person_db->del(person_db, txn,
        &key, 0);
```

```
if(retval != 0)
{
    person_db->err(person_db, retval,
            "error in delete_rec::del");

    retval = txn->abort(txn);
    if(retval != 0)
    {
        env->err(env, retval,
                "error while aborting transaction");
        return -1;
    }
    return -1;
}

retval = txn->commit(txn, 0);
if(retval != 0)
{
    env->err(env, retval,
            "error while committing transaction");
    return -1;
}.
```

Updating Records

Listing 12-13 shows how to update a record. The update operation is slightly more involved, because you have to read the record to be updated, make the necessary change, and then insert the record in the database. You have to do the update in three steps, because the Berkeley DB library doesn't provide a separate update method.

Listing 12-13. *Updating a Record*

```
int retval = 0;
int ssn = 111223335;
DBT key;
DBT value;
memset(&key, 0, sizeof(key));
memset(&key, 0, sizeof(value));
key.data = &ssn;
key.size = sizeof(ssn);
DB_TXN *txn;

retval = env->txn_begin(env, NULL, &txn, 0);
```

```
if(retval != 0)
{
    env->err(env, retval,
            "error in load_db::txn_begin");
    return -1;
}

//First read the record to be updated
retval = person_db->get(person_db, txn,
        &key, &value, 0);
if(retval != 0)
{
    person_db->err(person_db, retval, "error in get");
    return -1;
    retval = txn->abort(txn);
    if(retval != 0)
    {
        env->err(env, retval,
                "error while aborting transaction");
        return -1;
    }
}

//Change the Person record to include the middle name
//in the record
person *p = (person*)(value.data);
char *new_name = "Roland Tembo Hendle";
memcpy(p->name, new_name, strlen(new_name)+1);

//Insert the updated record
retval = person_db->put(person_db, txn,
        &key, &value, 0);
if(retval != 0)
{
    person_db->err(person_db, retval, "error in put");
    return -1;
    retval = txn->abort(txn);
    if(retval != 0)
    {
        env->err(env, retval,
                "error while aborting transaction");
        return -1;
    }
}
retval = txn->commit(txn, 0);
```

```
if(retval != 0)
{
    env->err(env, retval,
            "error while committing transaction");
    return -1;
}
```

It's possible to do the update with a single operation, by overwriting the existing record with your own record, if you know the exact bytes in the database that you have to change. Only one writer can update the database in that case. In a database with multiple concurrent writers, you can never assume that the record value you have with you is the one present in the database, because it's possible that another writer may have updated the record after you read it. Therefore, you can never know the exact offset and the length of the change when multiple concurrent writers are allowed to update the database. Since you performed this operation within a transaction, you can be sure that no other thread modified it while you were updating the record.

■**Note** You need to consider some locking issues for update operations. Please refer to Chapter 5 for a detailed discussion.

Reading Records

If you know the key of the record you're looking for, you can use the code shown in Listing 12-14 to read a record from the database.

Listing 12-14. *Reading a Record*

```
int retval = 0;
int ssn = 111223333;
DBT key;
DBT value;
memset(&key, 0, sizeof(key));
memset(&key, 0, sizeof(value));
key.data = &ssn;
key.size = sizeof(ssn);

DB_TXN *txn;
retval = env->txn_begin(env, NULL, &txn, 0);
if(retval != 0)
{
    env->err(env, retval,
            "error in load_db::txn_begin");
    return -1;
}
```

```
retval = person_db->get(person_db, txn,
        &key, &value, 0);
if(retval != 0)
{
    person_db->err(person_db, retval, "error in get");
    return -1;
}

retval = txn->commit(txn, 0);
if(retval != 0)
{
    env->err(env, retval,
            "error while committing transaction");
    return -1;
}
person p = *((person*)(value.data));

printf("Single read: Found for ssn: %d: name %s, dob %s\n",
        ssn, p.name, p.dob);
```

Note that a read operation doesn't modify a record, but if you want to ensure that get returns a value that doesn't get changed while you're using it, you should execute it within a transaction.

Using a Cursor to Read Records

To read the inserted records from the database, you can use a cursor to iterate through all the records. If you don't know the primary key of the record you're interested in, this is the only way to look for your record. Listing 12-15 shows how to use a cursor to dump all the records in a database.

Listing 12-15. *Using a Cursor to Read Records*

```
DBT key, value;
DBC *cur;
int retval = 0;

DB_TXN *txn;
retval = env->txn_begin(env, NULL, &txn, 0);
if(retval != 0)
{
    env->err(env, retval,
            "error in dump_db::txn_begin");
    return -1;
}

retval = person_db->cursor(person_db, txn,
        &cur, 0);
```

```
if(retval != 0)
{
    person_db->err(person_db, retval,
            "error while opening cursor");
}
memset(&key, 0, sizeof(key));
memset(&value, 0, sizeof(value));

int ssn;
person p;

while(!(retval =
            cur->c_get(cur, &key, &value, DB_NEXT)))
{
    ssn = *((int*)(key.data));
    p = *((person*)(value.data));
    printf("Found - ssn: %d, name %s, dob %s\n",
            ssn, p.name, p.dob);
}

retval = cur->c_close(cur);
if(retval != 0)
{
    person_db->err(person_db, retval,
            "error while closing cursor");
}
retval = txn->commit(txn, 0);
if(retval != 0)
{
    env->err(env, retval,
            "error while committing transaction");
    return -1;
}
```

It's important to close the cursor after it is no longer needed, because the database maintains a lock on every record visited by the cursor. The type of lock created by the cursor is determined by the lock mode used to create the cursor, and it isn't released until the cursor is closed.

Note that you didn't pass the transaction handle in the c_get method of the cursor, because you specified the transaction handle when you created the cursor. All subsequent operations on the cursor will be associated with that transaction automatically.

Error Returns

If you've been using the Berkeley DB C++ or the Java API, you'll notice a difference in the way the library reports an error. The C library doesn't throw exceptions when it encounters a runtime error, because exceptions aren't supported in C. An error condition is reported through the return value of the API calls. Berkeley DB–specific error codes are documented in the Berkeley DB documentation, while the generic system-specific errors reported by Berkeley DB can be found in the operating system documentation.

Documented Errors

Almost all C API methods return an integer value. All nonzero return values are errors. A negative return value is a Berkeley DB–specific error, and a positive return value is a system error, defined in your system's errno.h file.

Table 12-1 shows the list of error codes that the Berkeley DB C APIs can return; the descriptions are quoted from a Berkeley DB header file. I've extracted this from the db.h file. The other APIs wrap most of these errors within exceptions. For example, the C++ API has the exception DbDeadlockException, which is a wrapper around the DB_LOCK_DEADLOCK error value.

■**Note** You can get the error number associated with an exception using DbException::get_errno in C++ and DatabaseException.getErrno in Java.

Table 12-1. *Berkeley DB–Specific Error Codes and Their Meaning*

Error Code	Error Value	Description
DB_BUFFER_SMALL	-30999	User allocated memory too small for the byte array to be returned by the library.
DB_DONOTINDEX	-30998	NULL return from a secondary database callback.
DB_KEYEMPTY	-30997	Key/data deleted or never created.
DB_KEYEXIST	-30996	The key/data pair already exists.
DB_LOCK_DEADLOCK	-30995	Deadlock was detected.
DB_LOCK_NOTGRANTED	-30994	Lock unavailable.
DB_LOG_BUFFER_FULL	-30993	In-memory log buffer full.
DB_NOSERVER	-30992	Server panic return.
DB_NOSERVER_HOME	-30991	Bad home sent to server.
DB_NOSERVER_ID	-30990	Bad ID sent to server.
DB_NOTFOUND	-30989	Key/data pair not found (EOF).
DB_OLD_VERSION	-30988	Out-of-date version.
DB_PAGE_NOTFOUND	-30987	Requested database page not found.
DB_REP_DUPMASTER	-30986	There are two masters.
DB_REP_HANDLE_DEAD	-30985	Rolled back a committed transaction.
DB_REP_HOLDELECTION	-30984	Time to hold an election.
DB_REP_IGNORE	-30983	This message should be ignored.

Table 12-1. *Berkeley DB–Specific Error Codes and Their Meaning*

Error Code	Error Value	Description
DB_REP_ISPERM	-30982	A permanent log record written to the disk. This is not exactly an error message.
DB_REP_JOIN_FAILURE	-30981	Unable to join replication group.
DB_REP_LOCKOUT	-30980	API/Replication lockout now.
DB_REP_NEWMASTER	-30979	We have learned of a new master.
DB_REP_NEWSITE	-30978	New site entered system.
DB_REP_NOTPERM	-30977	Permanent log record not written.
DB_REP_STARTUPDONE	-30976	Client startup complete.
DB_REP_UNAVAIL	-30975	Site cannot currently be reached.
DB_RUNRECOVERY	-30974	Panic return.
DB_SECONDARY_BAD	-30973	Secondary index corrupt.
DB_VERIFY_BAD	-30972	Verify failed; bad format.
DB_VERSION_MISMATCH	-30971	Environment versions mismatched.

Handling Undocumented Errors

If you go through the C API documentation, you'll find the list of errors that a method can return. This list doesn't include the errors that the operating system can report. For example, if the operating system cannot allocate the required amount of memory while executing a method, it will return an ENOMEM error (this is also reported by the Berkeley DB library in some cases). This error is not listed in the documentation of any method.

The documented list also doesn't include all the errors that the Berkeley DB library can report. For example, almost any method can report the DB_PAGE_NOTFOUND error (it is usually returned when the database is corrupted), but you won't find it in any method description. The undocumented error returns can be hard to manage, because there are so many of them. At the very least, you should check for and log all possible error returns, not only the ones mentioned in the documentation. It would be impossible to take corrective action for all possible error returns in your code. The errors that you'll see will depend to a large extent on the nature of your application, the kind of platform it's running on, and the configuration you're using for the database. You can't determine all the errors in advance, but you can start by catching and logging all the error returns. When you notice that certain errors are being reported more consistently over time, you'll be able to handle them in a meaningful way.

Complete Code Example

It is sometimes difficult to follow the flow of a program when it has been broken up into pieces. In this chapter, you looked at numerous code snippets. Listing 12-16 lists the complete program from which the snippets were taken. It creates a database environment and a database to store

Person records. It then performs various operations on the database and finally shuts down the environment. The entire program is in a single file called tds.c.

Listing 12-16. *Using the C API*

```
#include <stdio.h>
#include <string.h>
#include "db.h"

typedef struct
{
    int ssn;
    char name[64];
    char dob[16];
} person;

person records[] =
{
    {111223333, "Manish Pandey", "jan 13 1971"},
    {111223334, "Shirish Rai", "dec 23 1974"},
    {111223335, "Roland Hendel", "feb 13 1973"}
};

int num_records = 3;

DB_ENV *env;
char *env_home = "./chap12_env";

DB *person_db;
DB *person_by_name_db;

int open_env();
int open_db();
int load_db();
int dump_db();
void close_env();
int get_sec_key(DB *db, const DBT *pkey,
        const DBT *pdata, DBT *skey);
int read_rec();
int update_rec();
int delete_rec();

int open_env()
{
    int retval = 0;
    retval = db_env_create(&env, 0);
```

```c
    if(retval != 0)
    {
        printf("Error creating DB_ENV handle: err: %d\n",
                retval);
        return -1;
    }
    env->set_errpfx(env, "chap_12_tds");
    env->set_data_dir(env, "./");
    env->set_cachesize(env, 0, 5000000, 1);

    int envflags = DB_CREATE | DB_INIT_LOCK |
                   DB_INIT_LOG | DB_INIT_MPOOL |
                   DB_INIT_TXN | DB_RECOVER;
    retval = env->open(env, env_home, envflags, 0);
    if(retval != 0)
    {
        env->err(env, retval,
                "Error opening the environment");
        env->close(env, 0);
        return -1;
    }
    env->set_flags(env, DB_LOG_AUTOREMOVE, 1);
    return 0;
}


int open_db()
{
    int retval = 0;

    //open the primary database
    retval = db_create(&person_db, env, 0);
    if(retval != 0)
    {
        env->err(env, retval,
                "Error creating DB handle");
        return -1;
    }
    person_db->set_errpfx(person_db, "chap_12_tds:person_db");

    int dbflags = DB_CREATE | DB_AUTO_COMMIT;
    retval = person_db->open(person_db, NULL, "person_db",
                             NULL, DB_BTREE, dbflags, 0);
    if(retval != 0)
    {
        person_db->err(person_db, retval,
                    "Error opening person_db");
        return -1;
    }
```

```
    //open the secondary database
    retval = db_create(&person_by_name_db, env, 0);
    if(retval != 0)
    {
        env->err(env, retval,
                "Error creating DB handle");
        return -1;
    }
    person_by_name_db->set_errpfx(person_by_name_db,
            "chap_12_tds:person_by_name_db");
    person_by_name_db->set_flags(person_by_name_db, DB_DUPSORT);

    retval = person_by_name_db->open(person_by_name_db, NULL,
            "person_by_name_db", NULL, DB_BTREE, dbflags, 0);
    if(retval != 0)
    {
        person_by_name_db->err(person_by_name_db, retval,
                    "Error opening person_db");
        return -1;
    }
    retval = person_db->associate(person_db, NULL,
            person_by_name_db, get_sec_key, 0);
    if(retval != 0)
    {
        person_db->err(person_db, retval,
                    "Error associating person_by_name_db");
        return -1;
    }
    return 0;
}

int get_sec_key(DB *db, const DBT *pkey,
        const DBT *pdata, DBT *skey)
{
    person *p = (person*)(pdata->data);
    skey->data = p->name;
    skey->size = sizeof(p->name);
    return 0;
}

int load_db()
{
    int retval = 0;
    DBT key;
    DBT value;
```

```
DB_TXN *txn;
retval = env->txn_begin(env, NULL, &txn, 0);
if(retval != 0)
{
    env->err(env, retval,
            "error in load_db::txn_begin");
    return -1;
}
int i;
for(i=0; i < num_records; i++)
{
    person p = records[i];
    printf("inserting: ssn: %d, name: %s, dob: %s\n",
            p.ssn, p.name, p.dob);

    memset(&key, 0, sizeof(key));
    memset(&value, 0, sizeof(value));
    key.data = &(p.ssn);
    key.size = sizeof(int);

    value.data = &p;
    value.size = sizeof(person);

    retval = person_db->put(person_db, txn,
            &key, &value, 0);
    switch(retval)
    {
        case 0:
            printf("put successful\n");
            continue;
        case DB_KEYEXIST:
            person_db->err(person_db, retval,
                    "%d already exists\n", records[i].ssn);
            break;
        default:
            person_db->err(person_db, retval,
                    "error while inserting %d error %d",
                    records[i].ssn, retval);
            break;
    }
    retval = txn->abort(txn);
    if(retval != 0)
    {
        env->err(env, retval,
                "error while aborting transaction");
        return -1;
    }
```

```
    }
    retval = txn->commit(txn, 0);
    if(retval != 0)
    {
        env->err(env, retval,
                "error while committing transaction");
        return -1;
    }
    return 0;
}

int update_rec()
{
    int retval = 0;
    int ssn = 111223335;
    DBT key;
    DBT value;
    memset(&key, 0, sizeof(key));
    memset(&key, 0, sizeof(value));
    key.data = &ssn;
    key.size = sizeof(ssn);

    DB_TXN *txn;
    retval = env->txn_begin(env, NULL, &txn, 0);
    if(retval != 0)
    {
        env->err(env, retval,
                "error in load_db::txn_begin");
        return -1;
    }

    retval = person_db->get(person_db, txn,
            &key, &value, 0);
    if(retval != 0)
    {
        person_db->err(person_db, retval, "error in get");
        return -1;
        retval = txn->abort(txn);
        if(retval != 0)
        {
            env->err(env, retval,
                    "error while aborting transaction");
            return -1;
        }
    }
```

```
    person *p = (person*)(value.data);
    char *new_name = "Roland Tembo Hendle";
    memcpy(p->name, new_name, strlen(new_name)+1);

    retval = person_db->put(person_db, txn,
            &key, &value, 0);
    if(retval != 0)
    {
        person_db->err(person_db, retval, "error in put");
        return -1;
        retval = txn->abort(txn);
        if(retval != 0)
        {
            env->err(env, retval,
                    "error while aborting transaction");
            return -1;
        }
    }
    retval = txn->commit(txn, 0);
    if(retval != 0)
    {
        env->err(env, retval,
                "error while committing transaction");
        return -1;
    }
    return 0;
}
int read_rec()
{
    int retval = 0;
    int ssn = 111223333;
    DBT key;
    DBT value;
    memset(&key, 0, sizeof(key));
    memset(&key, 0, sizeof(value));
    key.data = &ssn;
    key.size = sizeof(ssn);

    DB_TXN *txn;
    retval = env->txn_begin(env, NULL, &txn, 0);
    if(retval != 0)
    {
        env->err(env, retval,
                "error in load_db::txn_begin");
        return -1;
    }
```

```
    retval = person_db->get(person_db, txn,
            &key, &value, 0);
    if(retval != 0)
    {
        person_db->err(person_db, retval, "error in get");
        return -1;
    }

    retval = txn->commit(txn, 0);
    if(retval != 0)
    {
        env->err(env, retval,
                "error while committing transaction");
        return -1;
    }
    person p = *((person*)(value.data));

    printf("Single read: Found for ssn: %d: name %s, dob %s\n",
            ssn, p.name, p.dob);
    return 0;
}
int delete_rec()
{
    int retval = 0;
    DB_TXN *txn;
    retval = env->txn_begin(env, NULL, &txn, 0);
    if(retval != 0)
    {
        env->err(env, retval,
                "error in delete_rec::txn_begin");
        return -1;
    }
    int ssn = 111223333;
    DBT key;
    memset(&key, 0, sizeof(key));
    key.data = &ssn;
    key.size = sizeof(ssn);

    retval = person_db->del(person_db, txn,
            &key, 0);
    if(retval != 0)
    {
        person_db->err(person_db, retval,
                "error in delete_rec::del");
```

```
        retval = txn->abort(txn);
        if(retval != 0)
        {
            env->err(env, retval,
                    "error while aborting transaction");
            return -1;
        }
        return -1;
    }

    retval = txn->commit(txn, 0);
    if(retval != 0)
    {
        env->err(env, retval,
                "error while committing transaction");
        return -1;
    }
    return 0;
}

int dump_db()
{
    DBT key, value;
    DBC *cur;
    int retval = 0;

    DB_TXN *txn;
    retval = env->txn_begin(env, NULL, &txn, 0);
    if(retval != 0)
    {
        env->err(env, retval,
                "error in dump_db::txn_begin");
        return -1;
    }

    retval = person_db->cursor(person_db, txn,
            &cur, 0);
    if(retval != 0)
    {
        person_db->err(person_db, retval,
                "error while opening cursor");
    }
    memset(&key, 0, sizeof(key));
    memset(&value, 0, sizeof(value));
```

```
    int ssn;
    person p;

    while(!(retval =
                cur->c_get(cur, &key, &value, DB_NEXT)))
    {
        ssn = *((int*)(key.data));
        p = *((person*)(value.data));
        printf("Found - ssn: %d, name %s, dob %s\n",
                ssn, p.name, p.dob);
    }

    retval = cur->c_close(cur);
    if(retval != 0)
    {
        person_db->err(person_db, retval,
                "error while closing cursor");
    }
    retval = txn->commit(txn, 0);
    if(retval != 0)
    {
        env->err(env, retval,
                "error while committing transaction");
        return -1;
    }
    return 0;
}

void close_env()
{
    int retval = 0;
    if(person_by_name_db != NULL)
    {
        retval = person_by_name_db->close(person_by_name_db, 0);
        if(retval != 0)
            printf("error closing person_by_name_db\n");
    }
    if(person_db != NULL)
    {
        retval = person_db->close(person_db, 0);
        if(retval != 0)
            printf("error closing person_db\n");
    }
```

```
    if(env != NULL)
    {
        retval = env->close(env, 0);
        if(retval != 0)
            printf("error closing env\n");
    }
}

int main(int argc, char **argv)
{
    if(open_env())
        return;
    if(open_db())
        return;
    if(load_db())
        return;
    dump_db();
    read_rec();
    delete_rec();
    printf("dump after delete\n");
    dump_db();
    update_rec();
    printf("dump after update\n");
    dump_db();
    close_env();
}
```

Summary

In this chapter, you learned how to use the Berkeley DB C API. The C API is the lowest-level interface available in Berkeley DB; all the other APIs are thin wrappers around the C API. A large number of applications that use Berkeley DB are written in C. Hopefully, programmers not familiar with C++ will find it easier to relate to the material in the rest of the book after reading this chapter.

Berkeley DB is a difficult subject to write about. Not only are there too many interfaces to cover, but all of the interfaces are extremely flexible and open, making it impossible to discuss everything in detail without writing multiple volumes. This book is, by no means, a comprehensive reference of Berkeley DB. This book is intended to be a starting point for programmers interested in Berkeley DB. I hope that after reading this book, you'll feel comfortable investigating this complex and wonderful product on your own.

Berkeley DB was initially designed to serve as a replacement of the UNIX ndbm. However, it ended up being used in a lot more applications than ndbm was ever used in. One of the primary reasons for its wide adoption was the emergence in recent years of applications that require small, embeddable, fault-tolerant databases. Three trends in particular have produced devices and applications that require such databases.

The first trend is the miniaturization of gadgets. Commodity electronics are getting smaller, more intelligent, and more connected. Most modern gadgets, such as cell phones, MP3 players, and Pocket PCs, need to store and synchronize large amounts of data without squandering precious computing and storage resources on full-fledged RDBMS databases.

The second trend is commoditization. Applications that used to be primarily custom software solutions, such as firewalls and authentication servers, a few years back are now being designed and packaged as plug-and-play appliances. The main advantage of deploying appliances, as compared to software-based solutions, is that they have a significantly lower maintenance overhead. Appliances don't require users to buy and maintain separate hardware and software components. In order to reduce maintenance overhead, appliance designers prefer "programmable" databases, which allow database-management tasks to be programmed into the application code. And, of course, appliances have limited computing and memory resources too.

The third trend is the emergence of distributed applications. As networking and communication technologies are advancing, the enterprises are becoming more distributed. These days, it is not uncommon for even mid-sized and small companies to have offices and data centers in multiple cities and countries, so that they can fully utilize the resources spread across diverse locations. A distributed enterprise requires a distributed database technology. And since the modern enterprise is also rapidly adopting appliance-based solutions, the distributed database also has to have a small footprint and has to be "self-managing."

The existing database technologies, including Berkeley DB, leave a lot to be desired when it comes to fulfilling the requirements that I've mentioned. Even though Berkeley DB comes closer to meeting these requirements than most other embedded databases, it can be vastly improved. Features such as multimaster replication, partial replication, and the data-definition layer are absolutely essential to meet the needs of the next generation of applications. As a developer, you should not only use Berkeley DB, but you should also try to take advantage of the fact it's open source. If it doesn't provide everything that you need, enhance it.

Good luck!

Index

Find it faster at http://superindex.apress.com

Find it faster at http://superindex.apress.com

Find it faster at http://superindex.apress.com

Find it faster at http://superindex.apress.com

Find it faster at http://superindex.apress.com

FIND IT FAST
with the Apress *SuperIndex*™

Quickly Find Out What the Experts Know

Leading by innovation, Apress now offers you its *SuperIndex*™, a turbocharged companion to the fine index in this book. The Apress *SuperIndex*™ is a keyword and phrase-enabled search tool that lets you search through the entire Apress library. Powered by dtSearch™, it delivers results instantly.

Instead of paging through a book or a PDF, you can electronically access the topic of your choice from a vast array of Apress titles. The Apress *SuperIndex*™ is the perfect tool to find critical snippets of code or an obscure reference. The Apress *SuperIndex*™ enables all users to harness essential information and data from the best minds in technology.

No registration is required, and the Apress *SuperIndex*™ is free to use.

❶ Thorough and comprehensive searches of over 300 titles

❷ No registration required

❸ Instantaneous results

❹ A single destination to find what you need

❺ Engineered for speed and accuracy

❻ Will spare your time, application, and anxiety level

Search now: *http://superindex.apress.com*

You Need the Companion eBook

Your purchase of this book entitles you to buy the companion PDF-version eBook for only $10. Take the weightless companion with you anywhere.

We believe this Apress title will prove so indispensable that you'll want to carry it with you everywhere, which is why we are offering the companion eBook (in PDF format) for $10 to customers who purchase this book now. Convenient and fully searchable, the PDF version of any content-rich, page-heavy Apress book makes a valuable addition to your programming library. You can easily find and copy code—or perform examples by quickly toggling between instructions and the application. Even simultaneously tackling a donut, diet soda, and complex code becomes simplified with hands-free eBooks!

Once you purchase your book, getting the $10 companion eBook is simple:

❶ Visit **www.apress.com/promo/tendollars/**.

❷ Complete a basic registration form to receive a randomly generated question about this title.

❸ Answer the question correctly in 60 seconds, and you will receive a promotional code to redeem for the $10.00 eBook.

THE EXPERT'S VOICE™

2855 TELEGRAPH AVENUE │ SUITE 600 │ BERKELEY, CA 94705

All Apress eBooks subject to copyright protection. No part may be reproduced or transmitted in any form or by any means, electronic or mechanical, including photocopying, recording, or by any information storage or retrieval system, without the prior written permission of the copyright owner and the publisher. The purchaser may print the work in full or in part for their own noncommercial use. The purchaser may place the eBook title on any of their personal computers for their own personal reading and reference.

Offer valid through 3/08.